Chairman of the Fed

ROBERT P. BREMNER

Chairman of the Fed

WILLIAM McCHESNEY MARTIN JR. AND THE CREATION OF THE MODERN AMERICAN FINANCIAL SYSTEM

Yale University Press
New Haven &
London

Published with assistance from the foundation established in memory of
Philip Hamilton McMillan of the Class of 1894, Yale College.

Designed by Sonia Shannon
Set in Sabon type by Keystone Typesetting, Inc.
Printed in the United States of America.

Library of Congress Cataloging-in-Publication Data
Bremner, Robert P., 1940–
    Chairman of the Fed : William McChesney Martin Jr. and the creation of the
modern American financial system / Robert P. Bremner.
        p.   cm.
    Includes bibliographical references and index.
    ISBN 0-300-10508-8 (cloth : alk. paper)
    1. Martin, William McChesney. 2. Board of Governors of the Federal Reserve
System (U.S.) — Officials and employees — Biography. 3. Government economists
— United States — Biography. 4. United States — Economic policy — 1945–1960.
5. United States — Economic policy — 1961–1971. I. Title.
HG2563.M275B74 2004
332.1′1′092 — dc22
[B]   2004051626

A catalogue record for this book is available from the British Library.

The paper in this book meets the guidelines for permanence and
durability of the Committee on Production Guidelines for
Book Longevity of the Council on Library Resources.

10 9 8 7 6 5 4 3 2 1

Contents

Introduction: Who Was Bill Martin?

On 5 December 1965, President Lyndon Johnson was pacing in the office at his ranch in Johnson City, Texas, while he waited for William McChesney Martin Jr., the chairman of the Federal Reserve Board, to visit for what Johnson called "a trip to the woodshed." Two days before, Martin had led the Fed's board of governors to an increase in the Federal Reserve discount rate, the first in more than five years of uninterrupted economic growth. Through Henry "Joe" Fowler, his Treasury secretary, and Gardner Ackley, his Council of Economic Advisors (CEA) chairman, Johnson had advised Martin to delay the rate increase, and his instructions had been rejected. Few people ignored Lyndon Johnson's instructions, and he was furious when he heard of the Fed's move. He had growled at Fowler over the telephone: "Those marble tower boys. Joe, you find a tough guy to head the Reserve. If Martin resigns, it won't wreck the country."[1]

Their meeting was a classic confrontation. Johnson was a powerful and manipulative president who believed that a Fed tightening would jeopardize the economic expansion and the tax revenues he needed to finance the most important goals of his presidency: his war on poverty and continued involvement in the war in Vietnam, whose costs were growing. Martin was committed to defending the Fed's independence and dealing with the impact of administration economic policies that he considered irresponsible. When

Martin walked into the office, Johnson immediately accused him of placing himself above the presidency and totally disregarding Johnson's wishes: "You went ahead and did something that I disapproved of . . . and can affect my entire term here."[2] Martin later admitted that he was shaken but determined to stick to his position while not insulting the president of the United States.

As he so often did, Martin made the issue one of judgment—on which reasonable people could differ—and of the separation of powers: "I've never implied that I'm right and you're wrong. But I do have a very strong conviction that the Federal Reserve Act placed the responsibility for interest rates with the Federal Reserve Board. This is one of those few occasions where the Federal Reserve Board decision has to be final."[3] In the end, Martin's determination carried the day. After an hour of tough talk, Lyndon Johnson could see that he would not change Martin's position, and he had already concluded that the political cost of forcing Martin out of the Fed was too high. The Fed's independence from political interference, independence that Bill Martin worked so hard to define and defend, received a historic validation.

William McChesney Martin Jr. is not a well-recognized name in the economic history of theUnited States, although he had a highly public career from 1938, when he became president of the New York Stock Exchange at the age of thirty-one, to his retirement—as the longest-serving Fed chairman—in 1970. His anonymity in part reflects his modest and self-effacing nature. He tried, not always successfully, to avoid public controversy and to achieve his aims by working behind the scenes with those who opposed him. While Martin's service in the public interest includes a number of significant accomplishments, his great work is the creation of the modern Federal Reserve System.

Over the ninety-one years of the Fed's existence, its reluctance to provide extensive information about its policy-making activities has caused it to be criticized as secretive, and it is frequently the subject of public misunderstanding. To better understand the Fed, we need to know about its legislative mandate, the economic goals it strives to achieve, and how it pursues them. Last, but not least, we also need to appreciate the leaders who played critical roles in the Fed's evolution, and none played a more pivotal role than William McChesney Martin Jr.

To gain some measure of the scope of his transformation of the Fed, it is essential to appreciate the condition of the Federal Reserve System in 1951, when Martin became Fed chairman. At the time, the Fed was completing a disastrous quarter century, starting in 1928 with its widely acknowledged complicity in creating the conditions that brought about the Great Depression and extended its economic aftereffects. In 1941, the Fed entered into an agreement with the U.S. Treasury to help finance World War II that essentially suspended the Fed's monetary policy capabilities and continued in effect until 1951. The Fed's five-year struggle to end the arrangement put it in opposition to the Treasury and the Truman administration, and the conflict was so intense that it poisoned relationships and caused two Fed chairmen to lose their jobs. The Banking Act of 1935 centralized certain responsibilities under the chairman and the board of governors that had previously resided in the New York Reserve Bank, creating a tension between the two power centers that was still unresolved in 1951. Finally, the Fed had lost the confidence of the banking industry it regulated. One of Martin's immediate predecessors, Marriner Eccles, allowed official Fed-industry contacts to dry up and had proposed a severe anti-inflationary monetary policy that the banking industry successfully blocked. In almost every important respect, the Fed was a troubled institution.

In a sense, Bill Martin's journey to the Fed chairmanship began at his birth. His father, William McChesney Martin Sr., was the founding chairman of the Federal Reserve Bank of St. Louis, where he served for twenty-seven years. His son had an early role model for courage in the face of uncertainty, service in the public interest, and dedication to the potential of the Federal Reserve System.

Martin Jr. spent the early years of his career representing a St. Louis brokerage firm on the floor of the New York Stock Exchange (NYSE). There he accumulated a lifelong understanding of how financial markets work and learned the practices of those who made, and those who manipulated, the stock market in the freewheeling 1920s and 1930s. Martin, a member of a modest reform movement within the NYSE, landed in the NYSE president's chair when a spectacular financial scandal ended the rule of the "old-guard" members and swept the reform movement and Martin into office. As president, Martin was torn between the demands of Securities and Exchange Commission chairman William O. Douglas, a fiery New Deal reformer, and the unyielding resistance of his Exchange membership. Martin negotiated and tortuously implemented a compromise program of reform that introduced professional management, overhauled the regulatory and disciplinary processes, and strengthened the financial practices of NYSE members.

Ironically, Martin was brought back to the NYSE in 1971, over thirty years after his NYSE presidency, to help the NYSE deal with another series of financial and regulatory problems. After an extended analysis, Martin recommended steps to modernize operations, expand the regulation of its central market-making function, and rebuild public trust in the integrity of the NYSE. Recurrent crises of confidence in the ability of the NYSE to serve the public interest continue to the present day. Few of its leaders have been more dedicated or more steadfast in promoting the public interest than William McChesney Martin Jr.

Martin's preparation for the Fed chairmanship also included the presidency of the U.S. Export-Import Bank, the agency selected by the Truman administration as the first vehicle for financing the rebuilding of Western Europe's industrial base after World War II. His initial challenge was converting the bank from a sleepy bureaucracy into a businesslike financing institution. At the same time, he had to defend the bank from the pressures coming from powerful members of the Truman administration to make loans to prop up friendly, but destitute, political regimes. His experience in dealing with Truman and his cabinet taught him how to negotiate the political currents of Washington and encouraged Treasury Secretary John Snyder to bring him into the administration.

The event that put Bill Martin into the Fed chairmanship was the historic "Accord" that Martin engineered to end the feud between the Fed and the Treasury over the Fed's World War II financing agreement. The fundamental assumptions underlying the Accord were Martin's beliefs that the Fed and the Treasury could work together as equals and that freeing the market for Treasury securities would not cause interest rates to rise so much that the Treasury's borrowing costs would devastate the Truman administration budget. Both expectations proved to be correct.

Martin brought deeply held principles to the Fed that helped him rebuild it. He believed that the regional structure of the Federal Reserve System was one of its greatest strengths, and he increased the role of the twelve Reserve Bank presidents in monetary policy deliberations. He also believed that the Fed should not try to influence credit conditions by excessive intervention in the market for Treasury securities but should allow market forces to express themselves through interest rate changes. The Fed should limit its intervention to achieving monetary policy goals and maintaining orderly trading conditions. Martin's philosophy brought him into direct conflict with Allan Sproul, the influential president of the New York Fed and the most well-regarded central banker in the United States. Sproul had a profound grasp of the art of central banking and of the behavior of the financial markets. He virtually ran the Fed's monetary policy on a day-to-day basis. Martin and Sproul conducted a civil but relentless debate for four years until Sproul's underestimation of the appeal of a more democratic policy-making process forced him to admit defeat. Martin subsequently devoted considerable effort to selecting strong staffs for the Reserve Banks and building up their ability to conduct economic research in their districts. The regional structure remains a hallmark of today's Fed.

Although Martin came to the Fed at a time in which the value and impact of monetary policy were very much in doubt, he was convinced this conclusion was wrong. He believed that monetary policy could help reduce the cycles of boom and bust and provide more stable economic growth. The grain business of Martin's grandfather had been destroyed during a bust, and Martin's father led the St. Louis Fed to counteract business cycles in its district. To Martin Jr., the cycle began with excessive speculation in the financial markets, leading to the buildup of inflationary forces and the boom conditions that inevitably led to a collapse. The recovery process required the creation of conditions that would regenerate demand. At the Fed, Martin came under the influence of a remarkable economics staff, particularly Winfield Riefler. With Riefler's help, Martin developed the concept of a flexible monetary policy directed at achieving overall economic stability, which he described as "leaning against the winds of deflation or inflation, whichever way they are blowing."[4] The Fed would direct its monetary policy to cool down excessive demand by raising interest rates or, at the other end of the cycle, would help stimulate the economy by lowering rates and encouraging banks to lend. This monetary policy philosophy is still very much in evidence today.

Martin believed that in order to effectively pursue a flexible monetary policy, the Fed needed to be independent of political interference. The Fed's legislation created a system that was independent of the government, but its operational independence was never clearly defined. Moreover, Martin was well aware of Marriner Eccles's failures when he attempted to assert the Fed's operational independence. Martin's Export-Import Bank experience taught him that he could successfully assert independence when his institution's legislative mandate was clearly challenged and within a context of his well-known commitment to cooperation and consultation. Only when cooperation and consultation failed to resolve the situation would he lead the Fed to independent action. Once the impasse had occurred, he worked to resolve it and avoid any lingering hard feelings. Martin always believed that individuals of goodwill and sincere beliefs would eventually find a way to overcome their differences and once again work together. Martin's passionate commitment to these values enabled him to bridge very significant differences with each of the five administrations with which he worked. Today, the Fed's right to independent action is well recognized, if not always happily accepted by the incumbent administration.

At the end of his career, Martin felt he had failed in his role as Fed chairman. One of his early policy initiatives had been to make the control of inflation one of the Fed's highest priorities. The joint efforts of the Fed and the Eisenhower administration had shown that prudent fiscal policy and an active monetary policy could wring inflation out of the economy. During the Johnson administration, Martin learned that when the administration's fiscal policy was expansionary, the Fed could not attack inflation without causing a politically unacceptable downturn in the economy. In 1966, the Fed tightened the economy to a point at which the financial system began to unravel and yet achieved only a temporary respite in inflation. In 1967, Martin concluded that the economy could not stand a repeat of the 1966 crunch and redoubled his efforts to persuade the administration to seriously pursue a tax increase.

Martin engaged in a futile effort to pressure Congress to pass the tax increase by allowing the economy to grow and inflationary pressures to build. Similarly, he reinstituted credit ease in the second half of 1968 for a variety of reasons, including his promise to the administration and Congress that he would loosen credit once the tax increase was passed. In retrospect, both decisions were mistakes that inhibited the Fed's ability to deal with inflation during a period (1967–69) when a sustained campaign of restraint might have succeeded in bringing what became known as the Great Inflation under control.

Martin's associates on the Federal Open Market Committee told him that he was wrong to conclude that he had failed and that "given the circumstances, you have done a splendid job."[5] It is true that neither the Johnson nor the Nixon administration would accept the economic sacrifices necessary to deal decisively with inflation. Consistent inflation had begun only in mid-1967, and the public was not overly concerned with it. Finally, during 1968–69, a substantial minority of Martin's own board of governors was unwilling to risk a possible recession to attack inflation, and Martin led by consensus. Martin might have failed to bring inflation down on his watch, but he left behind a Federal Reserve System that had the public and political support, the monetary tools, and the capability to do it when the timing was right. The modern Federal Reserve System is the rich legacy of Bill Martin and is the reason he deserves the singular accolade of being called "The Chairman of the Fed."

I

A Family of Substance: The Early Years

Money, that seductive but treacherous commodity, has been woven into the history of the Martin family for three generations. It weighed heavily in the thoughts of Thomas L. Martin on 22 November 1894, as he stood at the back of a small crowd that had gathered for a public auction ordered by the Fayette National Bank of Lexington, Kentucky. The assets to be auctioned had once belonged to the McChesney & Martin Grain Company, of which Tom Martin had been a co-owner. For twenty years, McChesney & Martin had purchased the grain harvested by Kentucky farmers and stored it for sale to flour mills throughout the Midwest. Sadly, longevity and honest trading had proven no guarantors of permanence. Lexington remembers little about the unfortunate Thomas L. Martin, the grandfather of William McChesney Martin Jr., except that he was emotionally and financially broken by the bankruptcy of his business.

The failure of McChesney & Martin was the result of a national financial panic, an event that struck Americans all too regularly in the second half of the nineteenth century. Between 1893 and 1913, the American economy was mired in recession 55 percent of the time, and financial panics like that of 1893 were often the cause.[1] Years later, Thomas Martin's eldest son, William McChesney Martin Sr., referred to the problem: "Our financial system — and it is as important to the nation as the nervous system to the body — has been found to be unacceptably weak."[2] The panic of 1893 that doomed McChesney & Martin was caused in part by a bumper harvest and unusually large borrowing by grain-storage companies like McChesney & Martin. The huge crop put an enormous strain on the American financial system. Agriculture was the largest single element of the U.S. economy, employing nearly 30 percent of the work-force. To finance the harvest, banks in Lexington would normally turn to banks in Chicago and New York for temporary loans. In 1893, the demand for credit was so large that the great banks of continental Europe were asked to support their American counterparts.

Like many financial panics, the panic of 1893 was caused by rumors. Stories of financial problems at U.S. railroads and banks caused bankers across Europe to trim their lending commitments to the United States. With frightening speed, the European bankers began to reduce their U.S. loans, and within weeks McChesney & Martin's banker was asking for repayment of a portion of its loan. Thomas Martin tried to make a hurried sale of some of the company's inventoried grain, only to learn that grain companies across the Midwest were also selling, and grain prices were collapsing. Even liquidating all of the inventory at prevailing prices would not have enabled McChesney & Martin to pay off its debts. The company was ruined. The final episode in McChesney & Martin's existence was the sad little gathering around the auctioneer's platform in front of the company's building on the corner of Broadway and Water streets on that gray day in Lexington.

Thomas Martin's entrepreneurial fire was extinguished by the bankruptcy. For the remainder of his career, he worked as a bookkeeper for a trade association, and the family's financial circumstances never recovered. Thomas's change of fortune convinced two of Thomas and Hettie's children, William McChesney Martin Sr. and his younger brother, Louis, to seek greener pastures away from Lexington. William McChesney Martin Sr. was born in 1874, and after graduation from secondary school was accepted at Washington & Lee College, a school steeped in tradition and patriotism. The college traced its history through George Washington, who rescued it from financial troubles, and General Robert E. Lee, who served as its president after the Civil War. It was here, deep in the historic Shenandoah Valley of Virginia, that the notion of public service entered the Martin family consciousness.

After graduation from college in 1895, Martin decided to seek his future in the bustling city of St. Louis. He became secretary to his favorite uncle, William Samuel McChesney, a leader in the burgeoning railroad industry in St. Louis. After two years, Martin decided there was "no future in machinery" for him and began attending the Washington University School of Law at night.[3] In 1900, with his new law degree in hand, Martin encountered one of the men who would have a lasting impact on his life, Breckinridge Jones. Jones was a skilled lawyer and banker, a man of boundless energy and foresight, and one of those rare financiers who serve as midwives to the creation of a succession of businesses and industries. Jones had recently helped start the Mississippi Valley Trust Company and invited Martin to join its legal department. During the years 1900 to 1913, Martin became the smart young lawyer at Jones's side as Jones continued to promote new businesses and nurtured the upstart Mississippi Valley Trust into one of St. Louis's leading banks.

Breckinridge Jones also taught Martin about a banker's broader responsibilities. During these years, Jones served as president of the Missouri Bankers Association and founded the National Association of Trust Companies. Martin became the researcher and speechwriter for Jones's campaigns to recruit his fellow bankers on an endless list of progressive banking issues. Energetic and responsible bankers like Jones were an indispensable element in the overall economic development of their communities—a lesson Martin absorbed at firsthand.

By 1911, Martin's career had begun to take on a public-service character as he introduced the name of William McChesney Martin into American financial history. With Jones's encouragement, Martin stepped out from behind his anonymous speechwriting role and spoke out on banking issues in his own right. The burning issue of the day was the proposal for a National Reserve Association to strengthen the nation's banking system. The idea—to establish a federally authorized central banking institution with the power to provide credit during times of financial stress—had been conceived by a powerful group of bankers as an antidote to the financial panics of the nineteenth century. The proposal included a national board and a series of regional banks operating under a combination of private and public ownership. Their plan was comprehensive and resolved a conflict that had doomed all previous solutions by proposing a structure that balanced national and regional economic interests. Martin observed that the ownership structure would keep the Reserve Association independent of outside influence "by guarding against the politician and the plutocrat."[4]

In Missouri, as elsewhere, the Reserve Association idea was controversial with local bankers because they prized their independence and were suspicious of anything that resembled federal intrusion into the banking industry. The bankers' skepticism seemed to make Martin all the more determined to bring them around. Calling on bankers, "upon whom rests the chief responsibility for reform,"[5] he urged his Missouri counterparts to support the Reserve Association. He criticized the current banking system as incapable of handling temporary emergencies, which forced bankers "to call in loans and ruin our communities."[6] He was determined to do all he could to end the dismal cycle of prosperity and poverty that afflicted honest, hardworking men like his father. By this time, Thomas Martin had moved to St. Louis and was living in Martin's home. His presence was a constant reminder of the hidden costs of a financial collapse.

The Reserve Association became a campaign issue in the presidential election of 1912. The following year, the new president, Woodrow Wilson, and Virginia senator Carter Glass prevailed on Congress to pass what became known as the Federal Reserve Act. In 1914, St. Louis was chosen as the location for one of the coveted twelve regional Federal Reserve Bank headquarters. To head the bank, Treasury Secretary William McAdoo chose an influential Democratic Party politician and former St. Louis mayor, Rolla Wells. Wells had resumed his successful business career and declined the offer. In his place, he recommended a young banker whom he knew to be able and strongly committed to the idea of a Federal Reserve System, William McChesney Martin.

At age forty and only recently appointed a vice president of Mississippi Valley Trust, Martin was relatively young and untested for such a potentially important task, but Wells was determined to see him in the position. Few men could resist Wells when he was intent on a cause, and McAdoo did not. On 1 September 1914, a surprised St. Louis banking community learned that William McChesney Martin was the new chairman of the board and agent of the St. Louis Federal Reserve Bank.

The Federal Reserve System had begun operation a year earlier with a seven-man board of presidentially appointed governors working out of offices in the Treasury Department in Washington, D.C.[7] Most of the system's activities were to be carried out in the regional Reserve Bank headquarters, but few people outside Washington or New York knew how these banks would operate. St. Louis bankers regarded the idea of a St. Louis Reserve Bank with a mixture of curiosity and suspicion. Undeterred, Martin hung his spanking new federal charter in the suite of small offices he had rented in the ornate headquarters building of Boatman's Bank, a leading St. Louis bank. The first order of business was to arrange for the receipt of the bank's initial capitalization in the form of Federal Reserve notes. The newly issued notes were to serve as the official U.S. currency, replacing the "greenbacks" issued by the U.S. Treasury and in use since the Civil War. On 17 November 1914, Reserve Bank Chairman William McChesney Martin announced to the press that $3 million in crisp new Federal Reserve notes had been received, and the St. Louis Reserve Bank was officially open for business.

Most Missouri bankers were reluctant to consider Fed membership, and

Martin knew he had an immense job of salesmanship ahead of him. As soon as the bank's doors were open, he was out on the road to educate his fellow bankers on the virtues of the Federal Reserve System. Martin combined a solid intellectual understanding of the Fed's potential role in the U.S. economy with an ability to describe it in anecdotal examples taken from a banker's typical experiences. The Eighth Reserve District, for which Martin was responsible, represented the fourth largest banking concentration in the country, and building broad Reserve membership there was crucial to the success of the Federal Reserve System as a whole. Martin's black Ford sedan was a common sight on the highways of Missouri as he traveled from town to town to spread the Reserve System's gospel.

In countless meetinghalls filled with doubtful bankers, Martin attacked their concerns that the Fed might become too intrusive or bureaucratic. He defended the Fed's requirement that a borrower's financial statement accompany a request by a Fed member bank to sell, or "discount," that loan to the Fed. Martin cited his own banking experience in which the preparation of financial statements, far from being an unwarranted intrusion into the private affairs of a customer, often helped those customers to understand their financial position for the first time. Martin also promised that the St. Louis Fed would make it "extremely easy and, I think, pleasant to [discount] with us."[8]

The practices initially promoted by the Federal Reserve eventually became the hallmarks of modern banking in America. Within five years, Martin's indefatigable proselytizing had converted most of the larger banks in the Eighth Reserve District into members of the Federal Reserve System.

William McChesney Martin Sr.'s life consisted of more than work. In early 1901, he met a lively young woman named Flora Woods at the Memorial Presbyterian Church. Flora was one of four attractive daughters of a widowed purser on *The City of New Orleans,* a Mississippi riverboat. Martin began to court Flora, only to learn that she was soon to be engaged to another. Flora entreated Martin to consider her younger sister Rebecca as a replacement and, although he must have been disappointed, he took Flora's advice. Martin and Becky were wed in 1905. The couple had two sons: William McChesney Jr., born in 1906, and Malcolm Woods, born five years later. When the boys were young, the family moved to the suburb of Forest Park, buying a solid, two-story stucco house on a quiet tree-lined street. The family's turn-of-the-century life revolved around visits with relatives and the social and religious life at Memorial Presbyterian Church.

Becky Martin was a deeply religious woman who drew her circle of friends from the church, and together she and her husband played an active role in its good works. Biblical precepts and the Presbyterian theology of puritanical self-control and overriding spirituality formed the core of her lessons to her children about life. There was no drinking; the escapades of an alcoholic uncle served as an object lesson in its evils. There was no dancing, gambling, smoking, or card playing. Sundays were devoted to church and family. Despite their mother's best efforts, the devil sometimes won small victories with the Martin boys, inciting young Bill to launch marbles during quiet church services or to play tricks on surprised aunts and uncles. While Becky Martin insisted on an atmosphere of formality, it would be a mistake to conclude that life in the Martin home was emotionally austere. Both Martin boys were brought up with tolerance, good humor, and a great deal of freely expressed love.

William McChesney Martin Sr. was an all-encompassing figure in the life of Bill Martin Jr. Martin Sr. always looked young for his age, was slight in build, and usually wore a serious and attentive expression. Only the twinkle in his hazel eyes served notice of a sharp, dry wit. With rimless glasses, a starched, high collar, and his hair parted in the middle, he looked more like a bank teller than its chief executive. He was soft-spoken and rarely raised his voice, asserting himself at work and at home through the sheer force of his character and the keenness of his observations. He had not been close to his own father and was determined to be caring and supportive to his own children. He had a passion for classical literature, particularly Shakespeare, often expressing his observations about life through quotations from these sources. He was a natural teacher, a stern but loving taskmaster for his sons.

Martin Sr.'s personal style was formal, the formality overlaying an active mind and iron control over strong emotions. The curious way he taught discipline to his teenage sons reveals much about the legacy Martin Sr. passed on to Martin Jr. Once, when his sons argued at the dinner table, Martin Sr. required that in the future, no matter how much insult had been dealt or how serious the matter was, each boy had to address the other with "Sir, I perceive that you are in error. Allow me to explain . . . ."[9] Then each would have to lay out his best and most specific case for his side of the argument. In extreme situations, the boys were allowed to have recourse to "I perceive that you are in *gross* error." Occasionally, their father would sit in judgment on the matter, but usually the demands of marshaling their arguments would cool the boys' passions and conversation would move on to other topics. For the rest of their lives, the two brothers, only half in jest, addressed one another as "Sir." This self-control under pressure and reliance on specifics in arguments would become second nature to Bill Martin and award him a great advantage in a career that would have more than its share of controversy.

Throughout his career, Martin Sr. continued to serve as the roving ambassador for the Fed, traveling across his district to learn firsthand about conditions among his bank members and their customers. During Bill's teenage summers, he often accompanied his father on such trips. In part because of the Martin family heritage, Martin Sr. retained a special affection for farmers and agriculture. Often the two Martins and a local banker would travel down dusty, rutted roads to visit individual farms. Bill saw his father sweating in the blistering sun and often overheard him talking earnestly about the importance of studying new agricultural techniques and expressing his concern about excessive borrowing by overly optimistic farmers.

Bill's travels in the summer of 1921 made an indelible impression on him because of his father's leading role in organizing the St. Louis Fed's cotton-loan fund the previous fall. European demand for cotton had been strong since the end of World War I, and the 1920 crop was the largest in years. Unpredictably, the Europeans drastically cut back their purchases just as the harvest began and, with no other market for the crop, the situation of farmers, cotton brokers, and their banks quickly became desperate. The St. Louis Fed stepped in and, by borrowing the stupendous sum of $55 million from its sister regional Reserve Banks, enabled Eighth District banks to rebuild their liquidity and maintain the loans to their cotton customers. The Fed kept its financing in place until the next summer, when improved market conditions allowed the excess inventory to be sold.

Martin Sr. later described the decision: "In spite of much criticism, the Fed was a means of saving a critical situation from becoming a disaster . . . by banks' requiring loans to be paid up and merchandise sacrificed."[10] For Bill, acting in the public interest was not an abstract and distant virtue; it was the direct result of decisive and often courageous action taken in the face of uncertainty and controversy — by men like his father.

Martin Sr. traveled a great deal, but when he was in St. Louis, he often invited visiting Fed officials to share a home-cooked meal at the Martin residence. The men of the Federal Reserve System and their supporters were an impassioned group, vitally concerned that the young institution would fulfill the promise they all saw in it. Regular visitors included renowned Fed leaders such as Benjamin Strong, the legendary head of the New York Reserve Bank, and Fed supporters such as the redoubtable Senator Carter Glass, then known as "the father of the Fed," and H. Parker Willis, a leading advisor to Glass and the Fed board. Dinner-table conversation was lively and wide ranging, providing a continuing seminar in central banking and public service for Bill.

A picture of the formative influences on young Bill Martin would not be complete without mentioning his abiding passion for the game of tennis. Martin was fast and well coordinated. His attitude toward tennis was typical of his determined approach to many of his goals in life. His game consisted of strokes well schooled by constant practice, coupled with a bulldog tenacity that he applied to wear down stronger or more gifted opponents. Tennis taught Martin how to appraise opponents' strengths and weaknesses and gauge how they reacted to pressure and discouragement. The game taught him also the value of husbanding one's own physical and mental resources. Over the course of his teenage summers, Martin became one of the leading players in the midwestern junior tennis circuit.

Early in his tennis career, Martin was bedeviled by an uncontrollable temper, and it took him years and many distressing losses to learn to bring his emotions under control. Later in life, his temper could often trouble him professionally, but the lessons he learned on the tennis courts of his youth enabled Martin to rein himself in when the situation demanded it. Unlike many of his contemporaries who were also outstanding singles players, Martin became a skilled doubles player as well. In doubles, a willingness to subordinate oneself for the benefit of the team and the ability to develop an effective strategy against opponents are the keys to success. These are also characteristics one can discern in Martin's accomplishments later in his life. In his senior year of high school, Martin and his doubles partner, a lanky and crafty player named Clark Clifford (another young man destined to have a long career in Washington, D.C.), compiled a 16–1 won-lost record and were St. Louis city champions.[11]

Martin's experiences as a young tennis player are revealing. During a tournament in Memphis, Martin fought his way to the finals of an important junior tournament for the first time. The finals were scheduled for a Saturday, but a summer storm forced a day's postponement, posing a dilemma for Martin. He dearly wanted a shot at victory, but his mother's solemn admonition had always been that he not play tennis on the Lord's day. Martin knew there was really no choice between affirming the values he and his family held and a chance at an athletic honor: without hesitation, he defaulted the match. That afternoon, Martin related the story to the president of Memphis's largest bank, who was hosting Martin and his best friend, Presley Edwards. Some weeks later, the astonished banker, who had been unimpressed by Martin's justification for his decision, told Edwards's father, "that young man has no future."[12]

If the banker had known Bill Martin better, he would have not been surprised. The Presbyterian theology practiced by Bill Martin's parents was deeply woven into the way they lived their lives and raised their family. Their home provided an environment in which Bill Martin could come naturally to his own beliefs early in life. Religious values guided Martin's life choices as a teenager and, together with the ethical values he accumulated during his school years and from his father, sustained him during times of trial for the whole of his life.

Bill Martin graduated from public high school at the age of sixteen. Martin Sr. considered his son too young for college and signed him up for an additional two years at St. Louis Country Day School, a local private school. Here he came under the influence of classics teacher Eugene Hecker, exactly the inspirational teacher Martin Sr. wanted his son to encounter. A decorated World War I intelligence officer, Hecker led his classes with a dramatic flair. He vividly portrayed Paris desperately longing for Helen outside the gates of Troy and verbally re-created the chaotic fall of the mighty Roman Empire. Hecker was usually disheveled in appearance and was a lax disciplinarian in a starchy school, but he was a demanding taskmaster when it came to learning his material. Hecker challenged his students, most of whom were from wealthy families, by arguing that service to others was the only achievement that truly mattered in life. Martin never forgot Hecker and corresponded with him over the years.

In September 1924, young Bill Martin went off to Yale University and entered a world of Roaring Twenties' glitter, well-known professors, and energetic and privileged students. Over two-thirds of the students were from exclusive preparatory schools, and most were from New York and New England. Very few were on scholarship. On weekends, trains leaving New Haven for New York City were full of students making the two-hour trip to "The City" for fun and adventure. It was an era of raccoon coats, bathtub gin, and open-topped convertibles. Indeed, most Yale students had few worries. They were sufficiently primed for college academics by their preparatory schools so they could attain their "Gentlemen's C" with modest effort. Many were able to look forward to a career on Wall Street, where their fathers were making fortunes in the bull markets of the 1920s. This reality was a far cry from the picture painted by Eugene Hecker, in which the sons of Mother Yale were supposedly inspired by the classics and learning to practice noblesse oblige.

There were other sides to Yale, however, and it was there that Bill Martin found a home. There were remarkable teachers. William Lyon Phelps, Yale's most famous teacher, held forth about contemporary American novelists, and Maynard Mack, who would become the country's leading Shakespeare authority, challenged students to plumb the riches of the Bard. Entranced by their offerings, Martin majored in English and considered the possibility of teaching after college. The economics and finance faculty was equally distinguished. Raymond Westerfield, one of the professors of money and banking, taught at Yale and served as president of the New Haven Trust Company.

Irving Fisher, one of the world's foremost economists and a respected theorist of the financial markets, made his pronouncements from his offices at Yale. Martin was astonished to learn in his economics courses that his father and other Federal Reserve bankers were considered hopelessly out of date because of their misguided warnings about excessive speculation in the stock market. One of the few times Martin ever saw his father visibly struggling to control his anger was in response to his son's observation that he found the Yale economists' arguments persuasive.

Yale University's 223rd graduation, held for the class of 1928 during a rainy week in mid-June, was an august and tradition-laden affair. The baccalaureate address by Yale president James Rowland Angell included the usual call to pursue spiritual goals in life but was tempered by the realities of the post–World War I world: "To face and uncover the character of evil as it appears in human nature with its trail of suffering and misery, to fight it relentlessly wherever possible, and equally to seek out and understand the most significant good for our time, is to have some share in bringing in the better day for which men hope."[13] Angell's words resonated more with Bill Martin than with most of his classmates, for they echoed sentiments often expressed by William McChesney Martin Sr. to his son.

The graduation itself was held on Sunday, 17 June, and the drizzling rain held off just long enough to allow the colorful ceremony to proceed uninterrupted. The academic procession was led by President Angell, who was followed by ranks of professors wearing academic regalia emblazoned with the brilliant colors of their alma maters, with some carrying the gilded symbols of their office. Included in the procession was Chief Justice William Howard Taft, Yale class of 1878, the epitome of Yale's contribution to public service. Yale's strong tradition of graduates with notable careers in public service was certainly an influence on Bill Martin's choice for his life's work.

As Bill Martin and his friends gathered for commencement exercises under the spreading elms, they represented the promise of young Americans, full of optimism and preparing to go out into a world of possibilities. What they could not know was that they and the country were enjoying a last full year of unprecedented prosperity, and that long hardship was to follow close behind.

2

Into the Maelstrom: Wall Street in the 1930s

One of the people Bill Martin asked about career alternatives was his uncle, Albert N. Edwards, managing director of A. G. Edwards & Sons, a St. Louis stock brokerage firm. Edwards encouraged him to join the firm: "It's not a very complicated business and you can find out whether you like it."[1] Despite the booming stock market, there were only a few brokerage firms located outside the East Coast financial centers, and A. G. Edwards had grown to twelve employees. Martin joined the firm in November 1928 as a "board boy," responsible for updating stock prices on a large chalkboard in the firm's cluttered and noisy office. Two months later he became the sole member of a newly established research department.

The brokerage industry that Martin entered was enjoying the fifth year of an extended boom in stock prices. The *New York Times* stock index averaged an annual increase of 33.5 percent during the period, a figure rarely equaled in the 136-year history of the venerable New York Stock Exchange (NYSE or the Exchange). By 1928, annual trading on the NYSE was over five times the level of 1921, and much of this additional buying and selling came from hundreds of thousands of new investors. These new investors were drawn to the market by stories of spectacular investment results for those shrewd or lucky enough to benefit from the early stages of the market's explosive growth. As these new investors piled into the market, prices continued to increase, and the relationship between the price of a share of common stock and the underlying value of that share in terms of earning power became more and more tenuous.

As 1929 opened, the rise of the market began to take on a feverish momentum, and financial professionals in firms such as A. G. Edwards began to worry that the market could become dangerously overextended. During January, the *Times* stock index increased thirty points: almost an 11 percent increase in a single month and a clear indicator of an overheated market. The Federal Reserve was the only agency of the federal government with responsibility for the health of the financial markets, and its board was deeply divided over how to respond to the surging stock market.[2]

By the end of July, George Harrison, the capable president of the Federal Reserve Bank of New York, the most important regional Reserve Bank, determined that he had endured enough of the Fed's indecision. Although the New York Fed had requested an interest rate increase eleven times since the beginning of the year, the Fed board in Washington, which was dominated by the conservative and doctrinaire Treasury Secretary Andrew Mellon, had rejected every request.[3] Harrison was one of the few who fully understood the risks inherent in the Fed's inaction because he had worked closely with his legendary predecessor, Benjamin Strong, America's first true central banker. Harrison finally faced down Mellon at a climactic board meeting on 8 August 1929 and persuaded his fellow governors to raise the Fed's rediscount rate from 5 percent to an unprecedented 6 percent.

The financial markets quickly informed Harrison that his courageous stand had come too late. In the next full day of trading, the *Times* index lost 3 percent of its value, and a moderate selling panic occurred. For two brief days, it appeared that the warnings of Harrison's opponents that a rate increase would cause a broad market collapse might be coming true. Within four days, however, the stock market shrugged off the effect of the Fed's decision, and within a month the *Times* index hit an all-time peak of 310. The Fed took no further action. Its attitude was summed up by Fed Governor Roy Young, who observed that "while the hysteria might be somewhat restrained, it would have to run its course," and the Reserve Banks would have to brace themselves for the "inevitable collapse."[4] Neither the Hoover administration nor the Fed took any step during the remainder of 1929 to lessen or possibly avoid a stock market breakdown.

The end began quietly enough. During much of October, trading became more volatile, but prices usually firmed by day's end. On particularly bad days, the index might drop by as much as 5 percent, but over subsequent sessions, it would steadily recover its loss. Then, on an unremarkable Wednesday, 23 October, the index lost 7.5 percent. This was a significant loss, but the trading volume was low and many shaken investors hoped that the next day would bring recovery. The next day, forever to be known as "Black Thursday," ushered in the disaster everyone feared but few had prepared for.

A backlog of sell orders had built up over the previous evening, but the amount was not seen as threatening. As trading opened and brokers began filling the accumulated sell orders, without warning the floodgates were opened, and a tidal wave of new sell orders came in. Trading in the first hour was equivalent to a full day's trading on a normal day. The market plunge had a self-fulfilling quality to it. As prices fell, sell orders set to automatically trigger when certain price levels were reached would then launch another load of orders onto the market. The Exchange could not physically process the orders fast enough, and the ticker tape, the printed record telegraphed nationwide to inform brokers of the latest trades, began to fall behind. Frightened investors in chaotic brokerage offices such as A. G. Edwards were forced to view prices for their securities that were out of date the moment they were printed. "Sell at the market" became the uniform cry at the brokerage offices.[5] Brokers in the A. G. Edwards office tried to sell shares for their frantic customers, but they were told by the company traders on the floor of the Exchange that it was physically impossible to get close enough to the overwhelmed specialists to hand in their orders. Desks in the Edwards offices were overflowing with sell orders, but many remained unexecuted that day.[6]

The collapse of stock prices had a terrifying impact on investors in St. Louis and other cities who had been buying stock on margin. As prices fell, the value of the shares that served as collateral for their borrowings was no longer sufficient to offer full security for their loans. Under the terms of their borrowings, the investors had to replace the lost value with other assets or repay a portion of the loan. Those who were unable to take either step would find their shares sold by the broker, the loan repaid, and the losses deducted from the proceeds left in their account. Investors who had enjoyed the magnifying effect that leveraging their resources had on their gains discovered the ruinous effect when the market went down.

After the close of the market on Monday the 28th, Albert Edwards decreed that all twelve company employees would remain in the office until the deficits in all margin accounts were calculated and customers telephoned to inform them of any collateral shortages. For four straight days and nights, Martin and his associates made their calculations and their phone calls. Often there was a heartrending story on the other end of the line, and in the friendliest possible tone, the customer was gently but firmly advised to get his affairs in order as soon as possible.[7]

Although the agony of the company's margin clients was dreadful, it would have been far worse were it not for Bill Martin's father. As president of the Federal Reserve Bank of St. Louis, Martin Sr. had discretion in setting the terms on which St. Louis Fed member banks could make loans to stock-brokers. Brokers, in turn, were the major source of investor credit. Martin Sr. unsuccessfully urged his Fed colleagues in Washington to take a more active stance in controlling financial speculation, but back home he followed his own advice. Member banks in other Reserve cities were often lending as much as 75 percent of the value of stocks provided as collateral, but in St. Louis the range was 25 to 55 percent. The St. Louis banks initially complained about the more restrictive rules, but after late October 1929, their tune changed.[8] The partners at Edwards accepted the restrictions wholeheartedly, and because of the lower borrowing levels and the early calls to customers, the losses to Edwards's customers and to the firm itself were comparatively low.[9] Bill Martin had a ringside seat for viewing the catastrophic effects of excessive credit on his community and would never forget the experience.

By the middle of November, the market collapse had run its course. The *Times* index now sat at 50 percent of its September high and for the moment, share prices stabilized. The disaster was now changing shape, and the true scope of the calamity began to reveal itself.

Young Bill Martin saw the ruin caused by the Depression from a number of perspectives. He saw the accounts of his own brokerage customers "fade away to nothing" and a number of A. G. Edwards's largest and most active investors declare bankruptcy.[10] Martin listened to his father's description of his struggles to save the weaker Fed member banks in his district and the heartbreaking despair in the communities with failed banks.[11] In St. Louis, unemployment in 1931 grew to 24 percent of the workforce, much higher than the national average of 16 percent. St. Louis also had America's largest "Hooverville," a community of family "squatters" who lived in six hundred squalid tarpaper shacks between the muddy Mississippi River and an abandoned railroad yard. It was estimated that the city government fed 10 percent of St. Louis families that year. One historian described "small groups of desperate men, women, and children searching the St. Louis dumps for food scraps."[12] Those memories scarred millions of lives and convinced Bill Martin to do what he could to ensure that the U.S. government would never again stand idly by while the nation endured another boom and bust cycle.

In the summer of 1931, Bill Martin's life took on broader possibilities when A. G. Edwards & Sons asked him to move to New York and become the firm's representative on the floor of the Exchange. During Martin's early years at the NYSE, he encountered an institution trying to retrench while stock prices continued to slide. Hundreds of thousands of investors had abandoned Wall Street:

some no longer had the resources to invest, and others were afraid of another calamity. Daily trading volume and stock prices had shrunk back to the levels of 1923–24, giving up all of the growth in prices and trading volume generated by the Roaring Twenties. The brokerage industry was badly wounded. The staffs of these firms had been reduced and the net worths of the firms and their partners had been decimated by the market decline. Even the mighty house of Morgan had lost half its net worth.[13] The market-making mechanism, which depended on the specialists, was also weakened. The specialist firms were often small family-run businesses, and they could no longer afford to keep sizable inventories of the shares in which they made markets. Trading was often sporadic and disjointed for even the most well-known shares.

To make matters considerably worse, the management of the Exchange was in the hands of a group that clung nostalgically to a hope for the return of the good old days. For over one hundred years, control of the NYSE had been held by a group of specialists, floor traders, and partners of New York brokerage firms, collectively known as the Old Guard. Leadership of the Exchange was exercised by fifty-two governors who were chosen by a nominating committee dominated by the Old Guard. Candidates ran without opposition and were elected by a majority of those present to vote. Firms like A. G. Edwards, which made their business executing orders on behalf of individual investors, were known as commission houses and actually owned a majority of the membership in the Exchange. Because they were not part of the inner circle in New York, however, the commission houses were effectively disenfranchised and had little influence on activities at the Exchange. The reality on the Exchange floor was closer to the picture painted by commentator Richardson Wood: "The Exchange was run as a private club with little concern for the public welfare."[14]

The Exchange's governors managed daily affairs through a series of seventeen management committees, which often had overlapping responsibilities and indifferent leadership. Most important policy decisions came under the purview of the powerful Law Committee, which was also tightly controlled by the Old Guard. The governors were all part-time volunteers: the full-time Exchange staff was relegated to clerical and administrative duties. The leader of the Old Guard and president of the Exchange was Richard Whitney. Whitney was an imperious and tradition-bound broker who directed his formidable leadership talents toward forestalling a movement to reform the practices of the Exchange that was bubbling up in Congress and within the Exchange itself.

In early 1932, the U.S. Congress began to seriously consider why the stock market had crashed and how legislation might prevent a reoccurrence. Congressional appetites for investigation were whetted by an ample supply of rumors of manipulators who forced stock prices up during the boom and profited during the crash. The Senate Banking Committee initiated hearings in April 1932. The disingenuous responses of the bankers and the steadfast denials of NYSE leaders did incalculable damage to the reputation of Wall Street. The damning facts uncovered by federal investigators made it clear that many of Wall Street's leaders not only turned a blind eye to the self-dealing but also were actively participating in it. As the news accounts rolled across the country week after week, editorial commentary turned more solidly in favor of a legislative solution to the excesses of the financiers. One of the more effective campaign promises made by Franklin Delano Roosevelt, the Democratic candidate for the 1932 presidential election, was to reform the "mess on Wall Street by letting the light in."[15]

In December 1932, a brief four weeks after his election, Franklin Roosevelt asked his chief economic advisor, Raymond Moley, to "ignore the outcries of the Wall Street boys" and get on with the drafting of a securities law.[16] Moley turned to Harvard Law School professor Felix Frankfurter, who sent two of his ablest former students, James M. Landis and Benjamin V. Cohen, to Washington. They set about synthesizing the best ideas of comparable British legislation, unsuccessful past legislative proposals, and their own ideas. The keystone of their legislation was the creation of a Securities and Exchange Commission (the SEC) to establish standards for disclosure in the documents issued in support of new securities offerings. Landis and Cohen were skilled draftsmen, and the legislation sailed through both houses of Congress virtually unchanged and was signed into law by a beaming President Roosevelt in May 1933. The first shoe of regulation had dropped, even if some, like Felix Frankfurter, saw it as a "modest first installment."[17]

In January 1934, the other shoe of stock market regulation was dropped, a plan for legislation regulating the practices on the nation's stock exchanges. The final bill outlawed certain practices acknowledged to manipulate stock prices. One of the bill's most crucial features was to enshrine the primacy of "self regulation," which gave the exchanges the primary role in regulating their own activities. But if an exchange failed to address an issue that the SEC believed affected the public interest, the SEC was given considerable discretionary power to investigate and, if necessary, to promulgate its own rules, which the exchange would then have to obey. The promulgation process was potent but cumbersome, and knowledgeable observers concluded that as a practical matter, the SEC would depend on the leadership of the exchanges to implement reform. After considerable negotiation and compromise, the Exchange Act was passed on 21 April 1934, and a new era began for the nation's stock markets.

Unsurprisingly, the reform legislation did not have an immediate impact on practices on the floor of the Exchange. The steady improvement in the economy from 1934 to mid-1937 lifted corporate earnings, and stock prices began to recover. For many Exchange members and market manipulators, the improvement meant a return to business as usual. One of operators whom Bill Martin observed closely was the legendary "sell 'em" Ben Smith, famous for his revelations during the 1932 congressional hearings. Martin watched Smith manipulate Case Threshing Machine stock by spreading rumors about financial problems and creating selling pressure on the stock by selling it short, that is, by selling shares borrowed from other owners. Once the share price had been forced down, the manipulator would step in to buy those shares necessary to replace his borrowing and pocket the savings. Martin later described his reaction to Smith's practice: "[T]o me it was just a type of stealing and I thought it was terrible."[18] Martin was infuriated by the indifference of the Old Guard–dominated Business Conduct Committee, as "evidence in abundance of old-fashioned manipulation has been offered to the committee time and time again, only to be passed over as of absolutely no importance."[19] The more he understood the endemic nature of corruption at the Exchange, the more fiercely determined he became to help bring reform.

During these years, Martin complemented his education on the trading floor with a scholarly interest in finance and economics. In the spring of 1932, he had begun a night-school course at the New School for Social Research, an adult education institute with liberal leanings. His teacher was Alvin Johnson, the school's director of research and the future originator of the National Recovery Act, the first achievement of Franklin Roosevelt's New Deal. There Martin met Joseph Mead, an intense young economist employed by the Standard Statistics Corporation. After months of late-night talks about the need for a serious economic journal to give a voice to leading pro-capitalist economists to challenge "our friends on the left," they decided to start one. Johnson was taken by the enthusiasm of these two brash young men and offered the resources of the New School for their idea, and the concept of the *Economic Forum* was born.[20]

At an organizational meeting in May 1932 attended by over a hundred participants from major corporations and financial institutions, Martin and Mead enlisted the audience to join in small groups to undertake research on a range of economic issues, including monetary problems, world-trade issues, the future of financial markets, and unemployment. The two organized an editorial board and in September brought out their first issue of the *Economic Forum Quarterly,* featuring the first article by John Maynard Keynes ever written for a U.S. publication and another by the managing director of the Central Bank of England, Sir Josiah Stamp. The quarterly's credo was pure

Martin. It announced its interest in classic economic problems but also in "the more human side of economic life" and plans for America "to put her house in order."[21] It committed itself to relevant research, dissemination of economic thought and, reflecting Martin's pragmatism, encouraging the direct acceptance of new ideas by businessmen and legislators.

Martin's ambition to undertake the *Economic Forum* in the worst year of the Great Depression reveals much about him. It reflects his desire for a great calling, in this case to initiate a national dialogue about pressing economic issues, even though he was only a twenty-six-year-old junior stockbroker. The *Forum's* philosophy reflected Martin's thinking on how the United States should respond to the Depression. The editorials stated his belief that hard times require a rededication to steadfastness and "positive values." Hard-headed analysis would determine what needed to be done, and honest, open discussion would develop solutions that would preserve what was good and address that which must be changed. One of the quarterly's quotations submitted by Martin aptly summarized his outlook: "Yet, human, bravely hold thy course, firmly to pursue the gradual paths of an aspiring change."[22]

During 1935, Martin began to pursue a Ph.D. in finance at Columbia University, traversing the length of Manhattan to squeeze in classes around his hours at the Exchange. He took courses with Raymond Moley, once Roosevelt's closest economics advisor before the two had parted ways. Although Moley was a committed reformer, he encouraged his students to recognize the limits of government intervention in the economy and the importance of flexible governmental regulation. Another teacher was H. Parker Willis, a widely respected economist who had been instrumental in drawing up the Federal Reserve Act of 1913 and had served as the Fed's first research director. Willis taught that the Fed needed strong regulatory powers, but he was also an eloquent defender of free markets. He encouraged Martin to do his doctoral thesis on the workings of the NYSE, which Willis thought was misunderstood and had been poorly portrayed in the congressional hearings of 1932. Martin was eager to learn from men who combined a scholar's insight with practical experience in government, and he referred to their precepts often in the course of his career.

As the SEC began to play a more active role in the affairs of the NYSE, Martin's time for studies became compressed. In July 1934, Franklin Roosevelt had disappointed his liberal allies by choosing Joseph P. Kennedy as the first chairman of the SEC. Kennedy, known for his investing acumen, had admitted to participating in stock market "pools" with known manipulators in the early 1930s, although he had publicly apologized for it. Kennedy's first goal was to oust NYSE president Richard Whitney, who had tried to derail the

Exchange Act of 1934 and was thoroughly hostile to the idea of reform. Kennedy believed that the esteem with which Whitney was held at the Exchange made him the greatest barrier to reform. Kennedy discovered allies within the Exchange who were interested in reform; working with them, he pressured the Exchange governors to replace Whitney as president. The SEC chairman was well known for his skill at twisting arms, and he prevailed on the governors to nominate a new president for the 1935 election of Exchange leaders. After a bruising battle, Charles Gay, the senior partner of one of the oldest Exchange members, was ultimately elected. Gay's elevation represented the modest birth of reform at the Exchange.

Charles Gay was not the only anti–Old Guard candidate nominated in 1935. Bill Martin's disgust at the way the Exchange was run goaded him into campaigning to become the board of governor nominee of the out-of-town commission houses. Touching a wellspring of discontent, Martin found that "the out-of-town firms were glad to support me," and that he had amassed enough votes to assure his election as a member of the reform movement.[23]

On 12 May 1935, Gay, Martin, and Whitney were duly elected governors. Richard Whitney received more votes than any other candidate, reflecting the Old Guard's undiminished strength. Governor Martin was assigned to three management committees, only one of which had much influence on the affairs of the Exchange. In characteristic fashion, Martin carefully studied the minutes of past meetings and interviewed former members of the committees on which he was to serve. Before his first meeting, he knew the details of his committee's history as well as any incumbent and had plans to make it more effective. Despite his intention to "watch my step carefully and soft-pedal my too liquid tongue," Martin was often in the thick of the arguments between the Old Guard and the reformers that raged in nearly every management committee.[24]

Martin had been in office only three months when a crisis occurred over his stand on the issue of admitting a new member to the Exchange. Martin's experience crystallized the situation at the Exchange in 1935 and the problems of changing it. The proposed member, the partnership of Harrison & Peterson, had powerful Old Guard sponsorship in the form of Richard Whitney and the house of Morgan. Martin knew that Harrison had been pressured to resign from the NYSE years earlier, and Martin's review of the record indicated that while Harrison's affairs had been closed out "in good order," in fact there were many unresolved counts of dishonesty against him. Martin was not surprised at the crude whitewash, for he had seen it before, particularly when an ally of Richard Whitney or the house of Morgan was involved. Now he was in a position to keep men like this out of the Exchange, and he decided to call for a rejection of the application.

Martin laid out his case to the Committee on Admissions and thought he was well on the way to a unanimous vote when Richard Whitney entered the committee room. Not to be outdone by Martin, the Old Guard had gotten word to Whitney, and he brought the proceedings to a standstill by asking for a recess until the next day, when he wanted to appear as a witness. Despite Martin's angry protests that Whitney's appearance would be against the committee's rules, the request was granted.

As he contemplated the next meeting, Martin's anger was directed at Richard Whitney's influence: "He was a power, an arrogant power, unto himself."[25] Now Whitney was once again applying that power to protect his friends. Whitney's move was the essence of privilege and the private-club atmosphere that drew so much criticism from Congress and the public. When Whitney made his case to the committee, Martin could see his support melting away. Martin argued that if the Exchange "could not take a stand in this clear cut situation, it would never be able to raise its standards . . . and it will be just a matter of time before the SEC takes the matter out of our hands."[26] When even the two Exchange lawyers who had previously affirmed Martin's case backed away, he knew he had lost. Martin "fought a moral battle with myself as to whether I should be a Boy Scout" and call for a formal vote, in which he could record his dissent, or accept the consensus.[27] Conceding his loss by giving up the vote, Martin consoled himself that "I have made several prominent individuals, who are thoroughly sincere, do some thinking."[28] Martin's ability to see long-term progress in the midst of an agonizing short-term defeat gave him a capacity for resilience as well as a rare ability to avoid transforming an opponent on a particular issue into an implacable enemy.

During 1936, Martin continued to be frustrated by the Old Guard's ability to bottle up initiatives for reform, summarizing his experience as a governor with: "I got licked on all the things I struggled for."[29] His efforts did bring him to the attention of Exchange president Gay, and the two developed a close relationship. Charles Gay was over his head in the presidency, a job he had accepted only reluctantly in the first place. Gay had come up the hard way, starting as a teen in the 1890s delivering securities as a Wall Street runner. At sixty, an age when most Wall Streeters began to take things easy, he was working fifteen-hour days, caught between the demands for reform from the SEC and the steadfast resistance of his lifelong friends in the Old Guard. Martin saw Gay as "unfailingly honest . . . and he has done a magnificent job outside the Exchange, but he will not clean up the situation internally. On balance he is a whole lot better with his failings than if he had been more capable and ruthless."[30] A wise judgment for a thirty-year-old stockbroker.

Remarkably, Charles Gay relied on Martin for his knowledge of the inner workings of the Exchange. Although Martin had been a member of the Exchange for a relatively few years, he had amassed a broad knowledge of what actually transpired on the trading floor. He coupled this experience with his Ph.D. studies of the Exchange's regulations and research on the practices of its influential management committees. Now he was gaining firsthand experience with the problems of running the Exchange. One of Martin's assignments from Gay in late 1935 was to deal with James M. Landis, the new chairman of the SEC, on a variety of sensitive operational issues.

Martin met periodically with Landis and his staff, but he was disappointed with their understanding of how the Exchange actually functioned. He summarized the situation for his friend Presley Edwards, resident at the A. G. Edwards office in St. Louis: "Landis is a sincere public servant . . . and his judgments will be honest ones, but he is surrounded by people who are not really aimed at protecting the public interest, but more at how an ideal security business should be conducted."[31] Martin's experience in defending the Exchange in negotiations with the SEC convinced him that regulators needed to better understand the industries they governed and their cooperation should be enlisted whenever possible "because the objective of both is the prosperity of the citizen."[32] In Martin's mind, pragmatic regulation and industry acceptance, if not cooperation, were essential ingredients for long-lasting reform and effective government regulation.

Martin's awkward relationship with James Landis lost its relevance when Landis announced his departure from the SEC. Franklin Roosevelt, convinced that the SEC had lost the momentum toward reform begun under Joe Kennedy, had chosen a more committed reformer, William O. Douglas, to replace Landis.

Douglas brought an unusual background and exceptional personal qualifications to the SEC chairmanship. He was born in 1888 and lived a Horatio Alger story, beginning with his father's early death and the family's years of poverty. Douglas's brilliance and energy were captivating; he found sponsors and scholarships for his college education and Columbia Law School. After a few years of practicing law and teaching law at night, during which he found corporate law "a narrowing experience . . . that enslaves one because of its exacting demands," he joined the faculty of Yale Law School.[33] Douglas was teaching bankruptcy law when Joe Kennedy asked him to head an SEC investigation into a scandal in the oversight of corporate reorganizations. Douglas's report castigated "the old crowd of financiers which monopolized the bankrupt's real estate and squeezed out investors and, in addition, the bank trustees who sat idly by while this happened."[34] Kennedy was highly pleased with the report and promoted Douglas as an SEC commissioner. When Landis announced his departure, Kennedy persuaded Roosevelt to appoint Douglas as his successor.

It did not take much time for problems to pile up at Douglas's door. The economy had begun to slide into recession in June 1937 and carried the stock market down with it. Three months later, shortly after Douglas became chairman, the *Times* stock index had completed a 40 percent decline. The market's collapse wiped out six years of recovery and devastated the hopes of Wall Street. Exchange president Gay blamed the slide on "the overregulation of the market by the SEC."[35] On 18 October, a delegation of NYSE representatives arranged a meeting with President Roosevelt to plead for Douglas's removal. Anticipating their request, Roosevelt arranged for Joe Kennedy and Douglas to "drop by" the meeting in Hyde Park, and the embarrassed Wall Streeters never brought the subject up.

Douglas threw down the gauntlet of reform on 23 November 1937 in one of the most critical speeches ever delivered by the head of a government regulatory agency. Referring to a recently completed SEC study of the September 1937 market break, which had evaluated whether the NYSE specialists acted to moderate the market decline, Douglas berated "specialists who either create the daily price fluctuations or else contribute materially to their severity."[36] He harshly criticized Exchange members for short selling. The Exchange leadership, including Martin, had long maintained that short selling was a vital contributor to smoothing out trading in unstable markets and a fundamental support for the market-making mechanism. Douglas observed that in September 1937, "50 percent of short sales were members trading for their own account and [the SEC study] did not reveal any evidence of a market stabilizing influence."[37] He called for reform of trading practices on the Exchange floor "so that all elements of the casino are obliterated." He maintained that exchanges should be seen as public utilities, and "they must be tamper-proof, with no concealed springs and no laying on of hands."[38]

Having attacked the Exchange's practices, he moved on to its management. He observed: "The tasks of conducting the affairs of large exchanges are too engrossing for those who must also run their own businesses," and called for a paid full-time professional administration.[39] Douglas boldly challenged the Exchange to reform its practices in the public interest "or face an immediate and more persuasive administration by the Commission."[40] The speech publicly committed the SEC to control the management of the NYSE. Douglas knew full well that if the Exchange management resisted him, he would have to replace it entirely, and the financial markets could become paralyzed. It was a calculated gamble that the reformers could put more pressure on Charles Gay to cooperate with Douglas than the Old Guard could place on Gay to oppose the SEC.

Douglas won his bet. On 29 November, after an anguished Thanksgiving, Gay announced his willingness to work with "public authorities in every way for the better performance of the Exchange . . . under the supervision of the Commission."[41] On 8 December, Gay took another step that was to prove historic by forming a special committee to study the "organization and administration" of the Exchange under the leadership of Carle Conway, chairman of the board of Continental Can Co. Conway was one of the few businessmen recognized by New Dealers as open-minded, and Gay knew he supported reform. The eight other committee members included Kenneth Hogate, the president of the *Wall Street Journal*; Adolph Berle, an original New Deal "Brains Trust" member; and Charles Gay's right-hand man, William Mc-Chesney Martin Jr. Conway said his report would be finished in two months. The committee opened offices at 41 Broad Street and began to interview a wide range of Exchange members and nonmembers.

Conway's selection of Bill Martin as the committee's secretary gave Martin a significant influence on the final recommendations. The committee's routine called for various members to conduct interviews and deliberate during the day. Martin returned to his rooms at the Yale Club of New York, where he spent much of the night synthesizing the day's results in written minutes that updated committee members and set the agenda for the following day. Conway set the tone early in the process by meeting with Douglas and bringing back the SEC's recommendations for reform. They included "definite and suggestive proposals" that dealt primarily with establishing a full-time paid president, recruiting an "expert" executive staff, and reorganizing the board of governors.[42] Douglas's list made it clear that despite his threatening rhetoric about drastic reforms and taking over management of the Exchange, his primary goal was still to secure Exchange leaders with whom he could work. On that point, Carle Conway and Bill Martin agreed.

The committee interviews graphically revealed the split within the Exchange over the scope and speed of reform. Even the more broad-minded members of the Old Guard felt that relations with the SEC were "primarily a public relations problem" and did not see the self-perpetuating nature of the governing structure as a reform issue.[43] Paul Shields, the most eloquent reformer, accurately predicted the problems that would dog the Exchange's future. He saw the president as becoming caught "between the SEC and the rival factions in the Exchange."[44] He felt the public would not come back to the market "until it was convinced that the Exchange had ceased stalling on reform."[45] The Exchange needed to "call in an outstanding man, give him authority and immunity from our special pleas."[46] The committee discovered that bridging the gap between the two Exchange factions would be difficult, let alone overcoming the problems with the SEC.

The final report addressed the issues raised by Douglas and deftly laid ground rules for dealing with some less immediate but potentially explosive issues in the future. The report's general philosophy reflected the views of Bill Martin.[47] The recommendations included a paid president and professional administration as well a reduction of the Old Guard's control over the board of governors. In a move only Martin could have engineered, the Law Committee, the powerful committee the Old Guard had used to strangle reform initiatives for years, was abolished. The web of management committees was simplified and made more responsive to the presidency. The report addressed the hotly contested issue of the adequacy of the current securities trading mechanisms in a philosophical discussion that set a hurdle to reform which bore Martin's stamp. The report "acknowledged the criticism" of its current mechanisms but required that "if an existing piece of financial machinery is eliminated, an adequate method of [providing] liquidity must be substituted in its place."[48] Bill Martin played a vital behind-the-scenes role in shaping a response to Douglas's challenge that would serve as a blueprint for overhauling the operations of the Exchange.

On 25 January 1938, the governors met to discuss the report, but it appeared that Richard Whitney and the Old Guard would succeed in having the report accepted "in principle," with only a vague commitment for implementation. Charles Gay shed his usual equivocal posture and rose to the occasion. Leaving his chair as presiding officer, Gay lumbered to the well of the chamber and for the first time in his life spoke against Richard Whitney. The man who was lampooned as "Charlie McCarthy" Gay, an unflattering portrayal of Gay as the popular ventriloquist's dummy, now spoke with an unaccustomed passion born of his frustration with three years of conflict and stalemate. He advised Whitney that his proposal would goad Douglas to make good his challenge to take control of the Exchange. It was time to accept the inevitability of reform and for the Exchange to take control of the outcome.[49] It was Charles Gay's finest hour. Acceptance of Gay's logic and respect for his integrity overcame the Old Guard's resistance, and the report was unanimously approved with only Whitney abstaining. Acceptance of the Conway report put the Exchange on the path to reform.

Gay then proposed a committee of three to implement the report's recommendations. The members of the committee were a former Exchange president and certified Old Guard member, a leader of the reform movement, and Bill Martin. Martin had the obvious asset of his Conway Committee experience, and he knew how to modify the constitution to embrace meaningful reform. It was later said that the former president "jumped over the fence to the reformers so fast he left his pants hanging on the barbed wire."[50] Since there was no resistance to the Conway report, the bulk of the work was left to Martin. The report was presented on 21 February and approved overwhelmingly a month later.

The struggle for reform shifted to the selection of a new board of governors, and more particularly to the selection of a chairman of the board. The Old Guard was gathering its remaining strength to select a chairman who would give lip service to reform but protect their interest. The Old Guard was making considerable progress against the somewhat disorganized reformers until fate intervened with an event of colossal proportions: the financial collapse and disgrace of Richard Whitney

A man of pride and privilege, Richard Whitney was the quintessential Wall Streeter. Descended from a family that had arrived in America on the first ship after the *Mayflower,* educated at Groton, a preparatory school for New England's scions, and Harvard, through which he had come to know Franklin Roosevelt, he came to Wall Street in 1912. From his early days at the Exchange, Whitney enjoyed an expensive lifestyle and had a passion for investments in unproven companies. Making all the classic mistakes of an overly optimistic investor, Whitney poured money into his struggling companies even as the boom years of the 1920s passed them by. The demands of his lifestyle and his investments far outstripped the ability of Richard Whitney & Co. to support them, and beginning as early as 1931, Whitney began to borrow. His ability to borrow had been enhanced considerably by his courageous leadership during the dark days of 1929 and his determined, if misguided, marshaling of unceasing resistance to the SEC.

Even with his borrowings, Whitney could not keep up with his financial requirements, and in 1936 he took a fateful step. Whitney's firm was entrusted with millions of dollars of his clients' cash and securities. Whitney began to occasionally misappropriate these assets and temporarily pledge them as collateral for his personal loans. What began as occasional became more frequent, and between February and November 1937, Whitney took $1,121,000 of assets belonging to the Gratuity Fund of the NYSE.[51] This transgression proved to be Whitney's undoing and cast his criminality in its harshest light. These assets did not belong to Whitney's rich clients; they were to provide death benefits to the often-destitute families of Exchange employees. In mid-November 1937, Whitney realized the enormity of his predicament and confessed to his brother George, a senior partner in the house of Morgan, who had bailed him out in the past. George was horrified but loaned Richard the amount he said was enough to recover and restore the Gratuity Fund's misappropriated assets. Despite a promise to George that he would wind down Richard Whitney & Co., the borrowing merry-go-round resumed.

Bill Martin habitually reviewed the minutes of the Business Conduct Committee, and in December he noticed that attached to one of the minutes were summary reports of the financial condition of a number of member firms, including Richard Whitney & Co. Martin understood the arcane accounting system for Exchange member firms and could see at a glance that Whitney's firm was probably insolvent.[52]

Taking his concerns to the committee chairman, Howland Davis, whom Martin described as "not a strong man," Martin urged that Whitney be sent a request for a more complete financial disclosure. Davis was doubtful that the situation was serious, but this time Martin was not prepared to acquiesce on the subject of Richard Whitney. Martin pressed hard, and Davis finally gave in. In February, when the results came in, Martin and Whitney again faced one another in front of the Business Conduct Committee — but this time, Richard Whitney was on the defensive. When the extent of Whitney's financial distress became evident, the Exchange's disciplinary machinery finally began to close in on its former leader.

Whitney tried to extricate himself by using his old techniques of bluster and threats but, to his everlasting credit, Charles Gay once again stood firm: there would be no excuses or delays. That same afternoon Gay turned the matter over to District Attorney Thomas E. Dewey, and a few hours later, he and Howland Davis began the anguishing pilgrimage to Washington to inform William O. Douglas of the situation.

Douglas later referred to his meeting with Gay as the moment "the Exchange was delivered into my hands."[53] Douglas knew he now had a wedge to drive the reform process into the heart of the Exchange, and with Whitney gone, the resistance of the Old Guard would collapse. At midnight on 7 March, Douglas ordered SEC officials to be at Richard Whitney & Co.'s offices "at the crack of dawn" the next day to begin a thorough investigation.[54] On 23 March, a week after Whitney was indicted, Douglas told the Exchange nominating committee that the 1938 elections for the board scheduled for May "cannot provide a return of the Old Guard to power."[55] He also made it clear that the next board chairman had to be a convincing voice for reform. Fate had strengthened Douglas's position, and there was no question that he intended to exercise the opportunity the gods had given him.

As the Nominating Committee gathered on 9 April, it was in an awkward position to choose a chairman suitable to Douglas. The committee had been selected before the Whitney debacle and included many Old Guard members. Whitney's failure had indeed fractured the Old Guard's resistance to reform, but the Nominating Committee members could not bring themselves to select any of the reform leaders. The acrimonious debates over reform in the Exchange management committees had become highly personalized, and the reform spokesmen were bitterly detested by the Old Guard. The committee felt it had found an acceptable moderate in Edward E. Bartlett, who had been president of the New York Cotton Exchange and was a partner in the firm belonging to a reform leader. At the eleventh hour it was discovered that Bartlett's record was not sufficiently spotless to offer him to the public and the SEC as the spokesman for reform. When the out-of-town commission houses heard that Bartlett's candidacy was doomed, they began to pressure the committee to choose their spokesman, Bill Martin.

Martin's candidacy was neither widely supported nor vehemently opposed, which made him a suitable compromise, but one that few members actively supported. He was well known for his work in implementing the Conway Committee recommendations. Conway himself had recommended Martin in a letter to Charles Oakley, the head of the nominating committee: "He has intelligence, courage, indefatigable energy, intense spirit and great faith in the future of the Exchange as a public institution."[56] Charles Gay was known to think highly of Martin and had promoted him at every opportunity. Martin was seen as unusually skillful behind the scenes, but many could not envision a serious, modest, and somewhat humorless thirty-one-year-old as effectively representing the Exchange to the investing public.

Other committee members supported Martin's reputation for no-nonsense analysis of issues that most governors debated in emotional terms. He stayed out of controversies but was known to hold firm positions on disagreeable topics. The Old Guard members did not trust Martin but considered him a pragmatist and a reformer that they might be able to live with. The reformers recognized that Martin had taken on Richard Whitney when Whitney was still the power at the Exchange, but they hoped for someone more overtly committed to their cause. In the absence of a more popular candidate, the solid support of the out-of-town houses was sufficient to win Martin the nomination.

As Bill Martin sat in an Exchange anteroom on the afternoon of 11 April, awaiting the decision on the chairmanship, he was planning how he would become the first paid president of the Exchange. Some five months earlier, shortly after he had discovered Richard Whitney's financial problems, he had calmly informed his family that "events were taking place which have put me in the right place" to become president of the Exchange.[57] Events had worked out surprisingly close to his audacious plan. The chairmanship was one thing, but the presidency was quite another. It was here that the Conway Committee had placed most of the power, and even Douglas had told the Exchange leaders that their future depended on the capability of the president. Managing the Exchange and bringing reform would take knowledge, courage, and determi-

3

Cleaning the Augean Stables of Capitalism: The New York Stock Exchange Presidency

The formal capitulation of the Old Guard to the inevitability of reform took place on 9 May 1938, when the Martin administration and reform slate of governors were duly elected. If Martin were to use his Exchange chairmanship as the springboard to the presidency, he would have to move quickly. He invited the press to cover his acceptance speech, and despite his own awkwardness with reporters, Martin made himself available for innumerable interviews. The financial press had rarely been allowed into Exchange offices—and never into the inner sanctum of the mahogany-paneled chairman's office. A thirty-one-year-old chairman made good copy, and a typically overblown article described Martin as "The Symbol of the Wall Street Revolt."[1] Martin believed that if the public were ever to return to the stock market, it needed to see the Exchange as open to public scrutiny. At a time when few financial figures sought publicity, Martin was determined to become a very visible symbol of the Exchange's accessibility.

The road to the presidency ran through the office of William O. Douglas. The SEC chairman had publicly committed himself to an ambitious reform program at the Exchange, and Martin was worried that Douglas would not give the Exchange adequate time to come up with its own plan for reform. When Martin suggested an initial meeting, Douglas surprised him by proposing that they both meet with President Roosevelt. On 13 May, the three met at the White

House for a brief session in which the president genially encouraged the two to work together in the public interest. At an impromptu press conference after the meeting, Douglas was asked how he intended to pursue reform now that Martin was chairman. Throwing an arm around the astonished Martin's shoulders, Douglas replied, "We'll work that out together."[2] Martin had achieved his goal of getting Douglas's early public support, but only time would tell whether he would be suffocated by Douglas's all-encompassing embrace.

Martin then took a risky step. At the first meeting of the newly constituted board on 16 May, Martin proposed that he be elected president pro tem as well as chairman. The chairman lacked sufficient authority to initiate reforms, and Martin told his fellow governors that "the work of the Exchange must go on in any event."[3] Then he challenged them: "If you do not intend to nominate me, whom do you intend to select?"[4] Martin considered it possible that his election to the chairmanship might have been orchestrated by the Old Guard as a public relations ploy to give the appearance, but not the substance, of embracing reform. Now he was seeking real power. If he had misjudged his fellow governors' attitude toward his active leadership, his ambitious challenge would appear naive and overreaching. Martin's move could generate opposition to his presidential ambitions, and the Old Guard would unite to slap him down. All Martin's hopes hung in the balance.

Before the meeting, Martin had reached out to the reform group by offering to use his pro tem authority to promote many of its leaders to positions of influence. He also committed himself to give the out-of-town brokerage houses a voice in the management of the Exchange. At the meeting he called on their support. The unhealed wounds from previous reform battles were clearly visible in the acrimonious debate, but Martin's allies came through. In a close 14–10 vote, Martin was elected president pro tem. Martin had a foot in the door to the presidency and the power to move the Exchange along the path of reform.

Exercising his new authority, Martin initiated a formal dialogue between the Exchange and the SEC, and he soon came face-to-face with the full scope of Douglas's reform agenda. On 18 May, representatives of the SEC and Exchange met, and Douglas made it clear that he was unhappy about the safety of investors' assets placed in the hands of brokers. Douglas proposed the creation of a new "trust institution" that would process payments and deliveries for all securities traded on the Exchange and arrange financing for all margin (credit) lending by Exchange members to customers. To Martin's dismay, Douglas also revived an old complaint about the Exchange, that the brokerage business should be separated from the risks associated with the securities underwriting business. Douglas rounded out his agenda by suggesting that the Exchange give up its bond trading and transfer it to its rival, the New York Curb Exchange. From the Exchange's point of view, it was an appalling list and one guaranteed to inflame the membership. Martin said the issues raised were "serious ones for the Exchange" and that discussions with the SEC would continue.[5] Douglas had opened a Pandora's box of horrors, but it was too late for Martin to turn away from Douglas now.

Despite his setback in managing relations with the SEC, Martin made progress, or at least the appearance of it, on other fronts. In a style that would become a trademark, Martin personally announced all initiatives taken by the Exchange and quickly established himself as its spokesman. On 12 May, Martin appointed a Presidential Nominating Committee with Paul Shields as chairman. Shields, a man of firm character and the most knowledgeable of the reformers, understood the difficulty of reforming the Exchange. Martin knew Shields would demand a candidate forceful enough to bring about change. To buy time from the SEC, Martin announced that the Exchange would begin to gather data on the feasibility of splitting the brokerage and underwriting function. In early June, Martin introduced a program to assist unemployed financial district workers find jobs in other fields. Martin also authorized a study of how the interests of out-of-town brokerage firms could be better represented. Martin knew that he had only a limited time to make an impact, and he made the most of every day.

For its part, the Presidential Nominating Committee was buffeted by the conflicting interests of the Exchange factions and hobbled by the shoddy reputation of the Exchange. The committee began by looking at well-known leaders of industry or government—but they, understandably, declined to leave their posts to become the head of a polarized institution in a troubled industry.

Toward the end of May, the committee was running out of qualified and willing candidates, and by mid-June the only two viable candidates were Martin and O. Max Gardner. Gardner, an able and popular former governor of North Carolina, had reorganized the finances of that state and was known to be a friend of Franklin Roosevelt.[6] The Old Guard promoted Gardner, hoping that he could bring political pressure to neutralize Douglas and leave the details of running the Exchange to the Old Guard. The press breathlessly reported a close race between the two men.

The reality was quite different, for Martin's campaign had succeeded in convincing Douglas to weigh in on his side. Through their official negotiations and private conversations, Martin and Douglas began to establish a solid working relationship. Douglas's commitment to self-regulation was conditioned on the Exchange's willingness to address the SEC's concerns. Martin and Douglas reached an early agreement to reform the Exchange's lax disciplinary procedures. They discussed joint efforts to develop data on the financial resources and trading practices of Exchange members. Even on previously nonnegotiable issues such as Douglas's proposal for a "trust institution," Martin and the ubiquitous Paul Shields proposed a possible compromise. Even though he assured Douglas of his desire to work with the SEC, Martin regularly expressed his reservations about the practicality of Douglas's full agenda. Douglas recognized that Martin's most important accomplishment during his first hectic weeks as chairman was to earn a wary acceptance from the Old Guard for his various initiatives. It would do Douglas no good to have a compliant Exchange president who could not move his membership toward reform.

Once he was convinced about Martin's potential effectiveness, Douglas moved with his usual dispatch. He killed Gardner's candidacy by saying he "did not want a political hack" in the presidency.[7] When Shields visited Douglas in late June with the news that Martin was the nominating committee's preferred candidate, Douglas responded with, "now that's a man I can work with."[8] A Martin presidency, which had looked wildly improbable when Martin had predicted it in December, was now, with the aid of Richard Whitney and William O. Douglas, becoming a reality.

The Exchange Bill Martin took over on 1 July 1938 was still mired in the aftereffects of the market collapse of 1929 and the recession of 1937. Even though the economy had recovered from the low point of 1933, the gross national product was no larger than it had been in 1920. After six years of solid recovery, corporate earnings collapsed in 1938 and stock prices extended a decline that brought the major stock indexes back to the level of December 1919. Investors shunned the stock market, and trading volume was lower than it had been in 1921. The financial capacity of the market-making specialist firms had shrunk so much that they made little effort to stimulate market activity, and many shares simply did not trade on a daily basis. The issuance of new securities had slowed to a trickle. Exchange members were still retrenching in an unsuccessful attempt to bring costs in line with their shrinking revenues. The Exchange itself was on its way from a $141,000 loss in 1937 to a $1,550,000 loss in 1938. Unhappy with the decline in its transfer-tax revenue, the New York State Legislature was considering a large increase in the stock transfer tax. Worst of all, this terrible atmosphere was going into its tenth year.

Within the Exchange, there was an uneasy truce among the factions, since the Old Guard remained weak and the reformers Martin had placed in Exchange leadership roles were moving slowly.[9] The ongoing financial problems of nearly all Exchange members made them extremely apprehensive about the financial implications of the SEC's reform proposals. As he looked over a list of thirty-four "priority issues" prepared for him, Martin must have been painfully aware of the reasons that so many others had declined his new job.

As the responsibilities of the presidency dawned on him, Martin began to recognize "that he was just a kid" and how limited his experience really was.[10] He concluded that he needed the advice and support of some of the able and respected men in Wall Street. Replacing the Exchange's lawyers presented an opportunity, and Martin asked Jeremiah Milbank Jr. to take on the job. Milbank, then in his middle sixties, was one of Wall Street's wisest counselors. He was a senior partner of one of the most famous Wall Street law firms, a trusted advisor to the Rockefellers and American presidents, and the treasurer of the Republican Party as well. Martin told Milbank that he wanted him to work on the account personally because he was "desperate to do a good job at the Exchange" and badly needed an experienced advisor.[11] Milbank had been planning to cut back his practice but eventually agreed "because it's important for you to succeed."[12]

On 21 July, Milbank and Martin had a quiet dinner with John D. Rockefeller Jr. and J. P. Morgan Jr. "to talk over my [Martin's] plans."[13] About three weeks later, Winthrop Aldrich, chairman of the Chase National Bank of New York and the dean of the New York banking community, made an unannounced visit to say, "I know you have a tough job and I just wanted you to know that we all want to be helpful to you."[14] It was a heady dose of support for the young president. Just remembering Aldrich's visit brought tears of gratitude to Martin's eyes when he recounted it forty-six years later.

On 31 October, four months after he took office, Martin unveiled what he called his "Fifteen Point Program" designed to "promote the public interest and increase investor safety at the Exchange."[15] It contained the same combination of immediate steps and a framework for developing future actions that had characterized the Conway report. Martin created a document that set the tone for his presidency and defined the terms on which he would deal with the SEC. Martin's goal was to preserve the existing market mechanisms of the auction marketplace, with its stock specialist responsible for maintaining orderly trading and continuous pricing. Martin also remained committed to margin lending by brokers, which he knew to be vital to the economics of the securities business. To address the weaknesses in those mechanisms that had been the subject of SEC criticism for years, Martin proposed a series of measures that dealt with investor safety and inherent conflicts of interest. Martin anticipated that the SEC would be unhappy that the program did not go far enough and that his membership would consider it too revolutionary. He could not have imagined how correct he would be.

Some of the fifteen points dealt with self-dealing and the Whitney legacy of excessive borrowing. Margin borrowing by member firms and their partners would be prohibited, and members would be required to report regularly on all unsecured borrowings. The Exchange's supervisory powers would be upgraded and surprise audits authorized to confirm that members were adhering to Exchange rules. Martin appointed thirty-eight-year-old reformer Charles Harding to chair the Committee on Member Firms and to overhaul the Exchange's notoriously ineffective disciplinary process. Harding had an unusual combination of privilege and discipline, having gone to the exclusive Groton School before attending West Point and serving as an army officer. Harding was plainspoken and not subject to blandishment or pressure. He executed this sensitive role with such skill and fairness that he was elected chairman of the Exchange two years later. The Exchange now had a plan — but it remained to be seen if Douglas would buy it.

Douglas gave Martin's program a decidedly mixed review. He described himself as "very pleased with a practical progressive approach to some extremely complicated problems."[16] But he expressed his reservations about the failure to deal with the far-reaching reforms he had proposed: "We recognize that this program is an intermediate program to fill immediately a real need . . . overhauling the whole system is going to take time to work out."[17] Douglas's response to Martin's program reflected pressure on Douglas from the SEC's liberal wing to pursue fundamental reform at the Exchange coupled with Douglas's own sense of urgency to move decisively during the early years of his chairmanship.

The relationship between Douglas and Martin started to show the strain of their conflicting priorities. In early November 1938, Douglas sent Martin the final SEC report on the Whitney case. Douglas referred to testimony that two partners in J. P. Morgan & Co, Whitney's brother George and senior partner Thomas Lamont, had known of Richard Whitney's misappropriation of Exchange Gratuity Fund assets for months and had not informed officials at the Exchange of the crime. Instead, they had loaned him enough money to arrange the return of the cash and securities to the Gratuity Fund. Douglas asked whether these actions deserved punishment under the "[a]ctions detrimental to the Exchange" provision in the Exchange's constitution.[18] Martin presented the SEC report and comments to his board, and at an emotionally charged meeting on 14 December, it voted 27–1 that "no further action" was required in the case of the Morgan partners.

When he learned of the vote, Douglas demanded a meeting with Martin. The clash that took place on 16 December reveals the inherent complexities of government regulation of the financial services industry. Martin began by reviewing the stormy board discussion and stating that the upstanding character of the two Morgan partners and the reputation of the firm itself were so well known among the governors that the governors would never move for their expulsion or suspension. Martin himself agreed with his fellow governors that no legal basis existed for judging the men's actions as detrimental to the interests of the Exchange. In defending the Exchange's reasoning, Martin expressed a firmly held ethical viewpoint of his own. Two men of the highest integrity enabled a family member of one of them to straighten out his affairs and restore the assets of those who had mistakenly trusted him. In Martin's mind, a private action to protect the investing public's interest was hardly "detrimental" and should be protected by the Exchange — and by extension, the government as well.

Douglas saw the situation in a completely different light. His investigations of protective committees in the early 1930s had convinced Douglas that traditional investment banking firms such as Morgan had often used their immense power to act against the interests of the public. Douglas felt that investment bankers were "financial termites practicing predatory finance" and were indifferent to the interests of "the little people."[19] Douglas's position is best summarized in a letter to President Roosevelt on the issue of the Morgan partners, informing the president that "the reason for the inaction of the Stock Exchange was that influential and important people were involved in this case."[20] Douglas pressed Martin into admitting that if two unimportant brokers had aided Whitney, "the Exchange would have taken prompt and vigorous action."[21] Extremely unhappy with Martin's contradictory responses, Douglas offered to promulgate SEC rules that would "backstop" the Exchange when it could not pursue disciplinary procedures. Martin halfheartedly agreed this might be of help to the Exchange's administration. Predictably, the discussion fell apart over the difficulty of defining "standards of conduct" and "appropriate" penalties that would be the basis of SEC action.[22]

Douglas would not let the issue of the Morgan partners die. He was passionately determined to bring these two powerful men to justice and pushed for a Justice Department investigation. Douglas's last gasp was to write President Roosevelt, bringing up the "matter of Exchange discipline over its most powerful members," but once again his appeal fell on deaf ears.[23] Martin was deeply distressed that Douglas's single-minded persistence kept the divisive Whitney debacle alive at the Exchange and undermined Martin's patient campaign to get his Fifteen Point Program institutionalized. Despite the tensions over the Morgan issue, Martin and Douglas regularly telephoned one another to provide updates and deny rumors. In their public positions, both men continued to emphasize their cooperation; as Douglas put it, "[T]he Whitney case has not caused a change in the joint program we launched."[24] The public show of amity allowed both men to quietly negotiate their strong differences.

Martin's awkward relationship with Douglas ended soon after 20 March 1939, when Franklin Roosevelt announced that Douglas would take the place of Louis D. Brandeis on the Supreme Court. Douglas's departure would not necessarily make Martin's life any easier. Martin had initially been selected as Exchange president in great part because Exchange members felt he could deal with Douglas. Martin's ability to implement his reforms depended on the threat that Douglas would step in if the Exchange faltered. Martin would also miss the give-and-take he and Douglas shared behind the scenes. Douglas maintained an uncompromising public posture but in private had begun to appreciate that Martin's more cautious approach to reform was making steady progress. He recognized that it was preferable to have Martin accomplishing a more modest reform from the inside rather than have the SEC struggling unsuccessfully to force a more ambitious program from the outside. For his part, Martin tried to develop specific responses to Douglas's concerns that Martin could persuade his members to accept. In return, Douglas allowed Martin to back away from SEC proposals for changing the basic mechanics of the market. Though their disagreements were profound, both men felt it was in the interest of their respective institutions for them to cooperate.

Moreover, Douglas and Martin both realized that by 1939, the public's desire for reform had waned. The economy had recovered to 90 percent of its pre-Depression levels, and people were going back to work. Some New Deal initiatives had been struck down in the courts, and others had failed to achieve their ambitious goals. In addition, President Roosevelt, like most Americans, was focused on the coming war in Europe. Douglas was a poker-playing friend of Roosevelt and knew he could not necessarily count on the president's enthusiastic support if the SEC and the Exchange leadership came to an open rupture over the pace and extent of reform.[25] Douglas was also concerned that if he pressed Martin too hard, Martin's already precarious support from his membership might collapse. Finally, Douglas felt that his own contribution to reform of the stock market was largely fulfilled. A few months before his court appointment, he had advised Roosevelt of his intention to return to Yale Law School "by June, 1939."[26]

Douglas's worries about Martin's ability to remain in his position were not misplaced. During Martin's first year, a number of journalists, including Arthur Krock of the *New York Times*, predicted that Martin would be ousted.[27] One of the few serious efforts to do so that became public knowledge involved a financier named John Hancock. Hancock had a successful career in business, eventually rising to become the chairman of Jewell Tea Co., a well-respected supermarket chain. He was recruited to join the prestigious investment banking firm of Lehman Brothers and was the first outsider brought directly into the partnership. He had taken an aggressive anti-SEC position, which did not go unnoticed by the remnants of the Old Guard. A small group of Old Guard members and Hancock were plotting to replace Martin with Hancock when their plans were leaked by Douglas to the press on 26 March.[28] The coup collapsed in a fury of denials and finger pointing, but the incident revealed the deep-seated hostility that Martin endured throughout his term of office.

Like Kennedy before him, Douglas sought to handpick his successor. He eventually prevailed on Roosevelt to offer the chairmanship to Jerry Frank, one of Douglas's closest friends, a brilliant New Deal activist and fellow SEC commissioner. Although Frank had a great deal of intellectual affinity for Douglas's ideas, his chairmanship was markedly different from his predecessor's.

Jerry Frank brought a highly unusual set of capabilities to the SEC. He was gifted with one of the most powerful intellects among a group of highly talented young New Dealers. He had entered the University of Chicago at sixteen and its law school at twenty, graduating from the latter with the highest academic average of any student before him. Frank's intellectual capabilities were combined with a strong social conscience, and he was fully committed to the philosophy of the New Deal. After having a hand in drafting some of the New Deal legislation, Frank became counsel to the Agriculture Adjustment Administration. There he became known for his fierce attachment to the rights of small farmers. Frank's abilities were woven together in a personality that was both aggressive and sensitive. He often staked out strong positions but was unable to slough off the inevitable criticism they attracted. This characteristic, coupled with an unwillingness to negotiate political compromise, had caused him problems in the past and would dog him during his SEC chairmanship.

Frank was installed on 19 May 1939, and it did not take long for him to come into conflict with the Exchange. The Exchange invited Frank to make an introductory speech on 23 June and, as Douglas had done, Frank dismayed his hosts by unveiling a number of unpalatable policy initiatives. Frank gave new life to the concept of a trust institution, which he called "brokers' banks," to hold the cash balances of and provide margin loans to brokerage houses' customers. This was an issue on which even Douglas had been increasingly inclined to compromise. Frank chose one of the most divisive issues between the SEC and the Exchange as a platform to launch his chairmanship. In a single stroke, Frank had undermined moderate but steady progress toward reform. Worse yet, he chose to do it without giving Martin any warning of his intentions. It was hard to imagine a less promising beginning for the new SEC chairman.

Martin decided to deal with the brokers' bank idea by forming a board of independent financial experts to study the issue. Martin turned to Carle Conway, the industrialist with whom he had worked to produce the widely admired Conway report that had initiated the Exchange's reform process. Conway helped recruit Roswell McGill, a former undersecretary of the Treasury, as well as two leading commercial bankers. Armed with his committee, officially known as the Public Examining Board (PEB), Martin sought to persuade Frank of the PEB's independence and that both institutions should abide by its recommendations. Frank was understandably reluctant to commit the SEC in advance on such a controversial subject. After a tense negotiation, he agreed to "consider equally adequate alternatives" to a brokers' bank in return for Martin's commitment that the Exchange would accept the PEB recommendations regardless of the economic considerations.

Fortunately for Martin, the PEB's review called for an evolutionary rather than revolutionary solution. The report, released on 1 September 1939, recommended upgrading the current industry practices rather than "a thorough-going reorganization of the whole brokerage business . . . when the business is already unprofitable and disturbed."[29] It criticized the proposed institution as duplicative and doubted that one single institution could handle all the paperwork required when market volume was high. In effect, the PEB advised the SEC that their proposal simply wasn't practical. To deal with the SEC's concerns, the PEB recommended that customer cash balances be segregated into separate accounts within the brokerage firm and that Exchange member firms be required to provide more frequent reports on their financial condition.

Martin and Frank met in Washington on 15 September 1939 to resolve their differences over investor safety. The two men were very unlike in temperament and style, and their wariness bordered on open distrust. Martin, who hoped to control his temper, was unable to contain his resentment over Frank's handling of the brokers' bank proposal, and he and Frank were soon trading accusations before their embarrassed subordinates. The confrontation helped clear the air, and when the two men calmed down, they began the search for points of agreement. Frank conceded that a combination of segregating customer accounts and expanded insurance coverage could meet many of his concerns about the safety of investor assets. Martin agreed to implement the PEB's recommendations if the SEC would seek similar investor protections at those exchanges that competed with the NYSE. He told Frank that the NYSE could not afford to always "be the guinea pig for the entire industry."[30] Unfortunately, this fragile atmosphere of reconciliation was soon eroded by the corrosive realities of implementing these changes.

There is little in internal or public documents to indicate that SEC officials gave much consideration to the excruciating pressure that ten straight years of poor stock market conditions placed on Martin and other Exchange leaders. Trading volume for 1939 was the lowest in twenty-two years. The Dow Jones Industrial Average was still only one-third of its 1929 peak and only 10 percent above its value in 1919. The Exchange itself continued to lose money, although a painful cost-cutting program reduced the size of the loss. Exchange member firms retrenched and retrenched again. Employment in the financial industry had declined from almost 125,000 in 1929 to 33,000 in late 1939. The value of an Exchange membership had declined from a giddy $625,000 in late 1929 to an abysmal $52,000 in late 1939, taking the net worth of many brokers with it. One-half of Exchange member firms were losing money, and another quarter were just breaking even. Many firms were desperately seeking ways to increase their business just in order to continue in existence. Young men were no longer interested in entering the industry. Without a market recovery, the industry could not survive in its current form for many more years.[31]

The most crushing reality was that the reforms to date had not brought the public back to the stock market, and every Exchange member could see this fact in his firm's financial results. NYSE trading volume in 1939 was only 40 percent of its volume in 1933, before passage of the Securities Acts. It was also apparent that the additional steps proposed by Martin, and particularly those more drastic steps proposed by the SEC, would reduce Exchange members' margins even further in return for an uncertain improvement in customer safety. The SEC had prohibited trading by insiders, and Martin had eliminated margin buying by member firm partners, both of which hurt volume. Martin instituted independent audits and more financial reporting, which also increased member expenses. He was pushing for more employee training, more fidelity insurance, and more capital for the business, all of which would increase future costs. The SEC's proposal for a brokers' bank would effectively prohibit brokers from offering margin loans, one of the fundamental profit sources for the brokerage business. It is not surprising that many Exchange members did not support Martin — and that all were hostile to the SEC.

For the next six months, Martin tried to achieve his two highest goals: implementing his Fifteen Point Program and persuading the SEC that a moderate approach was the best route to lasting reform. On 6 March 1940, Martin and the five SEC commissioners met for another showdown on the issue of investor safety. Martin rehearsed the accomplishments of his Fifteen Point

Program but added that formal approval of the latest element, prohibiting trading on margin by partners of member firms, had taken the SEC's active support and a "resignation threat" by Martin. The financial difficulties of Exchange members were hardening the resistance to further reform, and Martin observed that the SEC could not ignore this fact. In addition, some of the PEB recommendations "were very superficial" and were proving very difficult to implement.[32] Martin returned to the issue that most angered his membership, the loss of NYSE business to other exchanges due to the increased costs associated with reform: "[T]he Exchange is by no means perfect, but it can no longer be a place where all untried ideas are worked out."[33] Martin also said that the Exchange committee charged with developing a plan for separate incorporation of the brokerage and underwriting business had not been able to reach agreement, and Martin was abandoning the idea.

Martin had occasionally been as candid about his situation with Jerry Frank but never had he been so brutal with the entire commission. His remarks did not sit well with Commissioner Healy, who felt even more strongly about the brokers' bank than Chairman Frank. After a vehement argument with Healy, Martin revealed his exhaustion and impatience by stating that "the best way to handle this matter from here on is for the Commission to proceed under its rules and, after giving us due opportunity to comment on your suggested rules, that you go ahead and put them in."[34] Martin concluded that he would "resist any efforts to increase safeguards which do not have the confidence of the financial industry."[35] This challenge was stronger than any his predecessor, Charles Gay, might have offered during his most recalcitrant periods. Martin was in effect saying that he had reached the limit on the reforms he could persuade his membership to accept. As the chief executive officer of the Exchange, he could go no further than his Fifteen Point Program. If the SEC wanted more, it would have to move on its own.

In a broader sense, the meeting of 6 March signaled the end of cooperation between the Exchange and the SEC over the New Deal reform agenda. The end was hastened by Jerry Frank's hard-line position on investor safety and his inability to engage Martin and other Exchange leaders in a continuing dialogue about where cooperation was possible. The end was also hastened by poor market conditions and the general public's declining sense of urgency about reform in general. There is some merit to the argument that the steps already taken by Martin to strengthen the administration and practices of the Exchange did convince the public and politicians that Wall Street had reformed. It is more likely that a combination of these factors persuaded the SEC commissioners that promulgating rules to force a brokers' bank would generate a fierce backlash from the Exchange. Without the support of the Exchange, the SEC would not be able to implement a broader agenda. On the other hand, if the SEC mandated broader reform and the brokerage industry's financial problems worsened, the damage to the SEC's reputation could be considerable. The SEC's reform agenda ground to a halt.

The standoff with the SEC offered Bill Martin scant relief because his administration was again under siege by unhappy Exchange members. Charles Harding, the reform governor who had been instrumental in institutionalizing the Fifteen Point Program, was nominated for board chairman. Unexpectedly, competition arose for the chairman's position. A group of Old Guard members had circulated a petition for Robert P. Boylan, an Exchange governor, for Exchange chairman. Their plan was to elect Boylan chairman and a year later oust Martin and replace him with Boylan. At the last minute, Martin's supporters managed to persuade Boylan that he couldn't win and to accept the vice chairmanship under Harding. The maneuvering was another reminder to Martin of those who remained hostile to him and his reform program.

Martin tried another approach to win his members' support for his agenda by addressing the critical issue of declining trading volume at the Exchange. Martin had introduced two programs to increase business: the first was nicknamed "baby portfolios," which were packages of shares in each of ten blue-chip companies, and the second was an installment payment plan for new investors to purchase shares. As Martin feared, the SEC, now highly antagonistic toward the Exchange, killed both ideas. Martin and Paul Shields proposed a national advertising campaign for the Exchange, scheduled to begin in November 1939, but they had to cancel it due to the Exchange's financial problems. Martin and other Exchange leaders knew that the war in Europe — for the Nazis were sweeping through Belgium and the allies were in retreat — kept American investors fearful and away from the stock market. Martin later described the position of the Exchange during this period: "We have Hitler on one side of us and the government on the other, and we are fighting to preserve our way of life."[36]

The issue of trading volume became a nightmare for Martin when his membership began calling for an end to "off-market trading" in NYSE-listed stocks. The prohibition on trading in NYSE-listed securities on other exchanges by Exchange members had been lying dormant in the Exchange constitution since 1865. An enterprising Exchange specialist had resurrected the provision in early 1940, and Exchange members quickly appreciated that by enforcing it, the Exchange could end a practice that was taking a growing amount of business away from the Exchange. It was well recognized by large investors that NYSE fees and commissions were higher than either the regional exchanges or the over-the-counter (OTC) market. Analysts estimated that as much as 30 percent of total trading in Exchange issues had migrated to other exchanges.[37] Martin realized that his membership would demand that he pursue the prohibition and that despite his misgivings, he would have to go along.

Martin knew that the ban would provoke an angry response from the other exchanges and the SEC, and he was proved right. All of the fifteen other exchanges complained and began to bring political pressure on the SEC. Goaded by the president of the Boston Stock Exchange, Representative John McCormack wrote to Chairman Frank on 15 April, describing the ban as "vicious and destructive of competition."[38] SEC Chairman Frank replied to McCormack on 17 April that "the Exchange's action may have consequences inimical to the public interest," but he cautioned that the SEC's "authority to take formal action is not free from substantial doubt."[39] The SEC began a study of the issue on 23 April, and for the remainder of 1940, the SEC and the Exchange conducted a tortured minuet over the ban.

Martin defended the Exchange's position before the SEC, but he did it with little enthusiasm. The SEC study concluded that without the growth of trading in NYSE-listed shares, at least six of the regionals would already have shuttered their doors.[40] Martin continued to press the Exchange's claims, but he knew he was in a poor position to sway the SEC on any subject. Eventually, the Exchange agreed to remove the prohibition provision from its constitution. Martin's real efforts to build volume had to be placed elsewhere.

This outcome was only one of the disappointments Martin encountered during the latter part of 1940. Trading volume continued its eleven-year decline, and it was beyond the ability of anyone at the Exchange to reverse it. Martin conducted a second painful reduction of Exchange expenses that increased staff reductions during his term to 30 percent. Martin even had to close the Stock Exchange Institute, the teaching institution for which he personally had raised money over the years. The value of an Exchange membership had fallen to $27,000, half the level of a year earlier and the lowest price in one hundred years. Martin's goal of reconciling the warring factions in his membership was as elusive as ever. Most of Martin's reforms under the Fifteen Point Program were finally implemented in one form or another, but further reform was problematic. Two of the most influential Exchange member groups, the specialists and the national brokerage firms, remained bitterly opposed on the issue of further reform.

The larger picture was little better. Martin was concerned that World War II would make private capital markets irrelevant for an extended period and that even when the peace was restored, the Exchange would never return to its pre-Depression prominence. He pleaded for a private role in wartime finance because the Reconstruction Finance Corporation (RFC) and its aggressive chairman, Jesse Jones, were expanding the government's role in financing industrial investment. Jones proposed RFC financing for the expansion of public utilities, although it had traditionally been the province of the Exchange and commercial banks. In reality, the capacity of the weakened capital markets would not meet more than a modest percentage of the nation's wartime capital needs, and both Martin and Jones recognized it.[41] Wall Street's financial distress and the enveloping specter of the war overshadowed Martin's success in achieving a functional level of reform at the Exchange.

Martin's worries about the future of the Exchange were interrupted by a notice from his draft board on 27 February 1941: he had been classified 1-A and could expect to be drafted in two months. Martin could not have been surprised; young men all over America were receiving similar notices. In a typical response, Martin decided to accept being drafted as a private in the army. Despite the arrangements negotiated by most young men in his situation, Martin did not believe that anyone in a leadership position should seek special treatment because of his status. His sentiment was summarized by his press statement, "All of us are subject to the selective service law and must expect inconvenience. Others have certainly been more adversely affected than I."[42]

With time growing short, Martin sought to leave his final imprint on the Exchange. On 5 March, he proposed a final installment of reform. He called for the virtual elimination of the committee system and transfer of all operating responsibilities to the paid staff of the Exchange. He revived his recommendations that members of the board of governors be relieved of any operational responsibilities and that the board be reduced from twenty-eight to sixteen members. To attract "ambitious younger men" to service on the board, governors would be paid an annual fee of $5,000. By recommending a corporate form of organization, Martin hoped to free his successor and his professional managers from the influence of various factions that had made his own term so difficult.

In another attempt to create a legacy, Martin gave new life to on-again, off-again discussion of a merger between the NYSE and the New York Curb Exchange. The Curb Exchange was sandwiched between the much larger NYSE and the less regulated, more freewheeling OTC market. An economic study indicated promising cost-savings possibilities, but like all of Martin's other last-minute recommendations, the merger died stillborn.

Martin gave a valedictory address on 5 March 1941 in which he summarized his presidency and his hopes for the future. Speaking from his heart, without notes, Martin gave vent to feelings he must have often experienced but never revealed. He observed that "we are facing a crisis in Wall Street that is worse than when I assumed office . . . despite our being able to render the best service to the public in our history."[43] Martin described the Exchange as beset by wartime conditions that "changed the political concept of capitalism" and frightened the "investing public as to the future."[44] Martin completed the dismal picture with: "I know many of you are starving," but members must realize that "Wall Street is not indispensable to the country."[45]

Martin then moved on to what must be done. He rejected the idea that bringing a much-admired individual in as Exchange president would help: "[I]t is utterly ridiculous for us to believe that any man, one man, can improve the volume of trading merely because the public thinks that he is honest."[46] Reflecting his own regulatory philosophy, Martin called on the SEC to judge the Exchange by "whether dishonest people in the business are being eliminated, whether standards are going up, and whether there is a flow of new capital into industry."[47] Finally, Martin encouraged the members to select as his successor "a man who is familiar with the business and has an honest viewpoint . . . to whom you will give the whole-hearted support that I have not gotten."[48] A reporter in attendance described the reaction of the eight hundred men in the audience: "Some faces grew red, some fidgeted, some stared straight ahead, thin-lipped, unsmiling."[49]

Martin left his Exchange membership much as he had first encountered it — badly split. Many of the comments Martin received on his departure represented the honest differences members had had with him, combined with their respect for Martin as an individual. Philip Russell, the president of Fenner & Beane, had often disagreed with Martin, but wrote: "I wanted to tell you that our differences, if they exist, are purely differences of opinion."[50] Lawrence Oakley, the man who had refused to renominate Richard Whitney as Exchange president, wrote: "Had your results been obtained under anything resembling normal times, even then the results would have been most satisfactory. But your management accomplished these results during a period of constantly declining business and general discouragement."[51]

Perhaps the best summary of Martin's role during these tortuous years was contained in a *Newsweek* article on 17 March 1941. "For ten years there has been a growing conviction in this country, fostered by those in high places, that the stock exchange performs no really useful service in our economy. Until this attitude is changed, our securities markets may have temporary bursts of activity, but fundamentally they will remain in the doldrums. All told, Martin has done a reasonably good job, and the Exchange will have to show rare wisdom if its next president is to leave office with as favorable a record."[52] The expressions of goodwill from his membership and press accolades would have been more useful to Martin if they had been expressed during his tenure rather than offered in the wake of his resignation.

In fact, Martin did bequeath an Exchange that responded to the public's demand for reform without reducing its ability to function as the nation's primary financial marketplace. Martin's ability to personify openness and integrity enabled him to serve as the visible symbol of reform at the Exchange and helped prepare the public to eventually return to the stock market. His detailed knowledge of the inner workings of the Exchange enabled him to help guide the Conway Committee in its pioneering reform agenda. It also enabled Martin to negotiate a subsequent program of reforms that were acceptable to the SEC and his membership. The reforms that he implemented, particularly a professional management structure and an effective rule-making and disciplinary system, ended many of the abuses that had contributed importantly to the crash of 1929 and caused the public to lose faith in the stock market.

One of Martin's signal accomplishments was his agonizing but effective working relationship with SEC Chairman William O. Douglas. Their mutual understanding prevented an adversarial relationship that could have led to more intervention by the SEC, possibly a radical restructuring of the securities industry, or the abandonment of self-regulation. The reforms accomplished during the Martin era have stood the test of time, and the NYSE has never experienced a recurrence of the widespread self-dealing practices that brought Bill Martin into the Exchange presidency.

Martin's chairmanship experienced its share of failures. The crisis at the Exchange thrust Martin into the chairmanship at a very young age, and his inability to develop many allies prevented him from building a broad-based constituency for reform. His Fifteen Point Program was directed at the ills highlighted by the Whitney debacle, instead of a more all-encompassing restructuring of the way Exchange policies were made and its operations managed. Martin recommended more far-reaching reforms only as he was walking out the door, and they were quickly abandoned. However, in light of the resistance he encountered in pressing his original program, it is unlikely that he could have achieved a more ambitious set of goals.

By the time Bill Martin went into the army, the forces arrayed against him at the Exchange were gaining strength, and the onset of the war would work against reform. Like Douglas's, Martin's best contributions were in his early years. The draft notice was a rescue boat—upon his departure, he never looked back.

4

From President to Private and Back Again: World War II and the Export-Import Bank Years

Martin's draft notice ordered him to report for basic training at Ft. Dix, New Jersey, on 21 April 1941. Nearly all his contemporaries were negotiating appointments as officers in the intelligence services or in the Pentagon — it was virtually unheard of for a highly visible Wall Street leader to go into the army as a private. The director of the Selective Service, General Lewis B. Hershey, was overwhelmed with thousands of requests for special consideration and welcomed Martin's straightforward response: "To convince people that we were dealing off the top of the deck [in selecting candidates for the draft] it helped to have some aces and kings come off as well as the deuces."[1]

A few weeks before his departure, Martin was interviewed by an enterprising reporter from the *New York World Telegram* who asked if he had a special girl. Martin was dating a young woman named Cynthia Davis at the time, and to protect her privacy, he replied: "No, but I sure wish I did."[2] When he arrived at Ft. Dix, there were two mailbags waiting for him, full of letters and proposals from young women, describing how they could help Martin remedy his situation. After some obligatory press photos showing Martin in his fedora and pin-striped suit waiting in line with his fellow inductees, he and hundreds of thousands like him were swallowed into the massive war preparation effort.

Martin's basic training got off on the wrong foot. He did not take to being regimented by his drill sergeants, and after one particularly bad session, his drill instructor shouted at him: "You are lucky to be in the Army because you are too stupid to earn a living anywhere else."[3] Martin retained a lifelong antipathy for the military hierarchy. During the war, he became a close friend of General George Marshall, later recalling that he told Marshall that to improve the army "[y]ou ought to make every one of those generals spend two weeks a year as a private. You have no idea what it would do for morale." Then Martin observed: "He [Marshall] used to love that. He'd tell people 'Here's my friend, Lieutenant Martin. He wants all you fellows to be privates for two weeks.' "[4] The story may overstate Marshall's reaction, but the close relationship between the two men was well known. Martin later served as the board chairman of the philanthropic foundation established to honor the great man.

It did not take long for Martin's peacetime contacts to help his military career. During his NYSE presidency he had met Henry H. "Hap" Arnold, the chief of the Army Air Corps, and Arnold recommended Martin for the intelligence unit stationed at the Army War College in Washington. Arnold's support was overly enthusiastic, for in order to assure Martin's eligibility for the intelligence unit, Arnold recommended that Martin be promoted to captain. The army personnel department reminded Arnold that Martin was only a private. The only other similar promotion, for James Roosevelt, the son of the president, "caused a furor," and a slower promotion schedule was now army policy.[5] Martin's rise in the military hierarchy would have to wait.

By December and the attack on Pearl Harbor, Staff Sergeant William McChesney Martin Jr. was engaged in analyzing the raw material resources necessary to prosecute the war in Europe. A report he wrote stressing the importance of providing materiel to the Soviet Union to enable its army to resist a German invasion brought him to the attention of General James Burns. Burns, a West Point graduate, had distinguished himself as an administrator in World War I and was responsible for the Russian component of the U.S. lend-lease program. In mid-1942, Burns offered Martin a promotion and the opportunity to join his staff. The new job required Martin to remain in Washington for an indefinite period, and this comparative stability encouraged Martin to propose to Cynthia Davis. They were married in a small wedding in eastern Maryland that June.

Cynthia Davis was and remains a tall, intelligent, soft-spoken woman with a gracious manner and a sly wit that she generally keeps hidden. The Davises were an old St. Louis family. Her father, Dwight F. Davis, had served as secretary of war under President Hoover. When he was appointed governor-general of the Philippines, Cynthia, whose mother had died when Cynthia was in college, had accompanied him to his new post and served as his official hostess for about a year. The Davis family members were tennis enthusiasts. When Dwight Davis was a Harvard University tennis star, he had initiated an annual international tennis tournament and donated the Davis Championship Cup, which assured his place in history. As a young man, Bill Martin had played tennis on the Davis family court, but he and Cynthia did not become interested in one another until they met again in 1932 at a dance in honor of Bill Martin's mother. But it was only when Cynthia moved to New York in 1940 and their paths recrossed that they began to date seriously.

It is easy to understand why Bill Martin was attracted to Cynthia Davis. She was twenty-nine, a willowy, lively Radcliffe graduate, and her Philippine experience gave her a worldly allure that was balanced by her midwestern common sense. She was at home in the traditional formality of the senior Martin household and yet shared Bill Martin's enthusiasm for new ideas and new experiences. She took delight in teasing Martin about his penchant for formality and his embarrassment when he tried to express his affection for her. When Martin proposed marriage, her only concern was that it be a small wedding to limit the presence of the press and her large and demanding family. They were married in Towson, Maryland, near Washington, D.C., in the home of a friend of Martin, with only a few family members present. They honeymooned in Atlantic City, New Jersey, because Bill Martin loved seaside resorts, but they could take only two days because Martin's army superior was unhappy that he had asked for time off.

By mid-1942, Soviet-U.S. relations were fraying at the edges. The U.S. war effort was gearing up, and the lend-lease organization was unable to obtain all the materiel to honor its commitments to the Russians. The Russians were unhappy with both the quantity and quality of U.S. goods they did receive. For its part, the U.S. military complained that the Russians were not honoring their commitment to share their intelligence with the Allies, nor were they "allowing American observers to report on the application of aid being sent to Russia."[6] The situation came to a boil in early March 1943, when William H. Standley, U.S. ambassador to Russia, told the press: "The Russian authorities seem to want to cover up the fact that they are receiving outside help. Apparently they want their people to believe that the Red Army is fighting this war alone."[7] Standley's comments became a cause célèbre back in Washington and the flap moved Harry Hopkins, administrator of the lend-lease program, to send Burns to the Soviet Union to see what the Russians were doing with U.S. economic aid. Burns scheduled a trip to Moscow for April 1943 and asked his principal assistant, Major William McChesney Martin Jr., to accompany him.

The trip made a deep impression on Martin and energized the rest of his military career, in which he became a principal defender of Russian lend-lease before Congress. Martin was astonished to visit a large airplane engine assembly plant staffed mostly with women and "almost no workers over the age of eighteen."[8] He was moved by the courage of the ordinary Russians he met: "Most of the people were living on black bread and tea, but were too proud to admit they were often hungry. They were determined to impress us with their hospitality and good spirits."[9] He never forgot the stories of tank battles told by a group of tank commanders who had previously seen service in the battle of Stalingrad: "They were all small, hard as nails, and unprepossessing looking. It was a depressing atmosphere. Very few of them could be expected to live through the summer."[10]

Unfortunately, Burns's trip did little to improve the situation. The army's request for its representatives to visit the Russian front continued to be rejected, and in retribution the army proposed to end the priority assigned to filling Russian lend-lease shipments. The administration was determined that Russia should assist in the defeat of Japan after the defeat of Germany and "adamantly resisted all proposals to alter policies for aid to the USSR."[11] The Russian lend-lease organization was buffeted by the conflicting views.

As the tide of the war began to change in the Allies' favor, a new issue arose that eventually engulfed the Russian lend-lease organization. In October 1943, a group of conservative senators, led by the redoubtable Richard Russell, who was already building a reputation for his knowledge of defense issues, returned to Washington from a visit to the war fronts. Their trip revealed waste on a grand scale and that the Allies were using American supplies to "secure commercial and political advantage at the expense of the United States."[12] Averell Harriman, who had recently served in the U.S. embassy in Moscow, made an even more inflammatory charge, that the Russians were using lend-lease supplies in their growing domination of Eastern Europe. Russian lend-lease, always controversial, was now losing its remaining congressional supporters.

General Burns was by this time quite ill and his deputy, General John York, and Lieutenant Colonel William McChesney Martin Jr. went to Capitol Hill to defend Russian lend-lease against the charges. It was not an easy task. The Russian strategy of expanding Communist control of the liberated Eastern European countries was an incontestable reality. Even if lend-lease materiel was not directly used to maintain the Red Army in Eastern European capitals, it was indirectly contributing to the process by allowing the Russians to divert resources from the eastern front. Franklin Roosevelt recognized the problem but ignored the pressure coming from Congress: "[A]ny attempt to use economic pressure [i.e., by terminating lend-lease] might jeopardize military cooperation at a time when it is obviously impossible to break with the Russians."[13]

A good portion of the burden of defending Russian lend-lease fell on Bill Martin. His writings and speeches during the war indicate that he struggled to find a rationale for a long-term relationship with a Communist ally. It is clear that Martin, who had served as a symbol of capitalism as president of the New York Stock Exchange and for whom the virtues of democracy were a fundamental value, had expanded his perspective on the relationship between capitalism and Communism. In a paper written during this period, he described the critical issue for the postwar world as whether America would return to isolationism. "Russia is the key to the situation. World peace requires understanding . . . of the importance of Russia to the world."[14] Reflecting his evolving viewpoint, he observed that the Russian-American relationship could be understood "only by fearless analysis, [a] live and let live [philosophy], and comprehension of the evolutionary flow of history."[15] In view of his previous public statements before the war extolling the strengths of capitalism, these words were remarkably broad-minded.

Martin further articulated his view in October 1944 in a speech to the American Institute Dedicated to American-Soviet Postwar Relations. He described what he had learned from his trip to Russia in 1943. He spoke of the "unshatterable qualities" of the Russian spirit as personified by two hardy ten-year-old boys he had met, both of whom had lost most of their family members but "hoped to join the Red Army shortly."[16] He spoke of how the government was "doing a complete job in [harnessing this spirit] and one realizes the power of Stalin's regime, both now and in the influence it will exert on the world of tomorrow."[17] He urged his listeners to look at both societies — American and Russian — from a realistic perspective: "Much as we love America, there are many things of which we are not too proud of. This situation is precisely the same in Russia. . . . At the same time there are real differences between our two nations. The Russians like their way of life, and we have no right to interfere with it; but likewise we Americans like our way of life and the reverse is true."[18] He was reaching out to the Russians as much as he possibly could.

Martin concluded his speech with a requirement he deemed essential but that was probably beyond the capacity of the two parties to achieve: "It is possible to be very good friends so long as each knows where the other stands. As long as the cards are placed on the table face up, disparities in point of view may actually broaden and enrich life. Once one or the other keeps cards under the table, it leads to distrust and inevitably, dislike."[19] For Martin, relations among nations were identical to relations among individuals: without trust, they are doomed to failure. He had done the best he could to approach the tenuous relationship objectively, but ultimately Martin concluded that the Russians had yet to prove their trustworthiness.

The controversy over Russian lend-lease ground on through the spring of 1945, with additional damaging revelations of Soviet misuse of lend-lease supplies in Eastern Europe.[20] The conflict was sharpened by the impending end of the war in Europe and the death of a heroically exhausted Franklin D. Roosevelt on 12 April 1945. The attitude toward Russia within the administration was already in the process of changing before Roosevelt's death. But after only a few weeks in office, Harry Truman had a celebrated confrontation with Russian foreign minister Vyacheslav Molotov, and soon thereafter U.S.-Russian relations deteriorated quickly. On 12 May, shortly after the war in Europe ended, the administration ordered that all Russian lend-lease shipments be halted. The Russians, who had no warning, were predictably angry. After a barrage of charges and countercharges, the United States resumed shipments.

Martin, by now a colonel, was placed in charge of the Russian lend-lease program in early July and tried unsuccessfully to improve relations with the Russians. Events soon overtook the situation: on 4 August, the first atomic bomb was dropped on Hiroshima. On 9 August, one of the primary goals of the Russian lend-lease program was realized when Russia belatedly declared war on Japan, and the Red Army drove into Manchuria.

Once the Nagasaki bomb had been dropped and the war's end appeared near, Truman advisor and Russian lend-lease opponent Leo Crowley lost no time in proposing a shutdown of all lend-lease activities as soon as the Japanese surrendered. Crowley persuaded Truman that when hostilities ceased, the U.S. government should convert outstanding lend-lease delivery obligations to commercial terms. Martin informed the Russian government that it could purchase undelivered items for cash or ask the U.S. Export-Import Bank (Ex-Im Bank) for financing. By this time, Martin and his Russian counterparts were barely speaking, and the end of the program came as welcome relief to the lend-lease staff.

With the victory over Japan complete, a unique experiment in American foreign relations came to an end. The marriage of necessity between the United States and the Soviet Union, forged by a common threat, had failed to overcome the dramatic differences in economic systems and political ambitions between the two nations. The buildup of trust that Bill Martin declared to be the ultimate test of the relationship did not occur. The Russian lend-lease organization orchestrated the delivery of $10 billion worth of equipment and supplies to the Russian war effort in the face of hostility from the U.S. military and Congress. As historian Robert H. Jones observed, "Lend-lease probably did not decide the outcome of the war in Russia, but the wartime statements of Soviet leaders make clear that it helped to make the nation and the Red Army a much more potent fighting force."[21] Bill Martin spent the bulk of his military career either dealing with representatives of a Russian government that was both grateful and resentful or lobbying congressmen who were increasingly dissatisfied with Russian lend-lease. He learned the hard way about the politics of Washington.

In September 1945, Martin wrote to a wartime friend voicing his concern about the future and a possible return to isolationism by America. Martin foresaw "a repetition of the cycle which followed the last war and its consequences that will result in the same bitter fruit when the next emergency arises. . . . The world which lies ahead is going to be a very difficult one."[22] But then his natural optimism returned: "During that [future] period, training, competence, and character will once again be looked up to and leadership of the right sort will assert itself. The experiences that you and I have had in the past five years . . . should offer a real opportunity for constructive service"[23] Martin's hopeful prediction would soon be tested.

In the weeks following the surrender of Japan, Bill Martin, like millions of other servicemen, faced returning to civilian life and resuming his career. His wartime experience had whetted his interest in public service, and one of those he spoke with about his future was Leo Crowley. During the war, Crowley had served as an advisor to Roosevelt and Truman as well as chairman of the U.S. Export-Import Bank. Martin and Crowley had worked together on the proposal to convert unfulfilled Russian lend-lease obligations into credit from the Ex-Im Bank. Crowley was intrigued with Martin because of his experience in the NYSE presidency and because Martin was a Democrat from Missouri, a considerable asset with fellow Missourian Harry Truman in the White House. Crowley suggested that Martin might want to join the newly reconstituted board of the Ex-Im Bank because Crowley was looking for a successor as board chairman.

On 31 October 1945, John Snyder, yet another Missourian and close advisor of Harry Truman, offered Martin the Ex-Im board position. Martin had barely taken office when he was invited to the White House to meet with the president and Crowley. There Cowley informed Martin that he had submitted his letter of resignation from the Ex-Im chairmanship and that the president had accepted his recommendation that Martin take his place. On 26 November, the White House issued a press release including phrasing that Martin had urged be included: "[The Export-Import Bank] has a unique role to play in the promotion, development, and preservation of the United States foreign trade. I am deeply interested in the Bank and want to see it operated prudently and aggressively."[24] Martin wanted to be sure that the White House was publicly committed to the idea of the bank as an economic, and not political, institution. Putting flesh on this commitment was to prove a Herculean task.

Though the Export-Import Bank was eleven years old, the institution Bill Martin inherited was still a work in process. The bank's initial purpose was to serve as the export-financing arm of the government. During World War II, Chairman Crowley focused the Ex-Im on financing new sources of essential wartime raw materials such as iron ore in Brazil and tungsten in Bolivia. As the war came to an end and the Foreign Economic Administration, Ex-Im's overseer, was to be dismantled, there was predictable bureaucratic infighting over control of the Ex-Im. Treasury Secretary Fred Vinson proposed that the bank become an adjunct of the Treasury Department, and the State Department and Commerce were also angling for influence.[25]

Crowley fended off the bureaucratic contenders by persuading Harry Truman that the Ex-Im Bank should remain an independent government agency and serve as the vehicle for responding to the pleas for postwar reconstruction assistance flooding in from America's allies. The policies of the Ex-Im would be guided by its relationship with the National Advisory Council on International Monetary and Financial Problems (the NAC). The NAC was established on 31 July 1945 as part of the Bretton Woods Agreements Act, the legislation authorizing U.S. participation in the International Monetary Fund (IMF) and the International Bank for Reconstruction and Development (the World Bank). The NAC consisted of the secretaries of Treasury (who served as chairman), State, and Commerce, along with the chairman of the Fed and the chairman of the Ex-Im Bank. The NAC's mandate was to "coordinate the policies and operations of the representatives of the U.S. on the IMF, the World Bank, and the Ex-Im Bank."[26] In July 1945, the Ex-Im's lending authority was increased from $0.7 billion to $3.5 billion. The bank had money and a mission. The question was what it would do with them.

The future policies of the Ex-Im evolved during the deliberations of the NAC. In its first meeting in August 1945, the NAC agreed that the fastest way to provide economic assistance to desperate U.S. allies was to send materials and goods already in the lend-lease "pipeline." The Allies could not afford to pay cash for these purchases, and Ex-Im Bank financing would fill the gap. By September 1945, $1.9 billion of the Ex-Im's $2.8 billion of new lending authority had already been "earmarked" for various allies. The major recipients were to be France with $555 million, Holland and the Dutch West Indies with a total of $200 million, Belgium with $100 million, and the Soviet Union with $1 billion. An additional $0.5 billion was tentatively reserved for loans to China, and Commerce Secretary Henry Wallace was pushing for a $400 million loan to the Philippines. If these proposed allocations were to become reality, virtually all of the Ex-Im's lendable funds would be spoken for, and Bill Martin had not even assumed the chairmanship.

Martin took office as chairman of the board on 3 December and saw his first tasks as reinvigorating the bank with fresh blood and implementing the bank's new mission. While Crowley had left day-to-day concerns in the hands of Wayne Taylor, the Ex-Im president, Martin intended to run the bank. He informed Taylor that the 1945 revisions to the Export-Import Bank Act made no provisions for a president of the bank.[27] Taylor, a low-key bureaucrat who had been undersecretary of Commerce during the war, was described as having "neither the intellect nor ability" to play a leadership role in the bank Martin was envisioning.[28] Taylor chose not to contest Martin's power play and resigned two months later. Martin promoted bank consultant August "Gus" Maffry to a vice presidency and hired Sidney Sherwood as his personal advisor. Maffry provided yeoman's service during Martin's term and remained a close personal friend for many years thereafter. Sherwood, who had previously served as assistant to John Snyder and Leo Crowley, was an old Washington hand and a shrewd judge of the politics of international finance. Martin had learned during his NYSE years that assembling a highly qualified staff was an essential element for administering public institutions.

At the end of March 1946, a delegation from the French provisional government came to Washington to negotiate for U.S. financial assistance for 1946 and 1947. This visit taught Bill Martin the difficulties of charting an independent course for the Ex-Im Bank. His first lesson came during a meeting of the U.S. negotiating team when he proposed that he should lead the team since the financial assistance consisted primarily of an Ex-Im loan. Martin was told firmly by Treasury Secretary Fred Vinson that a diplomat and not a banker would lead these negotiations: "The French are very sensitive and are interested just as much in the matter of treatment as in the loan itself."[29]

Martin got a second bruising lesson when he complained that Assistant Secretary of State William Clayton's estimate of a $750 million Ex-Im loan to the French was beyond the bank's financial capacity and that $300 million was a more appropriate number. Clayton bluntly advised Martin that the administration had decided that the full French loan had a higher priority than the amount the Ex-Im had reserved for Russia: "The French need prompt action and it has been decided not to continue earmarking the $1.0 billion [for the Russians]."[30] To make sure Martin knew where things stood, Clayton said: "All [NAC] members know we are not negotiating with the French about $300 million, but about $500 million or more."[31] Despite Martin's lone dissent, the loan was approved. The Ex-Im loan to the Republic of France for $650 million was announced on 13 July.

At the same time that the French tensions were mounting, Martin was under growing pressure for the Ex-Im to participate in the U.S. government's tortured support of the government of Chinese generalissimo Chiang Kai-shek. In late 1945, Harry Truman sent Army Chief of Staff General George C. Marshall to China to evaluate whether the United States should continue to support the Chiang Kai-shek government in its struggle against the Communist forces of Mao Tse-tung. Marshall returned to Washington in March 1946 and met with the NAC to present his case that the $500 million earmarked for China should be made available to the Chinese government in one global loan.

Martin protested strongly that Ex-Im policy provided only for lump-sum commitments for European postwar reconstruction. Any Ex-Im loan to China should be applied only to projects that were "analyzed by the Ex-Im bank to ascertain whether they are economically sound and conform to a general program of economic development for China."[32] Marshall responded by emphasizing the strategic importance of China, adding, "I am not opposed to flexible controls . . . [but] creating the impression that we are holding a gun to the head of the Government of China, the Government will lose so much 'face' that its power will be destroyed."[33] As the negotiations between Marshall and the NAC continued, Martin could see that his concerns were being ignored. He resolved to speak personally with Marshall about them.

Martin's opposition to Marshall's recommendations placed him in an excruciatingly uncomfortable position. General George C. Marshall, the man who had the ultimate responsibility for overseeing the vast allied effort in World War II, was one of the most admired men in the world. The president had asked him to find a way for the U.S. government to support Chiang Kai-shek in his struggle to keep the Communists from controlling the world's most populous nation. In addition, Marshall was Martin's friend. Later in his life, Martin often said that he revered George Marshall as he did few others.[34]

When the two men met to discuss the loan, Marshall did not accept Martin's position and pressed him to change his mind. In embarrassed exasperation, Martin responded: "I wish this were war-time and you could order me to do that, Sir. But you are not a general anymore, and I am not a Colonel. We are both just misters, and as two civilians we must try to be true to our respective institutions."[35] Marshall did not take this well but promised that he would think about the issue. The next afternoon, Marshall approved wording for the draft documents that was even stronger than that originally proposed by Martin. Though the Chinese did submit a few projects, the Ex-Im did not approve them, and the credit allocation expired unused.

The battle to protect the Ex-Im from making politically motivated loans continued throughout 1946. Sometimes the differences boiled over into heated arguments, and the issue of Ex-Im independence continued to roil NAC discussions until it ended up in the White House in December 1946. On

20 December, Bill Martin met with the president, Secretary of State James Byrnes, Treasury Secretary John Snyder (who had replaced Fred Vinson), and Undersecretary of State William Clayton to discuss the role and independence of the Export-Import Bank. Bill Martin was forty years old and had been in his position for all of one year. He knew he would be opposing two of Truman's most powerful cabinet members, but it did not stop him from standing his ground. Byrnes and Clayton justified political loans by arguing that "stimulating world recovery requires taking risks." Martin pushed for independence from political pressures when he observed that "The Export-Import Act of 1945 assigned some judgment of our [the Ex-Im Bank Board] own as to the dispersal of the funds placed in our care."[36] Martin also told Truman that if the Ex-Im did not receive repayments on its loans, "Congress will quickly crack down and put the Bank out of business."[37]

After listening to both sides, Harry Truman concluded that the Export-Import Board should be allowed to "make its own decision" on future loans.[38] Martin wrote to Truman later that day to thank him for his support, telling the president that in the future the Ex-Im would not necessarily support the financial commitments the administration might make to foreign governments: "We have no right to feel ourselves bound by decisions made without consulting us, particularly when we regard those decisions as economically unwise."[39] Martin's uncompromising posture reflects his acute sense of institutional purpose and his willingness to defend it regardless of the risk to his personal situation. As Ex-Im Bank historian Earl Mazo wrote, "He fended off attempts by the State and Treasury Departments at considerable risk to his own career to make the kind of lending decisions which he felt were the Bank's alone to make."[40]

Martin's determination to defend the bank's standards was expensive in terms of his relationships with other administration members. He had run-ins with Defense Secretary Robert Lovett and Undersecretary of State Dean Acheson. *Business Week* magazine later commented on Martin's Ex-Im's leadership: "The few enemies Martin has in Washington stem from his stubborn conviction that his institution not be used as a purse for relief purposes."[41]

Martin's successful defense of the Ex-Im's independence was undercut by a new reality: the Ex-Im was running out of money. In December 1946, Martin advised Truman that the additional $2.8 billion of new capital was "practically exhausted in emergency loans," and all that remained was the $0.7 billion of initial capital. Martin and the members of the NAC had been pushing legislation for a $1.25 billion increase in Ex-Im lending authority for almost a year, but congressional consideration had been repeatedly delayed. Martin concluded that additional Ex-Im funding was unlikely anytime soon, and that the bank would have to live within its existing resources. In view of the failure to achieve added funding, Martin informed the president: "Selections have to be made of many competing claims and . . . such funds as remain should be husbanded carefully."[42] Martin and the board cut new loan commitments sharply, from $1.1 billion in the first six months of 1946 to $255 million in the first half of 1947.

Even though new loan volume was declining, Martin was determined to establish the bank as an effective lending agency. He added engineers and economists to rigorously evaluate loan applications. He sent Ex-Im Bank staff into the field to review the financial prospects and repayment potential of its existing borrowers. By the end of 1947, he reported that "with only two exceptions, bank representatives visited every country in which major credits are outstanding."[43] Martin also strengthened the bank's financial position against potential loan defaults by expanding its financial reserves against future losses. By the end of 1947, the essential disciplines were in place to justify the Ex-Im's claim to be a permanent agency of the U.S. government.

It was not until late 1947 that an opportunity to secure solid administration support for a funding increase came along. Martin knew from his contacts with prospective Latin American borrowers that the Latin American governments were unhappy with the World Bank because most of its loans had gone for European reconstruction and ignored Latin America's development needs. The Latin Americans appealed both to the Ex-Im and the U.S. State Department for help. Martin began to work with General George Marshall, who had replaced James Byrnes as secretary of state, on a proposal for increasing the Ex-Im lending authority by $500 million, to be focused on Latin American borrowers. Marshall planned to announce the added funding proposal at a forthcoming meeting of the International Conference of American States in Bogota, Colombia, at the end of March 1948.

The main hurdle to securing administration support for the funding increase was overcoming the resistance of those concerned about potential competition between the Ex-Im and the World Bank. When Martin presented the proposal to the NAC on 25 March 1947, he expected the resistance of the World Bank representative, but he was surprised when J. Burke Knapp, the NAC representative from the Federal Reserve Board, joined in. Knapp argued: "If this action is taken on top of the International Bank's past record of not having acted on Latin American requests, the Latin American countries may withdraw from it. If they do this, there will be little to keep them in the IMF."[44] Martin responded that the Ex-Im referred its Latin American applicants first to the World Bank and "we intend to continue to cooperate closely."[45] Neither representative accepted Martin's arguments, and it appeared that this capital increase might suffer the same fate as its predecessors.

Fortunately for Martin, Secretary of State Marshall had personally persuaded the NAC chairman, Treasury Secretary Snyder, that the United States had much to gain diplomatically by supporting the Ex-Im funding request. After listening as the impassioned arguments continued, Snyder cut off debate by expressing his concern about the World Bank's priority for Latin America, concluding: "There is no intention to hamper the International [World] Bank or to indicate that the United States Government is not 100 percent back of the Bank. I will make a statement to this effect when hearings are held on this bill."[46] The NAC approved the Ex-Im proposal the same day. Three days later, Marshall, Martin, and Secretary of Commerce Averell Harriman flew to the International Conference of American States in Bogota.

The Colombia trip was another of Martin's formative experiences. On the flight to Bogota, Marshall told Martin that he had proposed that businessman Paul Hoffman serve as administrator of the European Recovery Program, the organization charged with implementing the Marshall Plan, but "[i]f he refuses the job, I hope that you will agree to serve."[47] On the second day, Martin encouraged Marshall to downplay the warnings from the U.S. ambassadors to Colombia and Brazil that the Latin Americans were unhappy with the United States and had unrealistic expectations about future American economic support. He encouraged Marshall to take the offensive by announcing the Ex-Im funding proposal and reminding the Latin Americans that the U.S. government could not finance all their development needs. To Martin's surprise, Marshall asked him to help write the speech Marshall would give to the conference. In the end, the speech was written and rewritten by many hands, but Martin's philosophy was plainly evident in the finished product.

Marshall's speech was to be given in the ornate house of state. Martin described it: "It was a tremendous occasion — every seat in the Capitolio was taken. There was no standing room any place and the room was tense with excitement."[48] Marshall began by complimenting the delegates on the progress on defining principles for regulating foreign investment. Taking on the sensitive question of the extent of potential U.S. economic aid, Marshall told the delegates, "We have poured out our substance to secure the [World War II] victory and prevent suffering in the first years of peace, but we cannot continue this process to the danger of exhaustion."[49] Marshall described the Ex-Im funding proposal, informing his audience: "My government is prepared to increase the scale of assistance it has been giving to the economic development of the American Republic. But it is beyond the capacity of the United States itself to finance more than a small portion of the vast development needed."[50] He went on to describe the importance of private capital, both foreign and domestic, to economic development and the importance of laws that encourage private investment.

The audience was stunned. General George Marshall, the father of the famous Marshall Plan, was telling them that there would be no Marshall Plan for Latin America. The applause was polite but unenthusiastic. Martin described the audience reaction: "He spoke to a hostile audience that wanted something for nothing and in essence he was telling them that Santa Claus was dead and he didn't intend to unbury him."[51]

The U.S. delegation remained in Bogota for two more weeks. A few days after Marshall's speech, the delegates were informed by the U.S. ambassador to Colombia, Norman Armour, that a military coup was occurring and they should seek safety in the U.S. embassy. That evening, the delegation, including Marshall, Martin, and Harriman, looked out on Colombian Army troops trading fire with supporters of President Espinosa. Harriman tried to make light of the situation by commenting that it was "one of those little South American revolutions," but Ambassador Armour advised them: "Please wear your flak jackets and helmets and stand away from the windows."[52] Armour's ambassadorial career could not have been helped if his secretary of state was mortally wounded when he was under the ambassador's care.

Perhaps it was the bloodshed in the streets, but whatever the reason, the atmosphere in the conference improved markedly. The delegates reached beneath the usual platitudes to address issues of real and immediate importance. The Latin American delegates agreed not to discriminate against foreign investment and to liberalize the treatment of income to be repatriated to foreign investors. The Americans agreed to provide more currency-stabilization lending and to explore ways of reducing the U.S. tax burden on U.S. capital invested in Latin America. The agreements were incorporated into an "Economic Pact of Bogota" that outlined specific principles to be implemented, replacing the vague statements of intent developed in similar conferences before World War II. There were many obstacles to be overcome before the signatures of fourteen nations would be put on this document, but it was a hopeful start.

Encouraged by the solid progress achieved in Bogota, Martin pursued the funding increase on his return to Washington. The Senate Committee on Banking and Commerce responded enthusiastically, but the House Banking Committee was far less supportive, and the hearings dragged on toward the summer recess. Martin tirelessly lobbied individual congressmen, but Republican members of the House committee remained unmoved. They did not want the U.S. government choosing which American company received financing in support of its Latin American business. In June, Martin learned that the House Banking Committee would not forward the proposal to the House floor, and that it was tabled for the rest of the session.

The failure to achieve the funding increase was a severe disappointment for Bill Martin. He felt keenly that he had broken faith with the spirit of Bogota.[53] His experience with congressional hearings during his NYSE presidency, and more recently in defense of Russian lend-lease, had taught him that influencing the political decision-making process was fraught with disappointment. Nevertheless, he had yet to learn to avoid investing too much of himself in the outcome of congressional deliberations, no matter how worthy his cause or how much support he might have from the incumbent administration.

The collapse of the funding request forced the Ex-Im back on its existing resources. Fortunately, the availability of grants and low-cost loans under the Marshall Plan encouraged some of the European recipients of Ex-Im's emergency relief loans to let a portion of their comparatively expensive Ex-Im loan commitments expire. The cancellations effectively raised the bank's uncommitted resources, and as of 30 June 1948, the Ex-Im still had $627 million of unused lending authority. Martin continued to husband these resources.

The efforts Martin made to turn the bank into a strong and effective lending agency received a vote of confidence in mid-1948 when Paul Hoffman, the administrator of the Economic Cooperation Administration (ECA), the operations arm of the Marshall Plan, determined that the loan component of the program would be conducted by the Ex-Im Bank. The bank would negotiate the terms and conditions under the guidelines of the Foreign Assistance Act of 1948 and assure the repayment schedule was met. By 1953, the bank processed $1.5 billion of ECA loans.

The issue of political loans refused to die. It was reignited in May 1948, when the Truman administration stuck its political neck out by recognizing the provisional government of Israel. Within a month, representatives of the provisional government were in Washington pleading with the Ex-Im to help finance its most pressing import needs. The prospects for the provisional government were uncertain at best. Israeli armed forces were engaged in a military standoff with several Arab neighbors, and a fragile cease-fire was in effect. The provisional government's budget was highly dependent on contributions from Jewish communities around the world, and if that were not enough, elections for a permanent government were not scheduled until 25 January 1949. Bill Martin was deeply troubled by the economic questions facing the new state, but in October he was bluntly told by the State Department and Harry Truman himself that the administration wanted the Ex-Im to make a loan to Israel. Martin continued to debate the issue and in early November cabled Truman congratulating him on his election as president and admitting that he "was wrestling with the problem about which we have spoken."[54]

In mid-November, Truman invited Martin to the White House to again discuss the Israeli loan. Martin was anxious about his inability to reach a decision on the loan and, according to Ex-Im historian Earl Mazo, "Martin expected to be fired or at least severely reprimanded."[55] Instead, the president "told him to negotiate the loan and approve it if he could do so in good conscience."[56] Harry Truman was as quick to apply pressure in pursuit of a political goal as any president, but he also could be fair and patient. Luckily for Martin, this was a time for patience.

Truman eventually got his way. On 18 January 1949, Martin advised the NAC that Ex-Im recommended a $100 million credit line to the provisional government of Israel, with the first $35 million installment for the import of irrigation equipment and services. Martin said that, despite the provisional government's budgetary uncertainties, the Ex-Im believed it would have "reasonable assurance of repayment" because "The United States is going to support Israel in every reasonable way."[57] He also indicated that, with the Ex-Im loan and continuing U.S. support for economic stabilization, a formally elected government might eventually be able to borrow in the private capital markets. The next day Martin wrote Harry Truman to inform him of the loan approval because "I thought [it] might be of interest to you."[58] Martin was not in the habit of informing the president about Ex-Im loans. The handling of the Israeli loan proved that under the right circumstances, even Bill Martin was willing to make a politically motivated loan.

As Bill Martin considered the future of the Ex-Im, he could take satisfaction from the bank's record. By and large, his determined effort to establish the bank's independence from political influence had been successful. By early 1949, the Ex-Im's loan portfolio consisted of quality credits with very few payment delinquencies. The bank was known to have a capable staff. Most important, it was profitable and able to live within the limits of its financial resources.

Through his leadership of a government agency with an important postwar role, and particularly through his active role in the NAC, Martin had become a visible member of the Truman administration with regular contact with its most powerful members. One of those members, Treasury Secretary John Snyder, had been in office since mid-1946 and knew he was over his head in his job. He decided to get some help and asked Bill Martin if he would become assistant secretary of the Treasury for International Affairs. In terms of independence, visibility, and pay, the job Snyder offered was a step downward. Nevertheless, Martin agreed to talk with Snyder about it.

5

From Crisis to Crisis:
The Truman Administration and the Fed

Bill Martin enjoyed recounting how he was persuaded by John Snyder to work for him at the Treasury Department: "He told me that he could only offer me a reduction in salary; he couldn't offer me any promotion and he could only offer me tougher work than I had had before, with no prospect of advancement."[1] Martin signed on nonetheless, becoming assistant secretary of the Treasury for International Affairs effective 1 January 1949. Martin took a cut in pay, from $15,000 to $10,000 annually. Eleven years earlier, Martin had earned $48,000 a year as president of the New York Stock Exchange. Then, as now, public service exacted a punishing financial sacrifice.

Treasury Secretary John Snyder was heavily criticized in the press, and viewed as a Truman crony who was in over his head. CEA Chairman Leon Keyserling spoke for many with these words: "I would regard John Snyder as an honest, hard-working, wily small town banker."[2] Snyder was cautious, insular, and conservative in a cabinet dominated by experienced political leaders such as George Marshall, Averell Harriman, and Henry Wallace, all of whom were comfortable with America's free-world leadership in the postwar years.

But Snyder was closer to Harry Truman than anyone else in the Truman cabinet. The two had first met in 1919 in the aftermath of World War I, when both were captains in the army. Back in Missouri, the two young men and their families became close friends, and Snyder began to offer advice during Truman's rise through the ranks in the state's Democratic Party machine. Snyder had served several tours in Washington, D.C., where he worked for various U.S. government agencies, but was a banker in Missouri when Harry Truman called in 1945, begging him to return to Washington to help him govern the country. Snyder briefly headed the Home Loan Administration and the War Reconversion Office before Truman appointed him Treasury secretary in June 1946. Snyder's influence on Truman's thinking was unequalled. Only he came in, often unannounced, to see the president in his office or living quarters to offer no-nonsense counsel on a broad range of political issues. The two men were the embodiment of the pragmatism practiced in the "show me" state from which they had come.

Snyder was a straightforward man of his word who assigned enormous value to honesty and honoring a commitment. He did not like to be taken advantage of, and he was quick to size people up, usually with skeptical evaluations. After almost fifteen years in government, Snyder had acquired a solid understanding of governmental finance and bureaucratic behavior. He was not afraid to challenge those in authority and in his earlier days had taken on Jesse Jones, his superior at the RFC and one of the most powerful men in the government. Nonetheless, Snyder was overwhelmed by his Treasury responsibilities. Despite being subjected to fierce lobbying, he plowed resolutely ahead, never publicly defending his decisions. Although he was vitally concerned about the attacks on his abilities, he did not let it show. His entire focus was on supporting his president and serving as a voice for hardheaded realism in Harry Truman's deliberations.

For the better part of two years, John Snyder had been engaged in a test of wills over the extent of American financial support for its European allies. Snyder, ever the prudent banker, wanted careful monitoring of and limits on all financial aid, in contrast to Secretary of State George C. Marshall's "insistence on quick, large-scale action" and multiyear commitments.[3] Snyder wanted help in countering the pressure on Truman to continuously expand foreign aid coming from Marshall and Harriman, and it was not surprising that he turned to Bill Martin. Snyder had helped place Martin at the Ex-Im Bank, and the two men had worked together on the National Advisory Council as it deliberated many of the international financial problems that bedeviled Snyder. Although Martin could not negotiate his salary, he did secure two conditions: Snyder agreed that Martin's role at the Treasury would extend beyond international issues — and Martin would have his lunch hours free to engage in his daily midday tennis game.

Martin had been in office about three months when America's closest ally, Great Britain, announced that during the first quarter of 1949, its foreign-exchange reserves had fallen to $1.63 billion, well below its safety level of $2 billion. The alarm was only the latest installment in a series of recurring exchange crises that had plagued the United Kingdom since the end of the war. Predictably, the news set off a chorus of conflicting accusations. Economists in continental Europe and in the United States declared the pound overvalued and called for devaluation. Congressional critics described U.S. financial aid to Britain as ineffective and proposed cutting it off. Officials at the Treasury Department knew that the bad news would bring their British counterparts to the United States with requests for added support. The parties could agree only that the United Kingdom's problem defied an easy solution.

Bill Martin advised Snyder that devaluation, not further U.S. financial assistance, was the only longer-term solution to the United Kingdom's balance of payments problem. Martin later described the advice he gave Snyder at the time: "How do you get [the United Kingdom] to cut costs and reduce expenditures if we cough up more dollars now. If you give a palliative, it makes it more difficult for them politically to take the needed steps. If Britain is to earn more dollars, she must cut prices; that means cutting exchange rates."[4]

Though Snyder agreed with Martin, he was reluctant to publicly propose devaluation. As secretary of the Treasury, Snyder did not want to give the impression that the United States was dictating U.K. economic policy. There had not been a wholesale currency readjustment since the Bretton Woods conference in 1945, and a devaluation of sterling would force adjustments in all major trading currencies. The Treasury Department's preferred solution was to accept the inevitability of a wholesale readjustment and to bring the process under the umbrella of the IMF. In a speech on 5 May 1949, Snyder referred to the timeliness of the upcoming annual meeting of the IMF in September and his expectation that a currency adjustment would be on the agenda. On 18 May, British Chancellor of the Exchequer, Sir Stafford Cripps, fired back his response: "Devaluation of sterling is not necessary, nor will it take place."[5]

The U.S. policy posture for the September meetings was debated within the National Advisory Council for most of the summer of 1949. As the discussions continued, Martin became the Treasury's spokesman for taking a firm position with the British. To put the British situation in the broad context of U.S. policy, Martin observed, "Our whole economic policy, on which we have spent billions, has the ultimate object of restoring multilateral trade and convertibility."[6] Martin argued that British policies were steps in the wrong direction and contrasted sharply with the progress being made in other European countries. Returning to his oft-stated conclusion, he argued: "The real problem is how Britain's cost structure can be brought into line to improve its competitive position in the dollar area."[7] Martin acknowledged that Britain had increased production and exports in recent years, but "the expanded exports have gone primarily to soft currency areas. Britain has been running a little Marshall Plan for the rest of the sterling area and, in so doing, is living beyond her means."[8] Martin believed that Britain had lost its ability to earn the dollars necessary to repay its postwar loans from the United States and urged the NAC to demand that the British address the issue. There was some opposition to Martin's arguments from the State Department and the Federal Reserve representatives, but over the course of the summer, they reluctantly accepted them.

Martin expressed his views directly to the British during a U.S. visit in June 1949 by Henry Wilson-Smith, a U.K. Treasury official and close advisor to Cripps. Wilson-Smith reported that Martin had taken a "kind but firm tone" to inform him that "the U.K. had agreed to work jointly with the U.S. toward a world of free convertibility and non-discrimination, but seemed to be moving in the opposite direction."[9] Further, Wilson-Smith reported that Martin told him that "practically all officials of the U.S. Government were firmly convinced that devaluation of sterling was inevitable."[10] Martin certainly took liberties in his claim that the U.S. government was united on a British devaluation, but he achieved his desired result. As economists Barry Eichengreen and Alec Cairncross wrote: "The talks in Washington had a powerful effect on Wilson-Smith, who was in a key position" and who "subsequently argued in favor of devaluation."[11]

British foreign minister Ernest Bevin and Cripps arrived in the United States on 1 September. The burden of negotiating Labour's unpopular agenda with its trading partners fell on Cripps who, as the most famous patent lawyer in the United Kingdom, was admirably suited for the role. For the better part of eighteen months, he staunchly defended the official value of the pound and watched as the U.K. dollar shortage worsened. Though he continued his public opposition to devaluation, Cripps listened to the advice of Britain's friends and the arguments of its critics and changed his mind. Shortly before Cripps and Bevin were to leave for the United States, the full British cabinet approved a devaluation.[12]

After his arrival in the United States, Cripps informed the tripartite representatives of the British government's decision. The American representatives were surprised and delighted. Deciding not to delay the announcement, the Finance Ministry announced a 30 percent devaluation, and the currency logjam was broken. As Snyder hoped, most of the new values for the world's other trading currencies were thrashed out during the IMF annual meeting. These negotiations were carried on in small meetings outside of the formally scheduled sessions, accompanied by frantic consultations with home governments. The IMF involvement in the currency realignment negotiations high-lighted the fact that the IMF was finally beginning to fulfill the vision of its founding members. A day after the announcement, Martin authorized John McCloy, the U.S. High Commissioner in Germany, to devalue the deutsch mark. Martin encouraged a devaluation that would "eliminate the present undervaluation in relation to other European currencies."[13] German indus-trial strength was rapidly recovering its export prowess and beginning to threaten its European competitors.

John Snyder and Bill Martin deserve a large measure of credit for the suc-cessful currency realignment. Despite the strong objections of the State De-partment, Snyder and Martin changed the U.S. government's policy away from relatively uncritical support for British economic policies. The British were encouraged to develop their own solution to their problem, but they understood very clearly that the United States was looking for decisive action. Bill Martin's vigorous defense of America's commitment to free trade and convertible currencies helped stiffen Snyder's backbone. Martin played a crit-ical role in shaping and communicating the U.S. government's policy, although he repeatedly denied that he "engineered the devaluation of the pound."[14] As late as 1951, *Business Week* reported that Martin's British critics "still feel he left them no alternative but to do what they didn't want to do."[15] The devalua-tion of September 1949 led to an immediate and sustained improvement in the U.K. balance of payments situation. The currency alignment that followed removed an important barrier to the implementation of an intra-European payments union and, ultimately, convertibility for European currencies.

Martin's days at the Treasury Department during late 1949 and early 1950 were typically filled with issues related to the financial aspects of the occupa-tion of Germany and Japan, progress toward convertible currencies, and the wind-down of the Marshall Plan. These comparatively orderly developments were upended on 24 June 1950, when North Korean soldiers swept into South Korea. The economic implications of the Korean War changed the trajectory of Bill Martin's career.

By this time, Martin had become a close advisor to John Snyder concerning a broad range of policy matters. Each morning before Snyder began his official day, he and Martin would enjoy an easy conversation about current issues facing the Treasury. In the middle of July, Snyder mentioned that the inflation-ary pressures coming from the Korean War buildup were reigniting a long-standing controversy between the Treasury and the Federal Reserve System. Martin asked Snyder if he might familiarize himself with the situation. Al-though Snyder gave little encouragement, Martin began with his usual schol-arly inquiry into the history of the dispute.

The seeds of the differences between the Treasury and the Fed were sown when Treasury Secretary Henry Morgenthau grappled with financing the costs of the World War II military buildup. Morgenthau wanted predictable interest rates for the billions of dollars' worth of Treasury securities he would have to issue. In February 1942, he negotiated a formal agreement with Fed Chairman Marriner Eccles that the Fed would support a range of fixed interest rates for the duration of the war. The Fed's commitment became known as the "peg." Unfortunately for the Fed, interest rates at the time of the agreement were still abnormally low due to the aftereffects of the Great Depression. The bank prime lending rate at the time the peg was set was 1½ percent, compared to an average of 4½ percent during most of the 1920s. Eccles reluctantly agreed to a 2½ percent rate for long-term Treasury issues but argued that the proposed ninety-day bill rate of ⅜ percent was too low. Eccles could foresee that all Treasury securities would be equally liquid, since the Fed would be supporting the market price of all the securities. In the face of uniform liquidity, investors would abandon Treasury bills and their lower yields. To support the market price for bills, the Fed would be forced to buy enormous amounts of them. Morgenthau remained unmoved and forced the ⅜ percent rate on the Fed.

Eccles's fears became a reality. Within sixteen months of the war's end, the Fed held virtually all of the outstanding Treasury bills, and its portfolio had ballooned from $2.5 billion before the war to $20.8 billion. The Fed's position was particularly painful because its purchases automatically created an equivalent amount of new reserves for the banking system. The added reserves contributed to a 300 percent increase in the money supply during the war years, and the purchasing power of the dollar declined by 47 percent. In the memorable words of Fed Chairman Eccles, the Fed became "the engine of inflation," and he pressed for the end of the peg.[16]

When John Snyder became Treasury secretary in mid-1946, he maintained the Treasury's unwillingness to modify the peg. Snyder was daunted by the task of refinancing the huge World War II debt and argued that even a ½ percent increase in long-term rates would raise the Treasury's borrowing cost by $1.25 billion, or 4 percent of the administration's budget. Of equal importance to Snyder was Harry Truman's absolute determination that long-term Treasury rates would not be raised. Truman cited the exigencies of war and his mistaken idea that savers who invested in wartime savings bonds would lose a portion of their principal value if long-term rates rose.[17]

By the middle of 1948, almost three years after the end of World War II, the Fed had achieved only a modest move away from the peg. The rates on bills and the one-year certificate had risen by ¼ percent, and long-term rates remained unchanged at 2½ percent. Marriner Eccles's constant petitioning for relief turned Treasury Secretary Snyder and President Truman against him, and when Eccles's appointment as chairman came up for renewal in 1948, he was replaced. Truman never revealed the exact reasons why he chose not to reappoint Eccles, but Eccles's constant criticism of the peg definitely contributed to the outcome.[18]

The new chairman, Thomas McCabe, had been chairman of the board of the Philadelphia Federal Reserve Bank, was a seasoned corporate executive, and was a friend of John Snyder. Snyder convinced the president that McCabe was a diplomat who could bridge the Treasury-Fed difference in a way that the administration could accept. To Snyder's anger and disappointment, it was not long before Tom McCabe was defending positions long advocated by his predecessor. Though McCabe's reputation for tact and persuasiveness was well deserved, he could not prevent the deterioration of his relationship with his old friend John Snyder.

The conflict over the peg was quiescent during the recession of 1949 but returned with a vengeance after the Korean conflict broke out in June 1950. The Federal Open Market Committee (the FOMC), the Fed's primary monetary policy-making committee, became alarmed by the inflationary potential posed by heavy defense spending that was flowing into an economy already strongly recovering from the recession. By the second quarter of 1950, the Consumer Price Index (CPI) was rising at an annualized rate of 7.6 percent, and the FOMC knew the time for temporizing was over. In July 1950, Mc-Cabe informed Snyder that "the System can not maintain the existing rate structure in the Government security market."[19] The FOMC followed that warning with an announcement on 18 August that the Fed's discount rate would increase from 1½ percent to 1¾ percent, the first rise in two years.

Snyder and Truman were strongly committed to the primacy of the Treasury over the Fed and were outraged at the Fed's show of independence. Truman had made his position clear late in 1949 when he told a meeting of the chairmen and directors of the Federal Reserve Banks: "Now gentlemen, you represent the greatest financial institution in the history of the world, *except* the Treasury of the United States."[20] In a similar vein, John Snyder advised Allan Sproul, the president of the New York Federal Reserve Bank, in September 1950: "In the long-run the administration in power must prevail, and that means the Treasury must prevail."[21] Between August and December, the Fed and the administration engaged in a delicate minuet of meetings and exchanges of letters.

Angered by the feuding, Truman launched a frontal attack on the Fed by issuing an unprecedented invitation to the entire twelve-man FOMC to meet with him at the White House on 31 January. Both sides restated their positions but in the vaguest of terms. McCabe reluctantly said he would work with Snyder but reserved the right to come back to the president if "an agreement . . . cannot be accomplished."[22] At the end of the meeting, Truman said he would issue a statement on the discussion the next day and asked the Fed representatives to await the White House release. On 1 February, Truman released a letter to McCabe in which he thanked the FOMC: "As I understand it, I have your assurance that the market on government securities will be stabilized and maintained at present levels."[23] The statement was amplified by a Treasury spokesman, who said that "the announcement means . . . these [current] levels will be maintained during the present emergency."[24] McCabe and the other FOMC members were stunned that the White House had so blatantly misinterpreted the Fed's position.

The dispute spilled fully into public view when Marriner Eccles released a Fed internal memorandum of the meeting, and any chance of a quiet reconciliation slipped away. The *New York Times*'s scathing editorial was a typical response: "The President has ordered the Federal Reserve Board to take its orders in the future from the Secretary of the Treasury. We can recall no instance where the independent central banking system in a democracy has been subjected to similar public degradation."[25]

If the administration had any thought that it might appeal to Congress for support, it was squelched by Senator Paul Douglas. The day before Eccles's sensational revelation, Douglas introduced a "sense of the Congress[']" resolution "that the primary responsibility for regulating the supply, availability and cost of credit in general shall be vested in the duly constituted authorities of the Federal Reserve System."[26] After Eccles's action, Douglas had all the allies he could use. The Senate Banking and Commerce Committee and the Senate majority leader, Robert Taft, both began to look into the matter, and their initial comments supported the Federal Reserve.

On 6 February, the FOMC rejected proposals for a mass resignation or going to Congress for a reinterpretation of the Fed's mandate. Instead, it wrote to Truman: "You as president of the United States and we as members of the Federal Open Market Committee have unintentionally been drawn into a false position before the American public: you for committing us to a policy which we believe to be contrary to what we all truly desire, and we for defying your wishes."[27] The FOMC promised to work with the administration to develop a policy that both maintained public confidence in government bonds and protected the purchasing power of the dollar.

To get the dialogue started, the FOMC also sent a letter marked "secret" to Secretary Snyder with the barest outline of a possible solution. The critical feature was the suggestion of a new issue of Treasury bonds carrying a "sufficiently attractive" but unspecified interest rate to be offered to investors in exchange for $20 billion of outstanding 2½ percent wartime bonds. Neither Snyder nor Harry Truman could accept the possibility that anyone who had contributed to the war effort by buying long-term Treasury bonds would experience a loss in principal value, even if it were a temporary condition. The Fed's proposed exchange offer reduced that likelihood by offering bonds that would not lose market value if rates rose. The proposal was purposely vague, but it was a beginning.

McCabe hand-delivered the FOMC letter to Snyder on the morning of 8 February. There he encountered Bill Martin, whom Snyder had asked to attend the meeting. Snyder and Martin had discussed the problems with the peg and financing the war in the weeks leading up to the current impasse. Martin advised Snyder that the peg's low interest rates would make it almost impossible for the Treasury to raise all the necessary war financing without significant Fed support, and that the Fed purchases were creating inflation. Martin recommended that the Treasury restart the dialogue with the Fed about a return to market-based long-term interest rates. Snyder rejected Martin's advice but continued to review the matter with him. Summarizing their discussions, Martin later observed: "It always seemed to worry the Secretary whenever I was in disagreement with him."[28] When Fed-Treasury relations ruptured after the White House meeting on 31 January, Martin asked Snyder if he might open up a backdoor communication with McCabe about staff-level discussions to seek a solution to the standoff. Snyder, who wanted to keep discussions at the policy level, discouraged Martin. Then fate took a hand.

On 11 February, Snyder entered the hospital for a long-deferred eye operation, and he informed McCabe that Martin would be the primary contact person for the Treasury. Three days later, Martin asked McCabe for permission to establish a small joint task force with staff from both institutions for "technical discussions" concerning the Fed's proposals contained in its letter of 7 February. To make the discussions more informal and to preserve secrecy, the initial meetings were held in Bill Martin's home.

The discussions between the longtime adversaries started well but soon bogged down. Winfield Riefler, Tom McCabe's assistant and the Fed's lead negotiator, amplified the Fed's proposal for the new Treasury bond to be exchanged for outstanding 2½ percent war bonds. The new issue would pay 2¾ percent interest and contained a well-conceived mix of features that allowed existing bondholders to earn higher interest and encouraged them to hold on to the bonds. The new bonds would be nonmarketable but would carry an option to convert the bond into a marketable security. A consensus formed around Riefler's proposal, but discussions collapsed when the group addressed ending the peg completely. George Haas, the Treasury's chief technician, was devoutly committed to the peg and argued that the Treasury could not afford the collapse of bond prices. After a few sessions, Martin knew he would have more problems dealing with his Treasury team than with the Fed representatives.[29]

Martin attempted to persuade his balky Treasury associates to support a plan for smoothing the transition to unpegged rates. Building on a Fed offer to work in concert, Martin proposed a joint market support program to be applied during a "testing period." The test would determine the likely level of market-based long-term interest rates. Martin argued that once it became clear the Fed and the Treasury were truly working together in the bond market, investor confidence in Treasury bonds would increase substantially. Given investor confidence, it was likely that unpegged long-term rates would stabilize at or near current pegged levels. If the test indicated higher rates might be necessary, the two institutions would work together to "consider the matter again" and, if necessary, modify the approach. The Fed's cooperative attitude helped Martin bring his associates around, and they agreed to write up a formal proposal.[30]

Before Martin could secure the agreement of the Fed representatives, Harry Truman added a new element of urgency to Martin's efforts. Truman recognized the failure of his attempts to force a solution on the Fed and was worried that the crisis would seriously damage his administration. On 26 February, the president gathered an interagency group under the leadership of Charles Wilson, director of the Office of Defense Mobilization, to recommend a solution to the conflict. By assigning the group a charter that covered the peg and several other knotty credit issues, Truman guaranteed a bureaucratic battle and months of negotiation before any results were achieved.[31] Disheartened by his tattered relationship with Snyder and Truman and anticipating an administered solution imposed by the interagency committee, Thomas McCabe went back to his office and wrote out a bitter resignation letter that he had delivered to Truman that afternoon.

If he were to head off the Wilson group and a cumbersome solution, Martin had to move quickly. At a meeting of Wilson, Martin, and Snyder in Snyder's hospital room the next day, Wilson "doubted whether the problem could be resolved by a committee set up" and was considering hiring a special consultant to develop a resolution.[32] Martin knew that Snyder was perplexed. Snyder did not want to leave Truman "holding the bag" by ignoring the interagency group, but he did not like Wilson's approach. After the meeting, Martin reviewed the Treasury negotiators' proposal, and Snyder unenthusiastically authorized him to negotiate the details with the Fed.

With Snyder's blessing in hand, Martin decided that the key to the Fed's approval was selling Winfield Riefler. In addition to serving as McCabe's assistant, Riefler held the influential post of secretary of the FOMC. Over two days of meetings, Martin and Riefler thrashed out the details of an agreement. The final product was a carefully crafted set of interlocking commitments. The new long-term bond was left much as Riefler had initially proposed. The short-term interest rate would be allowed to rise to the Fed's discount rate of 1 ¾ percent, and the Fed agreed to hold the discount rate steady for the rest of 1951. The Fed would keep the bond market "orderly" during the transition to unpegged rates but, in a crucial Treasury concession, would not be held to preserving par values for existing bonds. The relative contributions to a joint pool for funding purchases to stabilize the market were agreed. Finally, both parties agreed to consult prior to any changes in debt management or credit policy. Martin now had a complete package and, with Riefler's support, a persuasive ally at the Fed.

Armed with the full agreement, Martin made a final approach to Snyder. Martin knew Snyder was unwilling to abandon the ground rules he had stated in a highly publicized speech he had made in the early stage of the dispute. With the vital support of Treasury Undersecretary Ed Foley, Martin sold the agreement as being "within the framework of the 2 ½ percent long-term interest rate pattern announced by the Secretary in his address before the New York Board of Trade on January 18."[33] Martin emphasized the Fed's commitment to help stabilize the market during the transition to unpegged rates. He expressed confidence that when the Treasury and the Fed acted together, they could ensure an "orderly" market during the transition. Despite his assurances, Martin knew that bond prices could steadily decline, even in an orderly market, and make a mockery of his assurances that unpegged long-term rates would be close to those under the peg. The agreement was full of unknowns and Martin must have been aware that his assurances were taking him onto thin ice. But it appeared that even John Snyder's resistance was worn down by the struggle, for he gave his "unsmiling support to a smiling Bill Martin."[34]

On 1 March, Martin met with the FOMC to make his case for the agreement. Martin was in mid-presentation, emphasizing the importance of "continuous [Treasury-Fed] discussion . . . set in a broad picture of a joint Treasury-Federal Reserve debt management program" when he was interrupted by Allan Sproul, the powerful president of the Federal Reserve Bank of New York.[35] Sproul, the Fed's leading monetary policy maker, had borne the brunt of arguing the Fed's case against the peg during the years of conflict and was scarred by Snyder's repeated unwillingness to move away from the peg, despite promises to do so. Sproul observed that market forces, not the Fed, should determine interest rate levels: "If securities were offered in substantial amounts, and the FOMC chose not to buy . . . prices would go down and yields up."[36] In Sproul's opinion, the Treasury's proposal could still require the FOMC to "drive securities to a price or yield" by open-market purchases.[37] It was the moment of truth. Sproul was saying that the proposal would not prevent Snyder from forcing the peg back on the Fed. If Sproul were opposed to the working party's recommendation, FOMC approval would be unlikely.

Martin's answer focused on the heart of the issue: that the Treasury recognized that all rates would rise, and that bill rates might rise as high as the Fed's discount rate. He replied: "I agree with what you say about the operation of market forces. I have made it very clear to the Secretary that it is our understanding that [there will be] adjustment . . . we are under no illusions as to how far the adjustment might go. . . . We are talking about it [the discount rate] as a pivot."[38] Martin was saying that he had convinced Snyder to accept a fluctuating short-term rate, and even though bill rates might go above the discount rate, the Fed would not be expected to intervene. A freely fluctuating short-term rate was the foundation of a market-based interest rate structure and a guarantee that the peg was ended. It was also crucial to restoring the Fed's monetary powers. He knew Allan Sproul would accept nothing less. Martin believed that investor confidence absolutely depended on visible Treasury-Fed cooperation in the marketplace, and the proposed agreement was the only way that cooperation could be assured. Allan Sproul and Bill Martin were on the same side on the issue of trusting the market. Sproul, who had been the most effective spokesman in opposition to the Treasury, supported the proposed agreement from that day on.

On Saturday, 3 March, the FOMC unanimously approved the agreement. Tom McCabe concluded that: "in my opinion, the biggest hope in the agreement is the fact that it marks a new era in Federal Reserve–Treasury relations."[39] That afternoon, John Snyder telephoned Harry Truman in Key West and negotiated his approval. On Sunday, 4 March, a bland two-paragraph press release that the Fed specified to be "brief, financial, and non-political" announced that the Treasury and Fed had "reached full accord with respect to debt management and monetary policies to be pursued in furthering their common purpose."[40]

The Accord takes its place alongside the Banking Act of 1935 as one of the monumental events in the history of the modern Federal Reserve System. The Accord was constructed around the recognition that the Fed's responsibility for controlling credit and the Treasury's responsibility for managing its debt could come into conflict. To assure that the actions of the two institutions would be in the nation's interest, both had to recognize one another's institutional responsibilities and to act as partners and equals. The crisis galvanized the FOMC to defend its statutory responsibilities in the face of extreme pressure from the administration. The crisis also focused the attention of Congress on the respective roles of the Treasury and the Fed, and Congress reaffirmed its interest in protecting the Fed from excessive administration pressure. The Accord restored the institutional balance of power intended by the creators of the Fed's original legislation.

It is improbable that a solution based on the principles of the Accord would have evolved without Bill Martin. Harry Truman was seeking an administered resolution, such as an interagency consultative mechanism, when he called in Charles Wilson. Allan Sproul, the FOMC's intellectual leader, was pushing his associates to go to Congress for "a new set of rules." It is highly unlikely that John Snyder would have reopened direct negotiations with the Fed — a year after the Accord, he was still recommending an "advisory council" of outsiders who would oversee the reconciliation of Fed-Treasury conflicts. Bill Martin took the position from the beginning that the crisis was in great part a "breakdown in communication" concerning "our common problem," and that cooperation and prior consultation between equals was the only long-term solution. Martin had a well-developed mastery of persuading opposed interests to accept compromise that was honed during his years at the New York Stock Exchange and at the Export-Import Bank. He integrated existing ideas into a comprehensive program, and by applying his "pleasant implacability" squeezed agreement from the working group.[41] Martin won support for a plan that Allan Sproul aptly called a "human and natural solution," requiring "thorough discussion of divergent views by informed and responsible men" and the practice of the art of compromise "when positions become unyielding."[42]

As the reaction to the Accord died down, Snyder and Truman reviewed Tom McCabe's letter of resignation submitted ten days earlier. Throughout the conflict, neither man ever understood the depth of McCabe's diplomatically stated commitment to the Fed's independence. They simply felt he had fallen under the influence of Sproul and the New York bankers.[43] Moreover, Snyder felt that McCabe had given him a commitment to hold rates steady during Snyder's hospitalization and then had not lived up to it. Snyder convinced Truman to accept McCabe's resignation letter and called McCabe, advising him that "his services were no longer satisfactory."[44] On 9 March, McCabe obliged Snyder by sending a more statesmanlike version of his letter of resignation.

Truman was under pressure to find a replacement for McCabe. The Accord had to be implemented quickly and, in Truman's opinion, his last appointment to the Fed chairmanship had proven to be "just as bad as Eccles."[45] Truman proposed Harry McDonald, whom he had appointed chairman of the SEC a few years earlier. Truman believed McDonald would be acceptable to the financial community and was confident of his loyalty to the administration. John Snyder proposed his trusted assistant, Bill Martin, who had already demonstrated that he could work with the Fed. Martin was also recommended by Tom McCabe, who had made his resignation conditional upon having a say in the choice of his replacement. Truman was unmoved: he did not want another disappointment. In a situation reminiscent of his initial prospects for the presidency of the New York Stock Exchange, Bill Martin, the younger and comparatively unknown candidate, was about to come in second. At the eleventh hour, fate again intervened when it was discovered that Fed Governor M. S. Szymczak was from McDonald's home Reserve district. The Fed's legislation prohibited two Fed governors from the same Reserve district.[46] The debate was over. McDonald was out, and Bill Martin became the administration's candidate for chairman of the Federal Reserve System.

Still concerned about Martin's views, Truman called him to the White House. In an interview that Martin often described later, the president asked Martin if he would promise to keep interest rates stable so that government bonds would not fall below par value.[47] Martin replied, "Mr. President, unless the administration follows responsible fiscal and monetary policies, it [a rate increase] probably will happen again. Markets will not wait on kings, prime ministers, presidents, secretaries of the Treasury, or chairmen of the Federal Reserve Board."[48] Martin said he was sorry, but he could not make such a promise. Truman was taken aback by Martin's forthrightness and decided to take some time to think about Martin's response, saying he would contact him again. The next day he asked Martin to visit and said: "All I want is the assurance that whatever might happen, you will do the best you can."[49] Martin replied that he would and recalled, "even though I don't think he and I had the same understanding of the market process . . . he appointed me anyway."[50] Fortunately for Bill Martin, Harry Truman overrode his own skepticism and once again accepted the advice of John Snyder.

The press wrote that Martin's confirmation was "doubtful" in light of his closeness to Snyder and allegiance to the Treasury Department, his former employer. At his confirmation hearing before the Senate Banking and Currency Committee on 19 March 1951, Martin attacked the issue head-on: "[John Snyder] is not the type of individual who would want me to go into the Federal Reserve as a stooge for him."[51] Asked what he would do if Martin felt Snyder was "honestly wrong" on a disputed issue, Martin said, "If there was no give in him at all, and if the law gave me the right to [proceed in a certain direction] I would pursue that course."[52] Martin softened his response by observing that "I don't think you can say too often that 'I know he is 100 percent wrong and I am 100 percent right.' "[53]

Martin was asked how the Fed would interpret its vague Accord obligation to promote an "orderly market" for government securities. Referring to his experience at the New York Stock Exchange and the importance of the firms that made markets in a particular security, he replied: "[W]e insisted that a [dealer] was responsible for maintaining an orderly market . . . and that he had to [offer to buy] even if he lost his shirt on a [market] downswing. There never should be a point where people who have securities to sell cannot find buyers."[54] Asked if he had any concern that the post-Accord Treasury bond market might not operate this way, he replied, "None whatever."[55]

Martin's answer reflected the vital link in his success in achieving the Accord. He was confident that the bottom would not fall out of the Treasury bond market when the Fed stopped supporting rates. He knew that many in the FOMC and Fed staff felt the same and was able to convince his wavering Treasury counterparts and John Snyder to follow his lead. An unexpected chain of events landed him in the Fed chairmanship and now he had the opportunity of a lifetime: the chance to prove the adaptive capacity of free markets and to restore a flexible monetary policy to the Federal Reserve System — in short, to convert the promise of the Accord into a reality.

The committee met on 20 March and after a short deliberation confirmed Martin by a vote of 12–0. Senator Paul Douglas, who had upheld the Fed's independence as much as anyone in Congress, remained unconvinced that Martin would fully exercise that independence and abstained from voting.

The Federal Reserve System that Bill Martin stepped into was a relatively young institution grown beyond the vision of its original sponsors, including Bill Martin's father, but still in the throes of evolution. The Federal Reserve System is America's first sustained effort to deal with the boom and bust cycles that litter its financial history. The Federal Reserve Act of 1913 was a brilliant synthesis of modern thinking on banking reform and a novel approach to public-private cooperation. The operations of the system would be carried out in twelve Reserve Banks located throughout the country. The Reserve Banks would be corporations created in the public interest and owned by the banks that were members of the system. The member banks would not have an interest in the profits of the Reserve Banks, and bankers could hold only one-third of the seats on the Reserve Banks' boards of directors.

Even by the generous standards of legislation written in the early part of the twentieth century, the Federal Reserve Act was vaguely constructed. The Fed's initial mandate was modest: creating an "elastic" currency that could be expanded in times of high demand, establishing facilities for increasing the supply of credit by discounting member-bank notes, and supervising the banking system. The Fed might have a limited mandate, but it had enormous flexibility in implementing it. The provision of credit to member banks was limited only to considering "the maintenance of sound credit conditions, and the accommodation of commerce, industry, and agriculture."[56] The vagueness did not trouble the act's early sponsors, for their expectations for the Fed were as modest as the initial mandate. Treasury Secretary William G. McAdoo wrote that the Fed "is really a public utility in the service of the nation."[57] Senator Glass said: "Congress has created a Federal Reserve Board charged, not with conducting a central bank system, but charged merely with supervisory power to see that these regional Reserve Banks comply with the law."[58] From the beginning, the Fed would become what its leaders could make of it.

The experiences of William McChesney Martin Sr. during the early years of the Federal Reserve System were typical of the men who stepped forward across the country to win support for the Federal Reserve System and integrate it into the banking system of their regions. By setting uniform standards for providing credit to member banks and mobilizing credit during periods of financial stress, the Reserve Banks became vital contributors to strengthening the U.S. financial system. The initial influence of the Fed grew from its regional base, not from the board in Washington.

The board of governors began its early years under the thumb of the Treasury Department. For its first two decades, the Federal Reserve Board operated out of offices in the Treasury building, and the secretary of the Treasury and one of his subordinates, the comptroller of the currency, served as two of the seven board members. During the Fed's first decade, the twelve Reserve Banks began building a common approach to carrying out the Fed's mandate. The Reserve Banks' philosophy was defined by the president of the New York Reserve Bank, Benjamin Strong. Strong, whose experience as chairman of Bankers Trust Company, a leading New York City bank, and whose profound understanding of the financial markets coupled with a clear vision of the Fed's potential made him a natural leader. Strong was among the first to appreciate the impact of the Fed's purchases and sales of Treasury securities on bank resources and credit conditions. At his urging, the Reserve Banks began to coordinate their open-market transaction, and then formed the predecessor to the FOMC.[59] Within a few years, Strong led the Fed into the process of managing the U.S. economy.

The 1929 collapse of the stock market and the onset of the Great Depression revealed that the Fed had not yet developed the capacity to deal effectively with major economic disturbances. It also revealed the inherent vulnerability of depending too much on the leadership of a few outstanding central bankers, for after Strong died in 1928, the Fed was unable to mount a coherent response to the economic problems of 1929–33. The situation changed with the arrival of the New Deal and presidential advisor Marriner Eccles. Eccles, a self-taught economist of considerable ability, came to the Roosevelt administration from the presidency of a banking and industrial empire in Utah. From the beginning of Roosevelt's first term, Eccles served as one of the president's most valued advisors by providing much of the intellectual undergirding for the economic initiatives of the New Deal. Roosevelt asked him to take over the Federal Reserve System, and Eccles responded that he would be interested only if he could make fundamental changes to the way it was organized. Most of Eccles's recommendations were incorporated into the Banking Act of 1935, and the Fed took on its current organizational form.

Marriner Eccles made a singular contribution to the evolution of the Fed by designing and promoting the passage of the Banking Act of 1935, but he was not able to fully realize the powers he created for the Fed chairman. Eccles quickly learned that exercising his new responsibilities brought him into conflict with Treasury Secretary Henry Morgenthau. Morgenthau was Eccles's initial sponsor in the Roosevelt administration but had become suspicious of Eccles's influence with Franklin Roosevelt and about how Eccles would use his new position. Eccles and Morgenthau engaged in bitter conflicts, and although he lost most of them, Eccles retained Roosevelt's confidence. Eccles established a new level of visibility for the Fed within the administration, but much of his success was personal. He was not able to establish a comparable acceptance of the Fed as an institution. When Harry Truman became president, Eccles lost even his presidential relationship. Without presidential support, the Fed's influence began to wane, and neither Eccles nor his successor, Tom McCabe, was able to halt it.

It is not an exaggeration to describe the Fed as at a critical juncture in the spring of 1951 when Bill Martin first drove his favorite car, a white Cadillac convertible, into the chairman's parking spot. The institution was only thirty-eight years old, and for the past two decades its monetary policies had been ineffective or subordinated to the Treasury's debt financing needs. After Benjamin Strong's death, the Fed had been heavily criticized by economists and politicians for making the Great Depression worse by providing too much liquidity during the late 1920s and too little during the early 1930s. When Marriner Eccles became chairman in 1936, he downplayed the importance of monetary policy because he believed that fiscal policy was the most effective means of promoting economic recovery. The limitations on monetary policy inflicted by the peg reinforced problems the Fed was already having in exercising its monetary policy tools. When the peg neutralized the Fed's monetary tools, the Fed lost its ability to stabilize the economy, and an essential element of its institutional purpose was suspended.

The Fed's sense of institutional cohesiveness was also weakened by Marriner Eccles's strong personality and dictatorial leadership style. One of his associates described him thus: "He had little hesitation in telling anyone — his staff, senators, even presidents — what ought to be done, and even his friends called him abrasive with both superiors and subordinates."[60] Determined to support Roosevelt's New Deal initiatives, Eccles ignored those in the Fed who disagreed with him. Eccles's decision to remain on the board of governors after Truman removed him from the chairmanship created further dissension by forcing staff members to choose sides when Eccles and McCabe disagreed.

In 1951, the Fed also suffered from a lack of solid political support. Eccles never made an effort to cultivate relations with Congress. Political economist Donald Kettl wrote: "Eccles was far better at framing bold action than in negotiating his way through Washington's political avenues."[61] By the time Tom McCabe arrived at the Fed, relations with the administration were moving from distrust to hostility, and McCabe was unable to build congressional support as a counterweight. The only congressional supporter was Senator Paul Douglas. Douglas was a capable economist and a dedicated advocate for the Fed, but he was unpopular in the Senate and could not muster a broad base of support for his defense of the Fed.

The last, but certainly not the least, of the Fed's problems was that it had lost the confidence of the banking community. Despite his extensive experience as a banker, Eccles did little to convey his sympathy for the problems of the banking industry. He gave short shrift to the Federal Advisory Committee, a group mandated by the Federal Reserve Act consisting of leading bankers that periodically met with the board of governors to discuss economic and banking issues. The banks supported Eccles's forceful anti-inflationary stance but were aggravated when he proposed to achieve it through very large increases in required bank reserves. Eccles sought to "freeze" the excessive reserves created by the Fed under the peg, but the bankers saw it as an unwarranted restriction on their freedom to do their business. Tom McCabe tried to reach out to the industry during his chairmanship, but his lack of banking experience limited his effectiveness. The banking industry represented a national network of supporters with influence in every political jurisdiction. Losing this support took away a critical constituency that the Fed could call upon to help resist political pressure.

Robert Hetzel, a vice president and economist at the Richmond Reserve Bank, summarized the situation in 1951 when he referred to the absence of an institutional consensus on priorities and policies: "The Fed had broken free from the Treasury, but in many respects, it was a blank slate on which its future was to be written."[62]

Even before Bill Martin officially became chairman of the board of governors of the Federal Reserve System on 1 April 1951, he was drawn into the Accord implementation. The exchange offering for the new $2\frac{3}{4}$ percent bonds, one of the vital elements of the agreement, was scheduled to begin the week before Martin was to take office. The FOMC was in the throes of easing away from the $2\frac{1}{2}$ percent long-term interest rate peg and letting market forces influence prices. The FOMC was walking a fine line between allowing long-term Treasury prices to decline enough to attract active buying, but not decline so fast that investors began panic selling. The FOMC determined that prices on the bellwether $2\frac{1}{2}$ percent Liberty bonds would be allowed to decline from the pegged price of $101\frac{23}{32}$ to 99, at which point the Fed would step in with stabilizing purchases. Within two weeks of the Accord, the Fed and the Treasury had each purchased $500 million of long-term Treasuries in support of the 99 price limit. The Fed's open-market desk was nervously hoping that these enormous purchases would be enough to stabilize the market. The Treasury was already complaining about the amount of purchases it had been forced to make.

As he listened to the FOMC debate over how it should stabilize the market, Martin concluded that the Fed had lost its ability to carry out a program of price support in a freely functioning market. He believed that the future of the Accord hinged on the resumption of an active and resilient market for Treasury securities. The Fed's initial stabilization strategy was to choose a price limit and to resolutely defend it until the allocated support funds were exhausted. The Fed traders made little effort to work with the ebb and flow of the market. Martin urged the FOMC to "occasionally show an aggressive mark up of the market . . . and give leadership to it," while at other times, the Fed should step away from the market.[63] Martin had sold the Accord to the Treasury on the basis of "testing the market" to determine likely interest rates before making major commitments. To Martin, the FOMC's open-market strategy ran the risk of "simply establishing another peg."[64] He argued that more flexible open-market operations would introduce an element of healthy uncertainty for traders when they tried to predict future Fed moves. Investors and market makers would have to relearn the risks and realities associated with free markets.

But the full FOMC would not be easily won over to Bill Martin's philosophy. In the 17 May FOMC meeting, Martin requested a $250 million authorization to the open-market desk to "probe the extent of the underlying demand for government securities." New York Reserve Bank President Allan Sproul spoke out against Martin's proposal. The New York Bank president traditionally held one of the most influential positions within the Fed organization, and Sproul was highly regarded in the Fed for his strong grasp of the theory and practice of central banking. Martin had persuaded Sproul to support the Accord, but Sproul was wary about Martin's appointment as chairman. With more than a hint of patronizing, Sproul observed that the Fed's Treasury security purchases increased member-bank reserves and therefore carried important credit implications. Consequently, "stabilizing operations in the government securities market are . . . quite dissimilar to those of private interests in other securities markets."[65] In effect, Sproul was advising Martin that his experience in the equity markets of the New York Stock Exchange was not a sufficient basis for FOMC policy making. It was a challenge many on the FOMC had been expecting.

Marriner Eccles broke the awkward pause. With a verbal nod toward Sproul, Eccles said, "I agree with Mr. Sproul that there is a risk in adding reserve funds in the market, but feel it is worthwhile to undertake the proposed operation."[66] The tension immediately eased. Eccles, the only FOMC member whose opinion counted as much as Sproul's, came down on Martin's side. A strong majority of the FOMC eventually voted in favor of Martin's proposal, but Allan Sproul had fired an opening salvo to warn Martin that he would not be a pushover for the new chairman.

The combined efforts of the Fed and the Treasury to achieve the goals of the Accord produced encouraging results for the Fed over the remainder of 1951. The 2¾ percent exchange offer was more successful than anticipated, and even though the FOMC steadily reduced its stabilization efforts, long-term Treasury prices declined only a few more points over the course of the year. Martin's optimism that the bond market would respond positively to the end of the standoff proved correct. Investors and market makers gave the Fed high marks for negotiating the transition. The First National City Bank of New York observed that "the authorities handled the withdrawal [of the peg] with courage and skill."[67] The bond market was not yet truly free, but market forces were back in operation.

The results for the Treasury were less satisfying. John Snyder remained unwilling to pay more than 2½ percent on new long-term issues, and investor demand for long-term Treasuries at that yield remained lackluster. Watrous Irons, president of the Dallas Reserve Bank, spoke for a frustrated FOMC during its 4 October meeting when he said, "The system should not prevent rates from rising . . . because I doubt that present rates are sufficient to attract savings into Government securities."[68] The upward pressure on short-term interest rates was most severe, and over the year the Treasury bill rate moved from ⅝ percent to slightly above the Fed's discount rate of 1¾ percent. Martin acknowledged that the discount should be raised but doggedly held to the Fed's commitment under the Accord that it would not increase the discount rate during 1951.

The Fed had more success in reviving its reserve lending function. During the years of the peg, the Fed's open-market purchases force-fed reserves into the banking system. Awash in reserves, the banks had no need to borrow them from the Fed, and the Fed lost an important tool for influencing the banking system. It could no longer pressure individual banks to reduce their reserve borrowings when the Fed became concerned about the extent or inherent risks of their lending activity. Also, the peg had effectively frozen the Fed's discount rate, eliminating its ability to serve as an indicator of the Fed's posture toward short-term interest rates.

To resolve the situation, Martin and the FOMC set out in the fall of 1951 to reestablish reserve borrowing from the Fed. Traditionally, the demand for bank reserves rose toward the end of the year as members increased their lending for holiday retail activity and tax payments. By reducing its open-market purchases, the Fed provided fewer reserves to the banking system, and individual banks that were short on reserves found themselves at the Fed's "discount window" to borrow reserves. By the end of 1951, member-bank borrowing of reserves exceeded $1 billion, causing New York's First National City Bank to remark, "Member bank borrowing set an eighteen year record. . . . The Fed has sent a signal that more caution should be applied in adding to bank loan volume."[69] In early 1952, Martin described his philosophy at a congressional hearing: "Member bank borrowing at the Federal Reserve should be the principal means through which banks obtain additional reserves. Discount rate changes and open market operations should be the main instruments of credit and monetary policies."[70] Now that some of the Fed's commitments under the Accord had ended, Martin was previewing how the Fed planned to institute a flexible monetary policy.

The monetary policy concepts that Martin articulated in late 1951 reflected the ideas of Winfield Riefler, the assistant to the chairman and secretary of the FOMC. The wisdom of Riefler's policy advice made him the Fed's most influential staff member. Like Ernest Hemingway, Riefler had driven an ambulance on the French front during World War I, and after the war he earned a Ph.D. in economics. From 1923 to 1933 he served in the Fed's research department but left to organize a central statistical agency for the U.S. government. He was a highly original thinker who had helped create the Federal Housing Administration and, like John Maynard Keynes, promoted a plan to create an international agency to stabilize commodity prices after World War II. He wrote widely on financial topics and served on various government advisory panels. Riefler combined rigorous economic thinking with a practical appreciation of financial market behavior. He was equally capable of thinking quickly on his feet or developing a well-researched and closely argued recommendation. According to Robert Holland, who served as secretary of the FOMC at a later date: "He had a keen intellect, his reasoning was impeccable, and he had the chairman's ear."[71]

Riefler was also a dedicated free-market proponent and was the driving force for the resumption of flexible monetary policy at the Fed. Martin and Riefler had worked well together during the Accord negotiations, and when Martin became chairman, their common view of the Fed's role in the economy cemented their relationship. Riefler's advice helped Martin grow as a central banker and provided a solid theoretical underpinning for Martin's evolving monetary policy philosophy. Riefler remained at Martin's side until his retirement in 1958. As befits a confidential advisor, Riefler remained out of the public eye, but his philosophy and ideas are visible throughout the Fed's deliberations during his tenure. Riefler was one of a series of unusually capable Federal Reserve staff leaders who were able economists, experienced in dealing with monetary issues, and absolutely dedicated to the purposes of the Federal Reserve System.

It was not long before Martin had to draw extensively on Riefler's advice. In April 1952, Congressman Wright Patman, chairman of a subcommittee of the Joint Economic Committee, began a hearing to investigate "Monetary Policy and Management of the Public Debt." The hearing's primary focus was the role of the Fed since the Accord, and Patman's questioning gave Martin and John Snyder the opportunity to publicly describe their commitment to the spirit of the Accord. Senator Paul Douglas was skeptical about how conflicts arising from overlapping responsibilities would be resolved. He proposed a clearer demarcation of roles, quoting poet Robert Frost, "good fences make good neighbors."[72] Martin responded with a comment that summarized his view of governmental regulation of the financial markets: the best solution depended on men of goodwill working together, not through added legislation. He replied to Douglas, "We will sit around a table and hammer it out. Solutions require some experimentation, some probing, some accommodation of views. Constructive public policy in the financial field is something that can come only from long, tortuous, persistent, humble study."[73]

Later in the hearings, Allan Sproul responded to the subcommittee's inquiry about the independence of the Federal Reserve from the influence of the executive branch with a description that soon became widely quoted: "The independence of the Federal Reserve does not mean independence *from* the government, but independence *within* the Government."[74] Sproul and Martin emphasized that the Fed was a creature of Congress, and Sproul eloquently observed: "An independent Federal Reserve System is one that is protected from narrow partisan influence. It is a system with special competence in a difficult technical field, acting under the general directive of the Congress within the bounds of national economic policy as determined by the Congress."[75] Paul Douglas had the final word on the subject when he observed, "it sometimes helps, however, to have a little legislative protection."[76]

In a similar vein, Douglas asked Martin whether the Fed could remain independent of a strong Treasury secretary. Martin's response was revealing: "I think that public servants at some point have to stand up and be counted. If I am not strong enough to hold my own with the Secretary of the Treasury, then I am not entitled to the job I occupy."[77] Martin believed that when a public institution acted in the nation's interest and came under attack because of that, its leader had a duty to defend his institution to the limit of his abilities, even if it cost him his job. Martin believed that the public would support the Fed if it became convinced that the Fed was acting in the nation's interest. The character and integrity of the chairman were essential elements in building that public perception. Martin was raising the bar for the person chosen to head the Federal Reserve System.

The committee's final report was cluttered with minority dissents, but its message was clear. The majority affirmed its acceptance of the "team" relationship between the Treasury and the Federal Reserve and agreed that the Fed should have "a considerable degree of independence."[78] With a slap at Harry Truman, the majority called for "coordination of monetary policy, fiscal policy, and all other economic policies of the government. It is not merely the right, but the duty of the President to effect this coordination — by direction with respect to agencies under his control, and by persuasion with respect to the agencies which are not."[79] The committee's report was formal acknowledgment that the Fed's past was behind it. The open question was what its future would be.

By early 1952, the military costs of the Korean War were pressing on the Truman administration budget with their full force. The fiscal 1953 budget deficit was projected to swell to $14 billion from $4 billion the year before. The burden of raising the extra cash fell on the Treasury and the Fed at a time when they had yet to solve the problem of raising long-term money for the Treasury at a rate John Snyder would accept. Nearly all of the fresh money was to be raised during the second half of 1952. In mid-May, the Treasury offered a second exchange of the 2¾ percent nonmarketable bonds for the remaining Liberty bonds, but investor interest was minimal. The prospect for financing the fiscal 1953 deficit appeared bleak if Snyder did not change his mind on interest rates.

Although Martin felt he understood and could work with John Snyder, he could not persuade the Treasury secretary to accept the bond market's judgment on appropriate interest rates for new Treasury issues. As Allan Sproul had feared, despite Snyder's professed support for the Accord, the reality was he simply would not authorize the Treasury to issue long-term bonds at more than 2½ percent. To finance the deficit at acceptable interest rates, the Treasury was forced to issue shorter-term securities, and negotiations between the Treasury and Fed over the pricing of even these issues were often confrontational. Although Snyder was irritated by what he perceived as Martin's intransigence, he knew he could not go back to Harry Truman to complain about the Fed. Snyder had agreed to the Accord and now he was stuck with it.

Snyder took some satisfaction from the fact that, even though the peg was ended, the Truman-era Treasury financed its deficits without paying more than his self-imposed ceiling of 2½ percent for long-term funds. He sourly accepted Martin's justification that short- and medium-term rates had to rise in order to attract the savings needed for Treasury and private credit demands. Harry Truman, however, made no accommodation to financial reality, and he was bitterly unhappy that there was any increase in Treasury rates of any duration. Other than a formal quarterly meeting, Martin and Truman had little personal contact during 1952. Martin learned of Truman's displeasure with him only in late 1952, when he was visiting New York City and encountered the president and his entourage leaving the Waldorf Astoria Hotel. As Martin told it, "I said 'Good afternoon Mr. President.' The president looked me right in the eye and said only one word in reply, 'Traitor!' "[80] The successful implementation of the Accord depended on a spirit of cooperation, and the enduring resistance of both Snyder and Truman made Martin's task much more difficult.

Despite the lack of support from the leaders of the Truman administration, there was progress in the transition to market-based interest rates. The Fed regained a good measure of its ability to influence member-bank reserves through open-market operations. Member banks learned that the Fed would no longer expand bank reserves through open-market operations simply because banks were bidding for them. If the Fed's monetary policy was to restrain credit availability, banks would have to seek additional reserves from the Fed discount window. In addition, the FOMC was preparing to use the discount rate as a flexible monetary policy tool. Despite Snyder's hostility, relationships between the Treasury and the Fed were growing stronger. Treasury officials at the working level were learning to trust in the market's ability to price and absorb new Treasury issues. Investors and market makers were learning to trust that neither the Treasury nor the Fed would revert to some disguised form of pegging the Treasury bond market. The arrangements of the Accord had not yet encountered the stresses of inflation or recession, but there was a growing confidence that they would be up to it when that day came.

In retrospect, one of the reasons that Harry Truman did not pressure Bill Martin the way he did Martin's predecessors was that his popular approval had sunk to one of the lowest levels of any president, before or since.[81] Truman's unpopularity, a desire for a change from Democratic Party rule, and the universal admiration for the Republican presidential candidate, General Dwight Eisenhower, contributed to a Republican sweep of the presidency and both houses of Congress. Bill Martin was about to encounter an administration whose economic policies would be formed by the incoming Treasury secretary, George Humphrey, an outspoken and fiscally conservative industrialist. Martin's free-market economic philosophy appeared to be compatible with orthodox Republican economics, but it was uncertain whether the new administration was prepared to work with a Fed chairman appointed by its predecessor. Partisanship had a way of seeping into the relationship between the Fed chairman and the administration. Martin hoped to overcome that tradition, but the prospects were anything but clear.

6

By Fits and Starts: The Early Eisenhower Years

The Republicans who took the reins of the U.S. government on a raw, blustery January day in 1953 were dedicated to reversing twenty years of intervention in the American economy by successive Democratic administrations. Eisenhower's decision to run for the presidency had been heavily influenced by his support of Republican economic philosophy, and he was determined to achieve a thoroughgoing change in the way Americans viewed their government's role in economic affairs. A month later, the new president succinctly stated his administration's economic goals in his State of the Union message. Describing "immediate tasks," he listed "reducing the planned deficits ... handling the inheritance of debt ... checking inflation ... reducing the tax burden ... and encouraging the initiative of our citizens."[1] In the following weeks, the Eisenhower economic team set to work reintroducing "responsible fiscal management" to the nation's finances.

Their task was hugely complicated by the financial burden of the Korean War. The war began in July 1950, and military spending ballooned from $14 billion in fiscal 1950 to $42 billion two years later. Congress, following tradition, would not pass tax increases large enough to cover the full cost of the war, and deficit financing was expected to cover the shortfall. The Truman team departed, leaving behind a projected deficit for fiscal 1953 that approached $7 billion, a forecasted 1954 budget deficit of $9.9 billion, and a total of $5.5 billion of further planned deficits for the following two years. In addition, the wartime tax increases were set to expire in April and June of 1954. If the war were not going well at that time, the struggle necessary to extend the taxes would be fierce.

Joseph Dodge, Eisenhower's director of the Bureau of the Budget, compared the federal government's situation to that of a "family with an accumulated debt of four times bigger than its annual income, with only enough money in the bank to cover one month's living expenses, facing a ten percent reduction in income and with current bills coming due for C.O.D. purchases for an amount equal to a year's total income."[2] Even allowing for the normal tendency to blame the outgoing administration for leaving a mess, the Republicans had to move swiftly to stabilize a situation that many believed had become dangerous.

Following the president's admonition, "the first order of business is the elimination of the annual deficit," the administration's economic team began to pare the fiscal 1954 budget.[3] They quickly realized it would be impossible to balance that year's budget, but everyone knew the administration's initial credibility rested on reducing the size of the forecasted deficit. The budget-cutting exercise was led by Joseph Dodge, an exacting accountant with a genius for government finance. Armed with Eisenhower's complete support and a thick skin, Dodge set out to reduce the 1954 budget by $10 billion, or about 13 percent. The bulk of the cuts were to come from the defense budget, and the economic team prayed that the cease-fire negotiations in Korea would succeed and legitimize the reduction in military spending. After the dust finally settled in May, the fiscal 1954 budget deficit was reduced by $5.5 billion. The initial goal proved optimistic, but the administration had earned its first stripes in its campaign for fiscal responsibility.

The administration's emphasis on the virtues of fiscal responsibility and free markets provided a supportive backdrop for Bill Martin to expand his campaign to restore a "fully flexible" monetary policy at the Fed. The first step was to restore the variability of the discount rate. Martin firmly believed that changes in the Fed's discount rate could serve as a highly visible indicator of its policy posture, but this tool had not been used since 1934. During the Great Depression, member banks rarely borrowed from the Fed, and changes in the discount rate had little impact on the banking system. During the years of the peg, the discount rate was effectively fixed along with all interest rates. Neither banks nor the investing public paid much attention to it.

It was true that the Fed's open-market operations were visible to participants in the credit markets, but because the Fed's open-market moves could be influenced by the many forces affecting those markets, the policy implications of the Fed's actions were often obscured. To make his point, Martin often quoted a statement from the Fed's 1923 annual report: "The more fully the public understands what the function of the Federal Reserve System is, and on what grounds its policies and actions are based, the simpler and easier will be the problems of credit administration in the U.S."[4] On 15 January 1953, Martin persuaded his FOMC associates to increase the discount rate from 1 3/4 percent to 2 percent, the first increase since July 1950. In the previous FOMC meeting on 6 January 1953, Martin described the likely impact of a modest 1/4 percent increase as "mostly psychological . . . but it should not be underestimated in our operation."[5]

In the first week of February, Martin had his first meeting with Eisenhower. Though their life experiences were quite different, the sixty-two-year-old president and the forty-seven-year-old Fed chairman shared many of the same personal values. Many elements of the description of Eisenhower penned by Emmett Hughes, a presidential speechwriter and keen observer of the president, could easily have been made of Martin: "He bore marks of character and temper beyond doubt or qualification: a formidable honesty, a rare humility, a sense of dignity, an abhorrence of pretense, a distaste for all self-seeking, a tireless will to conciliate."[6] Although Martin's leadership experience had been on a much smaller stage than Eisenhower's, both men shared a lifetime of loyalty to democratic institutions and to service in the nation's interest. Both men had been profoundly influenced by their friendship with George Marshall and had modeled their lives on his example. As one of Eisenhower's biographers wrote, "Eisenhower found Marshall's modest, courtly personal manner and scrupulous professional principles the finest model for his own behavior."[7] In spite of their inherent compatibility, their first meeting was quite formal, since Eisenhower knew relatively little about Martin.

Martin knew that in comparison to many presidents, Eisenhower had a solid, if not extensive, education in public finance. He had studied the nation's economy at the Army Industrial War College. He had prepared the budget for the U.S. army when he served under General Douglas MacArthur in the 1930s and later, as Truman's army chief of staff, had defended it on Capitol Hill. Martin knew that as president, Eisenhower had begun to speak publicly about economic issues and had appointed a financially conservative Treasury secretary. For his part, Eisenhower saw economic issues as vital to his administration's success. To his brother Milton he wrote: "Maintenance of prosperity and economic stability is one field of governmental concern that interests me mightily and one on which I have talked incessantly."[8] Martin had every personal and professional reason to believe that the two men would work well together.

Martin advised the president that the Fed had recovered its monetary powers and stood ready to use them in the battle against inflation. Eisenhower, who had promised to deal with the "menace of inflation" in his inaugural address, thought he might have a useful ally in the Federal Reserve chairman, even though Martin had been appointed by a Democratic administration and had been Fed chairman for only two years.

As the administration's plans unfolded, it became clear that the secretary of the Treasury, George M. Humphrey, had the most influence on the administration's economic agenda. Humphrey had a solid middle-class midwestern upbringing. Trained as a lawyer, he had served as president of a supplier of minerals to smokestack industries. Humphrey's capabilities came to national attention when he chaired a committee for the Marshall Plan organization. Humphrey's work brought him in contact with General Lucius Clay, then American High Commissioner for Germany. Clay became a successful investment banker and advisor to president-elect Dwight Eisenhower. Asked to recommend a candidate for Treasury secretary who would be a forceful proponent for a Republican economic philosophy, Clay suggested Humphrey.

Like many successful businessmen, Humphrey had an analytical mind, an instinct for the heart of an issue, a decisive quality, and the capacity to break a complex problem and its solution into easily understood components. In addition, he advanced his ideas with a relentless energy. He exuded confidence, expressed himself freely, and often predicted dire results if his recommendations were ignored. Humphrey coupled these abilities with an open and welcoming personality that was free of pretense, and he possessed an easy willingness to admit error or ignorance. He would accept defeat in an argument only when faced by an overwhelming array of facts or argument forcefully presented. Speechwriter Emmett Hughes, who often saw Humphrey in action, compared Humphrey to his cabinet counterparts: "The very vigor of his person and conviction and speech allowed him to tower over most of his political neighbors . . . because those who might have more sensible views either fought for them only sporadically or lacked talents to make them persuasive."[9]

Because of a history of conflict that went back to the founding of the Federal Reserve System, the initial contacts between an incoming secretary of the Treasury and a sitting chairman of the Federal Reserve are inevitably wary and probing. Martin believed that an effective working relationship with a Treasury secretary, a relationship that could tolerate the inevitable policy differences, was one of the Fed chairman's highest priorities. Martin had enshrined the Fed-Treasury partnership in the Accord, and he believed that effective cooperation began at the top of the two institutions. Although Humphrey espoused a strongly conservative economic philosophy and was not known for his willingness to compromise, Martin was determined to build a relationship with Humphrey so the two could "sit around the table and hammer things out."[10]

Martin's first contact with Humphrey was in the early days of the administration, when Martin offered to resign as Fed chairman. Although his term as chairman did not run out until April 1955, Martin agreed with many Fed critics that a president should be able to appoint his own Fed chairman at the start of his presidential term. Martin later said that he "did not want to be a persona non grata" to the administration.[11] The only administration member who knew Martin well was W. Randolph Burgess, one of Humphrey's two Treasury undersecretaries. Burgess and Martin had a relationship that dated back to 1938 when Burgess had served on one of Martin's groundbreaking ad hoc committees at the New York Stock Exchange. Humphrey had begun to rely on Burgess's advice, and it is very likely that Burgess weighed in on Martin's behalf. In a spirit of nonpartisanship that had not been traditional in presidential appointments of Fed leaders, Humphrey informed Martin that he and Eisenhower wanted Martin to stay on. The relationship between Martin and Humphrey was off to a good start.

Now that a new and potentially cooperative Treasury secretary was in office, Martin was determined to restructure the relationship between the Fed and the Treasury. He began by addressing one of the issues that had bedeviled Fed-Treasury relationships, both before and after the Accord: reducing the Fed's obligation to support new Treasury bond issues. The peg required that the Fed serve as the underwriter of new Treasury issues and assure successful placement by supporting the market during and after the offering. The huge size and short-term nature of the national debt required Treasury issues every few months, and the Fed felt that it was regularly forced to temporarily abandon its monetary policy in order to support these issues. On the other hand, the Treasury felt that the Fed's status as underwriter gave it unwarranted influence over the government's debt-management policy. One of the goals of the Accord was to reduce the Fed's role in Treasury offerings, but there had been very little progress toward it.

The critical element in restructuring the Fed-Treasury relationship was the role played by Randolph Burgess. Humphrey had created a new position, undersecretary of the Treasury for Monetary Affairs, to develop the Treasury's internal capacity for managing the government's borrowing needs, and Burgess was his inspired choice. A commanding and universally respected figure, Burgess had had an outstanding career at the New York Fed and was a close second to Allan Sproul in the contest for that bank's presidency. Before joining the Treasury, Burgess served as an influential vice chairman of First National

City Bank, one of the three largest banks in the country. In his new Treasury role, Burgess was in an ideal position to act as the go-between for the Treasury and the Federal Reserve, much as Martin himself had done during his Accord negotiations.

Burgess and Martin agreed that if the Treasury abandoned its traditional insistence on low interest costs and paid competitive rates, it could place its new issues without substantial Fed involvement. The Fed would no longer serve as the Treasury's official advisor, and in return, the Fed would be released from its responsibility to assure successful Treasury issues. The Fed would continue to assist the Treasury by using its open-market operations to maintain stable market conditions during an offering under a policy that eventually became known as maintaining an "even keel" in the Treasury market. Burgess shared Martin's understanding of how the Treasury bond market worked and understood intuitively how the new relationship would work. Burgess also enjoyed Humphrey's complete confidence and soon had his agreement to the new arrangement. In a speech in April 1953, Martin referred to the new relationship: "The [Federal Reserve] System no longer needs to inject periodically into credit markets large amounts of reserve funds [by purchasing Treasury securities] which are difficult to withdraw before they have resulted in undesirable credit developments."[12] The promise of the Accord was finally becoming a reality.

Reducing the Fed's involvement in Treasury financing was only the first step in Bill Martin's bold campaign to completely overhaul the Fed's open-market operations. Martin believed that strong and unrestricted financial markets were vital to the capitalist economic system, and that the Fed's open-market practices disrupted, rather than strengthened, the market for Treasury securities. His commitment to free markets drove him to lead the forces of reform at the New York Stock Exchange when investment-pool operators and self-dealing traders were undermining the functioning of the stock market. It guided him in the negotiations for the Accord that had ended pegged interest rates and restored rates that were determined by free-market forces. After two years of cautious progress, Martin was ready to "complete the return from wartime necessities to the principles of the free market" by remaking the Fed's role in the marketplace for Treasury securities.[13]

Martin felt that during the years of the peg, the Treasury bond market had lost its "depth, breadth and resiliency" or the ability to provide investors continuous and unrestricted offers to buy or sell Treasury securities under all types of market conditions.[14] Martin based his conclusion on his New York Stock Exchange experience. His conversations with traders and brokers in the Treasury market convinced Martin that during the peg years, the Fed's continual bond purchases had "driven dealers to the sidelines," where they could make risk-free profits by buying Treasury bonds whenever they went to a discount and subsequently selling them to the Fed at par. In the two years since the accord, the dealers had not yet returned to continuous market making when markets were under stress. In Martin's mind, before dealers would take more risk during difficult markets, they had to be confident the market would operate freely and the Fed's open market operations would not unexpectedly distort the market, causing them to lose money. To restore the dealers' confidence, Martin wanted the Fed to change its practices "to encourage a Treasury securities market in which the market forces of supply and demand and of savings and investment are permitted to express themselves in market prices and yields."[15] Martin proposed modifying the Fed's open-market operations to achieve what he called "minimum intervention" in the markets and still enable the Fed to reach its open-market policy goals.

Martin began with a move reminiscent of his start at the New York Stock Exchange, in which he orchestrated an ad hoc committee to recommend the drastic changes he later implemented. In April 1952, he organized a small ad hoc subcommittee of the FOMC under his leadership to study the impact of the Fed's open-market operations on the Treasury bond market. Like the NYSE committee review fifteen years earlier, its conclusions were far-reaching and reflected Bill Martin's philosophy.

Martin described the report and its implications in a seminal speech titled "The Transition to Free Markets" given in April 1953. He described the subcommittee's overarching goal as making the Fed's open-market operations more understandable by "giving those who participate in the market a familiarity with how the Federal Reserve may intervene, when it may intervene, for what purposes it may intervene."[16] To minimize the impact of the Fed's operations on the Treasury bond market, the Fed would limit its open-market transactions to Treasury bills (subsequently described as the "Bills Only" policy). To reduce the frequency of Fed intervention in the marketplace, the Fed would end its commitment undertaken in the Accord to "maintain orderly conditions" in the credit markets and replace it with a less intrusive commitment "to correct disorderly conditions." To further limit the scope of open-market operations, the Fed would conduct them only to "provide or absorb reserves" and not to support any pattern of prices and yields in the bond market. Finally, the Fed created new limits on the extent and techniques it would apply in support of Treasury financings. Not only were the recommendations a substantial departure from traditional Fed practices, they were a direct challenge to the influence of the New York Reserve Bank and its powerful president, Allan Sproul.

The New York Federal Reserve Bank traditionally enjoyed a unique status in the Reserve System. Its position reflected its location in the heart of the U.S. financial market and the pioneering leadership of Benjamin Strong, the bank's first president, who orchestrated the Fed's first real monetary management activities. When the Banking Act of 1935 centralized Fed policy making in the board of governors in Washington, tensions escalated between the board and the New York Reserve Bank over control of day-to-day open-market operations. Open-market operations and their management continued to reside at the New York bank. While the operations manager nominally reported to the full FOMC in Washington, he reported through the president of the New York Reserve Bank. Sproul used this day-to-day operating relationship to dominate open-market policy.

By the time Bill Martin became Federal Reserve chairman, Allan Sproul already had achieved an illustrious twenty-seven-year career at the Fed. He was America's most well-known central banker in international financial circles, was the Fed's most articulate spokesman in congressional hearings, and had played a leading role in defending the Fed against President Truman's attack on the Fed's independence in 1951. He managed the Fed's open-market activities through his influence on the FOMC executive committee and direct supervision of the operations manager. The full FOMC met only four times a year, and while it made general policy recommendations, in practice, ongoing open-market operations were supervised by the FOMC's five-man executive committee. One of Bill Martin's first acts as Fed chairman had been to reduce the influence of the FOMC executive committee by scheduling meetings of the full FOMC every six weeks. Sproul accepted Martin's argument that air travel made frequent meetings possible, but he was deeply distrustful of Martin's intentions toward the traditional role of the New York bank.

The two men actually held similar philosophies about many aspects of central banking and had worked together successfully in 1952 during the Douglas hearings as they redefined the independence of the Federal Reserve. Their differences reflected the gulf between the views held in Washington versus those in New York. Sproul viewed the world from the trading rooms in New York where the Fed reigned supreme, influencing credit conditions through trading in the Fed's mammoth securities portfolio and through the discount window from which it dispensed temporary reserves and monitored the lending activities of the leading money-center banks. In contrast, Martin viewed the world from the hearing rooms on Capitol Hill and the conference rooms in the White House and the Treasury Department. Far from reigning supreme, Martin had to deal with his equals at the Treasury — or his superiors, as in the case of Congress.

Where Martin and Sproul differed most was in their view of the nature of the U.S. economy and the Fed's freedom in managing it. Sproul was skeptical of the concept of free financial markets, and he argued that "we have a mixed Government–private economy" and "haven't had a free market in government securities since . . . open market operations of the Federal Reserve system came to be used as a principal weapon of credit policy."[17] In such an economy, according to Sproul, the Fed should be a decisive presence. Sproul disagreed with the Bills Only policy and argued that the Fed's monetary policy objectives were best achieved when the Fed could freely intervene in all sectors of the bond market. The Fed should "not tie one arm behind our back by restricting transactions to the short term area."[18] The Fed should "have the freedom to put [reserves] where the pressures were the greatest in order to minimize the amount the committee would have to put in to achieve its purposes."[19] To realize its full potential as a central banking institution, the Fed "should be free to influence the supply, availability, and cost of credit in all areas in the market . . . to promote economic stability and progress."[20] Sproul also held the belief, traditional within the New York bank, that open-market policy should be made in New York, where it could be free of interference from political pressures and close to conditions in the markets.

Bill Martin, on the other hand, felt that the marketplace and the price mechanism were basic essentials of the American economy, and "interest rates are prices which perform vital economic functions and they should be responsive to basic supply and demand."[21] He believed that "there was no intention to place in the hands of the Federal Reserve Board or the directors of the Federal Reserve Banks the ability or responsibility to determine what the market [interest rates] ought to be."[22] "The market's objective measures of the forces of supply and demand give business and government alike a more reliable guide to policy and action than the subjective judgment of any man in government."[23] Martin believed that the Fed would be better protected from political pressure if it could say it was operating in a free-market environment rather than one in which it set the tone.

Bill Martin had spent his last fifteen years either dealing with government regulators or leading government institutions, and he accepted that economics and politics were no longer separate worlds. Even though the Fed was recovering its monetary policy-making freedom, it had to consider political realities in its deliberations. American politicians had a traditional distrust of its powerful financial institutions, which had cost Alexander Hamilton and his Treasury Department, Nicholas Biddle and his First National Bank of the United States, and even Marriner Eccles their political support.

Martin felt that a democratic Fed, operating in the public interest, would have the best chance of sustained political support. A more democratic Fed meant that the full FOMC, and not the New York bank president, had to control the open-market decision-making process. It would be much easier to defend decisions as being in the public interest if they were made by the full FOMC, consisting of the seven governors as well as the twelve Reserve Bank presidents. The Bills Only policy would also lower the Fed's political profile. By restricting open-market transactions to short-term bills, the Fed would stay out of the long-term Treasury market. Rates for residential mortgages and Treasury refundings were determined in the long-term Treasury market. The Fed could argue, with a certain amount of credibility, that market forces, and not the Fed, were determining those politically sensitive rates.[24]

Martin and Sproul also disagreed over the general philosophy of open-market operations. The subcommittee recommended that open-market transactions be restricted solely to increasing or decreasing bank reserves and not to achieve a particular interest rate structure. Sproul pushed for the broadest charter for open-market operations, arguing that the Fed's open-market purchases could be used "at the fringe of the market" to "touch up" or firm prices by buying certain long-term Treasury issues. Martin responded that the open-market trading desk would find it difficult to limit its purchases of a particular Treasury security if, for example, the market continued to weaken in spite of those purchases. Inevitably, the trading desk would be forced to decide the price and interest rate at which it would begin and end the intervention. Martin viewed this action as a return to pegging under a different guise. When Sproul argued that the subcommittee's recommendations were too restrictive, Martin implied that the recommendations would be applied flexibly by responding that "no tablets of stone were being written."[25] Throughout the debate, Martin's pragmatism and flexibility kept a number of conflicted FOMC members in his majority.

The debate in the FOMC over the recommendations raged for the first nine months of 1953. There were innumerable memorandums, personal discussions, and three contentious meetings of the full FOMC in which the recommendations were approved, the vote rescinded, and finally discussed one last time in September. The debate was driven by the gentlemanly but polarizing conflict between Martin and Sproul.

By September, Bill Martin's collegial style of leadership and earnest, considerate persuasiveness began to weigh in his favor. Allan Sproul combined an incisive mind with unusual verbal ability. He "[d]id not suffer fools gladly and did not make much of an effort to get along with his fellow FOMC members."[26] He was from the school of Fed leaders who initiated meetings by stating their own ideas first, and his presentations were lengthy and highly persuasive. In contrast, Martin described his early FOMC leadership style in a typically homely fashion: "I knew I wasn't the smartest kid on the block, but here I was, so I just had a 'go round' where everyone expressed their opinion, and I just summed things up."[27] Martin's negotiating style was described by a former associate: "[H]e would push on something, wait a little to give people time to absorb his argument, and then push again. He was never Machiavellian about it."[28]

The other FOMC members also realized that accepting the ad hoc committee's recommendations would bring open-market operations more under the supervision of the whole FOMC committee. Under Martin's leadership, each Fed governor and each regional Federal Reserve Bank president was asked to contribute to FOMC discussions, from which Martin forged a consensus. Martin was leading the Fed away from a tradition in which a few strong and capable individuals determined policy to a more democratic process, and the FOMC membership appreciated the change. According to Robert Holland, who was on the trading desk at the Federal Reserve Bank of Chicago in 1953, "Without the Bills Only restrictions, we could see that the open-market desk in New York would implement monetary policy pretty much as they saw fit. They were really good and could carry it off."[29] The more eloquently Sproul defended the status quo, the more isolated his position became.

In the end, the ad hoc committee's recommendations were accepted, with only Allan Sproul and one other bank president dissenting. The FOMC members agreed that operating only in the short-term market would help the Fed to take a further step away from pegging and support of Treasury issues. They accepted the importance of letting the long-term bond market operate as freely as possible and changing the philosophy for Fed intervention in the bond market from a preemptive to a corrective approach. Although much of the subsequent public analysis focused on the Bills Only decision, the recommendations should be taken in their entirety. While Bills Only has been subjected to more than its share of criticism, it is essential to note that to the current day, the Fed open-market operations are still carried out almost exclusively in the Treasury bill market. Considering all the subcommittee's recommendations together, the groundwork for distancing the Fed from the Treasury, lowering the political profile of open-market practices, and institutionalizing monetary policy making within the Fed, was laid during 1951–1953.

The FOMC's deliberations over its future operating policy were interrupted in April 1953 by a call of distress from the Treasury bond market, where prices were deteriorating badly. The seeds of the crisis were sown when the financial markets interpreted the Fed's January decision to raise the discount rate as an indicator that credit would be tightening. Martin contributed to the market's concern by a speech in which he described the Fed's new policy regarding new Treasury issues. The *New York Herald Tribune* reflected the news media's harsh interpretation: "Martin indicated that in the future the Reserve System will not interfere to help out the Treasury during periods of refunding."[30] Not surprisingly, investors took this to mean problems for future Treasury issues, and bond prices sagged further.

In a piece of unfortunate timing, the Treasury chose this moment to launch its much-heralded program to lengthen the maturity structure of the national debt. On the same day as Martin's speech, it offered $1 billion of thirty-year bonds at an unusually attractive interest rate of 3 ¼ percent. The market began to anticipate a flood of higher-yielding issues, and the market for existing Treasury bonds adjusted as prices fell sharply across all maturities. Uncertain about the extent of the price decline and unwilling to take further losses by adding to their bond inventories, bond dealers began to back away from the market. The market-making mechanism for Treasury bonds began to pull apart.

The atmosphere was tense as the FOMC gathered on 6 May for an emergency meeting. Robert Rouse, the manager of the open-market trading desk in New York, concluded his report with the comment that "there was virtually no market for Government securities at the present time."[31] In Martin's mind, to unravel the crisis, the banks had to step into the market and buy the bonds that others were selling. To do that, banks needed to know that the Fed would provide the necessary reserves for their purchases. It was critical for the FOMC to determine how many reserves the Fed had to pump into the market in order to meet this emergency requirement without creating an oversupply situation.

In a speech given a year later, Martin described the analysis the Fed went through in mid-1953, which reveals much about the environment in which the Fed operated and Martin's view of the difficulties of accommodating market fluctuations in the making of monetary policy. He described the first element the Fed considered, the Treasury's estimate of its borrowing needs for the rest of the year: "A group of intelligent men at the Treasury wrestled with that problem, but their views changed to the tune of $5 or $6 billion frequently. Money management isn't easy under this condition."[32] Martin went on to describe the inexact science of estimating the seasonal financing needs of the banking system: "[D]espite using the best Fed statisticians and the best talent from the banking community, we were just about a hundred percent too high."[33] Next, the Fed forecast the growth in the money supply needed to finance the economy, "which was projected at three percent, and it leaked to the press as these things do," and soon economists and analysts were voicing their concerns about excessive Fed easing and potential inflation.[34] Finally, the Fed predicted a rational psychological atmosphere, which meant that "if business were flat or declining, interest rates would be flat or declining. We didn't do very well here . . . our judgment wasn't equal to the task."[35] With so many uncertain factors, a reliable estimate of future reserve needs was impossible, and the FOMC simply advised the open-market account manager to "feel his way" as he sought to supply enough reserves to keep the market from tightening any further.

From 6 May to 22 June, the open-market desk flooded the banking system with $735 million of reserves, which it thought would be sufficient to stabilize rates. To the FOMC's dismay, credit markets remained weak, and interest rates moved higher. As they tried to understand the credit market's perplexing behavior, Martin and Winfield Riefler, the FOMC's chief economic adviser, decided that investors and bankers did not yet have confidence that the Fed would provide adequate reserves to the banking system. The steps the Fed had taken so far were not working. Something else had to be done.

In the FOMC executive committee meeting of 23 June, Martin asked the FOMC to recommend that the board of governors approve a reduction in member-bank reserve requirements. Traditionally, the Fed rarely resorted to changing reserve requirements because it was seen as a blunt tool when more surgical moves were usually needed. But Martin had no alternative: he had to move quickly, and he had to send an unambiguous signal to the banks "that reserves would be available."[36] Despite Allan Sproul's argument that such a move "would get the Board into the position of using reserve requirements in the tactical area rather . . . than for broad fundamental strategy purposes," the worried FOMC moved quickly to pass on the recommendation.[37] The next week, the governors unanimously approved a massive $1.1 billion reduction in required reserves.[38]

The Fed's forceful easing, together with a June decision by the Treasury to hold down the size of its issues, finally turned the bond market around. By mid-July, First National City Bank trumpeted "a bond market which regained its bearing."[39] The bellwether Treasury 2½ percent of 1967–72, which had been quoted at 97 in October 1952 and experienced a painful slide to 90½ by early June 1953, was trading at 93 by the end of the month.[40] Looking back on this period in 1965, author James Knipe wrote: "It is unlikely that any other easing during the System's existence has equaled the speed of this one."[41] The Fed had served notice that in an emergency, it would move quickly and decisively to restore liquidity to the bond market. While it had required very large additions to reserves, the credit markets did eventually respond.[42]

No one was more relieved with this outcome than Bill Martin. Though his life had its share of critical moments, the bond debacle of May–June 1953 was one of the most traumatic. In a time of crisis, the institution of which he was leader had failed, however briefly, in its primary obligation to the public. In the 11 June FOMC meeting, Martin admitted: "The money market in May got so tight across the board that it violated one of the cardinal principles of good central banking operations. It became so tight that money was almost unavailable."[43] It was an experience that made Martin doubt the FOMC's collective wisdom, the adequacy of the Fed's monetary tools, and his own reasoning and leadership. Martin referred to the "mistakes in judging public psychology" during this period, both publicly and privately, for years afterward.[44]

As the summer of 1953 made way for the fall, the credit markets continued to ease. The Fed's satisfaction with the condition of the markets turned to a concern that the easing was being driven by the economic slowdown that many had predicted. In the cabinet meeting of 23 September, Arthur Burns, chairman of the president's Council of Economic Advisors, delivered the bad news to President Eisenhower. His analysis confirmed that a "process of adjustment" had started that month. Burns was eminently qualified to make this judgment: he was the nation's premier business-cycle analyst. Burns was a brilliant student, having graduated Phi Beta Kappa from Columbia University in 1925 and received a Ph.D. from Rutgers University. As a result of his studies of the economic cycle, Burns placed considerable importance on the "leading indicators," a series of indexes of economic activity that predicted economic trends over the next six months. These indicators signaled when the government should move to counteract recessionary tendencies, and they were beginning to flash red.

Over on Constitution Avenue, the Fed's economists were also watching the economic slowdown. They expected a weakening economy to cool loan demand and create easier credit conditions. Despite the staff's optimism, Bill Martin was still haunted by the May–June tightness in the credit markets. He was determined to make it unmistakably clear that the Fed would keep credit conditions easy until the economy stabilized. He persuaded his FOMC associates to instruct the open-market desk to follow a program of "active ease" that would "avoid deflationary tendencies."[45] In October, Martin challenged his FOMC associates to be more aggressive in easing credit by asking "whether the system should be in the position of a leader or a follower."[46] Later, he answered his own question: "[T]he system should be in the lead in a program of active ease."[47] Some FOMC members were concerned that the financial markets had already "grown too easy," but the full committee could not resist Martin's pressure. By December 1953, the Fed's open-market operations sent bank reserves to the highest levels of the year.

In one of his most famous quotes, Martin later referred to his philosophy developed in dealing with the 1953–54 recession: "Our purpose is to lean against the winds of deflation or inflation, whichever way they are blowing."[48] This was the first time the Fed explicitly committed itself to stabilizing the economy and applying its monetary tools either to restrict or stimulate the economy, depending on the situation. At virtually the same time Martin was restricting the techniques through which the Fed would conduct open-market operations, he was aggressively extending how far the Fed was prepared to push those techniques in order to maintain the conditions for stable economic growth.

In early 1954, economists at the Fed and in the administration pored over economic statistics to determine any change in the pace of the economy's softening. The Fed's primary concern, articulated by Winfield Riefler, was "that the real problem is that Government outlays are going down; that the economy is finding it difficult to shift from defense to private demands."[49] In fact, calendar 1954 defense spending was projected to be $10 billion less than the preceding year and represented a 2.8 percent decline in GNP from that source alone. The expiration of wartime taxes amounting to $3.7 billion during 1954 would add to spending and saving, but it would offset only a portion of reduced defense spending. The so-called automatic stabilizers, such as unemployment benefits, in which Arthur Burns placed so much trust as contra-cyclical forces, had their work cut out for them.

The administration described the economy as experiencing "a rolling economic adjustment" in early 1954, and it appeared to be an apt term. Housing construction continued to be strong, capital spending remained stable, and consumer spending was surprisingly resilient. The administration's effort to maintain confidence appeared to be paying off with consumers and business spenders. In contrast, other elements of the economy were contracting. The Fed's index of manufacturing fell steadily as producers cut back operations to reduce their inventories of unsold goods. Unemployment surged from 2 percent of the workforce in August 1953 to 5.4 percent (3.3 million unemployed) at the end of March 1954. The CEA staff watched anxiously as the leading indicators continued downward.

The sharp increase in unemployment raised a recurring problem for the Fed. Whenever the economy slowed down and unemployment rose, editorial writers and congressmen questioned the Fed's willingness to combat unemployment. The slowdown of 1953 was no exception. Martin stated his position on unemployment in a hearing before the Joint Economic Committee in February 1954: "Men may differ over what is a tolerable level of unemployment. I do not subscribe to the harsh notion that some unemployment . . . is a good thing.

The man who wants to work and earn a livelihood cannot be expected to be tolerant about any statistical figure of unemployment if it includes him."[50]

For many years, Bill Martin had studied the causes of unemployment and what the nations of the world offered workers in the way of unemployment benefits and retirement security. For three years, beginning in 1935, Martin was a featured speaker at an annual seminar held at the University of Chicago on unemployment. His predecessors as speakers included John Maynard Keynes. At that time he concluded that the programs of the Roosevelt administration, because they provided no incentive for the private sector to expand employment, would not be effective in reducing unemployment. He also argued that job retraining was a crucial service for a government to provide.

Martin's 1954 remark about unemployment reflected his personal beliefs. He possessed an extraordinary interest in people, ranging from the chairman of General Motors, whom he might call to talk about car sales, to the taxi driver who might take him to the airport that same day. In his congressional presentations, he often described how the Fed's decisions impacted individual Americans, and his conception of unemployment was no different. Martin accepted the Fed's role in fostering stable economic growth as part of its responsibilities under the Employment Act of 1946. He believed that controlling inflation and avoiding deflation was the best way to "foster lasting employment." If cooling an inflationary economy caused occasional recessions, the resulting temporary increases in unemployment were a price to be paid by the unfortunate few in return for achieving the "greatest possible good for the greatest possible number." The Fed's responsibility was to use its powers to end the recession as soon as practical by restoring sustainable, inflation-free growth. Martin was painfully aware that his efforts to explain the Fed's position on unemployment failed to persuade the Fed's critics.

By March 1954, the slowdown entered its sixth month, and the watchers in the Fed and the administration became more determined to end it. Most economists in the government, as well as those in private and academic positions, had predicted a moderate recession. By the six-month point in the previous recession in 1948–49, the economy had turned around. To everybody's relief, the March statistics provided definite evidence that the decline was slowing. But as yet there were no signs of recovery. To an administration worried about losing control of Congress in the coming November elections, the situation called for more decisive action. To deflect some of the pressure on him, Arthur Burns cited "more abundant and cheaper credit to stimulate banks to make more money available" as the most important factor in reviving the economy.[51] To drive home Burns's recommendation, Eisenhower urged George Humphrey and Commerce Secretary Marion Folsom to put pressure on the Fed to lower interest rates.

It did not take a lot of pressure to persuade Bill Martin to push for easier credit. This was Martin's first recession experience as Fed chairman, and he badly wanted the Fed's flexible monetary policy to prove its capacity to help foster economic recovery. In early March 1954, Martin sounded out FOMC members on the question of another reduction in reserve requirements to energize bankers to make more loans. Typically, Allan Sproul spoke for the opposition: "I cannot agree that banks and other lenders need the impetus of increased liquidity to encourage them to seek loans and investments. If more vigorous action is needed, I wouldn't make monetary action carry too much of a load which should also be carried by fiscal policy."[52] The account manager chimed in, saying that a large addition of reserves would drive down interest rates without assisting the recovery. Martin knew enough about Dwight Eisenhower's aversion to budgetary deficits to conclude that any fiscal action that would increase the deficit would not be acceptable. Monetary policy was the only available tool to hasten a recovery. Martin had labored mightily to fashion a consensus-driven FOMC, and now he had to live with his creation. It would take more time and effort to build a consensus around further "active ease."

The debate on whether to reduce reserves was intense, as it often is when the FOMC is determining policy for an economy in a transition between recession and recovery. By early June, the economy continued to lag. Both the Fed and the administration were concerned that recovery might be many months away. Government spending was projected to decline by another 5 percent in fiscal 1955, and the question of whether growth in the private economy could offset the decline hung in the air. Although the FOMC remained divided on the question, Martin persuaded the board of governors to approve the reserve reduction on 21 June 1954. It had taken much longer than he had wished, but at last the Fed's monetary posture was where he wanted it. Martin hoped that it had not come too late.

The Fed had given the economy another shot of liquidity, but the economic recovery chose to march to its own drum. Manufacturers' inventories stopped declining and average hours worked began to inch up, but laid-off workers were not called back. Overall, the recovery remained stalled. Martin advised the FOMC that it should "keep in mind the limitations of any easy-money policy and what could be accomplished by it."[53] Martin regularly reminded the FOMC that the Fed's tools were much better suited for restraining an economy operating at too high a level than for reviving an economy operating at too low a level. Now that the Fed's program of credit ease was finally where Martin wanted it, he was able to counsel patience. Bill Martin's son later referred to this thought process as "establishing his 'base.' When that was square, he could be flexible and wait for others to come around."[54]

Not until September 1954, almost a year after the recession began, did the signs of a broad recovery become visible: housing starts had increased for three months in a row, operating rates for a range of basic industries had turned solidly upward, and loan demand expanded for the second straight month. Smiles replaced the worried frowns at the FOMC, and critics became converts.

Even Arthur Burns, in a major policy speech at the end of October, hailed the end of the recession and the policies that had produced the recovery. He marveled that a 9 percent decline in industrial production and a recession in which 2.2 million workers were laid off resulted in only a 3.8 percent decline in GNP and, incredibly, that personal after-tax income never fell during the entire recession. Burns ascribed the "unparalleled" results to the expiration of Korean War–related taxes, $2 billion in unemployment benefits paid out during the recession, agricultural price supports, and the Fed's "easing general credit conditions by reducing the reserves that the banks were required to hold against their deposits."[55] Burns concluded that "the Government must use monetary policy in a flexible manner and assign it a very high priority in the arsenal of contra-cyclical weapons."[56] The *New York Times* cited Burns's conclusions and observed, "If Government policy proceeds on these premises, we will avoid in the future the depressions that have marred the brilliant record of free enterprise in the past."[57]

The accomplishments in the life of a public servant are often marred by the enmity of unforgiving opponents, are appropriated by others for their own purposes, or are misinterpreted by an inadequately informed media. None of these outcomes occurred in this situation. This success must have given Bill Martin an unaccustomed pleasure.

The pleasure was not long lasting. By early November and before the recovery had made much progress, Martin's early warning system went off. When he was in a particularly self-deprecatory mood, he would describe himself as "just a bond man," referring to his thirteen years on Wall Street. That experience had given him an acute sense of the financial markets, and he believed strongly that they were an early predictor of future economic developments. The stock market had surged almost 40 percent during 1954, its best showing in decades, and Martin advised his fellow FOMC members, "There are a great many indications that the stock market is not alone in reflecting the existence of a speculative psychology."[58] He admitted that "there was no evidence in business statistics of a speculative movement . . . but we can not always wait until the statistical evidence is all in. A flexible monetary policy is again at the testing point."[59]

Bill Martin, along with two of his influential economic advisors, Winfield Riefler and Ralph Thomas, assigned singular importance to the role of inflation in creating the boom-bust economic cycle. Inflation created the economic distortions, such as excessive borrowing and declining savings, which could eventually lead to economic collapse. If inflation could be stopped at an early stage, the dismal cycle could be moderated or even avoided. The most reliable indicator of incipient inflation was speculative surges in asset values as reflected in the stock market. The stock market's expansion in the fall of 1954 was sufficient to convince Martin that despite the fact that the recovery was still in an early stage, the Fed had to move to tighten the credit markets.

Martin's focus on the buildup of speculative forces was in part a return to a traditional philosophy of monetary economics popular during the 1920s under the theory of "real bills." In this construct, the role of a monetary authority was to assure adequate credit so that "productive" lending could take place, but not so much credit that "speculative" borrowing would occur. Speculative credit created excess demand for assets and drove prices up to unsustainable levels. When prices collapsed, distress selling would create an "adjustment" process in which deflationary pressures forced prices down. Once the process of adjustment began, monetary authorities had to let it work its way through the economy toward a base from which healthy economic growth could begin. To stop this dangerous cycle from ever beginning, the monetary authority had to move quickly to stop speculative activity, and the financial markets were where those forces first appeared.

It was natural that Martin would gravitate to this theory. His father and Benjamin Strong had debated its virtues at the Martin family dinner table. In addition, Martin's experience on the floor of the New York Stock Exchange gave him firsthand experience in speculative fevers and their disastrous aftermath. In Martin's view, a flexible monetary policy enabled the Fed to move quickly and decisively to fight the boom-bust cycle.

Allan Sproul did not place the same importance on moving quickly to halt speculative pressures. When Martin pressed the FOMC to begin tightening monetary conditions at its meeting of 7 December, Sproul confronted him once again. Dismissing "surface manifestations of speculation," Sproul argued that he and his economic staff "found little or no evidence in credit data to support fears of generally unsound speculative developments."[60] Labeling Martin's argument as conjecture, Sproul said, "We do not want to make a guess about the future, which is too speculative. . . . We want to avoid nipping the bud of real recovery."[61] The conflict between Martin's reliance on the financial markets and Sproul's desire for broader statistical evidence paralyzed the FOMC. In mid-December, the committee finally directed the open-market account manager to adopt a posture of slightly less ease, but its reluctance to do more signaled at least a temporary victory for Sproul's position.

But Bill Martin was in no position to ignore the objections of Allan Sproul in order to push the FOMC on monetary policy. Martin was engaged in a delicate maneuver to transfer direct supervision of the Fed's open-market operations from the New York Reserve Bank to the FOMC in Washington. Arguing for the change, Martin observed that "in some ways the manager of the [open-market] account affects more people than anyone else in the System."[62] Acknowledging that the step would reduce the influence of the New York Fed president, Martin observed that the Fed must reduce its dependence on individuals: "Some of us may not be here tomorrow. . . . We have the problem of building an institution."[63] Despite Allan Sproul's argument that by reducing the New York bank's responsibilities, "we well may find that the days of our Federal regional system are numbered," the FOMC went along with the change.[64]

There would be one final step in Bill Martin's historic democratization of the Fed. In the summer of 1955, the full FOMC voted formally to eliminate the FOMC's executive committee. After four years of patient effort, Bill Martin ended the last vestige of the unrestricted influence of the New York Reserve Bank president over the Fed's open-market policy-making process. The New York bank president might continue to serve as vice chairman of the FOMC, but in the future he would have to argue for his monetary policy preference before the full FOMC.

By the spring of 1955, the pace of the economic recovery that had worried Bill Martin the previous November began to show up in economic statistics. Arthur Burns became concerned about "excessive enthusiasm" in the housing market. In the 25 March cabinet meeting, Humphrey agreed with Burns and urged action: "If we don't slow the economy now, we will pay for it in a year or two."[65] Both men promised to pressure the Fed to tighten the economy. Modern presidential administrations rarely support tighter monetary conditions, and Martin must have been pleasantly surprised as he listened to Burns's and Humphrey's requests. Remarkably, the administration was closer to Martin's position than the rest of the FOMC.

Martin was unable to move the FOMC in the direction of tighter credit because its members remained torn between Martin's concern about inflation and Allan Sproul's recommendation that the expansion be allowed to mature. In a presentation at the time, Sproul summed up his philosophy for guiding an expansion: "First, to make sure the character of the business recovery is broad-based and sustainable. Second, to assure that there are no speculative tendencies such as excessive consumer buying, evidence of an installment credit spree, or commodity price advances out of line with increased consumption. Third, to assure that bank credit appears to be sufficient to nourish recovery."[66] In the 2 March FOMC meeting, Sproul downplayed Martin's concerns and focused on the risks of premature tightening: "The general expectation in the market is that rates are bound to go up. If we do too much to confirm and inflame those expectations, they may get out of hand."[67] Sproul's mastery of conceptualizing and articulating the art of economic management was in full display at times like this. When he concluded that "nothing in the general situation needs to be curtailed by a generally restrictive credit policy," most FOMC members agreed with him.[68]

Although Martin failed to move the FOMC to significantly tighten the credit markets, he did persuade the FOMC and the board of governors to increase the discount rate in mid-April. Martin argued that the economic impact of a ¼ percent rate increase might be "negligible," but it would indicate that the Fed was not "operating on a perpetually easy-money philosophy."[69] Martin's determination to restore the flexibility and visibility of the discount rate was not an easy task. For five months of effort, he had only one ¼ percent discount rate increase to show for it.

By August, Martin's reading of price increases convinced him he could no longer accept the FOMC's continued reluctance to address the issue of inflation. Martin expressed his frustration with the inadequacy of the Fed's economic data: "I don't believe in intuitive judgments, but we cannot always wait for statistics."[70] For Martin, a flexible monetary policy enabled the Fed to move preemptively to halt the spread of inflationary pressures before they became embedded in the economy. Justifying early action, Martin concluded: "If a judgment is sufficiently wise, it is practicable to restrain a situation before it develops. It is much more difficult to restrain a condition after it has developed. By acting after the fact . . . your action becomes a form of punishment for what has happened, and that is not feasible in a democracy. We can never recapture the purchasing power of the dollar that has been lost.[71] In Martin's mind, the Fed's history was filled with too many examples of moving too slowly.

Martin's appeal, together with the staff's comments on the spread of price increases, proved persuasive this time. The FOMC supported a full ½ percent increase in the discount rate and a reduction in its primary monetary target, net reserves (excess member-bank reserves less reserves borrowed from the Fed) in the banking system. The FOMC was coming around, but Martin still felt the Fed was following trends in the credit markets rather than leading the markets toward tightening. To dampen inflationary expectations, the Fed had to make it very clear to the business community and to the financial markets that it would attack inflation with all its resources.

Despite the rate increases, the economy gave the Fed no respite. By the end of October, unemployment sank to 3.2 percent, and industrial prices rose 3 percent over the preceding twelve months, compared to almost no change in the prior year. In response, the board of governors approved another discount rate increase of ¼ percent in mid-November. This increase came at a time when investors expected a turn toward ease, typified by the First National City Bank's comment that "the Fed might ease credit for the presumed purpose of insuring a background of booming business for the 1956 Presidential election."[72] Another reason for the expected move toward ease was that Dwight Eisenhower's heart attack in September had unsettled the financial markets, and Fed ease would help calm them. When the mid-November discount increase exposed the fallacy in this thinking, disappointed investors moved massively out of Treasuries, and prices weakened across the board.

The undertow from the market's fallout engulfed the Treasury as it prepared to refund $12 billion of maturing notes on 8 December. Preliminary investor interest in the new notes was so low that the Treasury had to ask the Fed for help. This was the second time within six months that the Treasury had sought the Fed's support for a troubled issue. The previous May, Treasury Undersecretary Burgess had requested the Fed to reduce reserve requirements in order to assure that the banking system could purchase a substantial part of a refunding scheduled that month. Martin knew a reserve reduction would counteract his effort to turn the FOMC toward tightening and rejected the request. He had advised Burgess that to assure a successful issue, the Treasury would have to attract buyers by "offering rates substantially over the market," not by urging the Fed to reduce reserve requirements.[73]

On 28 November 1955, Martin told Burgess that he was leaning away from supporting the 8 December refunding, since any one-year note purchases would violate the Bills Only directive "he had explicitly approved."[74] That night, Martin was "up until after 5:00 a.m. making up my mind."[75] Several times during the last year, he had made it clear to Burgess that he did not agree with many of the Treasury's debt-management decisions, and he was exasperated by the Treasury's continued pleas for help. If the Fed were ever to confirm its disengagement from its entangling support of Treasury financings, now was the time. The Treasury requests for assistance had a divisive effect on the FOMC, and supporting this troubled issue would require the Fed to add significant reserves to the banking system at just the wrong time. If the Fed purchased the notes from banks, the additional reserves created would be in direct opposition to the Fed's current restrictive posture, a posture Martin had worked extremely hard to achieve. At the same time, Martin knew he could not refuse the Treasury's request. He concluded it would be "irresponsible to ignore the Treasury's problem."[76]

The next morning, Martin told an emergency meeting of the FOMC that he supported the Treasury's request because he "considered that the Treasury would have great difficulty in placing the entire issue," and "the money market banks have to be prodded for their responsibility to bid for bills and accept their role in the market."[77] Urging his fellow FOMC members to approve his request, he recommended: "We should make it clear that it is an exception" and said he would also inform the Treasury that "[i]t would be very unwise for the Treasury to think that at any time it gets into trouble on an issue the Federal Reserve will bail it out."[78] In a 9–3 vote, the FOMC gave its grudging approval, but even supportive members remained unconvinced that the Treasury would heed Martin's advice. From the Treasury's point of view, the operation was a success. Once the bond market knew that the Fed was supporting the issue, prices firmed and the Fed's actual purchases were less than half of the FOMC's $400 million purchase authorization. Martin's willingness to subordinate the Fed's institutional goals when he felt that larger interests were at stake earned him a great deal of goodwill within the Treasury Department. It also embodied the spirit of Fed-Treasury cooperation described so briefly but so profoundly in the Accord.

The Fed's support did not go unnoticed. In February 1956, Martin appeared before the Joint Economic Committee hearing on the 1956 Economic Report of the President. The committee's outspoken chairman, Senator Paul Douglas, criticized the Fed for yielding to pressure from the Treasury. Martin tried to get Douglas to understand his decision: "I have served faithfully and conscientiously with Secretary Humphrey, and have had to say 'no' to him on a good many occasions, but I also want to work with him. The Treasury and Fed are partners. We are trying to achieve the same general ends and we each have a 50 percent interest."[79] Later in the hearing, Martin responded to Douglas's accusation that the Fed was pressured to help the Treasury: "There has been no coercion on the Federal Reserve. I would not stand for coercion. Whenever a decision has been made, insofar as I am concerned, it has been made independently, and to the best of my ability."[80] Despite Martin's protestations, Douglas remained critical.

About this same time, Arthur Burns surveyed the economic prospects for the presidential election year of 1956, and did not like what he saw. He told the cabinet: "Economic activity has leveled off. Is this a pause or a beginning of a decline? I don't know the answer."[81] In the interim, the solution was clear. The Eisenhower economic team would press the Fed to ease monetary conditions. Burns generally believed the Fed was too remote in its "ivory tower" to respond promptly to economic changes, and he felt free to urge the Fed to take action. After calls from Burns and Humphrey, Martin advised Burns he would encourage the Fed to "ease up a bit."[82] At the 24 January FOMC meeting,

Martin observed that the "economic machine has reached a plateau and is wobbling . . . and although I do not favor relaxation of credit restraint at this time, we should have our foot on the brake, but not press on it."[83] Then, in a phrase that would prove more prescient than he could have imagined, Martin said, "We are going to have to deal with the political side of this all spring."[84] Arthur Burns would not have been very satisfied by Martin's response.

The Fed's tepid response did not satisfy Eisenhower either. In February, Eisenhower told Humphrey to press harder on Martin, and during the next few weeks, Humphrey and Martin had a series of heated discussions. On 27 March, Martin signaled his resistance to the pressure by advising Humphrey that he would propose a discount rate increase in April. As the decision neared, Burns, Burgess, and Humphrey pressed Martin to defer the action. Humphrey, always blunt, was the most menacing. He informed Martin that the president had called from Georgia to rail at Humphrey for an hour about Martin's intransigence. Humphrey said Eisenhower would have called Martin himself except that "he does not seek to dominate" the Fed.[85] Humphrey, building on Eisenhower's anger at Martin, brutally told Martin that if he were determined to oppose the president, Martin should resign. Martin retorted that if his leadership were to be "violently opposed by the administration, I will resign."[86] Martin knew his resignation would set off a firestorm of criticism at the administration and he wanted the Treasury Secretary to know that there was a price, and a high one, when an administration put excessive political pressure on Fed decision making.

Under normal circumstances, Martin had a more tolerant view of political influence on the Fed. Martin believed that, while the ultimate decision on monetary policy was the Fed's alone, the views of Congress and the administration could be freely offered and when appropriate, should be considered by the Fed. When Martin began to discuss his concept of the Fed's independence in the congressional hearings in 1952, he emphasized the partnership nature of the Fed's relationship with the Treasury and the importance of continual communication. Disagreements over economic policy were bound to occur, and sincere differences should be tolerated among reasonable men. In fifteen years of public service, Martin had ample experience with the give-and-take of political lobbying and was confident in his abilities to persuade congressmen and administration officials alike to accept, if not necessarily to agree with, the Fed's decisions. However, Martin had seen the conflict over the wartime interest peg at firsthand, and he was extremely sensitive to the implications of a standoff between the Fed and the president. Martin could endure the heavy-handed threats of a Treasury secretary responding to political pressure, but when his relationship with a president broke down, he would consider himself ineffective and offer his resignation.

On 13 April 1956, the day the Fed governors met to approve the discount rate increase, Martin discussed his possible resignation. Most of them had been through the standoff with President Truman and felt the Fed's independence was again under siege. They unanimously encouraged Martin to remain firm and approved the rate increase.

A week later, Humphrey reported to the cabinet on his negotiations with Martin: "Martin's response was so strong that we had to back off."[87] Humphrey repeated Martin's argument that eleven boards of the Reserve Banks had approved the rate increase, and that the boards were predominantly businessmen, not bankers (of whom Eisenhower had a low opinion). Humphrey continued, "[T]o go further would have put the story on page one if we had openly broke with the Fed."[88] Eisenhower was still angry and wanted to break his usual silence on Fed moves by criticizing the rate increases as "premature." Burns agreed, stating that the administration would not comply with the Employment Act of 1946 if it did not use its "powers" to avoid a recession. Humphrey opposed any action, stating that the only way to be certain they could change the Fed's policy was for Eisenhower to ask directly for Martin's resignation. After acknowledging the unanimity of the Reserve Bank Boards in support of the increase, Eisenhower cut the discussion off. He was not prepared to take that step.

Humphrey was not ready to admit defeat. A few days later, he drafted a stinging public statement condemning the rate increase and sent it to the president. During this period, Martin also met with Eisenhower to defend his position. Martin pressed the president to give priority to controlling inflation. If the financial markets became too tight, he offered that the Fed would move quickly to ease them. After two days of deliberation, Eisenhower made what Martin called "a remarkable statement from the President of the United States about the role of the Federal Reserve System."[89] At a press conference on 25 April, in response to a question about making the Federal Reserve responsible to the president, Eisenhower stated: "It is not under the authority of the President, and I really personally believe it would be a mistake to make it definitely and directly responsible to the political head of the state."[90] Humphrey's statement was never released, and the cause of an independent Fed received a historic boost from Eisenhower, who put the nation's interest in a stable economy over his own short-term political considerations. The pressure on Martin from Burns and Humphrey continued to be intense, but Eisenhower's comments had reaffirmed Martin's ability to resist it.

Martin's life at the Fed was also made easier by Allan Sproul, who decided to retire in late summer. His departure robbed the Fed of a giant who had done much to stabilize the Fed during the troubled period before Martin's arrival. He had subsequently served as a wise, if reluctant, mentor to Bill Martin during Martin's early years at the Fed. Sproul's ability to understand the economy, formulate an appropriate monetary policy response, and persuasively present it was equal to any of his predecessors, including Benjamin Strong and Marriner Eccles. He never doubted his own abilities or the importance of the Fed's powers to constructively influence the U.S. economy. He was the embodiment of the meritocracy that had set the tone at the Fed from its earliest days. But Sproul's confidence, often bordering on arrogance, cost him the support of his fellow FOMC members and ultimately limited his influence on Fed policy.

During his career, Sproul employed a pragmatic approach to policy making and appreciated the limits of the Fed's monetary policy tools, although he rarely admitted as much in the heat of battle. When Martin began to reshape the Fed, some of Sproul's challenges were polarizing and counterproductive. On the other hand, his rebuttals to Martin's policy recommendations were often extremely insightful and led to more thorough discussions of policy issues and more considered decisions by the FOMC. His parting observation on his complex relationship with Martin was "Bill was very easy to agree with and very difficult to disagree with."[91] Fortunately for Martin, Sproul wanted his insights to speak for themselves, was uncomfortable with political maneuvering, and never made an effort to organize a faction to oppose Martin's policies. Martin must have experienced mixed emotions when Sproul went home to California.

Despite the administration's concern about the Fed's policy of restraint during 1956, the economic expansion continued. The strength of the economy was certainly one of the many elements contributing to Dwight Eisenhower's reelection landslide. During the November FOMC meetings, the Fed economics staff described the economy as reflecting a broad-based "buoyancy and strength." Economic growth for 1956 was expected to be 5 percent, including a troubling 2.5 percent increase in consumer prices. The price pressures appeared likely to dissipate, however. A number of industries were announcing the availability of new manufacturing capacity, and the Fed staff reported that "the investment boom appears to be cresting out."[92] Most encouraging, inventories were maintaining a relationship to sales that was normal for the current stage of an economic expansion. It appeared that the Fed had been successful in avoiding speculative excesses during the expansion, and now the economy seemed to be cooling down at an acceptable rate. It remained to be seen whether the economy could continue to ease without sliding into a recession.

As 1956 drew to a close, Bill Martin surveyed a scene of unaccustomed calm. Criticism of the Fed's restrictive monetary policy, so harsh for the first eight months of the year, had diminished significantly. Martin's working relationship with Treasury Secretary George Humphrey had been badly strained during the year but was still intact. Martin and Dwight Eisenhower were brought into close quarters as they thrashed out their differences, and their relationship matured into mutual understanding, even respect. Eisenhower had reappointed Martin to a new fourteen-year term as a Fed governor and a new four-year term as Fed chairman. Despite his initial misgivings, Eisenhower had repeatedly voiced strong public support for the Fed's independence during the year, and Martin could look forward to four more years of dealing with him and his fiscally responsible administration. The contentious debates with Allan Sproul were ended, and the philosophy of Alfred Hayes, Martin's preferred choice for the New York Reserve Bank presidency, was more in keeping with that of Martin and the FOMC as a whole. There would be surprises and difficulties ahead, but this was clearly a moment to savor.

7

Trying to Manage Prosperity:
The Late Eisenhower Years

The second term of the Eisenhower administration began during a spasm of intensified postwar maneuvering. The Russians were suppressing the Hungarian revolt, and America's closest allies, Britain and France, were nursing their wounds after being forced by Eisenhower to abort their armed attempt to recover the Suez Canal from Egypt. At home, the U.S. economy was operating "close to capacity," and after four years of stability, consumer prices grew at a disturbing 3 percent annual rate during the last quarter of 1956. Any sense of accomplishment that Dwight Eisenhower or Bill Martin might have felt at the end of the administration's first term was buried under the onrush of challenging new developments.

Two of Eisenhower's highest economic policy goals for 1957 were balancing the federal budget and limiting the growth of federal government spending. Foreign policy problems kept Eisenhower from his usual involvement in the fiscal 1958 budget negotiations, and when he saw the 10 percent spending increase in the final product, he lamented, "I have never felt so helpless."[1] Treasury Secretary Humphrey held a press conference on 15 February 1957 to make an unusual request: he asked Congress to make the budgetary cuts the administration could not. At the end of the conference, Humphrey was asked about the economic importance of further cuts. He replied: "If we don't over a long period of time [reduce spending], I will predict that you will have a depression that will curl your hair."[2] Humphrey's unguarded remark, together with the apparent inability of the administration to control its own budget, fed the news media's portrayal of the administration as worried and confused. Humphrey was so embarrassed by the reaction to his comment that he canceled his plan to leave the administration at the end of January and spent the next six months trying to restore confidence in the administration's policies.

At the time of Humphrey's remark, the FOMC was evaluating the effectiveness of its program of restraint. Fed economists considered that it usually took a year for a Fed tightening to take effect, and this campaign was almost two years old. The recovery and expansion from the 1953–54 recession was about two and one-half years old, still middle-aged in comparison to the three-and-one-half-year lives of the two preceding expansions. During the FOMC meeting of 18 February, one of the Fed's economic staff appraised the impact of Humphrey's comments by observing sourly: "[T]here can be no doubt but that business sentiment was much affected by statements in January concerning depression."[3] A decline in business confidence and a corresponding falloff in capital spending would make it more difficult for the Fed to slow the economy down without risking a recession. The committee's indecision was summed up by the New York Reserve Bank's Alfred Hayes: "There is no clear evidence whether the present sidewise movement will be followed by further expansion or . . . by an appreciable economic recession."[4] The FOMC decided to maintain the status quo and took comfort from the fact that consumer prices were stabilizing after the worrying rise in the previous quarter.

Raymond J. Saulnier, the new chairman of the Council of Economic Advisors, looked at the same situation and reached another conclusion. Saulnier had previously served as one of the three members of the council and, as other staff members, he had been concerned about the recovery's loss of momentum. Saulnier relied heavily on the leading indicators, and they had been pointing to a slowdown since the fall of 1956. Moreover, CEA economists predicted that a recession would occur in the second quarter of 1957. Saulnier encouraged Martin to ease credit. When his advice was ignored, he tried again. On 12 April, he was blunter when he told Martin: "My feeling is that [monetary policy] is unnecessarily tight and that bank reserves should not be allowed to remain at the current [negative] level."[5]

Even if the gentlemanly Saulnier had used the rougher techniques employed by George Humphrey, he would not have influenced Bill Martin. Martin had been engaged in an all-consuming effort to eliminate inflation for almost two years. He had yet to see sustained progress and would not be diverted by pressure from the administration.

Two of Bill Martin's core beliefs, which he referred to as his "guiding principles," were that stable prices were a fundamental underpinning of a free-market economy and that the Federal Reserve System had the primary responsibility to preserve that stability. Martin had often heard his father observe that throughout history, one of money's purposes had been to serve as a "standard of value," and that preserving the value of the American dollar had been a primary operating goal of the Federal Reserve System since its earliest days. This lesson was reinforced during Martin's graduate studies at Columbia during the 1930s, particularly by Professor H. Parker Willis, the economist who had served as the intellectual godfather of the original Federal Reserve legislation and as the Fed's first research director. From a very early point in his career, Martin had a firm grounding in the practical workings of the American monetary system.

The impact of these influences on Bill Martin's thinking was reflected in a speech he gave in 1936, when he was only thirty, at the New York Stock Exchange Institute, an Exchange-sponsored school that educated young employees of member firms about the brokerage business. The subject of his speech was "A Financial Education," and in it he emphasized the importance of "stable money" by commenting that "money's ability to serve as a standard of value depends on confidence, and confidence is no greater or no weaker than the civilization upon which it is reared."[6] Using the example of the German empire, he attributed its historic economic growth to the development of its banking system and the nation's faith in its currency. When the government debased that currency to finance the costs of World War I, it unleashed an inflation that resulted in political upheaval and economic chaos. Germany's agony, according to Martin, was an example of "the political, social, and economic influence of a monetary policy."[7] Bill Martin was a dedicated inflation fighter many years before he joined the Fed.

Martin's views on the causes and control of inflation matured during his years at the Fed through his relationships with an exceptionally strong group of Fed economists: Ralph Young, Woodlief Thomas, and Winfield Rieffler. Martin considered it essential that he, as the Fed's spokesman, explain his philosophy and the Fed's policies to the public. He believed this was particularly true in early 1957, when Americans were worried about the slowing economy and ignoring the threat of inflation. In a series of speeches, Martin laid out his justification for the Fed's anti-inflationary posture.

Martin pictured inflationary pressures arising from a period of strong economic growth fostered by "imbalances in the economy" in which "rising costs and prices mutually interact upon each other over time with a spiral effect."[8] Describing the spiral as fed by both "rising wage costs" and "strong demand" enabled Martin to sidestep an issue, hotly debated by economists, of whether inflation was more likely to result from strong demand (known as demand-pull inflation) or from cost pressures (known as cost-push inflation). He simply stated: "[T]he problem is one of broad general pressure on all of our resources."[9] Once the spiral began, "more serious effects occur if the price rise brings with it an expectation of still other increases. Expectations clearly have a great influence on economic and financial decisions."[10] Inflationary expectations led to a series of distortions from normal economic activity: "Consumers are encouraged to postpone saving and instead purchase goods which they do not immediately need, the incentive to strive for efficiency no longer governs business decisions . . . and speculative influences impair reliance upon business judgment."[11] As different groups struggle to insulate themselves from the loss of purchasing power, "fundamental faith in the fairness of our institutions and our government deteriorates."[12]

Martin's focus on the buildup of inflationary expectations represented an evolution in Fed policy making. As economist Henry Wallich observed in 1958: "The U.S. has no experience of a prolonged inflation . . . price increases were not viewed by the public as a continuing process. An inflation that is expected to continue, one that everybody tries to stay ahead of, is a new phenomenon."[13] The Fed's research on expectations had been conducted in 1956 in a seminal study by Ralph Young, the respected head of research, and Martin incorporated it into his monetary philosophy.

Martin described full-blown inflation as carrying within it the seeds of its own destruction. The speculative influences unleashed by inflation generate investment in inventory and physical plant at a rate that cannot be profitably sustained and, inevitably, economic activity begins to decline. Unchecked, the decline leads to collapse. The person most likely to be injured in the inflationary cycle was the "hardworking and thrifty . . . little man" on fixed income who could protect neither his income nor the value of his savings. Often, he was also the unemployed victim of the collapse.

Having justified the Fed's anti-inflationary posture, Martin made a case for a policy of restraint. To Martin, the Fed "has a responsibility to use the powers it possesses over economic events to dampen excesses in economic activity [by] keeping the use of credit in line with resources available for production of goods and services."[14] Credit restraint would eventually lower economic activity and increase unemployment. Martin also admitted that capital spending would slow: "Naturally, these deferments [of capital projects] are of great concern to all of us."[15] Martin also accepted that the impact of credit restraint fell unfairly on a few sectors of the economy, but "all sectors suffer infinitely more from further bites out of the purchasing power of the dollar."[16] Martin emphasized the temporary nature of credit restraint, describing its economic costs as modest in comparison to the long-term benefits of noninflationary growth.

To describe the process by which a slowing economy brought supply into balance with demand, Martin used the economist's term, *economic adjustment*. The adjustment process included actions by the business community to squeeze inflationary excesses out of their costs, and Martin concluded that "we can have faith in the adjusting quality if we have character and intelligence on the part of our businessmen."[17] Martin described the Fed's confidence that the natural adjustment process would, if carefully monitored, "correct the economic imbalances" without the catastrophe of "another 1929."[18] In a statement that neatly summarized his philosophy, he concluded: "I have less faith in the power of money and credit policy than some people who criticize it, and more faith in the economy when it comes to its adjusting ability, so long as we let the law of supply and demand be the major factor."[19]

Martin's philosophy on the causes and cure of inflation was based on a pragmatic view of how the economy functioned. It called for the Fed to attack inflation by working with the natural functions of the economy and free markets. Martin honed his message so that it could be understood by Congress, the press, and the public. His guiding principles anchored his leadership of the FOMC as it attempted to manage a constantly changing economy. This steadiness of purpose was nowhere more evident than in his actions during the first half of 1957.

During that time, the FOMC maintained "a tone of restraint" in the credit markets and, reflecting strong bank loan demand, interest rates climbed steadily upward. By July, both short-term and long-term rates were at postwar highs, creating enormous pressures on the U.S. Treasury Department. Under the Treasury's congressionally authorized borrowing power, the Treasury could not pay interest in excess of 4¼ percent on obligations maturing beyond five years. If the Treasury could not issue long-term debt without exceeding the interest rate limit, it would have to issue new bonds at less than five-year maturities. The Treasury's program to lengthen the average maturity of outstanding Treasury issues was, at least for the time being, a dead letter.

More ominously, the Treasury was deeply worried that the owners of $55 billion of lower yielding Treasury savings certificates would begin redeeming them in order to reinvest their savings in higher yielding securities. Even if savers reinvested in Treasury securities, which was not certain, the Treasury's interest costs would go up and its maturity structure would worsen. Savings certificates represented the longest term, lowest cost form of Treasury borrowing. Describing the seriousness of the situation to the FOMC, Martin likened the redemption risk to that of a "run on a bank," the event that led to the collapse of the U.S. financial system during the Great Depression.

Resolving this thorny issue was complicated by the deteriorating relationship between Martin and Treasury Secretary Humphrey and their respective institutions. Two of the Treasury's 1957 long-term bond issues were near failures because of the rate ceiling. The Fed had to temporarily abandon its program of restraint to provide extra reserves so that commercial banks would purchase the issues. Humphrey and Burgess pressured Martin to avoid increasing interest rates so their problems with the debt ceiling would not worsen. These disagreements with the Treasury roiled the FOMC and in April, Martin acknowledged that the committee "might not approve the way in which the Treasury was running its affairs."[20] In July, the Fed's open-market manager took the unusual step of formally complaining to the FOMC, detailing his problems in conducting open-market activities with the flood of Treasury offerings in the short- and medium-term markets. Humphrey ignored the Fed's problems, but the situation changed in July, when Humphrey announced that he was returning to private life. His replacement, Robert B. Anderson, offered the prospect of a more conciliatory approach.

Anderson entered the Treasury with more political experience than George Humphrey, and he was no less committed to conservative Republican economic management. Anderson was born in the small Texas town of Burleson and marked himself as a young man of promise when he graduated from the University of Texas Law School and won a seat in the Texas legislature the same month. Anderson abandoned his political career at age twenty-six and spent the next two decades as general manager of a sprawling 500,000-acre cattle and oil empire owned by a wealthy Texas family.

Anderson appeared on the national stage when he was appointed to a commission organized by Columbia University president Dwight Eisenhower. Eisenhower, always on the lookout for executive talent, was impressed by Anderson's ability to summarize complex issues. During the presidential transition, Eisenhower urged Defense Secretary Charles Wilson to find a place for Anderson, and he was appointed secretary of the navy. He soon distinguished himself by quietly integrating the navy's huge installations in Norfolk, Virginia, and Charleston, South Carolina. The resolution of this potentially explosive issue won Dwight Eisenhower's "intense admiration."[21] Wilson promoted Anderson to deputy Defense secretary after a year in the navy post. When George Humphrey decided to leave the Treasury, he convinced Eisenhower to appoint Anderson in his stead. Humphrey described Anderson's abilities by saying: "Don't be misled about him just because he doesn't shout and pound the table the way I do. He can be firm as a rock."[22]

Unfortunately for Robert Anderson, his political skills failed to persuade Martin to back away from restraint. Martin did advise the FOMC that the Fed "had a very real obligation to consider the Treasury's problem" but did not recommend any policy change.[23] In April 1957 and again in June, the Fed's economic indicators revealed that credit conditions were tighter than the FOMC wanted, but consumer prices were still increasing at an annual rate of 3.4 percent. At the June meeting, Martin advised his FOMC associates that no policy change was called for: "[M]onetary policy is working at the moment."

Bill Martin's confidence about the Fed's policy posture was not uniformly shared by his fellow FOMC members and by July, the FOMC was split. Some members acknowledged the inflationary pressures, but were concerned about the obvious economic slowdown, and particularly about the 0.1 percent decline in second-quarter GNP. Alfred Hayes, president of the New York bank, said: "I do not agree that inflationary forces are in the ascendancy," later observing that the situation "calls for maintenance of restraint, but not any increase in intensity."[24] Malcolm Bryan, the respected president of the Federal Reserve Bank of Atlanta, joined in with the comment that the Fed's restraint was "pulling the rug out from under the market."[25]

The formation of a pronounced minority view was unusual in Bill Martin's FOMC. The FOMC's normal collegiality was the result of many factors, not the least of which was Martin's skill at building consensus. But during times of economic transition, such as in mid-1957, FOMC meetings were often marked by considerable debate, with some of it passionately expressed. At the end of discussion, Martin would regularly begin his summary with a deceptively bland comment: "Well, I think we are all in substantial agreement here."[26] From there, Martin would proceed to fashion a consensus that built on areas of agreement, no matter how small they might be, that his FOMC membership could accept.

Martin also enjoyed the chairman's traditional leverage over his fellow members. Eisenhower, like his predecessors, solicited the Fed chairman's views on potential board of governors candidates, and occasionally, as Martin had done for Governor James L. Robertson, the chairman proposed a successful candidate. The importance of the chairman's role in their selection was not lost on the governors. The presidents of the Reserve Banks were in a similar situation. Traditionally. they were recommended by the individual bank's board, but the Fed's board of governors had the final approval. Bill Martin took considerable interest in that selection process, and his role in the choice of Alfred Hayes as president of the New York Reserve Bank was widely acknowledged.

FOMC members were also influenced by the knowledge that the chairman's views reflected his contacts with the administration and the Fed's congressional overseers. In the 20 August 1957 FOMC meeting, Martin said: "In terms of the struggle against inflation, which is by no means won, the system gained during the past few weeks through the congressional hearings."[27] FOMC members understood that Martin had laid the political groundwork for a continuation of the Fed's policy of restraint. A final element in Martin's leadership was, as former governor and staff member Robert Holland put it, "that everybody around the table liked Bill. They trusted him and knew that he wanted to do the right thing."[28] During the first five years of Martin's chairmanship, nearly all monetary policy votes in the FOMC or the board of governors were unanimous or strong majorities.

The governors' vote on increasing the discount rate in August 1957 was one of the rare occasions when Bill Martin let his determination to control inflation override his desire for a consensus in the FOMC. The debate over a seventh discount rate increase simmered during the summer, and Martin repeatedly failed to persuade his opponents to moderate their concern about the weakening economy. Finally, at the 30 July FOMC meeting, Martin announced his intention to support a request from the Chicago Reserve Bank for a discount rate increase. He was willing "to assume the risk of being charged with precipitating a downturn, rather than take any action except one [that I] believe correct."[29] This remarkably blunt statement of Martin's deepest feelings reveals his exasperation with his inability to build a clear majority in favor of further restraint. It also indicates that as of mid-1957, Bill Martin was not willing to moderate his anti-inflationary philosophy in order to achieve a higher economic growth rate.

The discount rate debate reached a decisive moment on 6 August 1957, when the commercial bank prime rate was increased to 4½ percent. The ½ percent increase was higher than expected, and the rate stood at the highest level since 1931. The July statistics supported Martin's position that inflationary pressures had not abated and that economic growth was again rising. Two weeks later, in an unusually close 4–3 vote by the Fed's board of governors, Martin secured a ½ percent discount rate increase. The Reserve Banks in New York, Richmond, Cleveland, and St. Louis officially signaled their displeasure by refusing to raise their discount rate for several weeks after the other Reserve Banks adopted the new rate. Congressional reaction was a predictable roar of anger, led by Representative Wright Patman, subcommittee chairman of the House Banking and Currency Committee and a persistent Fed critic. Both houses of Congress had previously scheduled hearings for August to discuss monetary policy, and Martin used them to persuade his congressional critics of the necessity of higher rates.

To justify the Fed's action, Martin took on a growing number of economists who accepted incremental price inflation as endemic in the American postwar economy. The movement's leader was Professor Sumner Slichter, a respected

Harvard University economist known for his macroanalysis of the economy. Slichter believed extended prosperity was building an irreducible core inflation into the economy; he was dubbed the father of "the new inflation" by *Fortune* magazine. Slichter argued that costs for materials and labor were rising as low-cost supplies became scarcer. At the same time, "unions push up wages and fringe benefits faster than gains in the productivity of labor. The result is a continuation of the slow rise in prices."[30] He considered that the 3 percent increase in consumer prices during 1956 and the first half of 1957, despite the Fed's program of credit restraint, affirmed this thesis. He concluded that if the economy were to grow at a rate sufficient to generate enough jobs to keep unemployment low, the Fed would have to accept creeping inflation and follow a less restrictive monetary policy.

Martin was angered by the popularity of the Slichter thesis. In March, he had intemperately lashed out at it by saying: "I refuse to raise the flag of defeatism in the battle of inflation. If you take this [Slichter's] view, then another bust will surely come."[31] At the hearings, he took a more studied view, one that he had developed in cooperation with Ralph Young, the Fed's director of research. Martin observed that incremental inflation lowered the effective cost of interest and encouraged borrowing. Lower effective interest costs blunt the impact of the Fed's monetary policy when it attempts to slow the economy by restricting bank lending. Martin argued: "There is no validity whatever in the idea that any inflation, once accepted, can be confined to moderate proportions."[32] He concluded with his greatest concern, that the Fed could not do its job if the government were to accept incremental inflation: "[K]eeping a rising price level under control becomes incomparably more difficult when there is no clearly stated public policy to maintain price stability."[33] Martin's argument did little to sway those congressional opponents who were unalterably opposed to higher interest rates.

Martin could live with congressional criticism as long as he had the support, or at least the acquiescence, of the administration. On 8 August, he advised CEA Chairman Saulnier that a rate rise was coming. Saulnier had been worriedly watching the deterioration of the leading indicators since May but responded that he "saw nothing in the economic situation that would cause him to strongly argue" with the decision.[34] He told Martin, "I believe that Burgess and Anderson feel likewise."[35]

The administration's neutrality allowed Martin to breathe easier. He had brought a divided board of governors to accept the August rate increase. There could be no public misunderstanding about the Fed's commitment to control inflation, and Martin believed that understanding was essential to breaking the inflationary expectations that had taken root in the American mentality over the last three years. The Fed also served notice that it did not accept the theory of creeping inflation and would fight inflation until, as Martin put it, "it was licked." Martin readily acknowledged that the Fed's policy carried the risk of recession but, in his opinion, the risk was worth taking. Once again, Martin's faith in the tenets of the real bills philosophy led him to continue tightening the economy until it became widely evident that inflationary pressures were gone and would not soon reappear. The adjustments taking place in the economy, reflected in the declines in the leading indicators, were laying the foundation for noninflationary growth in the future. To Martin, the Fed was fulfilling the role for which it had been created.

The administration's silence on the Fed's policy of restraint ended in mid-October 1957, a victim of a devastating set of economic statistics for September. The downturn foreshadowed by the leading indicators was widely visible, and its presence was all the more disturbing because it had not been preceded by the usual indicators of a developing recession. Nevertheless, economists at the Fed and the CEA knew that a recession was indisputably under way.

The question of what induced the recession of 1957–58 has been debated over the years without resolution. There is general agreement that the administration's decision to cut back on Defense Department purchases in the first half of 1957 was a major factor. There is also consensus that the Fed's restrictive policy during 1957 was another contributor. On the other hand, there is also considerable agreement that without the Fed's restraint during 1955–57, the economy could have experienced an inflationary boom with much more serious aftereffects. There is no disputing the presence of strong inflationary pressures, as consumer price increases remained above an annualized rate of 3.4 percent from the second quarter of 1956 through the first quarter of 1958 despite the Fed's restraint. CEA Chairman Ray Saulnier, who had persistently argued for a Fed easing throughout 1957, did not assign a critical role to the Fed. He commented in his oral history in 1967: "The recession happened because a capital goods boom and a consumer durable goods boom, both too rapid to be sustainable, came to an end."[36]

As he reviewed the discouraging September numbers, Bill Martin had two objectives: to foster economic recovery and to assure that monetary and fiscal policy would be working in tandem. His ability to achieve the latter goal was aided by a giant step forward in the realm of economic policy coordination: the creation of what was called "the little four."[37] The idea was the creation of Dr. Gabriel Hauge, Eisenhower's influential assistant for economic affairs. He proposed that the chairmen of the Fed and the CEA, along with the secretary of the Treasury, meet regularly with the president to discuss economic policy issues. When Martin expressed his support for the idea to Raymond Saulnier, he said: "I was seriously handicapped by being unable to talk directly with the president, as happened during April 1956," referring to his tense standoff with George Humphrey during which the two had struggled over Martin's possible resignation.[38]

The first "little four" meeting, on 14 October 1957, represents a watershed in the coordination of economic policy making in the United States. These meetings provided an opportunity for give-and-take on policy issues that far exceeded Gabriel Hauge's modest goals. In these sessions, Martin carefully preserved the Fed's freedom of maneuverability by never revealing Fed thinking in advance of its policy decisions. He often advised the administration of impending moves, but he did this through direct discussion with the CEA chairman or Treasury secretary. As Fed economic historian Donald Kettl observes about these meetings, "They typically served less as a way of coordinating policies in advance than as a means of insuring that past problems, and sometimes public controversies, did not recur."[39] Martin's relations with the Eisenhower administration were enhanced by an unusual degree of common economic philosophy, but this would not be true for later administrations. There is no doubt that Bill Martin's longevity as Fed chairman owed much to these meetings.

Despite their promising start, even the "little four" sessions could not stop a growing disagreement between the Fed and the administration over how to respond to the recession of 1957. In early November, CEA Chairman Saulnier completed a new forecasting technique based on an detailed analysis of past recessions. The results confirmed that the recession could be relatively severe. Saulnier abandoned his usual civility and pushed Martin forcefully for easier credit. When Martin was noncommittal, Saulnier went first to Anderson and finally to Eisenhower. Both men shared his views but were not yet ready to increase the pressure on the Fed.

Although he gave little solace to Saulnier, Bill Martin was closely monitoring the slowdown. In the 12 November FOMC meeting, he commented on its beneficial effects: "The adjustments now taking place will prove to be salutary, and if the inflationary movement had gone farther, the unraveling process would have been much more difficult."[40] Urging his FOMC members to "help bind up and heal the [economy's] wounds," he led the way to lowering the discount rate and easing credit conditions.[41] The initial easing was relatively modest, however, because the FOMC did not want to undermine the adjustment process by creating excessive ease. A *New York Times* reporter quoted a Fed informant as saying: "We have been leaning against the wind of boom and inflation. Now we'll just lean a little less heavily without changing the direction."[42] This comment was unlikely to please CEA Chairman Saulnier, who was expecting a strong move toward ease.

By December, Saulnier was not alone in his desire for more Fed action. Eisenhower was moved by the increase in unemployment, and on 31 December he told Saulnier to advise Martin that the president "thought the Fed ought to put its shoulder to the wheel and do something dramatic . . . and if Martin had reservations about such a move, that he ought to have a meeting [of the little four] very soon."[43] These were strong words for Eisenhower, but the administration's inclination to pressure the Fed on monetary policy had lessened during Eisenhower's second term. Secretary Anderson's personality was typically less confrontational than his predecessor's. In addition, Anderson was not convinced that easy money was the best answer to the recession. In mid-October, he commented on the impact of Russia's successful launch of Sputnik, the first satellite to orbit the earth: "[C]onfidence in the economy is pessimistic, stemming from Sputnik, and easy credit will not work well now."[44] Saulnier continued to complain about excessive restraint, but he was more cautious than the supremely confident Arthur Burns and did not try to force his views on the Fed. In this case the president himself did not follow up his economic policy instructions as forcefully as he did in similar situations during his first term.

The Fed's response to the recession of 1957–58 was slower than it had been during the recession of 1953–54, but it was equally emphatic. A problem in the Treasury bond market in May 1953 had forced the Fed into an emergency program of ease, and the recession of 1953–54 began while the Fed was still in a position of active ease. There was no coincidental anticipation the second time around. The Fed did not initiate a sustained effort to deal with the 1957–58 recession until mid-January 1958, some four months after the slowdown began. Over the next two months, the Fed unleashed its antirecession arsenal in much the same way as it had in 1953. Two additional discount rate reductions were completed, and required reserves were reduced by a total of $1 billion, the same amount they were reduced in 1953. As commercial banks sought to convert their newly freed reserves into earning assets, they piled into Treasury bills, driving prices up and yields down. Between 1 November 1957 and 18 May 1956, Treasury bill yields plummeted from 3.6 percent to 0.6 percent. Trying to put the decline in perspective, the First National City Bank exclaimed: "There are few parallels in history for the rocketing advance in bond prices."[45] As early as February 1958, a satisfied Bill Martin was able to tell his FOMC associates that "the posture of the System is where it should be."[46]

Martin's pressure on the FOMC to move quickly and forcefully to ease credit conditions reflected a monetary philosophy that was an unusual blend of the old and the new, or as Fed economist Robert Hetzel said: "he had one foot in the 1930s and the other in the 1950s."[47] Martin's commitment to the traditional real bills theory motivated him to move quickly to damp down speculative forces. However, he also believed in the more modern monetary theory of aggregate demand management. That theory evolved in response to the fact that the Employment Act of 1946 assigned a shared responsibility to the Fed and the administration for promoting stable economic growth. To exercise this responsibility, the Fed had to respond both to inflationary booms and economic slowdowns. For Martin, a flexible monetary policy required symmetry: the Fed would be guided by the economy and would respond with equal vigor to slow an overheated economy or to stimulate a flagging one. This philosophy meshed perfectly with Martin's belief that the Fed had to work with the forces in the economy rather than try to control them. Martin's synthesis did not eliminate the difficult questions of when or how far to lean against the economic wind, but it provided the justification for action.

The question of when to lean was complicated by the difficulty of predicting the lag between the start of a policy change by the Fed and its impact on the economy. As the Fed's economists scanned the March 1958 statistics, it became clear that the Fed's moves were not yet having the desired effect. Research head Ralph Young commented: "The decline is now somewhat more rapid than the recessions of 1949 and 1953. By this point, those recessions had bottomed out."[48]

In April, Martin was back before the Senate Finance Committee. Although he could not offer immediate encouragement on the recession, he doggedly pleaded for patience from the committee members. He defended the adjustment process going on in the economy, observing that part of the economic problem resulted from "misdirected investment leading to excess capacity." He referred to a statement he had made in an earlier speech: "[W]e are dealing with waste and extravagance, incompetency and inefficiency, the only way we have in a free society of eliminating it is by taking losses from time to time. This is a loss economy as well as a profit economy."[49] To Martin, a free-market economy could not function effectively if the government insulated businessmen from the consequences of poor decisions. In a plea for a long-term view, he asked the senators to support "flexibility in stabilization policies that deal with today's problem and do not aggravate those of tomorrow."[50]

Unfortunately for Martin, his senatorial audience was thinking about its unhappy constituents and wanted the very short-term actions that Martin and the administration were trying to discourage. A growing number of congressmen were moving toward a tax cut. That step would have an immediate impact on the economy and, as far as they were concerned, tomorrow could take care of itself.

The pressure for a tax cut began in the Senate during February 1958, when Senator Paul Douglas proposed a one-year tax cut. Around the same time,

Arthur Burns began a series of letters to Eisenhower, urging a substantial tax cut on the basis of his forecast that unemployment would remain a continuing problem even after the recovery from the recession. Burns believed that without the stimulus of a tax cut, the economy would not grow fast enough to absorb the expected growth in the labor force and the projected displacement of current workers by automation. Ironically, both Democrat Douglas and Republican Burns used the argument that if their respective parties did not take the initiative on taxes, the other party would. With an off-year election only seven months away, the pro-cut forces found it easy to recruit supporters.

In a mid-May meeting of the little four, Treasury Secretary Anderson and Martin convinced Eisenhower to follow his own instincts and reject the notion of a tax cut. Martin argued that "business sentiment is rather good," and that recovery was coming without the need of a tax cut. Further, once the recovery process was under way, "a tax action will only add to the difficulties of dealing with the wage-cost spiral."[51] Secretary Anderson told the president that there would be "great difficulties in getting the kind of [investment-oriented] tax bill you can accept."[52] CEA Chairman Saulnier, the only voice for a tax cut in the group, was outgunned. A few days later, Eisenhower gave a speech in which he discussed the tax issue: "The timing of such [tax] reductions always poses problems. There is concern with inflationary effects. In a time like the present, with its rising government expenditures, we are particularly sensitive to tax burdens, but there is likewise great concern with the future impact of increasing deficits."[53] The indications of a recovery that began appearing in April soon made the tax issue moot. Labor Secretary James Mitchell told a reporter that he and Vice President Nixon had favored a tax cut, but had lost the fight to Anderson and the Federal Reserve Board."[54]

This outcome exemplifies the way in which discussions in the little four helped influence economic policy during the Eisenhower administration. Martin was vitally concerned about the impact of a tax cut on the economy once the recovery from the recession began. He repeatedly argued that the Fed had kept monetary conditions too easy following the 1953–54 recession. In Martin's opinion, overly easy credit in 1954 and 1955 had contributed to the expansionary excesses that led to the 1957–58 recession, and he was determined to avoid a repetition. A strong recovery, further fueled by a tax cut, would create expansionary excesses in 1959 and 1960. Martin believed profoundly that the Fed was most effective when fiscal and monetary policy were working in concert. The administration's decision to forego a tax cut was a crucial supporting step for Martin's campaign to foster noninflationary economic growth. On 27 May, when he advised the FOMC that "monetary policy was performing just about as it should," he truly meant it.[55]

As so often happens in monetary affairs, an appearance of calm can obscure the buildup of unseen, but potentially destabilizing, economic developments. Often these events have small beginnings but quickly mushroom into forces that overtake the financial markets. From a broader economic perspective, such a development may appear to be a narrow technical matter affecting only the financial market. From the viewpoint of the Fed, however, the financial market's reaction to that same event can have much broader significance. Changes in investor sentiment can occur quickly and spread rapidly, and if the trend is negative, investor confidence can be severely damaged and require a long time to repair. Bill Martin had firsthand experience in dealing with the repercussion from the loss of investor confidence in the 1929 stock market collapse, and he deeply believed that the Fed should move decisively whenever a major shock to investor confidence was possible. Such an event occurred during the summer of 1958.

In May 1958, a small New York City bond-trading house devised an investment idea based on the expectation that the continuing public pressure on the Fed to end the recession would lead to further monetary ease and lower interest rates. Lower interest rates meant higher bond prices and capital gains for savvy investors. Current margin lending rules allowed investors in Treasury bonds to buy bonds with a 5 percent down payment and to finance 95 percent of the purchase price. If a bond could be purchased at par and sold at a 2 percent premium, the return on the equity investment portion alone would be 40 percent. Over the course of a month, the tiny firm convinced its clients to agree to purchase $500 million of an upcoming issue of $7.4 billion of 2⅝ percent Treasury bonds. Other, larger investment firms jumped on the bandwagon, and when the 18 June offering was completed, total loans from banks and brokerage firms secured by Treasury securities totaled $7.1 billion, the highest level since 1946. The Fed's chief domestic economist, Woodlief Thomas, usually a master of understatement, advised the FOMC that the growth of security loans was "phenomenal." Most of the 2⅝ percent issue was held by profit-hungry speculators, and all it would take for investors to begin dumping Treasury bonds was the rumor that bond prices would fall.

It wasn't long in coming. The day after the placement, the *Wall Street Journal* carried an article forecasting a Fed tightening. Alarmed speculators, and particularly those who had large positions in the 2⅝ percent bonds, feared they now faced losses. Sales momentum began to build, and within three weeks the market value of the 2⅝ percent bond had declined by 3.5 percent. This decline wiped out 70 percent of the equity of those speculators who had borrowed the maximum 95 percent, and they were faced with having to sell their bonds or put up more collateral. Many investors simply sold their bonds, and the forced sales added to the "successive waves of selling pressure."[56]

Bill Martin was pounded by the onrush of events. In the space of a few short weeks, he went from believing that the Fed and the administration were on top of the economic situation to battling a confusing contagion affecting the Treasury market. At the 8 July FOMC meeting, Martin commented: "It is difficult to keep my sense of balance. The week after June 19 was one of the worst I have spent since coming into the system. In these times, forces are at work that are bigger than the System or the Treasury."[57] Martin was uncharacteristically dispirited. He was convinced that the Fed's sustained campaign to ease credit conditions had created excessive liquidity in the banking system and set the stage for the speculators' attempt to profit from further easing. On the other hand, Martin believed that a flexible monetary policy required that the Fed apply all its powers to assist in the recovery from recession. The Fed's monetary tools were simply not sensitive enough to allow it to moderate the speculative side effects of a policy of active ease. At times like this, Martin felt the full burden of responsibility for determining the Fed's "flexible" response to chaotic conditions in the financial markets.

At its 18 July meeting, the FOMC was faced with additional declines in prices for most Treasury bonds. After a heated debate, the FOMC agreed to a staff recommendation to temporarily suspend the Fed's "Bills Only" policy and publicly announce its intention to support the full range of Treasury securities. The decision was particularly painful for Bill Martin. He firmly believed that a bad precedent was being set and that the Fed would be on the slippery slope toward a resumption of "pegging" rates. The Fed had to support the Treasury bond market, and there was no time to consider alternatives.

In the middle of the strongest selling pressures in the Treasury market, a previously scheduled offering of one-year Treasury certificates came to market. Unsurprisingly, early subscriptions indicated that the issue would probably fail. A failure could have a devastating effect on what was left of investor confidence. Faced with this additional problem, the Fed could no longer afford to hold back on open-market purchases. On 22 and 23 July, the Fed desk purchased a total of $1.1 billion of the new certificates in what the First National City Bank called "a Herculean support of the refunding."[58] Investors concluded that the Fed was prepared to do whatever was necessary to stabilize the market, and the selling pressures stopped as quickly as they had begun. The Fed was fortunate that the difficulties of dealing with the Treasury refunding ended the FOMC's hesitancy to move forcefully into the market. The episode revealed the constructive impact of massive Fed intervention on investor confidence and established a pattern that would be used sparingly, but to great effect, in the years to come.

The relief that Bill Martin felt now that the siege was over was offset by the knowledge that the Fed's monetary policy posture was in tatters. It would be months before the reserves poured into the banking system as a result of the Fed's emergency purchases of Treasury bonds and certificates could be safely taken back out. The Fed's goal of fostering a noninflationary recovery from the recession would not be achievable until the Fed regained a measure of control over bank reserves.

Moreover, a residue of dissension remained within the FOMC over the decision to abandon the Bills Only policy. Malcolm Bryan, the Atlanta Reserve Bank president, criticized the decision: "It began on the presumption of correcting disorder, but turned promptly into one of the most massive support operations ever undertaken."[59] Martin, knowing that Bryan's charge would be repeated by the Fed's conservative critics, responded only that "it is well to have different views within the system."[60] There was little point in arguing. In hindsight, the dangers of the situation might actually have been overestimated. However, in the midst of the crisis, it was easy to envision a wave of investor losses followed by margin calls and individual bankruptcies, financial problems for selected brokers, and sizable portfolio losses throughout the banking and insurance industries. In Martin's mind, there was no question that averting a crisis in investor confidence in the Treasury bond market at the cost of a temporary lapse in monetary policy was a price well worth paying.

Bill Martin's scars from the speculative attack on Treasury bonds had barely healed when his attention was drawn to the surge in trading volume and stock prices at the New York Stock Exchange. By August 1958, the economy was only four months into a recovery from the recession, but the ease with which the financial markets erupted into a speculative fever troubled Martin. Financial speculation brought out the real bills element of Martin's monetary philosophy, and once again he was ready to move quickly. In the 18 August FOMC meeting, he began to press for a program of restraint. The transition to restraint following the 1953–54 recession had brought Martin and Allan Sproul to one of their most painful conflicts. Sproul might have retired, but his heirs would take up his battle. This time, the recovery had barely started and Martin was ready to put his foot on the brake. Martin knew he would encounter strong opposition on the FOMC, and he was not disappointed.

The recovery from the recession of 1957–58 put the FOMC in a dilemma. In contrast to the 1953–54 recession, the 1957–58 downturn was shorter, eight months compared to twelve, and steeper, as industrial production had declined 14 percent versus 9 percent. The 1957–58 recovery was also much more sluggish. Seven months after the bottom of the decline, unemployment had only declined by 0.5 percent of the workforce compared to 2.5 percent in

1953–54. Industrial capacity utilization was almost 10 percent less at this point in the current recovery, and corporate capital spending was also lagging badly. Despite a sharper decline, prices remained astonishingly firm during the 1957–58 recession, rising 2.6 percent compared to a 0.3 percent increase during the 1953–54 recession. Consumer prices had actually declined in prior recessions. Never had the Fed's principal goals of fostering postrecession recovery and heading off inflation been so opposed to one another.

At the 9 September 1958 FOMC meeting, New York Reserve Bank President Alfred Hayes spoke against premature restraint: "[T]here is surplus capacity, surplus labor, and surplus inventory . . . and neither the state of business activity nor price conditions convey a threat of higher inflation."[61] Rejecting one of Martin's arguments, Hayes said that "the assumption that the prospective Federal deficit for fiscal 1959 makes near term inflation inevitable, is erroneous."[62] Martin's response was defensive but reflected his undiminished determination to keep inflation under control: "In my seven years in the system, there is resistance all along the way when we move [interest rates] up. There is always the charge that the proposed action would result in [economic] collapse. The system has to assume a risk, for it will always be blamed if things go wrong."[63] A familiar split was forming within the FOMC, but Martin held together a majority of the FOMC to support restraint. With the support of the FOMC, the governors approved discount rate increases in September and again in November.

The FOMC's tensions over credit restraint simmered during the fall of 1958, but the stalemate was broken by a remarkable announcement from Dwight Eisenhower on 22 December. Unable to wait until the traditional mid-January release of the proposed budget for the coming fiscal year, the president enthusiastically reported that the proposed budget for 1960 would show a small surplus. The current year's budget deficit was expected to be $12.5 billion, or 15 percent of the total budget, and the swing to a surplus marked the largest year-to-year budgetary improvement in peacetime history. It was a triumph of fiscal prudence engineered by a persuasive Treasury secretary, a determined budget director, and a courageous president.

Martin was gratified by the administration's remarkable accomplishment but remained concerned that it might not be enough to completely subdue the inflationary pressures at work in the economy. In the 16 December FOMC meeting, Martin acknowledged that a balanced budget argued for a reconsideration of the prospects for inflation: "I saw some hazards in the situation that perhaps were not real."[64] Despite this concession, Martin was not ready to ease up on restraint even though his position was more awkward than ever. His majority on the FOMC would surely weaken and the administration, in the form of CEA Chairman Saulnier, was pressuring Martin to ease credit, arguing that the elimination of the deficit justified a change in Fed policy.

Martin had to make a further defense of his philosophy during the Joint Economic Committee (JEC) hearings in February 1959. The topic was the president's economic report, and Martin was preceded by a phalanx of economists who did not spare the Fed in their comments. Walter Heller, from the University of Minnesota, argued that unused industrial capacity and "manpower slack" would cushion the economy from inflationary pressures. He observed that "the obsession with Federal expenditure cutbacks and early budget balance as a prerequisite to price stability is unfounded. The cost of a restrictive budgetary policy is loss of production by slowing the pace of recovery and lower investment in public education and other public services that strengthen our long run economic potential."[65] Paul Samuelson, a well-known professor at the Massachusetts Institute of Technology, agreed with Heller: "My advice is to put the major emphasis on growth of real income . . . not letting concern over price inflation dominate decisions."[66]

Only Herbert Stein, the chief economist for the Committee on Economic Development and a spokesman for conservative economic policies, supported Martin's position: "We may either go up at a relatively mild rate without inflation, or we initiate another boom like that of 1955–56, in which we will have a resumption of fairly vigorous inflation. By accepting the inevitability of inflation, we will purchase only a brief respite from the basic problem, making high employment compatible with a predictable price level."[67]

In his presentation to the JEC, Martin tried to rebut the argument that the Fed's monetary policy restrained growth and caused recessions. He accepted the criticism that employment and prices had fluctuated too much: "We must moderate this [employment and price] instability so that losses in employment and output in recession periods will not depress our longer term rate of growth."[68] In the Fed's defense, Martin argued that the object of monetary policy was to promote economic growth by balancing growing demand with expanding supply. Monetary policy could encourage growth in demand by "sound credit expansion." It could also support investment in new capacity by achieving price stability because "savers can have confidence in the future value of their investments."[69] Summing up, Martin argued that the key to sustainable economic growth was low inflation: "What this Congress decides, what management, labor, agriculture, and the public decide to do will win or lose the battle against debasement of the currency."[70] Martin hoped his plea for understanding persuaded at least a few congressmen to keep an open mind toward the Fed's goal of balanced long-term growth.

Ironically, the willingness of many economists to push for more economic growth, even at the risk of generating inflationary pressures, reflected the success of postwar fiscal and monetary policy in promoting economic stability. As Fed economist Robert Hetzel put it: "Depressions were no longer an issue. Even recessions were shorter and shallower, and economists ratcheted up their expectations of what the economy could achieve [in terms of growth]."[71] Economists such as Paul Samuelson and Walter Heller used new statistical analyses with great skill and were articulate in presenting their conclusions. Martin and the Fed economists, by contrast, appeared to be fighting the last war with their focus on inflation and the need for continued restraint.

As often happens in congressional hearings, the responses of individual congressmen were shaped by political priorities. The Fed's monetary policy came in for some criticism for excessive restraint, but Congress's attention was elsewhere. It was focused on the impact of budgetary cuts on the military and the country's ability to respond to the Soviet Union's success with Sputnik. There was some cursory attention to disparity in growth rates between the United States and the Soviet Union, but that issue was left for future consideration. Serious congressional focus on the problems of economic growth and inflation would have to wait until they reached a more critical stage.

During the months that Martin battled over inflation, a new dynamic began to affect the economy. On 15 July 1959, the United Steel Workers, led by combative David MacDonald, walked out on its negotiations with the major steel producers. It was a familiar pattern. The steel industry had a history of awarding wage increases that were well in excess of productivity increases. To restore its profit margins, the industry simply raised prices. Economists generally viewed the industry as a leading contributor to inflationary pressures. As Saulnier wrote later, the administration viewed the steel strike as an opportunity to offer support for "an effort by the industry to keep wage increases within the limits of average productivity increases . . . and to win from the unions the right to make changes in the work rules that would permit productivity improvements and make it possible to pay higher wages [without contributing to inflation]."[72] The administration's plan was to avoid intervention, encourage "responsible negotiation," and hope that the parties would work out a noninflationary contract.

After waiting two and one-half months for a resolution, the administration could no longer ignore the strike's economic impact, and in mid-November it went to court for an injunction to put the union back to work. The workers returned, negotiations continued, and an agreement was finally reached on 15 January 1960. Acknowledging the economic cost of the four-month industry shutdown, CEA Chairman Saulnier concluded that the results justified the cost: "[B]y 1959–60, wage increases, on the average, were broadly in line with productivity improvement and unit production costs were stable."[73]

The decline in economic growth caused by the steel strike threw the FOMC into confusion because it could not agree either on the likely strength of the post-strike recovery or the appropriate monetary policy. A solid minority on the FOMC was concerned that the recovery would be slow and weak. Martin, on the other hand, referred to the Fed economics staff prediction of a strong recovery and urged his associates to continue a policy of restraint: "If the System does not stand firm, and gets pulled off base by what I regard as a temporary change in public psychology [resulting from the strike], I believe we will regret this later."[74] At times like this, Martin usually was able to step back from a current dilemma and put the Fed's situation into perspective. This time he could not. The strike had badly distorted the economy; with steel production resuming, the FOMC would have to tread water while the next economic movement took shape. At the 15 December FOMC meeting, Martin confessed his inability to recommend an effective policy: "What the System does will not really make too much difference."[75] Later, he summed up his position: "At this juncture, the problem is one of rolling with the punches."[76]

The FOMC was also confused by a report from the Fed's economics staff indicating that a decline in the money supply that began in the latter part of 1959 was continuing into early 1960. Ordinarily, the resumption of economic expansion would be accompanied by an increase in the money supply, and this unexpected behavior reignited a continuing FOMC debate over the role of the money supply in determining monetary policy. There was little agreement in the FOMC or the Fed's economics staff about how changes in the money supply impacted the economy. One widely held view of the money supply was described by Robert Roosa, the leading monetary theorist in the New York Reserve Bank. He argued that the money supply was a relatively small component of the economy and not a sufficiently reliable indicator either of the forces at work in the credit markets or of the impact of the Fed's monetary policy initiatives. Moreover, by the 1950s, the traditional definition of the money supply was becoming too confining. Both individuals and corporations invested a growing portion of their liquid resources in interest-bearing short-term investments. These investments were technically not included in the money supply, but they were used in the same way as bank deposits, which were included. New definitions of the money supply were being developed to reflect these changes, but they also were proving unreliable as indicators of the impact of Fed monetary policy moves.

The FOMC's dilemma over the money supply was part of a larger debate over which indicators the committee should use to guide and monitor its policy decisions. When Martin had arrived at the Fed, the primary indicator of credit conditions used by the FOMC was net reserves (total member-bank reserves in excess of the amount of required reserves less any reserves borrowed from the Fed).[77] By 1960, this indicator was generally considered inadequate for the Fed's needs. Atlanta Reserve Bank President Malcolm Bryan proposed that the FOMC focus on total member-bank reserves because they reflected the availability of bank credit throughout the economy. He argued that total reserves were also useful because they could be correlated with the projected long-term economic growth rate. Fed Governor Canby Balderston proposed a combination of currency in circulation and required member-bank reserves for similar reasons.

The FOMC staff advisors objected to tying bank credit or any other "monetary aggregates" to economic growth targets because the Fed's flexibility to influence credit market conditions would be compromised. Too often, they argued, open-market actions necessary to achieve aggregate goals would be in direct conflict with those required for influencing more immediate credit conditions. New York Reserve Bank President Al Hayes agreed with the staff, stating that the global total reserve goals would "not provide the kind of data that would provide a practical working guide to the account manager for day-to-day operations."[78] The pragmatists, including Hayes, Martin, the FOMC's economic staff, and a majority of the governors, resisted the new proposals.

The debate over monetary policy indicators and the difficult economic environment facing the FOMC in the early months of 1960 did move Bill Martin to reexamine his monetary policy precepts. Martin regularly encouraged his FOMC associates to focus on longer-term trends in the economy and not overreact to short-term changes. Often, in the midst of a heated debate, Martin would preface a comment with: "If a visitor from Mars were to look at this situation . . .". In other cases he would argue for delay: "If we step back, we can see that the economy has not reached a turning point." He was comfortable with the FOMC's use of policy position statements that did not change for months at a time and instructions to the open-market account manager that provided considerable latitude in achieving open-market policy targets.[79] Martin could push the FOMC to move quickly when he felt that inflationary pressures were building, but in between those transitions, he often moved cautiously, waiting for a definite economic trend to become established. As Martin considered the FOMC's difficulty in negotiating the recovery from the 1957–58 recession and the extreme uncertainty of economic prospects in early 1960, he decided it was time for a change.

At the 9 February FOMC meeting, Martin described his change of heart. He carefully stepped away from his normal focus on longer-term economic trends to observe: "The Committee must be prepared to take cognizance of minor shifts in the economy as well as major shifts."[80] Signaling another modification in his thinking, Martin observed that "the System ought to be looking at the growth of the money supply."[81] This was a most remarkable statement from the same man who two months earlier had told the FOMC: "I am unable to make heads or tails of the money supply."[82] Turning to the current situation, Martin advised the FOMC to encourage "orderly growth in the economy on the assumption that the country was not in a serious downturn, but was in a modest adjustment that would require picking up."[83] In a final departure, Martin suggested that the directive to the account manager be "mildly" adjusted. If the current conditions changed, the original language could be reinstated.

The most far-reaching aspect of the change in Martin's thinking was his call to action when it was clear to most FOMC members that the economy was not undergoing a transition. Inflation appeared to be modestly declining, credit conditions were easing, and manufacturing activity was stable. There were few winds of the strength that Bill Martin would traditionally lean against. By recommending a midcourse adjustment to "pick up" the economy, Bill Martin was acknowledging that the Fed could no longer ignore the economy's growth rate. It was the beginning of a new phase in his chairmanship.

In a larger sense, Bill Martin's change of heart revealed that he was not immune to the extended debate on the role of economic growth in the national political agenda. The question of how fast the economy should grow had been raised in the mid-1950s by Truman-era CEA Chairman Leon Keyserling, a notoriously pro-growth economist. The slow recovery from the 1957–58 recession brought well-known economists John Kenneth Galbraith and Paul Samuelson into the debate on the side of higher growth. During 1959, the deliberations of the Joint Economic Committee provided a pulpit for Senator Paul Douglas to rally Democratic congressmen to the cause. The JEC study "Employment, Growth, and Price Levels" raised the political sensitivity of the growth issue by analyzing the period from 1953 to 1958 to contrast the 1.3 percent average annual growth rate for the U.S. economy to the 8 percent rate for the Soviet Union. Although most serious economists disputed Nikita Kruschev's boast that in twenty years the Soviet economy would catch up with that of the United States, the threat lent urgency to the debate.

Much of the debate centered on how much the federal government should influence the economy's growth rate. The pro-growth economists believed that the historical growth rate of 3 percent was inadequate to preserve America's economic supremacy and "bring a higher quality of life and opportunity to American men and women."[84] Pro-growth economists were unhappy with the traditional estimate of the country's long-term growth potential of 3.5 percent, made up of average productivity increases of 2.3 percent and average increases in the labor force of 1.2 percent. These economists proposed a growth rate varying between 4 and 5 percent, which was over three times the

Eisenhower administration's record. They urged the federal government to provide more growth stimulus through a combination of increased spending and tax cuts. Like Sumner Slichter before them, pro-growth economists accepted the inevitability of a certain amount of inflation to achieve their goal.

Even more conservative economists, typified by Henry Wallich, a member of the Eisenhower administration's CEA, acknowledged that "the dominant challenge to be encountered by a conservative administration is to encourage rapid growth of the economy."[85] Wallich argued that simply by avoiding recessions, the long-term annual growth rate could be measurably increased, and increased federal spending was not necessary. Wallich and those like him seemed to be arguing for a status quo that was beginning to be viewed as unsatisfactory. In contrast, the vision of a more prosperous future for all, courtesy of higher growth, steadily gained adherents.

The Eisenhower administration rejected suggestions that it raise the rate of GNP growth by cutting taxes or more budgetary spending. The most it would promise was to achieve another budgetary surplus and to keep inflation low. Eisenhower defended the policy: "The expanding economy is a thing that I have talked more about than almost any individual that I know of, publicly. I believe that economic growth in the long run cannot be soundly brought about except with stability in prices."[86] CEA Chairman Saulnier promoted budgetary surpluses that would "reduce the need to keep money tight" and allow a monetary policy more conducive to economic growth.[87] Even pro-administration economist Herb Stein was moved to admit that the administration did not focus on the issue of economic growth effectively: "The administration did not distinguish . . . much between one degree of prosperity and another. The fact that the 1959 and 1960 prosperity was a significantly lower level of prosperity, relative to the economy's potential, was not recognized as significant."[88] The administration's reluctance to engage in the growth debate was becoming a political liability for the Republicans.

Bill Martin tried to remain above the public debate on economic growth. The Fed could ill afford to be accused of taking a public position on what was becoming a highly partisan issue. Yet under the terms of the Employment Act of 1946, the Fed was committed to promoting healthy economic growth. In his February 1960 presentation to the JEC, Martin readily acknowledged the importance of economic growth "because . . . only growth can produce the substance with which to achieve our individual and national aspirations."[89] Martin attempted to strike a politically neutral stance, but when he made comments such as "[S]atisfactory economic growth and reasonable price stability are not only compatible goals, but they are necessarily interdependent," he sounded like Dwight Eisenhower.[90] It is hardly surprising, since the economic philosophies of the two men were so similar, but the compatibility made it difficult for Martin to appear nonpartisan. When congressional inquisitors attempted to draw him into a discussion about desirable rates of economic growth, Martin refused to respond. By this time Martin had spent nine years defending the Fed before Congress, and his congressional opponents knew that his refusal was final.

During the first quarter of 1960, the economy finally delivered the results that Bill Martin had pursued for five long years, a sustained decline in inflationary pressures. The economy recovered fully from the steel strike and grew at an annual rate of 7.25 percent in the first quarter, but the consumer price increase remained below 1.8 percent. CEA Chairman Saulnier advised the Eisenhower cabinet as early as February that "a marked subsidence of inflationary sentiment has occurred."[91] It took economists at the Fed another two months before they remarked on the "continuing liquidation of inflationary psychology."[92] By early July, even Martin admitted that "inflationary psychology has somewhat diminished," but he was not yet prepared to ease up on a goal that had taken so long to achieve.[93] As late as the end of July, he was asking the FOMC for continued anti-inflationary vigilance: "The adjustments now going on have long been needed and are necessary if there is to be any real revival of business. . . . Price adjustments now taking place in business thinking and speculative psychology are always painful."[94]

Another reason Bill Martin was reluctant to abandon his posture of monetary restraint was the first eruption of concern over America's balance of payments deficit. For the first ten years after World War II, one of the great dangers to the international financial system was whether there would be enough dollars to support a recovery of world trade. Although the Marshall Plan grants were replaced by loans after 1949, transfers of dollars from the United States continued at a steady pace in the form of payments for troops stationed around the world, international aid, and private investment in foreign markets. These transfers more than offset America's positive balance of trade, causing the overall U.S. balance of payments to be in deficit virtually every year. The world was enjoying the fruits of recovery and paid little attention to the deficit.

World trade continued to expand and by 1958, America's trading partners had accumulated dollar balances well in excess of their commercial and currency reserve needs. In 1950, foreigners held $7 billion in U.S. dollars but by 1958, these balances had swollen to $16 billion. The continuing U.S. balance of payments deficit became a matter of concern to foreigners since it threatened the future value of their dollar holdings. As foreigners lost their appetite for dollars, they began exchanging them for gold, and by 1958, gold sales by the United States totaled $2.3 billion. Total U.S. gold reserves at the beginning of 1958 were $23 billion, and of that amount, $12 billion was legally required as backing for the U.S. currency. At the 1958 rate of gold sales, the United States would lose all its unrestricted gold in about four years. Since the entire international financial system was constructed around the U.S. commitment to exchange dollars for gold, reducing the U.S. balance of payments deficit became a critical administration issue.

The situation percolated throughout 1959. The overall U.S. payments deficit grew from $3.9 billion to $4.6 billion that year, but gold sales declined by 60 percent. Foreign official and private dollar holders were encouraged by the administration's determination to achieve a budget surplus in fiscal year 1960 and by the Fed's public commitment to control inflation. Europeans also supported an Eisenhower administration program to reduce the payments deficit initiated in late 1959. The U.S. payments situation showed improvement during the first half of 1960, but on 20 October, the issue burst back into the headlines. Prices on the London bullion market broke through the official trading ceiling of $35 per ounce and surged to $40.60. Even the London market — the world's largest free market — was relatively small, and a normal day's trading was about $1 million. A backlog of $7 million of buy orders was enough to cause the reaction. The price ceiling had not been breached for eleven years, and the market explosion came at a particularly awkward time.

Much of the market chaos was caused by rumors that John F. Kennedy, now the Democratic Party presidential candidate, intended to devalue the U.S. dollar. Kennedy tried to address the rumors by stating that he did "not intend to tinker with the dollar in order to maintain our competitive position in the world export market."[95] His statement was far short of an unqualified commitment, and gold sales from the U.S. Treasury swelled to an annual rate of $2 billion in the third quarter of 1960. The gold price surge was the speculative froth on top of a more serious economic issue: concerns about the dollar's future were becoming a recurring worldwide problem.

Martin and Treasury Secretary Anderson conferred on the first day of the crisis. Martin advised Anderson that European central bankers knew that the U.S. trade surplus had grown sharply so far in 1960, and they remained confident in U.S. economic policy. The issue was not the attitude of central bankers, however, it was short-term speculative money flows. That afternoon Anderson released a statement saying that "it is the department's firm position to maintain the dollar price of gold at $35 per ounce, where it has been for twenty-six years."[96] These statements had yet to become ritualized, and Anderson had reason to believe that his statement would help to calm the gold markets.

Five days later, Martin and Anderson met with the director of the Bank of England, who argued that the United States had been too passive in dealing with private gold speculators. If the price premium continued, others would come to believe devaluation was in the wind, and speculative flows from the United States could increase substantially. Martin and Anderson agreed with the director's request that the Bank of England be allowed to make limited gold sales in the London bullion market on behalf of the U.S. Treasury in order to punish these speculators. In return, the Americans asked that the Bank of England address the interest rate differential between the United States and the United Kingdom. On 27 October 1960, the British discount rate was reduced from 6 to 5½ percent. Three weeks later, the German Bundesbank reduced its rate by a half percent. These actions brought European interest rates closer to those prevailing in the United States. Within weeks, the gold markets were back to normal. The Bank of England gold sales and European rate reduction represented the first coordinated international effort to deal with currency issues in some years. This episode convinced Martin and Anderson that they no longer had the luxury of ignoring international financial considerations when they made U.S. economic policy.

As he spoke at the 22 November FOMC meeting, Martin reflected on the payments crisis. He observed that the 1960 improvement in the trade balance might not be long-lived because Europeans had been willing to "buy [U.S. exports] at any price" due to the boom conditions there. The primary problem was uncompetitive "pricing of goods and services" in the United States. Earlier, he had expressed his concern that Americans might not be willing to endure the pain of reestablishing international competitiveness: "People might get panicky, when what is needed is a little steadiness in the boat and recognition that there must be some adjustments. Where price adjustments have taken place, they unquestionably have been generating some demand, but the situation is painful for those concerned."[97] In his files, Martin had saved a quote by Lord Keynes in the late 1940s: "The U.S. is becoming a high cost, high living country."[98] He feared this might be another of Keynes's prescient comments. Referring to the international concern over the intentions of the Kennedy administration, he observed: "Until the whole world has a clear understanding of what the new administration contemplates, there will be great difficulty in following a proper [monetary policy] course."[99] Martin concluded somberly with: "[T]he balance of payments problem is the most important problem for the country to deal with at this time."[100]

As the country recovered from the extremely close election of 1960 and prepared for the installation of a new administration, the economy reflected the interregnum by continuing to slide sideways. Bill Martin did not look forward to the advent of the Kennedy administration with enthusiasm. During the campaign, John Kennedy had attacked the Fed for its complicity in what he called the "stop and go" and "slow growth" policies of the Eisenhower administration. Moreover, he had criticized Martin personally for leading a "tight money" Fed. There were rumors that Kennedy would ask for Martin's resignation, even though Martin's term as chairman ran through 1963. In December, Kennedy appointed liberal economist Walter Heller to chair the CEA. Heller was one of the most outspoken critics of the Eisenhower administration's economic growth record. He was also a leading proponent of using monetary policy to lower long-term interest rates and stimulate higher economic growth. It was not a promising outlook for a Fed chairman who was a dedicated inflation fighter.

As he looked back on the Eisenhower presidency, Martin tried to assess where the country and the Fed were headed. During the past eight years, the country had traveled from fear of a postwar economic collapse to a time of peace and stability at a high level of economic activity. The forces of economic growth now came from private consumption and investment rather than from the military spending of the early 1950s. Eisenhower achieved his goal of fiscal responsibility, and his administration's success in controlling government spending and balancing the government budget made it possible for fiscal and monetary policy to work in harmony to promote stable prices and moderate economic growth. Martin had worked effectively with a Republican administration. His relations with the secretary of the Treasury and the president had improved enormously over those with the Truman administration, and at various times, each of the three had subordinated his institutional prerogatives to act together in the nation's interest. The approval of the administration's economic and monetary policies by its major trading partners was apparent in the support given to the United States as it grappled with its balance of payments problem during 1959–60. Indeed, much had been accomplished.

There were shortcomings and missed opportunities, to be sure. There had been two recessions as well as the current economic decline, which would also be defined as a recession. The Fed applied its flexible monetary policy to move quickly to ease credit conditions as the recessions developed, and in the opinion of Fed economists, the economy had recovered satisfactorily each time. Despite this progress, Martin was troubled that the Fed's monetary tools did not appear capable of heading off a recession or preventing overly easy post-recession monetary conditions. The economic downturn of 1960 was particularly worrisome. Although Martin tried a midcourse correction to restore economic growth, the economy had not responded. Operationally, he encouraged the FOMC to move beyond its narrow focus on net reserves and to incorporate other indicators such as the money supply and total reserves, but no definable progress had been made.

It also appeared that the administration, with the Fed's strong support, had struck the wrong balance between price stability and economic growth. The American electorate selected both a Democrat president and a strong Democratic congressional majority that campaigned on a platform promising higher government spending to solve social problems and to generate faster economic growth. As economic historian John Sloan has written: "Although the standard of living steadily rose during the 1950s, people were not satisfied, but wanted more. Rising expectations were not confined to the third world."[101] Concerning economic critics, Sloan observed: "Democratic Keynesian economists believed that, though the administration had achieved modest success, the knowledge was available to achieve much more."[102] Americans appeared to want a bigger pie that came from higher economic growth. They wanted to see more people employed and to add to their own family incomes, and a little inflation was an acceptable price. Neither the Eisenhower administration nor the Fed had effectively made the case to the nation that stable prices and fiscal discipline offered better long-term growth prospects than a faster growing, but inherently inflationary, economy.

Bill Martin worried that the American people were no longer willing to endure the financial pain and economic adjustments that were occasionally necessary to keep prices stable and maintain America's competitiveness in the world economy. Despite the strength of his personal convictions about traditional economic disciplines, Martin was always willing to admit that new approaches might work better. Perhaps the critics were right, and the economy could be pushed faster without creating a devastating inflation. It was possible that this old-fashioned central banker was just out of date.

During a quiet week in late December 1960, as the Eisenhower administration packed up and prepared to turn its offices over to the Kennedy administration, Bill Martin asked the Fed's general counsel to prepare a memorandum advising him on how a Federal Reserve chairman might tender a midterm resignation.

Martin at about two. Courtesy Mary Institute and St. Louis Country Day School.

Martin in 1924 as a senior in high school. Courtesy Mary Institute and St. Louis Country Day School.

Martin with his father in July 1938, a few months after his election to the presidency of the New York Stock Exchange. The *New York Herald Tribune* mistakenly used a photograph of Martin's father to accompany its article about Martin's election as Exchange chairman. Courtesy AP Wide World Photos.

Martin with SEC Chairman Jerome Frank on 8 December 1938, after a sharp debate over the pace of reform at the New York Stock Exchange that was broadcast nationally. Courtesy AP Wide World Photos.

Private Martin, photographed in July 1941 during his U.S. Army basic training at Camp Croft, South Carolina. This was a publicity shot, since Martin had no known affection for cats. Courtesy AP Wide World Photos.

Martin, as Export-Import Bank chairman, signing a loan agreement in July 1947 with Francis Lacoste, representing France. Martin tried unsuccessfully to shrink the size of the loan to the French government. Courtesy AP Wide World Photos.

Martin being sworn in as chairman of the Federal Reserve System by Chief Justice Fred Vinson on 2 April 1951. His predecessor, Thomas MaCabe, looks on. Courtesy AP Wide World Photos.

Martin in his official "home" for nineteen years, the boardroom of the Federal Reserve System headquarters in Washington, D.C., April 1964. Courtesy AP Wide World Photos.

Martin and Lyndon Johnson meeting with reporters at the Johnson ranch on 7 December 1965, after discussing the Fed's increase in the discount rate. The administration had heavily pressured Martin to avoid an increase. Courtesy AP Wide World Photos.

An apprehensive Martin and Treasury Secretary Henry Fowler prepare to accompany Lyndon Johnson on a high-speed tour of the Johnson ranch in December 1965. Courtesy Corbis New York.

Bicycle Built For Two

An editorial cartoon by Herb Block in the 8 December 1965 edition of the *Washington Post*, portraying Martin in a favorite guise, the out-of-date and conservative banker. Courtesy the Herblock Foundation.

Portrait of the Martin family in the 1960s. Pictured with Martin are his wife, Cynthia, and children Cynthia, Diana, and William 3rd. Courtesy Mrs. Diana Martin Burgess.

Martin meeting with the international press in Washington, D.C., on 17 March 1968 to announce the agreement by seven leading central banks to support a two-tier system for pricing sales in the London gold market. Courtesy AP Wide World Photos.

Bill and Cynthia Martin at a dinner in the late 1980s in honor of the International Tennis Hall of Fame in Newport, Rhode Island. Courtesy Joseph F. Cullman, 3rd.

8

Gunfight on the New Frontier:
The Kennedy Years

During the interregnum between John F. Kennedy's razor-thin victory in the 1960 presidential election and his inauguration, much of the world watched in fascination, waiting to see what changes the appealing young senator would bring. The world's financial markets retained an uneasy calm following the central bank cooperation that had ended the run on the London gold market the previous October. European bankers believed that if Kennedy's campaign promises to increase spending and lower interest rates were realized, the dollar's value would be a casualty. Thoughtful American observers pictured Kennedy as stymied by an economy in recession, a surging balance of payments deficit, and without an electoral mandate for any of his campaign promises. A common view within the business community, at home and abroad, was that under any scenario, the prospects for the U.S. economy were not promising.

The view within the Fed was similar to its European counterparts. At the end of November 1960, the FOMC reviewed the prospects for the economy under the new administration. Martin observed that despite his statement about preserving the value of the dollar, Kennedy did not understand how foreign central bankers viewed the Fed: "The system is seen as playing fast and loose with the credit of the US . . . due to the easy monetary policy we have been pursuing."[1] Earlier, he had lashed out at the statements of several Kennedy economic advisors who proposed that "all our problems — the budget, the cost-price relationship, debt management policy, and the like — could be solved if the System would just raise short-term interest rates and lower long-term interest rates."[2] While Martin certainly understood that much of the criticism was campaign rhetoric, his remarks revealed his anxiety about dealing with the new administration. The compatible relationship between the Fed and the Eisenhower administration was over, and Martin could see increasing tensions between the Fed and the Kennedy administration.

These harsh comments, so unusual for Martin, also reflected his concern about his own status, which was more complicated than ever. Kennedy's criticism of Martin and the Fed during the campaign raised questions about Martin's future. The *New York Times* referred to "reliable reports that the President-elect wants Federal Reserve Board Chairman William McChesney Martin to resign by January 20."[3] In a moment of unguarded candor, Martin observed within the hearing of an alert reporter: "The president has a chip on his shoulder about the Federal Reserve System." A few days later the comment made its way into the press, and a transition spokesman responded that "the President-elect has remarked that 'Mr. Martin's got a chip on his shoulder and I'm going to knock it off!'"[4] The dueling statements caused so much press attention that Kennedy had to publicly disclaim the resignation request rumor. For two men who would have to work together on potentially divisive issues, Kennedy and Martin managed to get off to the worst start imaginable.

The public speculation on his possible resignation caused some internal conflict for Martin. The issue of having the Fed chairman's four-year term begin with the president's surfaced regularly, generated heated debate, and always fell victim to Congress's reluctance to begin tinkering with the legislative mandate of the Federal Reserve System. Martin himself had agreed in congressional hearings in the 1950s that changing the Fed chairman's term to coincide with the president's would be desirable. It was in that spirit that he had offered his resignation when Dwight Eisenhower became president and had been considering offering it to Kennedy.

The pressure for his resignation coming from the Kennedy transition organization had the opposite effect on Martin: it made him determined to remain in office. One of his most dearly held principles was that the Fed, and particularly its chairman, be seen as nonpolitical. Now that the Fed and he were under strong partisan pressure, the "best demonstration of this principle [of the Fed's nonpartisanship] is for me to remain in my position until my term is over."[5] In addition, he "had an obligation to my supporters in the System and to those in private life who have been defending the System" to fight for the Fed's independence.[6] No matter how difficult it might be to develop a working relationship with John Kennedy, Martin would "do the best he could" to establish one. The Fed and the nation deserved no less. If experience proved that it could not be done, that was a decision for another day.

As early indications of the likely economic policies of the Kennedy administration emerged, Martin began to reconsider the difficulty of cooperating with it. On 6 January 1961, the transition team released a long-awaited series of recommendations on economic policy authored by Professor Paul Samuelson, Kennedy's primary economic advisor. He described the economy as "sluggish and tired" but warned that "what definitely is not called for is a massive program of hastily devised public works whose primary purpose is merely that of making jobs and getting money pumped into the economy."[7] The *New York Times* applauded the report, saying that it "gives evidence of informed understanding of the problems we face and of willingness to take needed action . . . but is markedly cautious."[8] On 10 January, Treasury Secretary–designate Douglas Dillon told his Senate confirmation panel that the recession was expected to cause a budgetary deficit in fiscal year 1962, but that "balancing the budget is highly important."[9] He also stated his view that budgetary surpluses in boom times should balance out recessionary budget deficits. It was the kind of fiscal orthodoxy from a Treasury secretary that brought cheer to the heart of a Federal Reserve chairman. Despite Martin's apprehension about his personal relationship with John Kennedy, it seemed possible that Martin would be able to work with Kennedy's economic team, if their initial comments were reliable.

Martin first expressed interest in cooperating with the administration to Douglas Dillon in December 1960, and in mid-January he described his desire to Walter Heller. Kennedy had asked Heller to "visit with Bill Martin and assess whether he would be cooperative or obstructionist." Heller recounted that Martin said, "I am not going to give up the independence of the Fed," and Heller reassured him, "That's not what the President's going to ask you to do."[10] Martin told Heller that he had no intention of resigning and that "there is plenty of room for cooperation here."[11] Heller later advised Kennedy that Martin "went out of his way to be cooperative and he [Martin] foresees successful coordination of policy under President Kennedy."[12]

Martin remained worried as he approached his first meeting with the new president, for he knew comparatively little about John Kennedy. The presidents with whom he had previously worked, Harry Truman and Dwight Eisenhower, had leadership styles and general economic philosophies that were well publicized, but this was not the case with Kennedy. Douglas Dillon advised Martin that he had spoken to Kennedy on Martin's behalf and that the media had done Kennedy and Martin a disservice by describing Kennedy's general concern about monetary policy in terms of his unhappiness with Martin personally. Dillon's assurances were encouraging, but Martin would have to see for himself. Kennedy's staff described the president as "fiscally conservative, in that he prefers balanced to unbalanced budgets."[13] Kennedy had assembled a well-known group of economic advisors, all of whom were Keynsians.[14] Martin would have to put his trust in comments like those in *Time* magazine: "When his idealist professors give Kennedy advice, he listens attentively, blots up their words, and then makes his own decision."[15]

Martin and Dillon met with Kennedy in the Oval Office on 1 February. Martin's first words were to the effect that he had indeed made the reported statement about Kennedy and a "chip on his shoulder." He wanted the president to know that, as Fed chairman, he regretted publicly criticizing the president-elect. Martin affirmed his support for the administration's early policy statements and informed Kennedy that the Fed was in the process of reappraising its monetary policy. He mentioned his optimism about Fed-Treasury relations based on his conversations with Dillon and repeated his observation to Heller that there would be many opportunities for the Fed to cooperate with the administration.[16] The emphasis on cooperation was vintage Bill Martin. He believed that the Fed chairman's ability to work with the president set the tone for the relationship between the Fed and the administration. Martin had failed in his attempt to establish an effective working relationship with Harry Truman but had achieved considerable success with Dwight Eisenhower. He had to find a way to overcome a climate of distrust with John Kennedy, and he must have hoped his apology would create an opportunity for a fresh start.

John Kennedy's first impressions of Martin are unrecorded, but Martin's straightforwardness in his dealings with the president, so evident in that first encounter, became a fundamental element in their relationship. Kennedy is often quoted to this effect by Martin and several others.

If Martin had given a fuller picture to Kennedy, he would have admitted that the main reason the Fed was reappraising its monetary policy was not to find ways to cooperate with the new administration but rather reflected the FOMC's conclusion that its traditional policy approach was not working. To combat the recession that had begun in the second quarter of 1960, the Fed initiated a program of active ease and pushed reserves into the banking system. This action, coupled with the normal decline in required reserves as bank lending followed the economy downward, increased the net reserve position of member banks by $1 billion. The 1960 economic decline was shallower than its predecessors but was much slower to respond to the Fed's easing.

Ordinarily, the Fed would have continued to push down on short-term rates until the economy began to exhibit a decisive response. The Treasury bill rate fell to a low of 0.9 percent during the 1953–54 recession and 0.6 percent in the 1957–58 recession. In the fall of 1960, the bill rate was still at 2.14 percent, but the Fed faced a dilemma in pushing it lower.

Historically, the Fed concentrated only on the domestic impact of the decline in short-term rates, but because of the balance of payments deficit, the international impact of Fed monetary policy could no longer be ignored. As the Fed pursued a program of active ease, its open-market operations pushed Treasury bill yields down. As short-term rates fell, U.S. investors looked to foreign money markets for higher short-term returns. The outflow of these funds increased the balance of payments deficit. In the 25 October 1960 FOMC meeting, New York Reserve Bank President Alfred Hayes warned the committee: "[T]he sharp decline in bill rates has doubtless been a significant factor in the serious deterioration in the balance of payments deficit in the third quarter."[17] The culprit was the Bills Only policy, which forced the Fed to limit open-market operations to the bill market. Everyone on the FOMC understood the issue, including Bill Martin.

As he did so often, Martin formed an FOMC subcommittee to study whether to end the Bills Only policy. This was one of the rare times that Martin was unenthusiastic about the likely outcome. He observed that "there is a very real question whether the System can operate in longer maturities for more than a very brief period without running into difficulties. I do not want us to fall back into [setting] a pattern of rates."[18] He was deeply concerned that once the Fed entered the long-term market, it would open itself to administration pressure to force long-term rates down. Martin believed that the Fed could move easily in and out of the bill market because the market was broad and trading was active. Because trading in individual Treasury issues was much less active, Fed officials were not confident they could predict the impact of open-market operations in this end of the market. In addition, long-term interest rates were dominated by mortgage financing and debt issues by corporations and municipalities, and price changes in Treasury issues were not the major factor in determining long-term interest rates.

Setting his own reservations aside, Martin joined other subcommittee members to recommend suspending the Bills Only rule by implementing a program of "transactions outside the bill area." The recommendation was accepted by the FOMC in early February 1961. Martin's description of what persuaded him to support the recommendation reveals how he reached his important decisions. First, he accepted the argument that "in view of the very heavy barrage, both from within and outside Government, against the System for its unwillingness to change its own operating procedures and policies, . . . the System has to give some tangible indication of open-mindedness and willingness to experiment."[19] Second, he told the FOMC that "no progress can be made [on the issue] by the device of papers, studies, or committee reports. There has to be evidence accumulated from actual experiment, and the sooner the System gets busy obtaining empirical data, the better it will be."[20] Martin also told the FOMC that his interviews with dealers in the treasury market indicated "they were divided in their judgments" about the potential impact of the proposed change.[21] In Martin's mind, as long as some knowledgeable market professionals thought the plan was feasible, it should be tried.

Martin's thought process was a textbook example of pragmatic decision making: be willing to modify or even abandon long-standing practices when they cease to work, be sensitive to the views of outside critics as well as those who would be affected by the decision, and before making a final commitment, test critical assumptions by careful experimentation with the new approach.

Despite Martin's conversion, many FOMC and staff members remained firmly unconvinced, and feelings ran high. The most serious challenge came from those who argued that the bond market's response to a Fed "experiment" would not provide a true indication of market behavior. The Fed should announce a permanent policy change to get a reliable reaction, and then it would have to publicly reverse its decision if the new policy failed. Martin's most trusted advisor, FOMC Secretary Ralph Young, argued that trying to affect long-term rates at the same time the Fed was influencing short-term rates would inevitably force the Fed into "continuous administration of the [entire] interest rate structure and continuous intervention in the market. . . . Continuous use of this authority will result in something pretty close to, if not actually, a peg."[22] Undeterred by the doubters, Martin won a majority of the FOMC by emphasizing the experimental nature of the policy change and by maintaining that "I have doubts about the outcome."[23] Martin's skepticism convinced the proposal's opponents that the test would truly be objective and that they were not facing a foregone conclusion.

Ever since the inception of Bills Only in 1953, Fed critics had doubted its wisdom. Referring to a personal poll, Paul Samuelson wrote in 1960: "I recall that out of 20 supposed expert economists, only 3 were in favor of bills only, with another few willing to reserve judgment."[24] Fed critic Daniel Ahearn wrote in 1965 that "there seems to be little doubt that monetary policy did create too much liquidity in the 1954 and 1958 recessions and that 'bills only' was a major reason why this happened."[25] It is also true that Martin repeatedly defended the policy within the FOMC and prior to 1961, never formally considered a serious reexamination of its validity. The rule periodically came up for FOMC reauthorization, and each time Allan Sproul or Alfred Hayes suggested that the rule be qualified by adding "as a general rule" or "primarily," Martin strongly opposed it. While the Fed unofficially called its practice "bills preferably," during the period 1953–60, the fact remains that the Fed's open-market desk rarely dealt in anything but bills. Martin downplayed the differences over Bills Only: "This is more of a new technique than a new policy."[26] While Martin's comment is disingenuous in minimizing the implications of the change, it does reflect his pragmatism in accepting the reality of changed circumstances.

As the Kennedy administration's first year unfolded, a sustained economic recovery began, but the unemployment rate remained frozen at 6.8 percent. Kennedy's political aides worried about the political cost of failing to "get the country moving again" sufficiently to bring unemployment down. The man who provided Kennedy with the answer was CEA Chairman Walter Heller. As is often the case with presidential appointments, the decision to appoint Heller was made on the basis of a first impression, and in this case it proved to be an exceptional choice. During a campaign stop in Minneapolis, Kennedy had a brief encounter with Heller orchestrated by Senator Hubert Humphrey and Paul Samuelson. The candidate peppered Heller with questions for "about ten minutes."[27] Kennedy was impressed with Heller's "approach to problems and his ability to field questions swiftly."[28] Without any additional contact with Heller, Kennedy offered him the chairman's job in mid-December 1960.

Heller brought talents and ambitions that were very different from those of his four predecessors in the CEA chairmanship. He was the first Keynesian economist to hold the post and as such was the first to assert the dominance of fiscal policy over monetary policy for achieving the economic growth needed to fully utilize the economy's productive capacity. He also believed that as long as there were unused productive capacity and unemployed labor, the government could pursue expansionary spending policies and incur budgetary deficits without fear of igniting inflation. He had ambitions for the CEA that were well beyond those of his predecessors. From the very beginning, Heller served as an influential advisor to Kennedy and inserted the CEA in an instrumental role on a variety of economic policy issues.

But what made Heller uniquely effective were his personal qualities. He possessed the ability to describe complicated economic ideas in layperson's terms, and he had a feel for the political implications of economic policy decisions. In contrast to many of his predecessors, he was not doctrinaire, and he combined a pragmatic flexibility with a modest, easygoing personality that generated cooperation rather than battles over bureaucratic turf. Beneath his calm exterior were enormous reserves of energy, a zeal for educating and persuading others, and an appetite for work. He also attracted two extremely able associates to serve with him: James Tobin, a highly regarded and original economic thinker who would go on to win the Nobel Prize in economics, and Kermit Gordon, a former Rhodes scholar specializing in labor and economic development issues.

Heller was fortunate to have an apt and willing pupil in John Kennedy. Before becoming president, Kennedy had had limited interest in economic issues. Kennedy aide Ted Sorensen recalled that Kennedy told him that, in his pre-presidential days, "he could remember the difference between fiscal policy and monetary policy only by reminding himself that the name of the man most in charge of monetary policy, Federal Reserve Chairman Martin, began with an 'M' as in 'monetary'."[29] Heller soon learned that Kennedy was interested in economic issues: "One could write a ten-page memo and not feel that his interest would flag . . . and he was willing to penetrate and find out what lay beneath some of the recommendations."[30] As the president responded positively to Heller's advice, Heller became more forceful about the need to lower interest rates and raise the economy's growth rate. By late March 1961, the CEA chairman was prodding Kennedy to tell Martin that "the time has come not for nudging [interest rates] but for a real shove . . . to make investment funds abundant and inexpensive."[31]

Walter Heller's growing influence on John Kennedy and his determination to achieve an easier monetary policy would have created an early conflict between the administration and Bill Martin were it not for the countervailing influence of Treasury Secretary Douglas Dillon. Dillon's route into the Kennedy administration was much more predictable than Heller's. Kennedy was well aware that his campaign pledges had not been well received in U.S. or European financial communities. He wanted a Treasury secretary who could generate political support for his administration's economic program and, equally important, would be fully accepted by the financial establishment. He asked two giants of the World War II generation of public servants, John McCloy and Robert Lovett, if they would serve as Treasury secretary, but both demurred, citing their ages.

When Kennedy looked for a younger Treasury candidate, Dillon's name surfaced at the head of the list. There had even been rumors that Richard Nixon would have asked Dillon to serve as his Treasury secretary had the opportunity presented itself. Despite a leading position in the Eisenhower administration, Dillon was convinced that its economic policies had restricted economic growth and that it had failed to encourage individual initiative by reducing wartime tax rates. His candidacy offered Kennedy two critical assets, a solid reputation in Republican and financial circles and an economic philosophy that fit well with Kennedy's.

Dillon brought unusually broad government service to a cabinet position too often filled by men like John Snyder and George Humphrey, whose past experience did not adequately prepare them for the conflicting demands in a high-profile public position. Dillon's government experience began in 1940, when he was thirty-one and served three years as assistant to Navy Undersecretary James V. Forrestal, who was beginning his own distinguished public service career. After a career in investment banking at the firm founded by his father, Dillon was rewarded for his enthusiastic support of Dwight Eisenhower's presidential campaign by being appointed ambassador to France. Through hard work and his innately diplomatic personal style, he became well regarded in France and in the State Department. In 1957, Dillon was brought back to Washington, ultimately to serve as undersecretary of state for economic affairs. His highest achievement in that position was to convert a disintegrating relic of the Marshall Plan, the Organization for European Economic Cooperation (OEEC), into a refocused international economic development body, the Organization for Economic Cooperation and Development (OECD).

Once he was confirmed as Treasury secretary, Dillon quickly established his imprint on the new administration's economic policies. His style was not to dominate meetings by his personality, which was modest and unpretentious, but by his ideas, which were calmly and carefully presented. He was usually the best-informed person in the room, and he had a passion for facts that meshed perfectly with John Kennedy's thought process. Dillon supported Heller when he told the Senate: "I believe there is no contradiction between sound fiscal policy and a more rapid rate of growth."[32] At the same time he supported the Fed by telling Kennedy: "The Fed was right when it restricted credit late in the 1958–59 boom."[33] Dillon threw cold water on Heller's proposal for a temporary tax cut if the economy did not respond to the spending increases in the fiscal 1962 budget. The expansionary rhetoric of the campaign, which was still incorporated in Heller's memorandums, began to lose out to the advice of Dillon and JFK's political aide Ted Sorensen. Dillon recommended the benefits of fiscal discipline for the balance of payments, and Sorensen emphasized the fiscal conservatism of congressional leaders who would decide the fate of the administration's legislative proposals.

Dillon's presence in the cabinet offered crucial support to Bill Martin in the early months of the Kennedy administration. Martin and Dillon shared many personal characteristics: both were modest, diplomatic, and pragmatic. The description of Dillon's negotiating style — "he had a clear concept of what is attainable . . . believing it is better to give a bit today and leave the way open to victory tomorrow" — could have easily been written about Martin.[34] Both men were equally committed to market-based solutions to economic policy issues. They first met on Wall Street in the late 1930s, and their common experience led them to place a high value on retaining the confidence of the financial community in the prudence of the government's fiscal and monetary policies. Dillon's statement "The US should continue as banker for the world" echoed similar comments by Martin.[35]

Douglas Dillon's calming presence could not smooth all the differences among Kennedy's economic advisors, and it was not long before the Fed and the CEA were in open disagreement. The issue was one of the administration's most pressing problems, reducing the unemployment rate. The CEA was unanimous in its view that as long as the economy performed under its potential, there would be excess unemployment. The only solution was to expand the economy at a higher rate of growth through an easy monetary policy and Keynesian fiscal action in the form of a temporary tax cut. Heller justified his approach to the JEC in March 1961 by arguing that "unemployment pockets that now seem intractable will turn out to be manageable in an environment of full prosperity."[36] Using arguments that skillfully combined economic and political goals, Heller privately urged Kennedy to ignore budgetary deficits and if necessary pursue a tax cut because a "vigorous use of fiscal policy would be greeted as a bold and pioneering stroke, in keeping with the magnitude of the recovery problem and the activist image of the administration."[37]

Fed economists and officers viewed the unemployment issue from a very different perspective. The orthodox view at the Fed was that most unemployment resulted from structural problems — that is, unemployed workers who were without needed skills or were unwilling to move to where the jobs were. The Fed monitored employment and output in manufacturing and concluded that strong productivity increases were reducing the demand for unskilled manufacturing workers. In that case, job retraining programs and relocation assistance were the most cost-effective solution to the problem. The Fed was concerned that seeking an unrealistically low unemployment rate would force fiscal and monetary policy into an overly expansionary posture. In his presentation before the JEC in March, Martin outlined the Fed's view on the causes of structural unemployment and identified the nonstructural portion of unemployment as cyclical, predicting it "should prove only temporary."[38] Martin defined the Fed's responsibility as "to do our share in combating the cyclical causes as effectively as we can by fostering the financial conditions favorable to growth. Attempts to reduce structural unemployment by massive monetary and fiscal stimulation of over-all demands likely will have to be carried to such lengths as to create serious inflationary problems."[39]

The views Martin and Heller presented to the JEC in March 1961 were in such stark contrast that the committee chairman, Senator Paul Douglas, threatened to call the two men back to the hearing room to reconcile their differences. When John Kennedy heard of the problem, he hurriedly summoned his economic team and Martin to the White House. Both sides presented their arguments once again, but Kennedy cut the meeting short by observing that he did see much of a difference between the positions. Heller later told his associate Tobin that "we papered over our differences of opinion" to accommodate the president.[40] A week later, Kennedy told a press conference: "I do not think that regardless of whether the unemployment we now have is structural or not, and some of it is structural and some of it is not, I do not believe we should live with the present rate of unemployment."[41] Kennedy achieved a truce, but as in many truces, neither side was prepared to abandon the conflict.

The potential rift sensitized Heller and Dillon to the importance of improving communication with Martin, and Dillon pressed the president to resume meetings of the Eisenhower administration's "little four." That grouping, consisting of the president and the Treasury secretary along with the chairmen of the CEA and the Fed, had played a vital role in Eisenhower's economic policy planning. Heller proposed adding the director of the Bureau of the Budget, and he sought out a new name. He decided on the Quadriad, based on Webster's definition, " 'A union or group of four. Rare.' That's us," he concluded.[42]

It was not long before the Quadriad began to prove its usefulness. During his first year in office, Kennedy became more confident about the wisdom of the CEA's advice, and Heller used his access to the president to push harder for an expansionary monetary policy. When he felt that Martin needed prodding on monetary policy, Heller would urge Kennedy to call a meeting of the Quadriad, as he did in May 1961, informing him: "Your announced policy [of pursuing lower] interest rates is in jeopardy . . . because of the Fed's loss of conviction and heart in applying the present policy. Martin's back needs to be stiffened."[43]

When the Quadriad actually met, however, Heller and Martin tended to moderate their differences in deference to the president, and Dillon usually weighed in on the side of the Fed. Kennedy's comments often reinforced the majority view expressed by Dillon and Martin, but he usually couched his support in the context of achieving higher economic growth or reducing the balance of payments deficit. Heller and the CEA were often frustrated that they could not force Martin to actively support the CEA's plan to raise short-term interest rates (to discourage the outflow of short-term funds) and simultaneously lower long-term interest rates (to promote economic growth), which they dubbed "Operation Nudge." They took comfort from the fact that their analysis showed the Fed to be more active in supplying reserves (and easing monetary conditions) during the days preceding Quadriad meetings.[44]

The Quadriad meetings, which took place about every two months, offered Martin and Heller an opportunity to make their respective cases to the president, and neither man had to resort to politicking in order to be sure that Kennedy heard their views. Heller later described his conviction that "it [the Quadriad] isn't too bad an arrangement, provided there is good will, competent people, and reasonably systematic consultation and presidential participation."[45] Bill Martin was equally succinct: "It is a very good device to make it possible for me to talk to the president at convenient intervals without being forced into it."[46] Reflecting on Martin's performance in the Quadriad, Walter Heller observed: "Bill Martin knew how to strike a balance between safeguarding his independence and being a team player. He felt he was having some influence on other policies of the government, especially fiscal policy, and we felt that we had a right to have some influence on Fed policies."[47]

Walter Heller may have been disappointed in the results of his effort to directly influence the Fed, but he had more success in a flanking movement: influencing the president's choice of candidates for the board of governors of the Federal Reserve System. Heller was the first CEA chairman to see the value of placing activist, pro-administration economists on the Fed's board of governors. Again, John Kennedy was a willing pupil, and Heller quoted the president on the subject: "About the only power I have over the Federal Reserve is the power of appointment, and I want to use it."[48] In May 1961, Heller focused on the position that would be open when Fed Governor Mike Szymczak's term ended that August. Heller was determined to promote the selection of a trained professional economist who would be a "liberal expansionary influence" on the board.[49]

The Banking Act of 1935 not only centralized the Fed's policy-making powers in the board of governors and its newly created position of chairman, it also gave the governors a majority of seats on a more powerful FOMC. Nevertheless, the Roosevelt administration and Chairman Marriner Eccles ignored the governors. Subsequent administrations also downplayed the importance of choosing them, and typical candidates tended to be men with a limited range of experience. By the time Heller looked into the matter, the governors consisted of two former college deans, a former deputy in the office of the Comptroller of the Currency, two former small-town bankers, and Martin. Szymczak had been the controller of the City of Chicago. The majority of these men had experience in governing public or banking institutions, and with rare exception, politics did not play a decisive role in their selection. There had never been a governor who was trained as an economist, nor did any governor come to office with any particular background in monetary policy issues.

During the period after 1935, the Fed chairman and the Treasury secretary discussed the opening, and the ultimate appointee usually emerged as a result of their combined effort to identify potential candidates. This practice continued into the 1960s, and Martin and Treasury Secretary Dillon were discussing a proposal that one of Dillon's assistant Treasury secretaries, Joseph W. Barr, be the candidate for the governorship. When Heller heard of their deliberations, he knew he would have to work fast to offer Kennedy an alternative. Heller combed through his professional contacts and settled on George W. Mitchell, a vice president and chief economist at the Chicago Reserve Bank. He was an inspired choice.

Mitchell was from Chicago, the same Federal Reserve district from which Szymczak had come, and held a Ph.D. in economics. He had earned his liberal stripes by serving as economic advisor to Adlai Stevenson during his unsuccessful presidential campaign in 1956. He had been in the Chicago Reserve Bank for eleven years. Heller determined that Mitchell had Keynesian leanings and yet was well regarded within the Fed. Heller promoted Mitchell's candidacy with Kennedy, advising him: "His [Mitchell's] general sympathy lies strongly with the president. He is not prepared to accept every move that Bill Martin makes."[50] Leaving nothing to chance, Heller asked Richard Daley, the influential Chicago mayor, to call the White House and support Mitchell. With Kennedy's approval in hand, Heller informed Dillon and Martin of the president's decision to propose Mitchell. Martin could see that Heller had done his homework: Martin could hardly object to the appointment of the chief economist in the Chicago Reserve Bank. Heller later described the reality that faced Martin: "At that very late stage of the game, it was virtually a fete [*sic*] accompli."[51] George Mitchell was appointed a Fed governor on 27 June 1961.

It should be noted that by securing the appointment of George Mitchell, Walter Heller permanently raised the standards for successful governor candidates in terms of their professional background and exposure to issues of economic or monetary policies. Within a few years, there were so many professional economists on the board that Martin was moved to push the president for the appointment of noneconomists to secure a better balance in the makeup of the board. There is no question that the increasing complexity of the Fed's open-market operations, the sophistication of the analytical tools used to evaluate monetary policy options, and the importance of international operations all argue that a solid background in economics is necessary for a Reserve Board governor to be an effective contributor to monetary policy decisions.

From mid-1961 to mid-1962, the economy entered one of those benign periods during which economic policy makers prayed that their policies were responsible for bringing it about and that it would continue indefinitely. The administration got the economic growth it was seeking. The GNP expanded at an average rate of 6 percent during the period, although the quarterly rate of increase was slowing by mid-1962. Even unemployment moved grudgingly downward, and by the end of June 1962 it fell from its peak of 6.8 percent to 5.4 percent. The Fed noted that bank credit had increased at an annual rate of 8 percent, while inflation remained quiescent at 1.3 percent. Moreover, "Operation Twist," as Walter Heller now called the administration's intention of manipulating both ends of the yield curve, was enjoying modest success.[52] Treasury bill yields had risen from 2.23 percent to 2.79 percent during the twelve months, while long-term Treasury bond rates had declined from 3.74 percent to 3.6 percent. An editorial in the *Journal of Commerce* congratulated the Fed on the "professional dexterity" of its trading operations and its ability to assure the bond market that it "has no intention to maintain any specific yield rate level, but is merely making more funds available in the long term market."[53]

One of the most important developments during this twelve-month period was the Fed's decision to maintain a policy posture of credit ease. By a comparable number of months after the low point of the recessions in 1953–54 and 1957–58, interest rates had already moved steadily upward, and the money supply and bank credit were no longer increasing. During these prior recoveries, the Fed had been highly concerned about the rekindling of inflation and had tightened credit conditions in order to "sop up" much of the liquidity it had previously injected into the banking system in order to combat the recession. Analysts ascribed the low inflation rate during the recovery of 1961–62 to a number of factors: the sharp increase in productivity, the existence of substantial excess industrial capacity and unemployed workers, and the hard-won lowering of inflationary expectations achieved by the Eisenhower administration. The increase in the CPI remained below 1.5 percent and enabled the FOMC to maintain a policy of ease throughout the period.

Other elements contributing to an atmosphere conducive to low inflation were the administration's policy on wages and prices and a spectacular confrontation over pricing with the U.S. Steel Co. The administration's wage-price policy began in early 1961 when Walter Heller and Arthur Goldberg, Kennedy's secretary of labor, convinced the president to establish an Advisory Committee on Labor-Management Policy. The committee served as a forum for the two men to engage management and labor in a dialogue about wage and price issues. During the rest of the year, the CEA refined its theory that limiting wage increases to the level of historical productivity increases should stabilize labor costs per unit of production and eliminate any need to raise prices to offset labor cost increases. In January 1962, Heller persuaded Kennedy to formally announce a set of "guideposts" that laid out the "conditions" under which management and labor were to negotiate noninflationary wage contracts and price increases. The guideposts were not supported by legislation or enforceable sanctions, and it fell to Heller and Goldberg to convince management and labor to consider the public interest in their deliberations. The two worked tirelessly through personal contacts and public speeches to build public support for the guideposts.

It was not long before the guideposts bumped into the hard realities of the bargaining table. The administration decided in mid-1961 that the upcoming wage negotiations for the steel industry would be a crucial test case. The 1959 steel strike had wrecked the Eisenhower administration's economic policy for recovery from the 1957–58 recession, and Kennedy's advisors were determined to avoid a repetition. In the fall of 1961, the administration quietly lobbied the industry and the union, and on 6 April 1962, the negotiators announced a contract with an annual wage increase of 2.5 percent. The annual increase was only one-third of the average increase over the last twenty years and was well below the industry's historical annual productivity increase.

Four days later, the administration was still enjoying its success when U.S. Steel CEO Roger Blough presented Kennedy a copy of an announcement of a 3.5 percent across-the-board price increase, to "catch up" for an increase proposed in September 1961 but deferred at the insistence of the administration. Kennedy, feeling that he had been double-crossed by management and made to look like a fool before the union negotiators, exploded in anger. Special assistant Ted Sorensen later wrote that after Blough left "Kennedy recalled his father's fight with steel industry leaders when he was on the Federal Maritime Board and said 'My father always told me that steel men were sons-of-bitches, but I never realized till now how right he was.' "[54]

The administration quickly mobilized to force U.S. Steel, and the other steel producers that immediately joined in the price increase, to reverse their decision. The Justice Department, the Defense Department, and Congress all began investigations. The media spotlight shone incessantly on the besieged steelmen. A tense forty-eight hours later, U.S. Steel threw in the towel and announced that it rescinded the price increase. Roger Blough bitterly observed that "never before in the nation's history have so many forces of the Federal Government been marshaled against a single industry."[55] The rescission was hailed as a victory for the presidency, for John Kennedy, and for the guideposts.

As he stood on the sidelines, Bill Martin worried about the price John Kennedy was paying for his victory. Businesspeople had generally favored Richard Nixon in the 1960 election and were fond of saying that the "jury is still out" on President Kennedy. Business leaders generally appeared shocked at the all-out attack on the steel industry. The *Wall Street Journal* decried what it termed Kennedy's use of "naked power."[56] Martin was convinced that the fallout from the conflict could permanently damage the confidence of the business community in the Kennedy administration and put a damper on business investment, a crucial underpinning for economic growth. Martin encouraged Kennedy to meet with Blough and offered to use his personal friendship with the U.S. Steel CEO to bring the men together.

After some initial resistance, Kennedy finally agreed to a meeting, and on 17 April Martin and Blough met secretly with Kennedy in the White House. Blough revealed his political insensitivity by admitting that he was "genuinely surprised" by Kennedy's response to the price decision.[57] Now that he had prevailed, Kennedy could afford to be gracious and assured Blough that "he bore no grudges."[58] At his next press conference Kennedy announced that Blough had accepted Kennedy's offer to head a Business Council Presidential Advisory Committee. Martin was pleased that he had brokered a reconciliation between the two men, but he knew that it would be a long time, if ever, before the business community forgave Kennedy.

Martin's concern about business sentiment was reinforced by a steady stock market decline that brought the Dow Jones Industrial Average (DJIA) down 10 percent between 11 April and 3 May 1962. The administration began to worry about a "Kennedy Bear Market." Walter Heller tried to reassure the president that the decline occurred because "the stock market has been highly valued by historical standards . . . and because the outlook for price stability, reinforced by the steel episode, and lowered inflation expectations take some of the steam out of stocks."[59] The DJIA slid downward another 10 percent over the next three weeks, and on Monday, 28 May, the index lost almost 6 percent in the largest one-day drop since the 1929 crash. Kennedy's shaken economic advisors met the next morning to discuss how to respond to the situation.

Dillon and Martin began by relating that in their Wall Street experience, sharp declines of this magnitude almost always proved temporary. Heller reiterated his conclusion that investors were digesting the prospects for a more competitive industrial price environment and the market would soon adjust to the new level of expectations. Kennedy was unmoved and persisted with his concern that "the market fall will drag the economy down with it."[60] Alternatives were developed, including a "fireside chat" to reassure the nation, announcing a speedup in federal spending for public works, a "quickie" tax cut of $5–10 billion, and finally, a reduction in the margin requirement for borrowing to purchase stocks on the New York Stock Exchange. A consensus began to form around a margin reduction, but setting margin requirements was the responsibility of the Fed. Martin argued that the move would appear "panicky" and would not stabilize the market. When the exasperated president asked him why he would not agree with his other advisors, Martin responded that he and Dillon were the only ones who understood the stock market and that he was the only one in the room who did not work for the president.[61]

In what must have been a stunned silence, Martin proposed that he sample opinions at a gathering of presidents and directors of the Reserve Banks that was taking place that morning in Washington. Kennedy said he would also make some calls and that the advisor group should reconvene later that day. Kennedy called Robert Lovett, a former presidential advisor, secretary of Defense, and Wall Street veteran, who advised him that the correction was long overdue and repeated his advice of the previous day, that Kennedy should "say nothing."[62] When Martin reported that the overwhelming advice of the regional directors was to ignore the market gyration, Kennedy grudgingly accepted the collective wisdom of the financial community that a minimal administration response was called for. On 31 May, the market began to recover, and with recovery the accusations of blame receded from the front pages.

June 1962 also brought a reminder that the efforts to strengthen the fraying international monetary system could not slacken. During the first half of the year, the Canadian dollar came under severe pressure by investors and speculators expecting a devaluation. The Canadian government responded with a 10 percent devaluation, but the selling continued. By early June, fully 45 percent of the country's reserves were "swept away." The Canadians turned to the IMF and the U.S. government for help. Fortunately, a structure the Fed had placed in operation only a few months before was available to serve as one of the cornerstones for an aid package. The story of how that structure, known as the swap network, came into existence is another example of how Bill Martin's experience and outlook made him the right man at the right time.

The most serious weakness in the international monetary system was uncertainty over the future value of its linchpin, the U.S. dollar. The deficit in the U.S. balance of payments that had surfaced in the last three years of the Eisenhower administration totaled $11.2 billion, and $4.7 billion of the cumulative deficit was financed by the sale of U.S. gold to foreign central banks. At the end of 1961, U.S. gold reserves were down to $16.5 billion, including the $12 billion that was legally required to back outstanding U.S. currency. The Fed could waive this requirement on an interim basis, but without it, the $4.5 billion of unrestricted gold was a small amount compared to $22.5 billion of outstanding dollar claims held by foreign private and official holders. Foreign bankers and finance ministry officials worried that the U.S. might have to devalue in order to restore equilibrium in its balance of payments. The broad-ranging deficit reduction program begun by Eisenhower and expanded under Treasury Secretary Dillon included increased financial compensation by U.S. allies for U.S. military outlays for troops stationed abroad, tying U.S. economic aid to purchases in the United States, and expanded export financing. The administration's program succeeded in reducing the 1961 deficit to $2.5 billion in comparison to the 1958–60 average of $3.7 billion. The decline represented progress, but the problem was a long way from being solved.

The international monetary system was also laboring under the strain of an enormous increase in financial and investment capital moving through the system. By 1961, U.S. industry had a total overseas investment valued at $37 billion. During the five years 1956–61, a total of $17 billion of U.S. long- and short-term private capital went abroad. During 1960 and 1961, U.S. private capital movements out of the United States averaged $3.9 billion, while foreigners moved an average of only $1.3 billion into the United States. The importance of these numbers is that, at any given point in time, a great deal of private money was available to investors and speculators. These numbers are particularly large when compared to the gold and foreign-exchange reserves of individual countries such as the United States, with $4.5 billion of unrestricted reserves in gold; West Germany, with $6.2 billion in gold and foreign exchange; the United Kingdom, with $3.4 billion; and Japan, with $1.6 billion. When companies and individual speculators have access to hundreds of millions of dollars, pounds, or marks with which to speculate or hedge their investment exposure, it is not hard to understand how individual countries such as Canada can easily come under unmanageable speculative pressure on their currencies. It is hard to criticize the framers of the Bretton Woods monetary system for not being able to see beyond the rubble of World War II in order to anticipate the growth of private wealth and the impact it would have on a fixed-rate exchange system.

Finance ministers and central bankers joined together in various piecemeal efforts to address the system's problems. In 1960, the facilities of the London gold market were expanded under an informal pooling of gold by the leading European central banks and the United States. In mid-1961, Dillon, Martin, and Dillon's undersecretary for monetary affairs, Robert V. Roosa, proposed an increase in the resources of the IMF specifically to deal with temporary currency problems. The creative and indefatigable Roosa orchestrated its approval under the title of "General Agreements to Borrow" — and by the end of 1961, the arrangements were in place. While the IMF agreements were being negotiated, there were intermittent exchange crises among the European currencies that were contained by short-term credits extended by consortia of European central banks. The United States had no role in these informally organized consortia, but as Dillon, Martin, and Roosa discussed how the United States could contribute to further strengthening the international monetary system, they agreed that these short-term credits offered a useful model.

Dillon and Martin turned to their respective organizations to develop a vehicle for the United States to support the dollar. Martin asked Ralph Young, the secretary of the FOMC and his closest advisor after the retirement of Winfield Riefler, to study the problem. Described as a "polished old professional, wise in the ways of Washington," Young was an accomplished economist who possessed considerable persuasive powers, along with an acute sense of the Fed's capabilities.[63] From the very beginning of the study, Martin pushed the Fed into the international arena. On 12 September 1962, he introduced the subject to the FOMC: "There is no question but that this country is going to be in the business of foreign-exchange operations in one way or another . . . and I would like to see the Federal Reserve in the posture of contributing what it can to the development of the soundest possible method of handling the matter."[64]

Martin knew that only a few FOMC members had any experience in international finance and that the FOMC would be reluctant to accept unfamiliar risks that might involve financial losses and new political pressures. There were substantial legal questions to be resolved, and the general support of the Treasury Department and Congress would be essential. There were many unknowns in this new role, but Martin believed the Fed was the only instrumentality that could undertake the task without new legislation and the inevitable horse-trading that went with it. He was committed to persuading his FOMC associates to embrace this new role and was uniquely qualified to do it.

Martin's experience in international financial matters was both intense and long-standing. It began in 1945, when U.S. Army Chief of Staff General George Marshall selected Lieutenant Colonel William McChesney Martin Jr. as the U.S. Army representative to the Bretton Woods international monetary conference. There is no record of Martin's role in that historic gathering, but it could not have been significant. He was, however, "present at the creation" of the international monetary system and, as a member of the U.S. delegation, was exposed to the battles over its ultimate structure and the hopes the delegates had for it. Martin's lifelong commitment to cooperation with America's European allies must have sprung in part from this experience and the acquaintances he made at Bretton Woods. One of those acquaintances was John Maynard Keynes, whom Martin had persuaded to write an article for his *Economic Forum* in 1932.

In 1946, after he became president of the Export-Import Bank, Martin authorized some of the early U.S. postwar reconstruction loans to France, Italy, and Holland. Ex-Im was also deeply involved in helping meet the drastic shortage of U.S. dollars for rebuilding European industry. Martin's real grounding in the international monetary system began in 1946 when, as Ex-Im president, he became a member of the National Advisory Committee on International Financial Problems (the NAC). The committee served as the ultimate policy authority for evaluating and negotiating direct U.S. government loans for reconstruction, supervising the finances of the Marshall Plan and the Economic Cooperation Administration, and establishing the International Monetary Fund and the World Bank.

Martin continued to serve on the NAC even after he became assistant secretary of the Treasury for International Finance in 1949. His Treasury years rounded out Martin's six years of intense involvement with the international monetary system. These years taught him two important lessons: that worldwide confidence in the U.S. dollar was crucial to the international monetary system, and, that international monetary problems could usually be resolved by the cooperative efforts of people of goodwill. By the time he took the Fed chairmanship, Bill Martin was well experienced in dealing with the issues and personalities in international finance.

Martin's expectation that it would be hard to persuade the FOMC to support international operations proved correct. The vehicle ultimately recommended by Young was a "swap" in which the Federal Reserve would enter into an agreement with another central bank — for example, the Bank of England — for the right to borrow a certain amount of pound sterling at the prevailing exchange rate for a term of ninety days, subject to renewal. At the same time, the Fed agreed to lend an equivalent amount of dollars, again at the prevailing exchange rate, to the Bank of England. When the funds were actually borrowed, the proceeds were immediately included in the U.S. and U.K. reserve positions, respectively. The Fed usually used the British loan to purchase dollars held by the Bank of England. The two banks gave cross-guarantees protecting one another in the event of devaluation during the period of the loan. The swap was a flexible and quick way for central banks to temporarily add reserves at a time when short-term funds outflows, speculative or otherwise, were taking reserves away. When Martin began his campaign of persuasion in the FOMC meeting of 12 September 1961, the committee members' initial reaction was dubious. They were concerned about the risk of financial loss, potential conflicts with the Treasury, and whether the Fed's legislative mandate allowed such transactions. It was an inauspicious start to a long campaign.

Martin gave his FOMC associates almost three months to study and think about the proposal before he addressed the subject again. This time he asked Ralph Young to express the staff's view of the proposal. Young reviewed the accomplishments of the Bretton Woods monetary system and concluded: "We are now in a critical phase, with the risk that gains made will be lost. A breakdown in the system would take years for recovery."[65] He described the danger of "a confidence fission in which a chain reaction will have to run its course."[66] The solution was "to brace the foundation . . . with an enduring solution which will have to be as free of political bias as practicable . . . through central bank cooperation with Federal Reserve participation."[67]

The debate was as passionate as any that Martin experienced in his term as chairman. Dallas Reserve Bank President Watrous Irons wanted specific legal authorization via an amendment to the Federal Reserve Act. Governor Abbot Mills said: "I have no great faith that operations of this kind can be conducted successfully or without serious danger to the independent status of the System."[68] Governor James Robertson observed: "It [the proposal] involves very sensitive international diplomatic relationships with which the system is not in the best position to cope . . . while the Treasury can."[69] Atlanta Reserve Bank President Malcolm Bryan said, "[A] great deal more harm can be done by intervening to save the patient some pain than by letting him realize he is sick. The fundamental problem can be dealt with only by prudent fiscal and legislative policies."[70] Governor George King argued that the Fed was well advised always to avoid exposure to political pressure, and "a political agency [the Treasury Department] is the proper place for these . . . operations to be conducted."[71] Governor Robertson spoke for other governors and staff members when he summed up his position: "There are no gimmicks by which the position of the dollar can be maintained in the world. It would be unwise to resort to devices designed to hide the real problems. The United States must practice what it has long preached about the need for monetary and fiscal discipline [dealing with the balance of payments problem]."[72]

Of the twelve voting FOMC members, the only vocal supporters other than Martin were New York Reserve Bank President Alfred Hayes and Governor George Mitchell. Martin could see that sentiment was running strongly against the proposal. Covering over his awkward position, he blandly stated that "the committee is not united."[73] Martin advised the FOMC that since a number of members had suggested that the Treasury should run the swap program, he would secure the Treasury's views on the issue.

At the FOMC meeting on 19 December, Martin introduced a letter from

Treasury Undersecretary Robert Roosa. A few words about Roosa's remarkable contribution to U.S. international monetary policy are in order. Roosa was gifted with a prodigious intellect and was a Rhodes Scholar with a Ph.D. in economics from the University of Michigan. After service in the intelligence corps during World War II, he joined the research department of the Federal Reserve Bank of New York. His talent for original and insightful thinking brought him to the attention of Allan Sproul, much in the same way Sproul had been picked out by Benjamin Strong in his day.

Roosa became one of Sproul's most trusted advisors and was appointed head of the research department in the early 1950s. From that position, his thinking and writing earned him a distinguished reputation among academicians and bankers alike. His analysis of how institutional investors treated Treasury bond investments changed the way the Fed approached its open-market trading strategies. For all his contributions to thinking about the U.S. bond markets, it was on international monetary issues that Roosa had his greatest policy impact. Roosa became involved in international issues in 1958 and was a frequent observer to meetings of the Bank for International Settlements, the Basel-based organization that brought representatives of the European central banks together on a monthly basis. Before long, Roosa was applying his talents to proposals to strengthen the international monetary system.

When the Kennedy administration was being assembled, the demand for Roosa's services was so strong that both Douglas Dillon, as Treasury secretary–designate, and Walter Heller, CEA chairman–designate, separately claimed that they were responsible for appointing Roosa to his position. Roosa stepped easily into the position of Treasury undersecretary for monetary affairs, the position that had been so ably filled by Randolph Burgess when it was established in 1953. Like Burgess, Roosa earned impeccable credentials during his Fed career and brought to the Treasury his ability to balance the interests of the two agencies. In addition, he originated and advocated new approaches to old problems. As Charles Coombs, who worked beside Roosa at the New York Reserve Bank for years, wrote: "Roosa was a truly gifted advocate of whatever cause he espoused. He spoke with flowing eloquence and, as a Bank of England man put it, his appeals for decisive action took on almost a biblical quality."[74] It did not hurt Fed-Treasury relations that Roosa had a deep admiration for Bill Martin, writing later: "Chairman Martin was a really great man, one of the great men of the century, in my view."[75]

Roosa's impact at the Treasury was immediate. He smoothed the potential friction between Kennedy and Martin over the administration's desire for ever lower long-term interest rates and the extent of the Fed's support for "Operation Twist." By the fall of 1961, Roosa had already experimented with forward purchases of foreign exchange in transactions that were similar in structure to the swaps being proposed for the Fed. Dillon, Roosa, and Martin had previously discussed the limited funds available in the Treasury's Exchange Stabilization Fund, the vehicle used to fund the Treasury's forward purchases. They agreed that in contrast to the Treasury, the Fed's financial resources could be expanded sufficiently to provide meaningful support for the international financial system. When Martin told Roosa he needed help in persuading his FOMC associates, Roosa was quick to respond.

Roosa informed the FOMC: "Only the central bank can make the prompt, smooth adjustments [during a currency crisis] that are called for. The very existence of a central banking capability for coping effectively with volatile flows can give confidence to international traders and investors and further the orderly evolution of international market processes."[76] He assured the FOMC that the Treasury would work with the Fed, and "[t]he Treasury would naturally want to avoid impinging on the independence of the Federal Reserve System within the government."[77] It is difficult to imagine what more the Treasury could have promised in the way of support, short of agreeing to underwrite any potential losses.

Martin put off any further consideration of the swap issue for two months while he built support for the proposal. He reviewed the issue with the chairmen of the Senate Finance Committee and House Banking and Currency Committee and determined that pursuing specific legislative authorization for foreign-exchange dealing would open a Pandora's box of legislative initiatives.[78] Working with, and occasionally leaning on, their respective legal counsel, Martin and Dillon concluded that the Fed's existing legislative mandate would allow undertaking the swap program, and the U.S. attorney general agreed. Finally, as he always did, Martin met personally with each governor and spoke with each bank president to present his case and listen to their concerns.

When the FOMC gathered on 13 February 1962, five months after their first discussion on foreign currency transactions, Martin was ready to push for a resolution. He tried to ease the committee's concern that the Fed's foreign-exchange objectives might conflict with its domestic responsibilities: "It is not possible, with the world developing as it is, to separate domestic and international considerations" in formulating monetary policy.[79] He reassured them that "committee members will not have to become foreign-exchange experts . . . but you will have to understand the broad principles. We will feel our way."[80] He concluded with a forecast that "ten years from now, operations in foreign currencies will be just as much a part of the system as open market operations in government securities."[81] It was Martin's usual style: offering a broad view of the issues involved, couching his arguments in unthreatening terms, and proposing a careful, experimental unfolding of the new departure.

FOMC members reiterated some of their concerns, but the results of the extended review process and the weight of Roosa's arguments changed the tenor of the debate. This time there were more questions about the mechanics of supervising the swap activity and coordination with the Treasury. In the end, the approval was unanimous; as Charles Coombs, the man who was to supervise the swap program, carefully described it, "The FOMC somewhat apprehensively approved the undertaking."[82]

FOMC members went along with Martin and the Fed staff even though most of them realized that they could not foresee what lay ahead in the complex world of foreign-exchange dealings. They had been convinced of the seriousness of the problem and that the Fed was the appropriate agency for undertaking the program. They knew from past experience that Martin was very careful to keep the Fed's activities within its legislative mandate, and believed him when he said: "I do not think that the System should be seeking 'power,' instead it should seek the best end result."[83] They accepted Bill Martin's promise that the Fed would "feel its way" and would not take unreasonable risks before it built up its experience base. Martin's unique contribution to the swap approval process was to build a climate of trust in which FOMC members, congressional leaders, and Treasury officials could support a carefully designed plan for what appeared to be evolutionary rather than revolutionary change.

Bill Martin finally won the approval he sought, but he fully recognized the risks he was leading the Fed to undertake. Douglas Dillon told Martin that when he advised Kennedy of the Fed's new program, he took pains to emphasize the "great sensitivity that prevails with respect to the independence of the Federal Reserve System within the government."[84] Despite this assurance, Martin shared the concern of his FOMC associates about future conflicts with the Treasury and the administration over the politics of which currencies were supported and how much support they received.

Under the proposed arrangements, either the Fed or the Treasury could veto a potential transaction. Martin was confident he could resolve any related issues with Dillon and Roosa, but it was impossible to foresee the pressures these arrangements might put on future Fed chairmen and Treasury secretaries. Martin also acknowledged his FOMC critics' argument that the Fed's program could enable the world financial community to avoid dealing with the real issue of trade imbalances when he observed: "[T]hese ideas, as good as they are, are not going to solve the whole problem . . . it is still necessary to deal with the fundamentals."[85] Despite these legitimate concerns, the United States could not afford to ignore the weaknesses of the international financial system. Additional defenses were absolutely necessary, and Martin believed that "every practical device should be used."[86] The United States stood to gain more than any nation from a strong international monetary system. If the Fed were to truly act in the nation's interest in preserving the system, it would have to take on the risk of additional political pressure and the possibility of failure.

The initial authorization limited total outstanding swaps to $600 million, but the eventual importance of swaps came much closer to Martin's forecast that the program would become as integral to the Fed's role as open-market operations. When Charles Coombs retired in 1975, the ceiling on swaps outstanding had increased to $20 billion, and the technique had become a crucial support for the international monetary system. By that time, the total resources available under the swap program were comparable to the Fed's $35-billion Treasury portfolio. Commenting on the program's start, Coombs observed: "I suppose that it was just as well that neither the FOMC nor I could even remotely imagine all that lay ahead."[87]

What lay immediately ahead was the collapse of the Canadian dollar. Armed with an initial Federal Reserve swap of $250 million and a $400 million standby credit from the U.S. Export-Import Bank, the Bank of Canada put together a credit package of $1 billion in only four days. The package was announced on 25 June 1962, and within four weeks fully 55 percent of its previous reserve losses had been recovered. The value of the Fed's swap program was already proving itself.

The continued growth of the economy and the Fed's unwavering commitment to easy credit throughout 1962 brought the relationship between Martin and the Kennedy administration to a condition of stasis by early 1963. Heller did not get the full expansionary thrust from monetary policy he sought, but the goals of "Operation Twist" were generally being achieved. It was in this period of relative calm that Bill Martin's term as Fed chairman expired, and Martin's early apprehension about his relationship with Kennedy resurfaced.

Walter Heller viewed the expiration of Martin's term with decidedly mixed emotions. He had initially hoped that Martin would resign when Kennedy came into office, and during the last two years he and Martin had been on the opposite side of most economic issues. All three CEA members were frustrated by Martin's ability to outmaneuver Heller in the Quadriad. As CEA member James Tobin described it: "Martin would indicate a certain amount of agreement and at the same time he would not really promise anything or give any indication that he could do much."[88] Nevertheless, Heller believed that for all Martin's equivocations, the Quadriad worked effectively: "[T]he relationships were in essential harmony . . . we were able to reach consensus much more than our predecessors."[89] Heller's posture was aptly described by a *New York Times* reporter: "vigorous New Frontiersmen view Martin with a mixture of admiration, irritation and wonder."[90] Tobin flatly predicted that Kennedy would ask Martin to stay on. When Heller recognized that Kennedy still depended on Martin and Dillon for the support of the international financial community, he gave up his opposition to Martin's reappointment.[91]

Douglas Dillon had no such reservations. He advised Kennedy that "during the past two years Martin has always cooperated wholeheartedly with the Treasury. One cannot find fault with either his policies or his attitude."[92] Referring to Kennedy's continual concern about the U.S. balance of payments, Dillon argued: "Martin's support of our fiscal policy will be of vital importance in holding foreign opinion in line during the coming months and avoiding any foreign loss of confidence in the dollar."[93] Finally, Dillon referred to Kennedy's intention to ask Congress for a tax cut in 1963: "He can be a tower of strength in support of our tax program."[94] It was a rare display of outright enthusiasm by Dillon, who was famous for his circumspect personal style. Dillon's support could not have surprised Kennedy, since Martin and Dillon had taken similar positions on virtually every issue debated in the Quadriad.

Kennedy and Martin met in the Oval Office on a snowy Saturday morning, 26 January 1963. Kennedy listed Martin's supporters in the administration and asked him if he would accept reappointment. Martin asked, "Are you offering the reappointment only because of my political value to your administration, because in that case I wouldn't like to be re-appointed."[95] The president was taken aback but responded, "That certainly is one reason. It would be politically damaging to me if you were to leave, but it is certainly not the only reason. I know you don't always agree with what we're doing and that my people don't always like what you're doing. But in our dealings, I've found you to be independent-minded and willing to speak up for your position. There are too few of such people and they are what a president needs above all."[96]

Now it was Martin's turn to be taken aback. He had walked into the Oval Office "not particularly anxious to continue."[97] Building a relationship with the administration had not been easy, and perhaps it was time for a change: for himself, for the Fed, and for the administration. He had been approached by several corporations and offered "excellent opportunities," and his wife, Cynthia, had been urging him to end the twelve-hour days and unrelenting demands on his time. On the other hand, he now enjoyed a highly cooperative relationship with the administration. He could work with Walter Heller and had the strongest possible personal and philosophical compatibility with Douglas Dillon. Martin could talk to the president, and Kennedy had made a real effort to understand the Fed's position on a number of important issues. Now the president was pointedly saying that he could accept a difference of views between the Fed and his administration and that he valued a virtue that Martin held most highly, his willingness to speak his mind in defense of what he saw as the public interest. Whether it was calculated or not, Kennedy appealed to Martin in terms he could not resist. Bill Martin agreed to four more years.

The press reacted positively to Martin's reappointment. The *New York Times* editorialized that the reappointment "assures a continuation of the cooperative spirit in the Federal Reserve that has been the hallmark of Mr. Martin's career."[98] Then it made an observation with which Martin, who constantly admonished the FOMC not to overestimate the importance of monetary policy, would have agreed: "Though there have been occasional disputes, Mr. Martin has always recognized that the ultimate power and responsibility for the nation's overall economic policy, of which monetary policy is but a part, lies with the chief executive."[99] The loudest disapproval came from India, from which U.S. Ambassador John Kenneth Galbraith sent his missives castigating Martin's policies, and Capitol Hill, where Wright Patman grumbled about four more years of dueling with Martin.

Bill Martin had barely grown accustomed to his reappointment when his next dilemma emerged in the form of Walter Heller's long-deferred dream of a tax cut. As good Keynesian economists, Heller and Paul Samuelson believed that the new administration should place primary emphasis on fiscal policy for achieving its goals for long-term economic growth. Beginning in early 1961, both men encouraged Kennedy to consider a temporary tax cut if economic growth remained inadequate. Later in that year, Heller focused on the "performance gap," or the shortfall in GNP caused by operating the economy at less than full capacity, and argued that a tax cut was the only way the performance gap would be overcome. Throughout 1961, Kennedy was hesitant to consider a tax cut. He was already having problems persuading Congress to pass his social legislation, and adding a tax cut to the list was unlikely to improve his congressional relations.

By June 1962, the economy's slowing rate of growth changed the situation. Paul Samuelson advised Kennedy: "A majority of economists inside and outside the government have shifted toward the view that . . . a tax cut this year can do much to avert the developing recession."[100] This news, along with lobbying from a variety of traditional Democratic Party interest groups, caused Kennedy to reconsider the tax cut idea. On 7 June he announced that he intended to introduce a bill "including an across-the-board reduction in personal and corporate income taxes."[101] To build a broader base of support, the reduction was to be coupled with tax reform, but there would be "a net tax reduction."[102] When Congressman Wilbur Mills, the head of the House Ways and Means Committee, spoke out against a tax cut, Kennedy again hesitated.

On 15 November 1962, Paul Samuelson sent another memo to Kennedy, criticizing the administration for its delay and reporting the dismal statistics that confirmed the economic slowdown. Samuelson concluded that a sizable tax cut was the only assurance that "by early 1964, events will be working clearly and strongly our way."[103] Kennedy got the unsubtle message that his reelection chances depended on a strong economy and the only way to achieve one was to move soon on taxes. In a speech to the Economic Club of New York three weeks later, Kennedy committed himself to introducing tax cut legislation in early 1963. As speechwriter Ted Sorensen wrote of this period, "The president's own enthusiasm [for a tax cut] grew. He began to look to the tax cut as his most potent weapon against the persistent unemployment still plaguing him."[104] On 24 January 1963 Kennedy sent a special message to Congress proposing an across-the-board permanent cut in personal and corporate taxes, with a loss of government income of $13.5 billion, coupled with tax reforms that recovered $3.5 billion. The die was cast: the proposed cut was large, amounting to 2 percent of GNP, and its timing, during a period of economic expansion, was unprecedented. There would be no turning back.

Bill Martin was conflicted about the administration's tax cut proposal. Under somewhat different conditions in 1958, he and Treasury Secretary Robert Anderson had convinced Dwight Eisenhower to reject a tax cut proposed by former CEA Chairman Arthur Burns. Martin and Anderson had argued that it was essential to eliminate budget deficits in order to achieve long-run, non-inflationary economic growth. Their prescription had produced low inflation, but at the cost of slow growth in 1959 and a recession in 1960. Martin cannot have been unmoved by the extended criticism of monetary policy for being too restrictive during the late 1950s. By early 1963, the economy had been growing for two years, but Martin was troubled by the string of budgetary deficits that the Kennedy administration was creating. The deficit for fiscal 1962 was $6.3 billion, the deficit for the current fiscal year was forecasted at $7.8 billion and, with the first installment of the proposed tax cut, the fiscal year 1964 deficit was expected to be $11.9 billion. These deficits, together with an economy that was still growing, albeit more slowly, would ordinarily have motivated Martin to oppose the tax cut because it would add to the economy's inflationary potential. However, this was not 1958 and the inflationary pressures were modest and getting weaker. The pragmatist in Martin had to recognize this fact.

Another reason Martin came out in favor of the proposed legislation was that monetary policy had gone as far as it could in support of economic growth: it needed help from fiscal policy. The Fed was still pursuing an easy monetary policy, and yet the economy's growth rate was clearly slowing down and unemployment remained stuck at 5.8 percent. A few weeks earlier, he had advised his fellow FOMC members: "For the past few months I have done my best to try to convince myself that additional monetary ease would alleviate unemployment and aid economic growth, but it is my conviction that additional ease will do just the reverse."[105] New York Reserve Bank President Al Hayes spoke for others on the FOMC when he complemented Kennedy's New York speech: "The speech put in good perspective the need for fiscal policy to share with monetary policy the burden of growth stimulation."[106] The challenge for Martin was to make a public case for the tax cut that would encourage Americans to use their additional income constructively and to convey the Fed's goals for future monetary policy in light of the tax cuts.

Martin began his campaign on 1 February 1963 in his annual presentation to the JEC on the Economic Report of the President. He downplayed the effects of the cut on consumption by stating that the tax cut and the increase in the deficit "can only be justified if they create incentives for people to do and to save more than they are doing and saving at the present time."[107] He then said that the inflation potential of the tax cut would depend on the way in which the increased deficit was financed. "The System would be derelict in its responsibilities were it — in the light of a large deficit — to add to bank reserves and to bring about substantial credit expansion solely to facilitate the financing of the deficit."[108] Martin was saying that the Fed would provide bank reserves to enable the banks to meet legitimate credit needs associated with an expanding economy, but not just to enable banks to purchase the added Treasury debt. If the Treasury financed the deficit through private savings, there would be no net addition to the money supply. On the other hand, if banks purchased the added Treasury securities, the deposits automatically created would increase the money supply and the inflationary potential. Finally, Martin tried to prepare JEC members for a possible rise in interest rates as the tax cut stimulated continued expansion: "[A]ccelerated growth will lead to larger credit demand and a gradual rise in interest rates, not through a restrictive monetary policy, but through the influence of monetary forces."[109]

Try as he might, Martin was not able to achieve much sympathy in the JEC for the Fed's point of view. Senators Douglas and Proxmire were concerned that the likely stimulus of the tax cut would not be felt until late 1963 at the earliest, and yet the Fed seemed to be expecting higher interest rates well before then. Proxmire summarized the Democratic majority's attitude: "As long as we have 5.8 percent of the work force out of work . . . there is no reason in the world why monetary policy and fiscal policy should not pull in harness — both expansionary."[110]

Martin was more successful in persuading the administration. As he expected, Walter Heller argued against the Fed's position: "A deficit arising from reduced tax rates will cause incomes to rise and will produce increased demand for money and credit. Unless bank reserves are increased, credit will be restricted. If the deficit is financed under conditions of monetary restraint, the tax program's stimulating effects will be partly offset."[111] Fortunately for Martin, Dillon again weighed in on Martin's side, both in the Quadriad and through the actions of the Treasury Department. Dillon's commitment that "efforts will be made to insure non-inflationary financing of the sizable deficits with which we are confronted" was applauded as "right and proper" by First National City Bank and greeted with relief at the Fed.[112] Dillon also indicated that the Treasury was prepared to pay attractive interest rates in order to assure investor interest. What is most remarkable about Dillon's support is that he firmly disagreed with the importance Martin assigned to this issue.[113] Rather than create the impression of a policy conflict, Dillon smoothed over the differences. Throughout his term as Treasury secretary, Douglas Dillon supported the Fed at critical junctures. The 1951 Accord between the Treasury and the Federal Reserve System was built on a spirit of cooperation among equals. Douglas Dillon's leadership exemplified the highest achievement of those principles.

As the battle for Kennedy's tax cut moved into the halls of Congress, an old nemesis returned to the scene in the form of the balance of payments deficit. The administration's payments program of 1961 reduced the official balance of payments deficit for that year, but much of the improvement represented one-time transactions. By 1962, the payments deficit surged to $3.5 billion, and Fed economists foresaw no improvement in 1963. In March, FOMC Secretary Ralph Young reported on his visit to a recent meeting of an Organization for Economic Cooperation and Development (OECD) working party. "The tone of the meeting was highly critical of U.S. financial policy. Confidence in the dollar is waning."[114] Martin requested that the FOMC increase the discount rate to keep investment funds from flowing out of the country, but the committee remained focused on the possibility of a slowdown in the U.S. economy and would not support him. Expressing his frustration, Martin told the FOMC: "The balance of payments has become the real shadow over the domestic economy. Too much attention is . . . being paid to stimulating the domestic economy through monetary policy and not enough to dealing with the balance of payments."[115]

In the following months, Martin waged a campaign with two objectives: to persuade the FOMC to support a discount rate increase and to prepare the financial markets for it. He asked the FOMC staff to analyze the impact of different degrees of credit tightening and discussed the results at the FOMC. He and Al Hayes, who was also in favor of a rate increase, lobbied individual FOMC members. By May, Martin felt that a majority of the FOMC would vote for tightening, and typically he promoted a policy of gradualism. The discount rate had remained at 3 percent for nearly three years, and a meaningful rate increase would require portfolio adjustment by banks and other institutional investors. At the FOMC meeting on 7 May, Martin urged the committee to prepare the markets for a tightening: "[T]he balance of payments problem is growing worse . . . [and] it might become desirable for the committee to make a decisive move. Such a move is not feasible unless monetary policy has been trending for some time in a [similar] direction."[116] Martin knew that financial markets can overreact to unanticipated events, and he believed that they must be prepared for changes in Fed monetary policy. He always tried to communicate the Fed's new posture, either through public statements from Fed officials or through carefully orchestrated open-market moves.

Another principle that guided Martin in dealing with the balance of payments was his desire to work in concert with the administration. In March he advised the FOMC that the Fed needed administration help: "If the System does not have the support of the administration, we will be defeated psychologically almost at the start on moves that monetary policy might make on the balance of payments."[117] Anything the Fed does "should be part of a package deal" along with an administration balance of payments program.[118] A few weeks later, Martin, Dillon, and Roosa drew up a plan for Fed-Treasury cooperation, including a rise in the discount rate and a new Treasury debt-management policy to confine new Treasury issues to the short- and medium-term markets in order to reduce pressure on long-term interest rates. On 17 April, Dillon wrote to the president: "A ½ percent increase in short term rates . . . may well become the key to the success of our [balance of payments] efforts."[119] The Treasury and the Fed were in concert, but success depended on convincing the rest of the administration to go along.

Dillon proposed a novel approach to overcome Walter Heller's objections and win Kennedy's approval. The Treasury would form a joint working party to evaluate the likely impact of a rise in short-term rates on the domestic economy. The working party would consist of a senior representative of the Treasury, the CEA, the Budget Bureau, and the Fed. If the group unanimously confirmed the conclusions of the Fed analysis that showed only a modest impact, Dillon believed that Heller's objections would be compromised, and

Dillon and Martin could persuade Kennedy to go along with the rate increase. The representatives began work in mid-June, and submitted a unanimous forecast incorporating the Fed's conclusions on 8 July 1963. The Quadriad was scheduled to meet a week later.

Despite his philosophical compatibility with Dillon, Martin was apprehensive as the Quadriad meeting approached. He had allowed the Fed to become an integral part of an administration decision-making process to an extent he had carefully avoided during his first twelve years as chairman. Had he undermined the balance between cooperation and independence he had worked so hard to establish? He had succeeded in achieving closer relations with the administration, but each cooperative effort generated higher expectations on the part of the administration. In March 1963, he told the FOMC of the downside of teamwork: "The System is considered off the team when it does not do everything that is wanted by the administration."[120]

Martin's dilemma was caused by his agreement to incorporate a discount rate decision into a more comprehensive administration economic policy. A rise in the discount rate, a decision that was the province of the Fed, had been integrated into the administration's policy formulation. At a FOMC meeting to set the stage for the discount rate increase, Martin told the committee that he feared the Fed would overplay its hand in dealing with the situation: "We have to be careful about approaching the idea of team play in the sense of the System wanting to play a leading role or to become the driving force. The system must be careful that it does not get itself into the position trying to do more than monetary policy should do."[121]

The Quadriad met on 15 July to complete the administration's review process. When Kennedy came to the discount rate increase, he asked: "Is it Federal Reserve policy to prevent a rise in long term rates?"[122] Martin replied: "Yes. I cannot be certain that the effect of the action will be confined to short term rates, but we will make a major effort to achieve this goal."[123] At the end of the meeting, after Kennedy had given his approval to the program, he pointedly said: "The rate increase makes the passage of the tax program even more urgent. It would be especially useful if Bill could offer his public support for it."[124] Kennedy did not directly ask Martin for an answer, but it was exactly the kind of quid pro quo thinking that Martin feared. Even though he had tried repeatedly to offer his carefully qualified support for the tax cut, any future support would be interpreted by the White House as a repayment. Also as Martin expected, the press commented on the close coordination of the discount rate and the balance of payments program. The *New York Times* announced the discount rate rise on its front page. "To the political observer, this marks an open liaison between the Federal Reserve System and the New

Frontier."[125] Martin knew he would have to spend considerable effort to tactfully restore the balanced independence he had previously created.

Walter Heller accepted his setback on the discount rate question by rededicating himself to detecting any wavering in the Fed's commitment to open-market operations in longer-term Treasuries.[126] His irritation with the Martin-Dillon partnership was about to experience a sharp rise over the next opening on the Fed's board of governors.

Martin and Dillon knew they had been outmaneuvered by Heller when George Mitchell was appointed to the Fed's board, and they were determined to avoid a repetition. There were rumors that Walter Heller favored Harvard economist Seymour Harris when the next opening on the Fed board occurred. Martin viewed a Harris candidacy with considerable alarm. Harris was well known for his liberal economic views and was a long-standing critic of the Fed, and particularly of Bill Martin. He was currently serving as an advisor to Dillon, and he had clashed repeatedly with Treasury Undersecretary Robert Roosa.[127] It was unlikely that Martin knew it, but Harris had written Kennedy in September 1962 to recommend that Martin not be reappointed.[128] If this were not sufficiently problematic, he also took a dim view of the Fed's independence.[129] Harris was outspoken and used to defending liberal views against the arguments of more conservative economists. Once on the board, he could unite with Mitchell and Robertson to tie the board of governors in a polarizing liberal-conservative split.

Martin and Dillon agreed that Harris would be an undesirable selection and settled on Robert Roosa's deputy, J. Dewey Daane, as their preferred candidate. Daane had been appointed to the Treasury by the Eisenhower administration but had quickly impressed Dillon and Roosa. On 16 September 1963, before Walter Heller had any idea of what was going on, Martin and Dillon met with Kennedy to discuss the upcoming board vacancy. They knew that Daane was not an outspoken Keynesian and would be unlikely to meet Walter Heller's criteria for a successful candidate. Dillon emphasized Daane's prior experience as a vice president in the Federal Reserve System and his "nearly three years of close association with all aspects of the economic and financial program of your administration."[130] Both Martin and Dillon praised Daane for his work in their respective institutions. Dillon then made an eloquent case for nonpartisan competence in the leadership of the Federal Reserve: "Mr. Daane is one of several prominent Federal Reserve career men of the post-depression period who have judged that they could best serve the public interest in central banking, throughout one administration after another, by denying themselves affiliation with either political party."[131] Coming from Dillon, these were not words of empty praise. Kennedy listened but kept his counsel.

When he found out about the Daane candidacy, Heller moved with dispatch. He wrote Kennedy to praise Harris's virtues: "He has an international reputation . . . as a specialist in monetary and international economics. He would strengthen the minority group in the Fed that wants to avoid a restrictive monetary policy. He has been a faithful defender of this administration. The net gain on the Hill, particularly among Senate liberals, will be distinct."[132] Heller appealed to Kennedy's aides and to Kennedy himself. He made a full court press on Harris's behalf.

In the end, Heller lost the argument. It is surprising that he, who could read Kennedy so well, would push for such a controversial candidate. At the time of his decision, Kennedy was under a stinging public attack by Truman-era CEA Chairman Leon Keyserling, another well-known liberal, who accused the administration of an inadequate commitment to economic growth. It is unlikely the president was feeling particularly generous toward liberal economists. When Paul Samuelson referred to those economists who influenced Kennedy in planning for his administration, he observed that "the president had a definite lack of confidence in Seymour Harris. This came out in a number of occasions."[133] As Heller saw failure looming, he appealed to Kennedy to keep the Harris candidacy alive for the board opening that would occur when Governor James L. Robertson's term ended in early 1964. Perhaps that is how Kennedy actually left the matter, for that is how Heller informed the press about the decision.[134] The Daane appointment was met with approval in the press and relief in the office of the Chairman of the Board of Governors of the Federal Reserve System.

As the second half of 1963 unfolded, the U.S. economy began to grow faster. As usual, macroeconomic trends beyond human control drove events, but the results of the Kennedy administration's economic initiatives could justly claim some of the credit. By 30 September, the expansion entered into its thirty-third month and economic growth, which had all but ceased in the fourth quarter of 1962, returned to an annualized rate of 6 percent for the first three quarters of 1963. Walter Heller remained distressed by the 5 ½ percent unemployment rate, but he was pleased with the economic growth rate and an inflation rate averaging only 1.4 percent for the first nine months of the year. In the 1 October FOMC meeting, the Fed staff noted "a relatively high degree of business optimism" due in part to the passage of the administration's tax cut legislation by the House of Representatives. When the third-quarter payments deficit came in much lower than forecast, those who had struggled to put the balance of payments program in place celebrated and hoped for more of the same. Similarly, the 0.5 percent discount rate increase was fully reflected in short-term rates, but long-term rates were only up 0.03 percent. The future was always uncertain, but economic policy makers in the administration and at the Fed could bask in a brief moment of satisfaction.

The ever vigilant Walter Heller monitored the Fed's summary of open-market transactions to make sure it did not backslide on the commitment to operate in the long-term end of the Treasury market. He sent the president press clippings referring to possible interest rate hikes due to Fed actions. It became Dillon's chore to reassure Kennedy that "the Fed is taking the actions we expected them to."[135] Though Heller did not accept Dillon's assurances, he resorted to calling for a Quadriad meeting only once between mid-July and mid-November.

But as Martin often said, "A Fed chairman is paid to worry," and he did. He had been concerned for some time that the notion of excess industrial capacity had the potential to deceive policy makers. Conventional economic wisdom held that excess industrial capacity was a crucial factor, along with unemployment, in holding down inflationary pressures during an economic expansion. In fact, economists often compared December 1956, twenty-four months after the 1954 recession, with mid-1963, twenty-six months after the 1960 recession. In mid-1963, plant utilization rate was 80 percent, unemployment was 5 ½ percent, and inflation at less than 1.4 percent. The corresponding numbers for 1956 were plant utilization of 90 percent, unemployment at 4 percent, and inflation at 3.5 percent. The presence of excess plant and manpower was used by the CEA to justify both an expansionary monetary policy and the Kennedy tax cut. Martin, on the other hand, felt that "the volume of unutilized plant capacity that could pay its way is getting very small."[136] He believed that the traditional definition of plant capacity included uneconomic facilities, and that the incremental costs of using these facilities put pressure on manufacturers to raise prices to preserve their profit margins.

Martin was also concerned about other inflationary pressures that were not evident in the statistics. He often complained, as he did at the 12 November FOMC meeting, about inadequate consumer price information: "[P]rice indexes always tend to lag behind actual price changes. Inflation can be unnoticed for a period and then suddenly become evident."[137] Because he distrusted the price data, Martin used his network of business contacts to seek anecdotal evidence about price developments. In addition, he advised the FOMC: "The unemployment statistics do not indicate an adequate response to the stimuli that are being applied."[138] Martin believed that the budget deficit, along with more than adequate credit availability and the business community's confidence, were already working to bring unemployment down. As he tied these various trends together with the expansionary thrust of a tax cut, Martin was convinced that the economy's capacity for low inflation growth was coming to an end. He summed up his position with a blanket statement in November 1963: "For the first time in a long while, the committee might find itself faced with serious problems with prices and with an incipient expansion at an unsustainable rate."[139]

Martin's concerns about inflation, along with the hopes and fears of millions of Americans, were suspended on the afternoon of 22 November 1963, when the news came that John Kennedy had been assassinated during a visit to Dallas. Soon after the news hit the wire services, New York Fed President Al Hayes called to advise Martin that prices on the New York Stock Exchange were falling sharply, and the Exchange would be closing early. Martin and Hayes agreed that the Fed needed to issue a statement and that, while the event was a terrible human and political tragedy, its economic impact should be manageable. A few hours later, the Fed issued a statement that concluded with: "There is no need for special action [by the Fed] in the financial markets."[140] To head off any panic selling of U.S. dollars in foreign-exchange markets, Hayes contacted selected European central bankers. Later that afternoon, he announced to the public: "The Fed is confident of continued cooperation with foreign central banks."[141] The Saturday morning papers offered a picture of a solemn and haggard Lyndon Johnson being sworn in as president on Air Force One as it flew back to Washington with Kennedy's torn body. The visible symbol of the American democracy being carried forward helped stabilize markets in Europe, and Saturday trading in the London gold market was calm.

American financial markets were closed on Monday for a day of mourning, and Tuesday's trading began on a confident note. That morning the FOMC met by telephone. Robert Stone, the head of open-market trading at the New York Reserve Bank, told the committee that he had advised Treasury dealers: "We are picking up where we left off on Friday [before the news broke]."[142] Eager investors, buoyed by the developments over the weekend and looking for bargains, placed large buy orders on the NYSE. By the end of the day, the Dow had more than recovered Friday's losses. Foreign central banks, "in a dramatically heightened sense of political solidarity," stepped in to support the dollar, and exchange rates returned to their Friday levels.[143] In the following days, the financial markets confirmed their return to normalcy. Official Washington, including the Federal Reserve System, put on a brave public face over its private sorrow and resolutely soldiered on. For Martin, as for all of those who had worked with John Kennedy, the sense of loss was palpable. It was as though a vital and irreplaceable part of their own lives had also come to a tragic end. In a moment of reflection, Martin spoke with CEA member James Tobin of his admiration for Kennedy's quick grasp of economic matters: "I had better communication and more interest and understanding, if not always agreement, from Jack Kennedy than from any president under whom I have served."[144]

As he tried to envision the future, Martin's fears about inflation returned. He had come to respect Kennedy's willingness to debate economic issues and his healthy pragmatism. Despite Martin's initial fears about Kennedy's economic instincts, he had come to judge him a "pretty conservative fella."[145] Now the nation would be led by an easy-money man from the Southwest who had inherited a rapidly expanding economy reaching the limits of its capacity and a growing budget deficit, and who had just announced that securing the Kennedy tax cut was his first political priority. Martin summed up his gloomy feelings in the last FOMC meeting in 1963: "If the present euphoria is translated by a tax cut into a real surge in the economy, we might be faced with the need for some . . . drastic action to be taken at the first opportunity."[146] The era of Camelot was indeed over.

9

Sowing the Wind: The Early Johnson Years

For Bill Martin, as for the other leaders of the U.S. government, the terrible days after John Kennedy's assassination were filled with questions about the likely course of a Johnson presidency. Johnson's early public statements were full of references to "carrying on the work of John Kennedy," but little else was known.[1] In his personal style, Lyndon Johnson was the exact opposite of John Kennedy. A *New York Times* reporter contrasted Kennedy's "detachment, understatement, irony, sophistication and coolness" with Johnson's "flamboyance, folksiness, emotion and earthiness."[2] The son of a failed Texas farmer and former state legislator, Lyndon Johnson grew up poor. After graduation from West Texas State Teacher's College, Johnson began his career as a teacher in an impoverished neighborhood school in Houston. It did not take long for the siren song of politics to call out to Lyndon Johnson, and soon he was in Washington, D.C., serving as an influential assistant to Jack Kleberg, congressman from Texas.

Lyndon Johnson entered electoral politics in 1937 by winning a special election for an unexpired term in the House of Representatives. After eleven years in the House, Johnson won a hard-fought primary for a Senate seat by a meager eighty-seven votes, earning him the sobriquet "Landslide Lyndon," but went on to overwhelm his Republican opponent. There were lawsuits alleging vote fraud in the primary, but his friend, lawyer Abe Fortas, and a member of Harry Truman's staff helped shunt them aside.

In the House and later in the Senate, Johnson was known as a hardworking, glad-handing politician who pushed for government-sponsored spending programs and was skilled in bringing home the "bacon" for his oil industry constituents. Gifted with a passion for persuasion and a talent for knowing when to compromise, along with membership in the powerful Texas congressional Mafia, Johnson worked his way into the leadership of Senate Democrats after only six years in the Senate. With a continuing Democratic majority in the Senate, Lyndon Johnson wielded enormous power in political Washington. He became known as a man who could stand up for principle, but who also could be vindictive — and possessed a very long memory.

Astonishingly, Johnson left this pinnacle of influence to assume the mantle of anonymity reserved for all vice presidents. He had worn it with unexpected grace. Now, as president, Johnson inherited Kennedy's extensive list of legislative initiatives, all of which were stalled in Congress. He also inherited an economy that, in the view of the Kennedy administration economists, was growing steadily with an enviable record for low inflation, but still had too much unemployment and underutilized industrial capacity.

One of the first to whom Lyndon Johnson turned for help was Walter Heller, and Heller was ready for him. The two men had participated in the sessions that John Kennedy used to prepare for his press conferences and had struck up a friendship. On the second full day of his presidency, Johnson met with Heller and gave him the unsurprising news that "I'm no budget slasher . . . I am a Roosevelt New Dealer."[3] Already on Johnson's desk was a memorandum that Heller and his staff had prepared on the evening of the day of the assassination, stressing the importance of securing Senate approval of the Kennedy tax cut. Johnson had not been on the front lines of the battle to get the tax cut passed, but he was well aware of the arguments in favor of it. Heller was quick to capitalize on his understanding that, as he put it later, "Johnson never really got involved in economic reasoning . . . he was interested in the conclusion, the results and the politics."[4]

One of the pillars of political philosophy is that incumbent presidents need a strong economy to remain in office. Johnson understood that prompt passage of the tax cut could extend the economic expansion at least through 1964, when he would be running for the presidency in his own name. Moreover, the bold government programs that were already taking root in Johnson's imagination would take increased tax revenue, and a lot of it. The Johnson administration would need a growing economy to generate that tax revenue. In a speech to a joint session of Congress on 27 November, LBJ urged the Senate to "remember President Kennedy by the early passage of the tax bill for which he fought all this long year."[5]

Once Heller knew that Johnson would push for the tax cut, he wanted to make sure the tax cut would have the desired impact on the economy. Heller's biggest worry was that Fed would become concerned that the larger budget deficit caused by the tax cut would be inflationary and begin to tighten credit. On 31 December, he advised Johnson that tight money "could kill off a substantial part of the expansionary economic impact of the tax cut" and pushed for an early meeting of the Quadriad to put pressure on Martin and the Fed for more monetary ease.[6] Heller was determined to break the stranglehold Dillon and Martin exercised on the Kennedy administration's economic policies.

The Johnson Quadriad held its first meeting on 10 January 1964, and Heller and Martin repeated arguments they had made for Johnson in writing. Heller, the first to speak, focused on the Fed's role in encouraging higher interest rates: "The Fed manages money and, together with the Treasury, can determine interest rates."[7] He argued that prices and wages might creep upward but "it won't be 'inflation' and particularly not the kind that tight money can stop."[8] Heller also knew from his FOMC informants that Martin was indeed pushing the FOMC for an increase in the discount rate. Taking Martin on directly, Heller argued that a ½ percent rise in interest rates would increase the federal government's borrowing costs by "well over $1.0 billion a year" and could not be justified.

Bill Martin was put on the defensive by Heller's well-organized arguments. He gamely tried to downplay the Fed's influence on interest rates, but it sounded technical and unpersuasive. Martin was also frustrated by his ineffective description of two of the Fed's greatest accomplishments during the Kennedy years, consistent economic growth and stable long-term interest rates: "The fact is that ample credit has been available to finance an expansion in GNP, which was substantially larger than most private and Government observers anticipated. . . . Corporate and municipal rates are still below the levels they reached in 1961, the first year of recovery."[9] Lyndon Johnson was justly famous for his ability to forge a consensus around his point of view, and as he went around the table seeking opinions, the other administration members fell in line behind Heller. Even Douglas Dillon was unusually noncommittal about inflation. Martin realized that inflationary concerns would not receive much support from a Johnson administration. Martin, who had intended to distribute a memorandum titled "Monetary Policy and Cost-Push Inflation," was sufficiently disheartened by the discussion that he chose not to distribute it.[10]

A month later, Lyndon Johnson's strenuous efforts to cut the budget convinced Majority Leader Robert Byrd and the Senate to pass the tax cut of 1964. A weary Johnson complained: "I worked as hard on that budget as I have ever worked on anything,"[11] The U.S. economy would receive a thrust of additional consumption and, if it worked, Lyndon Johnson would receive the extra tax revenues he so eagerly sought.

As Walter Heller suspected, Bill Martin's posture in the January Quadriad meeting was intended to lay the groundwork for a possible credit tightening if the tax cut proved too stimulating. The campaign got off to a poor start in the Quadriad meeting and went further downhill when the president's annual economic report was issued in mid-January. In an unusually blunt admonition, Walter Heller wrote on behalf of the administration: "A strong upswing in the economy need not bring tight money or high interest rates. It would be self-defeating to cancel the stimulus of the tax reduction by tightening money."[12] This highly visible warning, clearly aimed at the Fed, generated intense speculation in the press about a possible Fed-administration conflict. Martin was no stranger to political pressure from politicians determined to see lower interest rates, but he was disturbed by the unmistakable hardening of the administration's position so soon after Lyndon Johnson's arrival in the White House.

While the implications of the tax cut were worrisome, Martin had a more immediate problem demanding his attention. Wright Patman, an easy-money congressman from Texas, was in his first year as the chairman of the House Banking and Currency Committee, the House committee with primary responsibility for overseeing the Fed's activities. Patman was an idiosyncratic legislator who had voted to impeach President Herbert Hoover in 1932, had quarreled bitterly with Franklin Roosevelt over bonuses for World War I veterans, and was often at odds with his fellow members of Congress. Patman had become a passionate crusader for the "small man" against what he saw as the evil influence of big-city bankers and their ally, the Federal Reserve System. With the pulpit of the chairmanship at his disposal and buttressed by economists, consultants, and the power of subpoena, he began what the *Wall Street Journal* called "fulfilling a life-time dream: his own full-scale investigation of the money-regulating Federal Reserve Board."[13]

Martin and Patman had engaged in a running argument about the Fed's activities over the last thirteen years, and they made an odd couple. The fifty-eight-year-old Martin, usually tanned and fit from his daily tennis regimen, would be seated at the witness table, clad in banker's pinstripes and round metal-rimmed glasses, listening intently, regularly breaking into his trademark smile during his responses. Answering in his gravely voice, often using folksy terms, he always chose his words carefully and often ended his sentences with a friendly "you see." In his debates with his congressional interrogators, Martin applied a skill honed by over thirty years of dealing with hostile Congress members. He had debated with Congress about the activities of the New York Stock Exchange, the Russian lend-lease program, the U.S. Treasury Department and, for the last thirteen years, the Fed. Over the years, Martin had developed an ability to endure just or unjust criticism with equal stoicism, and he always anticipated that his responses would not satisfy his critics.

Peering down at Martin was seventy-one-year-old Wright Patman, sitting behind a raised mahogany-paneled facade with his committee compatriots. A balding sharecropper's son whose southwestern drawl was softened by thirty-five years in Washington, Patman's only financial background consisted of contacts with the small businessmen in his Texas congressional district and his unflagging support for small savings & loan companies. Over his thirty years on the committee, he had accumulated a broad understanding of the Fed's operations, but his suspicion of the Fed's motives often drove him to make unsupportable accusations that alienated his committee members. He would often read statements or questions delivered to him by unobtrusive aides. Patman would pepper Martin with hostile questions, occasionally reddening with anger at his answers. Their duels had become legendary in the Capitol.

To parry Patman's attacks, Martin used the Fed chairman's traditional right to obscure the Fed's monetary policy intentions, along with an unthreatening defense of basic Fed policies and a ready admission that "we could have done better." Their debates could become heated, but Martin never let it become personal because he knew he had to maintain a viable relationship with Patman no matter how difficult it was. Martin was the first Fed chairman to devote substantial effort to cultivating relationships on the Hill and, with the notable exception of Wright Patman, it had paid off in improved relations, if not understanding.

The Patman hearings ground on, consuming thousands of hours of Fed staff time in dealing with the committee's requests. Patman launched numerous legislative proposals designed to undercut the Fed's independence and force it to be treated like any other government agency. As an embarrassment to Martin, Patman asked that Martin's personal financial information be made available to the committee so it could be reviewed for possible conflicts of interest. Ironically, Martin's Fed salary in 1963 was less than half of the salary he had received twenty-six years earlier as president of the New York Stock Exchange. Martin and many others who felt called to public service knew that the financial sacrifice required might limit the length of their tenure. Martin had accumulated financial resources during his Wall Street years, and his wife, Cynthia, was from a wealthy St. Louis family. He could accept public-servant pay levels longer than others. Martin's assets were conservatively invested and grew modestly during his years of public service. His experience was in sharp contrast to politicians like Lyndon Johnson, who built considerable wealth while serving in public office.

Patman's legislative proposals included many that had been previously defeated, but this time he added several new weapons to his repertoire. He now proposed eliminating the FOMC, increasing the Fed board from seven to twelve and, in an attempt to reverse the outcome of a twenty-two-year strug-gle, advocated returning the secretary of the Treasury to the Fed's board of governors. He also proposed eliminating the Fed's right to retain any of the interest earned on its Treasury portfolio to cover its operating expenses, in-stead subjecting it to an annual budget authorization process. In the view of Martin and other Fed officials, Patman had dangerously raised the ante in his periodic forays into Fed oversight. To their dismay, the hearings continued without a clear end in sight. It appeared that Patman might simply wear down the opposition and, as *Time* magazine put it in February 1964, "he could buck through at least a few of his proposals."[14]

By early May, the Patman hearings had entered their fifth month. Martin knew that Patman had lost the support of the committee's Republicans and that members of his own party were also beginning to defect. Despite the erosion of support, Patman labored on, and no one on the committee would openly challenge him. Martin knew he had to do something or "Patman would win support for his long-standing campaign to make the Fed just another government agency."[15] Martin rarely requested personal appointments with his presidents, since they always entailed a sense of obligation. This would certainly be true for Lyndon Johnson, who was justly famed for trading favors. Martin had endured considerable administration criticism over the years in order to achieve a reputation for nonpartisanship. He was extremely reluctant to cede any of his hard-won gains. As much as it went against his philosophy, Martin concluded that he had no alternative, and he reluctantly called the White House for an appointment.

As Martin followed aide Jack Valenti into the Oval Office, Johnson proposed a walk in the May sunshine. They began to pace around a macadam circle be-hind the White House, one of Johnson's legendary venues for his arm-twisting sessions, dubbed the "LBJ treatment" by the press. LBJ started off by asking Martin to tell him about interest rates and how they worked. Taken aback, Martin gave a brief summary, knowing that the punch line would be Johnson's desire to see them come down. It came, and Martin gave a polite but firm answer: "I think we're heading toward an inflationary mess that we won't be able to pull ourselves out of."[16] Johnson replied, "Now I have some pretty good people here and they don't agree with you . . . but we'll talk about it later."[17] Then they discussed Patman and his hearings. Johnson listened, returned to the Oval Office to call John McCormack, the Speaker of the House, and asked him to help resolve the issue. Two weeks later, after an angry valedictory by Patman, the hearings ended without any agreement on the disruptive proposals. Martin wondered how he would respond when Johnson inevitably asked him to "see if he could help" the next time they discussed interest rates.

Another reason that Lyndon Johnson preferred the macadam circle for his walks was that the press corps could survey who was receiving the Johnson "treatment." Martin's little visit was the subject of lively speculation in the next morning's papers. An old hand at the politics of the press, Martin used the attention now focused on him to offer a few selected in-depth interviews. The 16 May 1964 issue of *Business Week* described him thus: "[S]itting in his favorite olive leather chair, feet propped on a marble table, he is jovial, even voluble."[18] Martin highlighted the "Fed's own reform program," which put trained economists in the presidencies of most of the regional Federal Reserve Banks and led to the appointment of a permanent academic consultant to the board whose role was to increase contact between the board and academic economists. Although Martin hoped that his interviews would counteract some of the sting of Patman's angry accusations, he believed the issue would soon fade from the front pages. He was not disappointed.

Much of the general public's view of Bill Martin was conditioned by the indelible impression made by Herblock cartoons in the *Washington Post*, which usually showed Martin in a celluloid collar, bowler, and 1890s-era suit. Martin had learned to accept that this caricature was nourished by the tenor of many of his public comments over the years. Like his predecessors, Martin served as the nation's schoolmaster, using his public speeches to praise the virtues of financial discipline and warn about the dangers of inflation. Unlike his predecessors, who had traditionally disdained the press, Martin tried to maintain open and friendly relations with selected financial writers, a practice that dated back to his days as president of the New York Stock Exchange. At that time, Martin's widely broadcast public image as a reformer had been a useful element in the campaign to restore the public's confidence in the integrity of the stock market. Since he had assumed the Fed chairmanship, Martin and the Fed had frequently come in for harsh commentary, often reflecting the views of congressional or academic economist critics. But the in-depth articles and profiles were generally more balanced. Martin knew that to deal with an administration that was masterfully managing the press, he and other Fed officials would have to devote time and effort to getting their side of the story out.

During the summer of 1964, the economy continued to grow steadily. In his usual felicitous phrasing, Walter Heller described the economy as "being blown along by the gentle zephyr of the tax cut."[19] Fed economists concluded that the initial impact of the tax cut was milder than expected and must have been "anticipated by consumers" who began spending at higher levels earlier in the year.[20] The FOMC's chief economic analyst, Daniel Brill, reviewed the economy's achievements in the 17 June FOMC meeting: a real growth rate of

5 percent for the last six months, unemployment down to 5.1 percent, capital spending increasing at a 12 percent rate, and wholesale prices actually declining slightly. He concluded: "[I]t's trite, but I have to say it: it's just too good to be true."[21] The surge in capital spending created new manufacturing capacity, so that capacity utilization was still only at 86 percent, an unusually low number for an expansion that was over three years old. The absence of inflationary pressures allowed the Fed to avoid tightening the economy. The money supply expanded at a 3.1 percent annual rate for the first half of 1964 and, most remarkably, bank credit was growing at over 12 percent. The Fed willingly provided the reserves needed to sustain that growth.

The forces at work in the U.S. economy could not sustain that perfect balance achieved in the first half of 1964. On 12 September, the leaders of the United Auto Workers announced wage contracts with Chrysler and Ford containing annual increases of 4.7 percent. The increase was well in excess of productivity increases in the industry and knocked a giant hole in the credibility of the wage-price guidelines. Even Walter Heller was moved to conclude that "auto price increases are on the way."[22] Prior to the settlement, Heller, Dillon, and Defense Secretary Robert McNamara had been pleading with auto industry executives to pressure their suppliers to hold the line on prices and wages. Now that effort was in ruins. Martin weighed in on the side of price and wage restraint and again turned to reporter Hobart Rowen, who quoted him as saying: "I would be slightly skeptical about the notion that the industry's new contracts are not inflationary, particularly if they spread to other negotiations."[23]

Martin faced an uphill battle to convince Americans that inflation was a potentially serious issue in mid-1964. By traditional postwar measures of longevity, the current expansion was exceptionally long-lived, and most economists and the popular press were predicting a slowdown in the second half of 1965. Inflation for the twelve months ending 31 March 1965 was a quiescent 1.56 percent. Martin was concerned that the administration would move too quickly to counteract any slowdown and sow the seeds for future inflation. He knew that Walter Heller was promoting a combination of increased expenditures and additional tax cuts if a slowdown threatened, and Lyndon Johnson could be expected to go along with Heller.[24] In addition, the full expansionary impact of the 1964 tax cut would be felt in 1965. These factors raised the possibility that economic growth, and inflationary pressures, could be stronger than expected in 1965.

In view of these possibilities, Martin pushed the FOMC to move toward restraint before problems arose: "If the committee ignores inflationary tendencies at a time when something could be done about them . . . monetary policy will bear the entire blame for events."[25] The Fed would have to walk the narrowest of tightropes. Too much restraint could damage the economy and bring a hailstorm of criticism down upon the Fed, while too little restraint would fail to alert the financial markets about the Fed's true concerns.

As he nudged the FOMC, Martin also carried his message to the public. In his interview with Rowen, he not only acknowledged the inflationary potential of the auto settlement, he also observed: "Over the course of the next six weeks we will have to make some judgments on whether there is to be a major shift in monetary policy."[26] To reassure the public that the Fed was not ready to clamp down on the economy, he added: "The Fed hasn't the slightest desire to get tagged with causing a decline."[27] It was a mixed message, but it was the best he could do when the economy might be entering a transition.

Bill Martin often advised his fellow FOMC members that the fate of the U.S. economy could not be separated from that of the world economy, and another crisis for the British pound proved him all too correct. On 16 October 1964, by the narrowest of margins, British voters elected the first Labour Party government in fifteen years. International bankers watched in horror as Prime Minister Harold Wilson declared his "first 100 days" agenda, which included renationalizing selected industries and vigorously expanding the welfare state. The British balance of payments was in a critical situation before the election, and the Labour Party's plans triggered a flood of sterling selling. Much like president-elect John Kennedy in 1960, Wilson was forced to announce his intention to defend the value of his nation's currency. The Labour government announced a surtax on imports, and the Bank of England began to support the pound in foreign-exchange markets. After a brief hiatus to digest the news, currency speculators decided that the Labour government lacked the willpower to prevent devaluation, and by mid-November, the selling again rose to a floodtide. The Bank of England exhausted nearly all of its short-term credit lines with other central banks, and it was frighteningly clear that extreme measures were necessary to control the speculation against the British currency.

On Sunday, 22 November, the Bank of England advised Martin, Dillon, and Roosa that it would raise the bank's discount rate from 5 percent to 7 percent the following day. *Time* magazine later quoted a Swiss banker as saying: "A seven percent rate will drag money from the moon."[28] The three Americans agreed that a ½ percent increase in the Fed's discount rate would help reduce the incentive for speculative short-term funds to flow from the United States to the United Kingdom. That night, Martin canvassed members of the FOMC to pave the way for the increase, and Dillon and Roosa informed Lyndon Johnson about the proposed rate change. As they expected, the president erupted.

He demanded to know how the Fed and the Treasury "would guarantee that the higher rates will not hurt the economy," but Dillon and Martin advised Johnson that no such guarantees were possible.[29] To help calm the president, Martin offered to hold an unprecedented press conference at the time of the rate increase announcement in order to assure the public that the move was purely precautionary and should not impact the availability of credit. The press description of Johnson as "unhappy and upset" hardly did justice to his frame of mind.[30]

Dramatic as it was, the British rate increase was not enough to stem the tide. On the morning of Tuesday, 24 November, sellers of sterling returned in force. A worst-case scenario, the collapse of one of the two reserve currencies, was unfolding. The Fed's point man was the sardonic and unflappable Charles Coombs, manager of foreign-exchange operations at the New York Fed. In an emergency telephone meeting of the FOMC on the afternoon of 24 November, Coombs argued that "the situation is extremely dangerous and a 'now or never' effort should be made."[31] Coombs proposed a $3 billion rescue plan, twice as large as any previous package, with the United States providing $1 billion and other nations supplying the remainder. Coombs proposed that the Fed and the Bank of England organize the central bank consortium, with the Fed increasing its swap credit line with the Bank of England to $750 million. Martin had already asked the U.S. Export-Import Bank to provide another $250 million. Those FOMC members who had opposed the recent discount rate increase began to question the wisdom of supporting the British during their recurring exchange problems. Martin moved to Coomb's defense, and the FOMC reluctantly approved the Fed commitment.

Martin also had mixed emotions about the frequency of British exchange problems. He had personally led the move to force a British devaluation in 1949 and was distressed that successive British governments had not taken the difficult decisions to make their economy truly competitive. But the British pound was one of the linchpins of the international monetary system, and devaluation would cause chaos in world exchange markets. The selling might begin with the pound, but it could easily extend to the dollar. Confidence in the British currency had to be quickly rebuilt if the Labour government were to have any chance of securing a lasting solution. Each day of delay added enormously to the cost of achieving a long-term recovery for Britain. That afternoon, Martin advised Lyndon Johnson that the Fed would move decisively to rebuild confidence in the dollar and sterling in the exchange markets: "We're not fooling around on this. If need be, we'll make all our payments [for international reserve settlements] in gold."[32]

Once the Export-Import Bank commitment was in hand, a group of officers in the Federal Reserve Bank of New York and their counterparts in the Bank of England conducted a nonstop negotiating process to bring other central banks into the rescue package. Within twenty-four hours, the consortium was in place, earning Robert Roosa's accolade for "the biggest and quickest monetary rescue job ever seen."[33] International speculators were put on notice that the world's financial officials were willing and able to mobilize large-scale defenses of their currencies. The rescue had succeeded, but the sheer size of the package indicated that the speculative forces arrayed against the stability of the international monetary system had grown substantially. As he reflected on the ferocity of the crisis, Martin concluded that the unwillingness of Britain or the United States to deal decisively with their respective balance of payments deficits was threatening the continuity of the fixed-rate international monetary system.

Martin was able to express this concern directly to Harold Wilson and Lyndon Johnson in a meeting two weeks after the rescue, but this rare opportunity ended in an embarrassing standoff. On 7 December 1964, the British prime minister met with the president, Dillon, and Martin. When it was Martin's turn to speak, he minced no words and criticized Wilson's refusal to accept the higher interest rates needed to deal with the British balance of payments deficit until it was too late. Martin also accused Labour government ministers of publicly undercutting the only real policy the Wilson government initiated to deal with the exchange crisis, its emergency surtax on imports. Martin concluded: "It is vitally important that the United Kingdom re-establish confidence in its [balance of payments] program."[34] Unlike the more diplomatic comments from Secretary Dillon and the president, Martin delivered a stern, unmistakable message.

Lyndon Johnson broke the uncomfortable silence that followed Martin's comments by asking him whether the United States was doing all it could about its own balance of payments. Martin answered no, and LBJ, who was surprised by the answer, was even more surprised when Treasury Secretary Dillon agreed with Martin. The president, now red-faced and with his voice growing louder, ordered Defense Secretary Robert McNamara to leave a meeting in the next room and join the discussion. McNamara immediately disagreed with Martin and Dillon, and a "rather sharp debate" started among Johnson's key advisors.[35] When Johnson angrily rejected Martin's assertion that the overseas military commitments of the United States would eventually force a devaluation of the dollar, Martin challenged Johnson "to declare yourself [on the valuation of the dollar], as President Kennedy did in 1963. It is important that the whole world know where you stand on this basic question."[36]

Lyndon Johnson's freewheeling leadership style pushed Bill Martin to the edge of his patience, and he addressed a president of the United States in a way he never had before. The Johnson White House was a continuum of negotiation and intense emotional pressure, and it reminded Martin of his days at the New York Stock Exchange. This rough-and-tumble environment might be suitable to political horse trading, but it was not very conducive to dealing constructively with long-term economic problems. As the argument in front of the British prime minister wound down, Martin despondently observed that the Johnson administration was in no position to lecture Harold Wilson or any other government leader about the virtues of financial discipline or cabinet unity.

A few months later, Martin went public with his discomfort with the economic situation. On 25 February 1965, he appeared before the Joint Economic Committee. Referring to the prospects for continued strong economic growth and the full impact of the tax cut, he said, "There is an element of brinksmanship in our laudable efforts to push our economy closer and closer to its full potential without straining it."[37] Then, focusing on the balance of payments problems, he observed: "The chronic payments deficits have undercut the U.S. bargaining position in international economic affairs. We are dealing from a position of weakness."[38] In a response that cannot have pleased Johnson, he said that if the president's balance of payments program introduced on 10 February did not work, "we will have to look at our military forces abroad, our foreign aid, and of course, a less expansive overall credit policy."[39]

Having so openly differed with the assumptions underlying the administration's economic policy, Martin could have expected an early Quadriad and a debate with Walter Heller. But this did not take place. Following Johnson's true landslide victory in the 1964 presidential election, many of the stalwart holdovers from John Kennedy's administration were resigning. Walter Heller had already been replaced, and Douglas Dillon had announced that his resignation would be effective in April. Lyndon Johnson would soon have an economic team of his own choosing—given Johnson's instincts, it was not a particularly comforting thought for Bill Martin.

Finding a compatible Treasury secretary was not as easy as Lyndon Johnson had hoped. The few businessmen he considered, such as his friend utility executive Donald Cook, were judged too liberal by the financial community, and candidates from the financial community, such as New York banker David Rockefeller, could not be persuaded to join the administration. He finally turned to Dillon's undersecretary, Henry Fowler, and "enveloped him in ardent patriotic Johnsonian persuasion and squeezed out an acceptance."[40]

Fowler was a courtly Virginian, the son of a railroad engineer, who had joined the New Deal when he was fresh out of Yale Law School in 1933. He started as a junior lawyer at the Tennessee Valley Authority and cut his teeth on regulatory issues in a series of governmental agencies. During World War II, Fowler served as assistant general counsel for the War Production Board, which eventually landed him as Harry Truman's choice to run the Office of Defense Mobilization and the National Production Authority during the Korean War. In the years between his defense-related posts, he founded a Washington, D.C.–based law firm known for its government contacts and blue-ribbon clients. His successful legal practice enabled him to play a leading role on a variety of governmental policy task forces. When economist Paul Samuelson gathered a group to advise candidate John Kennedy on possible economic policies, Henry Fowler was a natural selection. When Treasury secretary–designate Douglas Dillon was seeking a number-two man who was politically astute and capable of managing the daily activities of the Treasury, Henry Fowler was again the natural candidate.

After two years of competently minding the store for Dillon, Fowler became the man of the hour in 1962, when the Kennedy tax cut legislation was bogged down on Capitol Hill. Dillon asked him to organize a nationwide campaign to develop business support for it. For a steady six months Fowler was on the road, "speaking to any business group that would listen."[41] As *Fortune* put it: "Within months there were 3000 top executives enrolled in [Fowler's] Business Committee for Tax Reduction."[42] Business support proved to be crucial in persuading the House to pass the legislation in 1963, and Lyndon Johnson, who had put together a few legislative campaigns himself, took notice of Fowler's accomplishment. Henry Fowler might not have a Wall Street background, but Johnson placed a very high value on his ability to persuade members of business and Congress alike.

Johnson turned to another deputy, Gardner Ackley, to replace Walter Heller as the chairman of the Council of Economic Advisers. Heller had known Ackley as another midwestern Keynesian economist and in late 1961, asked him to take a leave of absence from the chairmanship of the economics department at the University of Michigan to replace the departing James Tobin on the CEA. Ackley was not as prominent in the field of economics as either of his immediate predecessors, Tobin or Kermit Gordon, but he was known to be a hard worker, a solid researcher, and a clear writer. He did have prior experience in the federal government, having served as an economist in the Office of Price Administration during World War II. During his early years at the CEA, he covered monetary policy and regularly commiserated with Heller about the council's problems in pushing a more expansionary policy on the Fed.

Ackley brought the most anti-Fed attitude to the chairmanship of the CEA since Leon Keyserling, the CEA chairman in 1950. In his oral history in 1973, Ackley admitted: "I was critical of the Fed in those days and I am still."[43] "I don't believe that the Federal Reserve System ought to have any real independence. It is part of the government and should be responsible to the administration."[44] While Martin and Ackley had had relatively little contact before Ackley became CEA chairman, Ackley saw Martin's lack of background in economics as a serious liability for someone in the Fed chairmanship: "I don't think we'll ever have a chairman of the Federal Reserve who is so completely out of the mainstream of economics."[45] Furthermore, he felt that "the tradition of independence which Martin cultivates very strongly means that discussion of policy [between the CEA and the Fed] is much more difficult."[46] Bill Martin might even have accepted some of Ackley's complaints about him, but their future relationship would depend on the extent to which Ackley let his anti-Fed attitude affect his policy recommendations to Lyndon Johnson.

Martin's concern about his ability to work with the new administration team crystallized in early March 1965, when Fowler's appointment was announced. Martin would miss Dillon: his was a voice of moderation and independent thought in a cabinet that Johnson had inherited from John Kennedy but had bent to his own will. Martin would lose an ally he had often counted on for crucial support. Henry Fowler did not have Dillon's standing in the business or financial communities that might enable him to stand up to Lyndon Johnson. Martin's relationship with Ackley was uncomfortable and, to Martin's mind, Ackley was not capable of differing with the president. In the absence of any restraining influences among his advisors, Lyndon Johnson's single-minded determination to realize the benefits of continued economic growth regardless of the cost weighed heavily on Martin. The Quadriad met less frequently during Heller's last year, and Martin no longer enjoyed the give-and-take with the administration that was so essential in working out complementary monetary and fiscal policies. In the dangerous period that Martin saw ahead, that give-and-take would be more important than ever. The time had come for him to make way for someone with whom the president could work. A brief handwritten letter of resignation had lain in Martin's desk drawer for a month.

Martin decided to discuss his resignation with the president privately before a Quadriad meeting scheduled for 10 March. As the two men sat down, the president's favorite beagle jumped into Martin's lap. Johnson told Martin, "You look very good with the beagle and I think I should have a picture taken."[47] As the amused president undertook a fruitless search for a photographer, Martin realized that he was running out of time before the meeting was scheduled to begin. Finally he said, "You know Mr. President, you and I have talked about this before, and now I wish you would try to find someone for my place."[48] Johnson, without giving it any thought, said, "I can't lose more than Doug at the moment," and turned to engage in banter as Dillon and the other Quadriad members entered the room.[49] It was hardly a vote of confidence, but it was clear that Martin's awkward relationship with Johnson would continue, at least for the present.

Another factor that contributed to Martin's decision to offer his resignation was his disappointment over the most recent selection for the board of governors. Abbott Mills, the last governor with any banking experience, was retiring and leaving Bill Martin as the only governor with practical experience in the financial markets. From the Fed's inception in 1913 through the Eisenhower administration, governors had come both from the private and public sectors, reflecting the Fed's original legislative mandate that the president, when selecting governors, "shall have due regard to a fair representation of the financial, agricultural, industrial and commercial interests and geographical divisions of the country."[50] Martin believed that the spirit of this mandate was being undermined by the governor candidates selected by the Kennedy and Johnson administrations. The Kennedy candidates had both been economists from the public sector, and Martin knew that Gardner Ackley was pushing another economist.

Martin had proposed possible candidates from the banking industry, but without Douglas Dillon's support, he could not persuade the administration to consider them. On 1 April 1965, the president announced the appointment of Sherman Maisel, the first academic economist to be appointed since 1914. Maisel was from the mold of Seymour Harris, an outspoken Keynesian economist who Ackley hoped would, along with James Robertson and George Mitchell, push the FOMC toward expansionary monetary policy. When he learned of Johnson's decision, Martin could foresee that the composition of the board of governors would make it difficult for him to persuade the FOMC to undertake restrictive monetary policies under anything less than unarguably inflationary economic conditions. Although Martin could count on a few reliable supporters, he would have to work for every vote to forge a consensus for restraint.

In the months after his aborted resignation effort, Martin felt more isolated from an administration than he had ever been as Fed chairman. He worried that the traditional differences between the Fed and the administration over the future of the economy were growing dangerously wide under Johnson's single-minded focus on growth. Fed officials foresaw strong economic growth and all the problems that usually attend it. Economists at the Fed reversed their forecast of a slowdown in the second half of 1965 and now anticipated that for the full year, GNP would grow at a faster rate than the 5.3 percent recorded in 1964. FOMC members were concerned that, while the official budget numbers for the fiscal year ending 30 June 1965 reflected modest spending growth, it was common knowledge that the administration's supplemental budgetary requests for education and the war on poverty totaled $6 billion and were growing.

The credit markets indicated soaring bank lending, with a growth rate of 13.8 percent during the fourteen months ending February 1965. Most ominous of all, inflationary pressures were becoming visible. On 13 April, a representative of the New York Reserve bank told the FOMC: "The prospect of price increases is more imminent, and the problem of keeping down unit costs is more precarious that it has been for several years."[51] Martin persuaded the FOMC to approve a "modest" move toward tightening in late March, and sentiment was growing for a further tightening in May.

The viewpoint of the administration could not have been more different. In early February, Gardner Ackley advised the president: "The economy is advancing rapidly, but this is a temporary situation."[52] He also commented on Martin's statement that if the president's balance of payments program did not work, higher interest rates might be needed: "The balance of payments benefits of higher interest rates do not justify higher interest rates."[53] In the 10 May Quadriad, Ackley pressed Martin for more ease in the credit markets. In a press conference after the meeting, Ackley said, "The general consensus is that the economy is progressing extremely well. . . . There is no evidence that inflationary pressures are building up to threaten the healthy growth that has characterized the economy for a record-breaking fifty-one months."[54] There was little about the prospects for the economy on which the CEA and economists at the Fed agreed.

Martin determined that it was again time to take the Fed's side of the story to the public and did so in a speech to the Society of American Business Writers on 13 May 1965. Referring to the budget deficits of the last five years, he observed: "I am not at all sure that the present political climate of perpetual growth will be vindicated in terms of perpetual deficits and easy money."[55] He attempted to build support for the Fed's past tightening: "There have been two discount rate hikes in the last two years and reserves have moved from a substantial plus to a moderate minus without slowing the rate of economic advance or impairing the health of the economy."[56] Finally, in a comment that reflected his remarkable humanity, he mocked his own sense of isolation: "I know people say, 'There's old Martin again. He thinks the economy is overheating. He's always saying that.' "[57] Martin was uncomfortable taking his differences with the administration to the public, but he felt an honest debate over economic policy was in the public interest. If it could not take place in the White House, it must take place in the public arena.

Undeterred by a noticeable lack of response to his speech to the business writers, Martin tried again in a commencement address to the graduates of Columbia University on 1 June. He used financial history to justify the Fed's concerns about the economic risks inherent in an extended period of economic growth. Comparing economic conditions in 1965 with those prevailing in the years before the Great Depression, he found "disquieting similarities."[58] In a series of "then, as now" comparisons, Martin highlighted the expanded use of consumer debt, the balance of payments problems for the world's primary currencies, and an uninterrupted prosperity restricted to a handful of rich countries. He finished off with: "Then, as now, government officials, scholars, and businessmen are convinced that a new economic era has opened, an era in which business fluctuations have become a thing of the past."[59]

Martin went on to list a series of economic factors that represented strengths of the current economy, including reduced borrowing for stock purchases, organizations responsible for stabilizing commodity prices, better understanding of the impact of monetary and fiscal policies, and an international monetary system strengthened by the IMF and bilateral credit arrangements. He concluded with the admonition: "Most observers agree that to a large extent the disaster of 1929–33 was a consequence of maladjustments born of the boom of the twenties. Hence, we must continuously be on the alert to prevent a recurrence of maladjustments — even at the risk of being falsely accused of failing to realize the benefits of unbounded expansion."[60] Unfortunately for Bill Martin, the positive economic comparisons of this prescient speech were totally lost in the media's coverage. The press reported that the chairman of the Federal Reserve Board was warning about a possible depression, and the speech caused a sensation.

Martin touched on a nerve and the body politic suffered a spasm. As soon as the news appeared on the ticker tape, prices on the New York Stock Exchange, which had been trending downward, swung into the sharpest decline since the Kennedy assassination. The next day the speech became page-one news in papers across the United States and world financial capitals. Not surprisingly, Representative Wright Patman immediately called for Martin to "do the decent thing and resign."[61] Fed Governor James L. Robertson took the highly unusual step of publicly disagreeing with Martin: "We are not suffering from inflation . . . and tight money is not an appropriate prescription for our domestic problems" was his rejoinder.[62]

The speech generated considerable editorial commentary as well. The *New*

York Times weighed in with "Martin has exaggerated the parallels between the 1920s and the present and has mistakenly raised the specter of another 1929. His doubts clearly seek to temper Washington's . . . confident consensus."[63] Reporters had a field day, playing up the historic nature of a conflict between a powerful president and a Fed chairman. Even *Isvestya,* the Russian official newspaper, commented: "The speech was . . . an attempt to preserve the hegemony of the US dollar, despite the desires of the French and other western powers that it change."[64]

The commotion over the speech required Martin to execute a delicate minuet with the administration. Henry Fowler visited Martin personally to confirm LBJ's visceral anger, despite his public silence. Gardner Ackley, sent out for public damage control, argued: "We have not been able to find overheating, even in the booming first quarter. There is no evidence of inflationary pressures."[65] At a noisy press conference following the 10 June Quadriad meeting, Johnson stated that there was no reason for "gloom and doom" about the economy and that his administration was "united on that fact."[66] The press pool turned expectantly to Martin for a show of his renowned independence. In a careful response, he said: "I don't think any of us here agree with every shade or emphasis with what the president said. I don't think he would want us to."[67] Asked if he wanted to change his speech in view of the reaction, Martin admitted that he was surprised by the attention but that "[t]here is nothing in the speech that I would want to change."[68] Martin summed up his difficult position: "I find that I am in the position of having advocated safe driving, and now I am accused of causing all the accidents."[69] He had focused the public's attention on the economy to an extent that he could never have imagined, but at the cost of making his differences with the administration into an international incident.

As the weeks passed, the uproar over the speech gradually died down. Martin's astonishment that his cautionary remarks had generated such extended exposure was equaled by his disappointment that the debate on the issues, the original motivation for his speech, quickly disappeared from the public consciousness. Lyndon Johnson, on the other hand, regretted that he had not paid more attention to Martin's offer to resign a few months earlier. In mid-July, the president asked Attorney General Nicholas Katzenbach to review the conditions under which a Fed board member could be removed. Advised that "termination for cause" did not include disagreement with administration policies, and that in the Fed's fifty-one years of existence no attempt had ever been made to remove a sitting Fed governor, Johnson let the matter drop.[70]

The public interest in the future of the economy might have faded, but

Martin's concern about the sustainability of the expansion did not. The expansion, now close to fifty-three months old, was being fueled in part by a virtuous cycle of complementary forces. One element was that the Fed was accommodating an unusually large increase in the assets of the banking system. From late 1960 to mid-1965, total nonborrowed reserves (total bank reserves minus any reserves borrowed from the Fed) of the banking system grew at an average annual rate of 4 percent, compared to almost no increase in reserves during the expansion following the recession of 1957–58. The availability of reserves enabled the banking system to accommodate a strong surge in loan demand. During the period from late 1960 through mid-1965, bank loans grew at an average annual rate of over 8 percent, compared to a 3.5 percent average following the 1957–58 recession. Many of the loans financed new and low-cost manufacturing capacity that helped corporations keep costs and prices from rising. The final and most important element in this cycle was that stable costs and minimal price inflation enabled the Fed to refrain from tightening credit. The economic statistics analyzed by Fed economists indicated that this virtuous cycle might be unwinding.

During the second quarter of 1965, the CPI increased at an annualized rate of 2.6 percent, the highest quarterly rate since the fourth quarter of 1960 and well above the 1.1 percent increase over the previous twelve months. Most analysts saw it as a short-term phenomenon, but it was a bad omen. A Fed economist warned the FOMC: "A number of wage increases in the first half of 1965 have exceeded the guidelines of the Council of Economic Advisers by a significant amount."[71] FOMC Secretary Robert Holland remembers that the FOMC staff worked with economists at the Brookings Institution to determine why the real economy was so strong, since the Fed's economic model did not produce this result when the actual economic data were fed into it. Their conclusion was that unacknowledged war spending must be rising.[72] At the staff's urging, Martin met with Defense Secretary Robert McNamara to discuss the subject, but McNamara denied that Vietnam commitments were increasing.

McNamara's answer did not satisfy Martin. After many years of public service, Martin had developed strong friendships throughout official Washington. Two of those friends were Senator Richard Russell, who had opposed Martin on Russian aid many years earlier and was the chairman of the Senate Armed Services Committee, and David Packard, the deputy secretary of Defense. They both confidentially advised Martin that the cost of the Vietnam War was actually rising fast and that defense spending would be many billions of dollars over budget. In July 1965, Martin had advised Fed Governor Dewey Daane: "I have been talking to Packard. These things [Vietnam spending] are going to go way beyond what the administration has admitted."[73] When Martin broached this issue with Fowler and Ackley, it was clear that neither official understood the true situation.[74] Lyndon Johnson was deliberately keeping this added spending a secret, and the two men most responsible for the administration's economic policy were not prepared to delve into this issue. Martin knew that if he were to act on this information, he would end up in a direct conflict with the administration.

By the fall of 1965, Martin was worried that some of the deeper fears that he usually kept submerged under his professional calm would become a reality. His dark visions saw economic consequences in black and white, even though his experience taught him that grays predominated. It now appeared that the grays were giving way to blacker hues. At the 28 September FOMC meeting, Martin warned: "I cannot believe that all periods of prosperity float on constantly rising levels of credit . . . or that one can ignore credit quality."[75] Martin had a foreboding sense that momentum in the economy was building, and the Fed was not dealing with it. If the Fed and the administration began to modify their monetary and fiscal policies now, it might eventually be possible to bring the economy under some measure of control. If these policies were not put in place, the impact of the war spending on an economy that was almost at full employment and already stimulated by growing government social spending would create an inflationary economic boom. That boom would be unlike anything the United States had experienced since World War II and in Martin's opinion would be followed by the inevitable bust.

The pragmatist in Martin knew that he had little chance of persuading the Johnson administration to support a plan to slow the economy. The Fed must act on its own to tighten credit, and the timing was becoming terribly urgent. By mid-December, the season of heavy Treasury refinancings would begin, and any monetary policy changes at that time could severely disrupt the financing of government operations. Even more important, Fed Governor Canby Balderston, one of Martin's staunchest supporters on the board of governors, was retiring in late January, and his vote would be critical. Martin was already canvassing his governors about a possible rise in the discount rate. He knew that the liberal minority of Robertson, Mitchell, and Maisel were against it, while hard-liners Balderston and Shepherdson were in favor of it. Governor Dewey Daane was the swing vote and, although Martin was working on him, Daane's allegiance was unclear.

Throughout his chairmanship, Martin made certain that the administration was "apprised about the thinking within the FOMC."[76] A discount rate increase would be the Fed's first widely public move to tighten credit since the current expansion began fifty-eight months earlier. Prior to the 6 October

Quadriad, Martin tried to persuade Johnson to accept a rate increase by emphasizing that the current interest rate structure and statutory ceilings on interest rates on savings certificates were too low, putting small banks at a disadvantage in attracting savings. An increase in the discount rate would "open up a freer, more effective flow of funds . . . and the position of smaller borrowers would clearly be improved."[77] He also argued: "Rising [inflationary] expectations evidenced in financial markets and price warnings suggest slightly higher interest rates would sustain and stretch out the expansion."[78]

Predictably, Gardner Ackley took the other side of the argument, observing that the economy "was not moving ahead too rapidly."[79] In Ackley's opinion, "interest rates are already inching up across a broad spectrum" and did not need the added impetus of a discount rate increase.[80] Martin and Ackley were preparing for a face-off when the president announced: "I'm scheduled to go into the hospital tomorrow for a gall bladder operation. You wouldn't raise the discount rate while I'm in the hospital, would you?" Martin waited a second and, in a reply that became legendary within the Fed, said: "No, Mr. President, we'll wait until you get out of the hospital."[81]

Martin's campaign became further complicated on 1 November, when a long-awaited study on the future of the economy was completed. The influential authors were Paul Volcker, the deputy undersecretary of the Treasury for Monetary Affairs; Daniel Brill, director of research for the Fed; CEA member Arthur Okun; and Charles Zwick, assistant director of the Budget. The report concluded that "prices would creep upward, but the rise was not likely to accelerate."[82] Arthur Okun described the report's conclusion as "basically a policy recommendation that we ought to keep monetary policy about where it was, and should not tighten for the remainder of the year."[83] In the report, Volcker and Okun proposed that any monetary policy decision be deferred until the fiscal 1967 budget was completed in January, and monetary and fiscal priorities could be announced in the State of the Union address. When Martin received the working party report and saw that it "considered a step-up in Federal spending to be unlikely," he knew that Lyndon Johnson was still unwilling to divulge the true extent of Vietnam War spending.[84] Martin concluded that the report was based on incorrect assumptions and could not serve as a basis for Fed policy, so "he chose to sit on it," never distributing it to FOMC members.[85] It was an atypical decision for a man who believed in maximum disclosure and reveals the tremendous importance Martin assigned to gaining board approval for a rate increase.

During this period, Martin worked closely with Al Hayes, the president of the New York Reserve Bank, to bring the five Reserve Bank presidents with a vote on the FOMC around to Martin's view. FOMC staff advisor Bob Holland remembers: "Those five presidential votes were very important to Bill's majority. He needed Reserve Bank support in the form of a rate increase request. Hayes was with Bill all through the process."[86] The presidents of the New York and Chicago Reserve Banks were in Martin's corner, and since they were the two largest banks in the System, the other presidents were influenced by their views. The Reserve Banks were closer to the financial markets and further from the political pressures in Washington; according to Holland, "they disliked the idea that the Fed was inhibited for political reasons."[87] Though the board of governors, not the FOMC, made the final decision, by late November, the governors were well aware of the Reserve Bank presidents' feelings and could not ignore the probability that requests for a discount rate increase were coming to the board for approval.

At a long and contentious FOMC meeting on 23 November, Dewey Daane revealed that he would support a discount rate increase. Martin knew then that he had the votes within the board of governors to approve a rate increase. With Daane's vote in his pocket, Martin tried again to inform the administration of his intention. That afternoon, he advised Fowler that "an increase is in the wind."[88] Fowler replied that it was "premature" and reemphasized the importance of waiting until January. Fowler was irritated with Martin's lack of "cooperation" and had recommended to Johnson earlier in November that Martin be replaced by Paul Volcker.[89] As his efforts to communicate with the administration failed, it was becoming more obvious that Martin would be put squarely and publicly into opposition to the president.

The course he was pursuing was profoundly troubling to Martin. When he could not sleep, he would walk around the darkened streets of his neighborhood, sometimes until dawn.[90] This was such a time. Martin knew he was leading the Fed into a very public defiance of one of the most manipulative and powerful men ever to enter the presidency. Johnson had regularly voiced his opposition to higher interest rates and had specifically asked for a delay in the move Martin was about to take. The president was known to seek revenge, and a combination of Lyndon Johnson and two anti-Martin allies — Russell Long, the chairman of the Senate Finance Committee, and Wright Patman, the chairman of the House Banking and Currency Committee — could persuade Congress to limit the Fed's independence. If, on the other hand, Martin lost his majority and the Fed did not act, there would be no stopping Lyndon Johnson until the economy was out of control. By then it would be too late to avoid the economic collapse Martin had predicted. He would go ahead, and when the challenge to the Fed came, he would pray that a lifetime of honest service would secure the public and congressional support needed to fend off any onslaught from Lyndon Johnson.

On the morning of 3 December, the day of the board's vote, Martin told Fowler: "We will act later in the day if the board will support me."[91] At 1:20 in the afternoon, the governors gathered in the ornate boardroom to discuss the requests from the New York and Chicago Reserve Banks for a discount rate increase. Governor Mitchell spoke for a number of governors concerned about the political risk of opposing the president: "The Federal Reserve appears to be on a collision course with the administration."[92] Governor Maisel observed that the administration had requested a delay; by going ahead anyhow, the Fed "would be saying that it does not want a coordinated monetary-fiscal package."[93] Governor Robertson argued: "Price pressures to date have been small and selective. They are not the types of increases appropriately dealt with by a dampening of aggregate domestic demand. The wholesale price index has slowed since mid-year."[94] The opponents argued passionately for delay.

Before he cast the tie-breaking vote, Martin acknowledged the concerns of those opposed to the increase. "We should be under no illusions. A decision to move now can lead to an important revamping of the Federal Reserve System, including its structure and operating methods. This is a real possibility and I have been turning it over in my mind for months."[95] Reviewing his past efforts, Martin said: "I started as early as August to try to negotiate," and he reminded has fellow governors that at the 12 October FOMC meeting he had said "the administration is strongly opposed to a change in policy."[96] He told the governors that Fowler and Ackley "seemed to be saying that if given another month or two, perhaps they can agree with my position."[97] Martin had already dismissed this possibility in the 23 November FOMC meeting when he observed: "If the System waits until mid-January, and if the budget turns out as I think it will, it will be too late for monetary policy to have any effect on the course of events."[98]

Martin's final argument focused on what he saw as the heart of the issue: "There is the question whether the Federal Reserve is to be run by the administration in office."[99] He told the governors: "Many people in the market with whom I have talked are convinced that the Federal Reserve has been prevented from taking action on the discount rate."[100] The timing of any increase had been argued fiercely, and Martin admitted that it was a very close issue. For Martin, the essential reason to move now was to decisively remind the world of the Fed's independent status. Martin believed that its independence was the unique contribution of the Federal Reserve System to American democracy. If Balderston's retirement cost Martin his majority, the Fed could lose its will to act independently at a critical juncture in its history. He finished: "I hope the Board will act today."[101]

In a few more minutes it was over. Martin had previously urged his FOMC opponents to support a strong majority with the argument: "When the System is united it occupies a strong position in the ranks of the government."[102] But committee members would not change their previously stated positions, and the final tally was 4–3 in favor of the increase. Rarely in Martin's experience had so important a Fed decision been made by such a close vote. The economy would finally receive a highly visible dose of monetary discipline, and the Fed had made a historic reaffirmation of its independence.

When he heard about the rate increase, Lyndon Johnson was as angry as he could possibly be. Aide Joe Califano described Johnson as "burning up the wires [from the ranch] to Washington, asking one member of Congress after another, 'How can I run the country and the government if I have to read on a news-service ticker that Bill Martin is going to run his own economy?' "[103] Johnson fumed at Fowler: "Those marble tower boys. Joe, you find a tough guy to head the Reserve. If he [Martin] resigns, it won't wreck the country."[104] Fowler tried to reason with Johnson. "He [Martin] has already thought of this possibility, and Martin told me 'Although I don't believe it, people tell me that I'm worth a billion in gold.' He [Martin] believes that if he left it would be damaging."[105] Fowler ended the conversation by promising to think of suitable candidates to replace Martin.

The next day, Martin and the other Quadriad members flew to Johnson's Texas ranch, where he was recuperating from his gall bladder operation. Arriving at the ranch, Martin encountered Lady Bird, the president's wife and confidant, who advised him: "I hope that you have examined your conscience and you are convinced that you are on the right track . . . because this is terribly important to the president."[106]

The meeting that took place in Johnson's simple office at the LBJ ranch was a classic confrontation; two determined men, both of whom believed that the goals for which they had worked all their lives were at stake. Johnson wasted no time before he went on the attack. "You've got me in a position where you can run a rapier into me and you've done it."[107] Johnson accused Martin of placing himself above the presidency and totally disregarding his wishes: "[Y]ou went ahead and did something that I disapproved of . . . and can affect my entire term here."[108] He finished: "You took advantage of me and I just want you to know that's a despicable thing to do."[109] As he so often did, Johnson had personalized the issue and brought the full force of his physical and presidential presence to bear on his adversary. Martin admitted later that he was shaken but determined to stick to his position and not to insult the president of the United States.

In his quiet but determined way, Martin fought back. "Mr. President, we were not precipitous about this. I warned you about it. We discussed this [increase] and you asked me to give you another chance. I did, and we couldn't wait any longer."[110] At another point Martin tried to reduce any possible threat to Johnson's presidency by saying, "Now you're the president and I'm just a worker in the vineyard, way down the line. I have no constituency. I have a board that supports me sometimes and sometimes it doesn't. In this they supported me, but only by a four-to-three vote."[111] Finally Martin said, "I've never implied that I'm right and you're wrong. But I do have a very strong conviction that the Federal Reserve Act placed the responsibility for interest rates with the Federal Reserve Board. This is one of those few occasions where the Federal Reserve Board decision has to be final."[112] Lyndon Johnson rarely heard such stern words delivered to him during his presidency. It was one of Bill Martin's finest moments.

But would it goad the president into retribution? Lyndon Johnson was not well placed for revenge against the Fed. Despite his Democratic Party majorities in both houses of Congress, attacking the Fed was far from a sure thing. Neither Russell Long nor Wright Patman commanded the loyalties of the conservative Southern Democrats who were so influential on financial and economic issues. The Fed had its congressional defenders and could be expected to launch a nationwide lobbying campaign to protect its interests. Lyndon Johnson was also well experienced in using the principle of the separation of powers to defend a decision in the face of presidential opposition. He had used it often when he was Senate Majority leader, and he knew Martin was right about the Fed's responsibilities. A public campaign against the Fed would be intensely divisive, and success could not be guaranteed. No matter how painful it was to him, Johnson would have to accept the Fed's independence. There would be no presidential telephone calls to congressional aide Larry O'Brien or House Speaker John McCormack demanding that they find ways to clip the Fed's wings.

After the meeting, the president and the Quadriad members were ushered to a line of folding aluminum chairs hastily set up on the porch of the LBJ ranch house for a press conference. In a skillful and statesmanlike performance, LBJ appeared calm and accepting of the Fed's decision. Responding to the tenor of the president's comments and glossing over their conflict for the benefit of the press, Martin said that Johnson "in no way placed me in the role of defying the President or the Johnson administration."[113] Even Bill Martin could dissemble if he felt it served the nation's interest. Johnson quipped: "I make no pretense to being a monetary expert. Even experts have a division of opinion, 4 to 3, and we do have division all the time within the government."[114] Lyndon Johnson was not given to understatement, but the division he blithely alluded to ran very deep. Martin and Ackley's relationship had deteriorated so badly that they had ceased speaking to one another in late November. Treasury Secretary Henry Fowler and Budget Director Charles Schultze eventually negotiated a guarded reconciliation between Martin and Ackley.

Johnson's only retribution for the distress that Martin had inflicted on him was taking Martin around the ranch for one of his famous hair-raising tours. Piling his honored guest in the front seat, LBJ would take the wheel of his armor-plated Lincoln convertible and rocket over the dirt roads of the ranch at sixty miles an hour. He would point out the sights and bark orders to his staff on his walkie-talkie, often driving one-handed, facing backward to talk with those in the backseat as they bounced over the dusty Texas hill country. It was an experience his terrified guests would never forget. The official picture of Martin and LBJ before their trip reveals Martin with an expression that any condemned man facing execution would instantly recognize. Martin did use the opportunity as they sped along to point to a large boulder blocking the flow of the Pedernales River, telling Johnson that the Fed's discount rate was like the rock, blocking the river's flow. Only by raising the rate, like removing the rock, would credit move smoothly. Johnson seemed to understand the analogy. When Martin told this story to the Fed staff, they argued that this wasn't the way it really worked. Martin responded, "Well, it did this time."[115]

Not surprisingly, the period that followed the confrontation was one of the lowest points in Martin's relationship with Lyndon Johnson. When Johnson was angry with an aide, he withdrew completely from the relationship. For those who dealt regularly with the hyperactive president, this change was immediately apparent. In January 1966, Martin complained to Joe Califano that he felt "closed out of the decision-making process."[116] Martin feared that his stand had cost him his relationship with his president and that the Fed would suffer because of Martin's show of independence. The only consolations during this difficult period were the strong performance of the financial markets as they responded to the discount rate increase and a surprise letter from Dwight Eisenhower. The former president wrote of "the intense pride I have in seeing you stand 4-square for what you know to be right" and predicted that "history will evaluate your career in the Federal Reserve Board something like it does for John Marshall on the Supreme Court."[117] Eisenhower occupied a place in Martin's pantheon of heroic leaders of the nation, and the former president's encouragement came when it was most needed.

As Martin considered how to heal his damaged relationship with the president, the contentious issue of replacing retiring Fed Governor Canby Balderston clamored for his attention. Unknown to Martin, the fine hand of Walter Heller reinserted itself in the governor selection process when he suggested a young economist, Andrew Brimmer, to Johnson in early January 1966. At thirty-nine, Brimmer was young for a Fed governor, but he was one of the most visible African Americans in the Johnson administration, where he served as assistant secretary of Commerce for Economic Affairs. Despite his youth, Brimmer had a record of considerable accomplishment. He had gone to the University of Washington on the G.I. Bill while he worked part-time as an assistant editor of the local newspaper. He began a Ph.D. program in monetary economics at Harvard, completing his thesis while he worked at the Federal Reserve Bank of New York. Before joining the administration, he taught at the Wharton Business School, where his research on the civil rights aspects of public accommodation gained national attention. In the administration, he was a primary spokesman for the Commerce Department on balance of payments issues. This time, Heller had chosen a governor candidate who was a capable Keynesian economist but also offered other attributes that enhanced his candidacy.

On 1 February, Martin and Johnson met to discuss the vacant governor position. It was their first meeting since the blowup in December. Martin promoted the candidacy of the current chairman of the Federal Reserve Bank of Minneapolis, industrialist Atherton Bean. Bean, a Rhodes Scholar, was the chief executive of a middle-sized food processing company. Martin rehearsed his argument that the Federal Reserve Act mandated a broad representation from diverse fields of endeavor, concluding that Kennedy and Johnson had "ignored the law" by appointing "a majority from a single profession."[118] Martin's arguments against Brimmer were his youth and comparative inexperience, and he proposed "a top position on our staff" as a way to help him gain the needed experience. Martin offered Bean's experience as a contrast and, in an open invitation to Johnson, concluded that Bean would have "every qualification you would want, not only in a member of the Board, but also its Chairman."[119]

On 26 February, Martin and Johnson again discussed the Brimmer appointment, and in this case the responsibilities of the president prevailed. Many of Lyndon Johnson's finest accomplishments were in the service of civil rights in the United States, and once again he put his political skills to work on that task. He informed Martin: "I have instructed Brimmer to forget that he is a Democrat . . . and to become non-partisan and support you as much as his conscience will permit. He is not to be the President's man or Martin's man, but to serve the best interests of the country."[120] He asked Martin to put himself in Brimmer's shoes by imagining that he (Martin) had been "just appointed to a high post at the Central Bank of Ghana."[121] It was ironic that Martin focused only on Brimmer's comparative lack of experience and was so insensitive to Lyndon Johnson's larger concern about creating a groundbreaking opportunity for a well-qualified African American. During his army days in World War II, Martin had argued often with General George Marshall about the army's treatment of African Americans.

This time, in contrast to the December interest rate decision, the president's word and vision were final. Johnson's adroit intervention enabled Brimmer and Martin to get along well from the start. In a break with tradition, Brimmer requested that Martin be allowed to administer the oath of office, rather than the president or chief justice of the Supreme Court. In April, Martin wrote to the president commending Brimmer for his "constructive contributions to the Board."[122] With Brimmer's appointment, four of the seven Fed current governors had been selected by Kennedy or Johnson. Bringing this group into consistent opposition to the Johnson administration would be a nearly impossible task.

The misreading of the Brimmer candidacy was not the only distressing element for Martin during the early 1966. He and the president were experiencing continual disagreements despite both men's effort to put the best face on it. A man who believed that the Fed and the administration should work together, Martin must have been deeply troubled by his personal conflict with Lyndon Johnson. He felt that the impasse should not continue and yet, in personal and professional terms, he could choose no other course. In late January, he told Treasury Secretary Fowler, "I continue to be a LBJ man. If there is any desire for me to go, all that is needed . . . is a quiet nudge and I'll resign."[123] Martin expressed these thoughts to Johnson the day after his unsuccessful negotiations on the Brimmer candidacy. "[D]espite our difficulties . . . I am earnestly desirous of aiding your goals, since they are the proper goals of us all. . . . But as I think over our talk [of 1 February], I become more discouraged with the prospects as I see them."[124] Martin put his future in the president's hands.

Bill Martin honestly wanted to be an LBJ man. Perhaps it is more accurate to say that he wanted to be a president's man. He had seen four very different presidents labor under the crushing burden of leading the country. He watched Lyndon Johnson struggle to put into practice his lifelong dream for a government that truly helped others escape poverty as he had. Despite his sympathies for Johnson, Martin was in complete disagreement with him over the management of the nation's economy. Martin had personally orchestrated a move that brought the Fed into open conflict with the administration, but he could not persuade a FOMC majority to formulate a consistent response to the administration's policies. He had by now been in office for fifteen years, longer than any predecessor, and he could well have overstayed his time. It was probable that his nightmare of a world financial collapse was unrealistically pessimistic. His many critics might be right; perhaps the economy had entered a new cycle that Martin did not appreciate. He tried to give the president every opportunity to make the decision about Martin's future that Martin himself could not.

Johnson's response revealed that he had calmed down from his anger over the rate increase and had come to terms with his relationship with Martin. In a late February conversation with Martin on the Brimmer candidacy, Johnson told Martin: "I have great respect for you and business and bankers have a high regard for you. You have educated three presidents before me . . . and I want you to continue to be frank with me."[125] While this reasoning did not convince Martin that he would be able to change Johnson's economic thinking, the president had invited Martin to continue to press his case. Martin concluded that he would do what he felt must be done, and do it to the limits of his ability.

While the CEA and independent economists grappled with the perplexing signals of an economy in transition, the staff of the FOMC monitored the credit markets for signs that that they were adjusting satisfactorily to the Fed's turn toward restraint. By February 1966, Fed economists were concerned about rising government spending and the impact of financing a growing budget deficit on the Treasury bond market. They agreed with First National City Bank when it observed that the fiscal 1967 budget "either underestimates actual expenditures or accelerates tax payments to narrow the deficit. Without these fiscal devices the budget deficit might well have amounted to $10 billion."[126] Fed economists also anticipated strong demands on the capital markets coming from a worrisome 16 percent projected increase in corporate capital spending. One of the primary justifications for the Fed's December rate increase was to facilitate the higher interest rates needed to draw out sufficient savings to meet future credit demands. That decision was looking increasingly far-sighted.

By mid-March, Martin was sufficiently encouraged about the response in the financial markets to the rate increase to write Lyndon Johnson about its benefits: "increased pressure on banks to ration credit, less ebullience in stock prices, a balance of payments dividend via investment by foreigners in U.S. securities and . . . the prospect of tempered [corporate] spending plans."[127] Within the FOMC, the majority for tightening was growing. Even the expansion-minded governors now supported tightening because they were concerned that inflationary pressures might goad Congress into pressing the administration to cut social expenditures. Martin was able to build a consensus for gradual tightening and argued for giving the desk manager considerable leeway so that he could achieve "a smooth flow of funds so that any [open-market transactions] would not prove disruptive."[128]

The next month a conflict broke out in the FOMC that challenged Martin's assertion that monetary policy might be performing adequately. The conflict represented the widening division between the "old school" and Keynesian FOMC members. The FOMC was reviewing recent results of monetary policy at its 12 April meeting when Governor Sherman Maisel, the most outspoken Keynesian on the board, launched an unusually broad attack on the effectiveness of the Fed's monetary policy. He pointed out that between mid-December 1965 and early April 1966, the FOMC had implemented a policy of less ease, and by the traditional criteria used by the FOMC, the financial markets had tightened. The interest rate on Treasury bills increased from 3.85 percent to 4.5 percent, and net borrowed reserves increased from $110 million to $230 million. Maisel observed: "The committee might believe it has brought about a changed monetary policy," but when broader measures of the economy are applied, "they paint an entirely different picture."[129] Bank credit had spurted from an annual increase of 7.2 percent prior to December to 15 percent between December 1965 and April 1966, and the money supply had grown from a 5.9 percent annual increase to 8.3 percent during the same period. He concluded: "The Committee has given the manager poor instructions and . . . as a result of a poor directive, the Federal Reserve is not really battling inflation."[130]

Maisel's assault elicited similar conclusions from a number of other FOMC members. George Mitchell agreed that the committee was "losing ground": "Unless strong pressure is maintained, the Committee's whole program of monetary restraint will fail."[131] Governor Charles Shepardson, normally a solid supporter of traditional policy analysis, agreed that "the growth rate of total reserves is quite high and should be slowed down. . . . The rate of increase in aggregate reserves should receive attention."[132] Even FOMC staff member Robert Holland was moved to admit: "We may be in a period when a given dollar of borrowed reserves will not represent quite as much restraint as before."[133] Maisel's comments revived a long-standing debate over how to monitor monetary policy. Two years earlier, the committee had informally downgraded specific net reserve targets for open-market operations, but after extended debates on the subject had not agreed on replacement criteria.

The younger and Keynesian-oriented staff and FOMC members continued to push for using the monetary aggregates (i.e., total bank reserves, the money supply, and the bank credit proxy) as the criteria for evaluating the impact of monetary policy. They argued that over a longer period of time, changes in the monetary aggregates did reflect the impact of the Fed's policy moves. The Keynesians also noted that economists of all stripes generally agreed that the aggregates should increase in concert with the growth rate for the economy as a whole. The Keynesians argued that if the aggregates were growing at a different rate than the economy required, the Fed should direct its open-market operations at restoring this alignment.

The traditionalists, led by Bill Martin, believed that the broader market forces at work in the economy were constantly evolving and changing. The Fed's open-market operations manager needed considerable latitude to work with these forces rather than in opposition to them. In the opinion of the traditionalists, using economic forecasts to determine monetary policy targets that were too specific and applied too rigidly would lead the open-market desk into moves that could destabilize markets. Moreover, the traditionalists, and particularly Bill Martin, had little faith in the reliability of economic forecasts. Describing the atmosphere in the Fed in the mid-1960s, one latter-day economist observed: "The making of forecasts was prohibited . . . on pain of being fired."[134] There was a balance between the traditionalists and the Keynesians in 1966, but it could not be expected to last much longer. Keynesians were steadily filling the ranks of the Fed economics staff and FOMC members, and the traditionalists would become an embattled minority.

This debate was taking place during a period when the Fed's economic staff was making considerable progress on improving the analytical basis for FOMC policy making. The statistical analysis used to brief FOMC committee members for policy discussions was greatly expanded. The Reserve Banks increased their ability to analyze their regional economic conditions. Despite Martin's skepticism, Fed staff economists were improving their econometric models used for forecasting the economy and analyzing the potential impact of alternative monetary policies. In an attempt to respond to Maisel's complaint, the FOMC staff added a "proviso" to the formal directive produced at the end of each FOMC meeting and issued to the open-market desk manager. The proviso modified the instructions to include additional criteria. For example, the primary directive might be "no change in existing conditions of restraint," but the proviso might add "provided, however, that if required reserves expand considerably more than seasonally expected . . . further gradual reduction in net reserve availability shall be attained."[135] The inclusion of additional criteria satisfied the Keynesians, and the absence of numerical targets satisfied the traditionalists.

By the summer of 1966, the broader market forces that Martin often spoke about were buffeting the money and credit markets. Reinforced by the Fed's tightening, these forces were creating conditions that few in the financial community had ever experienced. Ironically for the Fed, the federal government was a major contributor to the problems. Lyndon Johnson was a master of budgetary manipulation, and in order to hold down the official budget deficit, he prevailed on Treasury Secretary Henry Fowler to capture a one-time tax collection windfall of $6.3 billion by moving from a semiannual to a quarterly corporate tax payment schedule. He also pushed Fowler to authorize $3.2 billion of debt issuance by government housing finance agencies, since the proceeds could be credited against budgetary spending.

These tactics obscured the true budget deficit and the government's requirement for deficit financing. The higher level of federal government borrowing would add to existing demand for credit described by First National City Bank as "borrowings by corporations, state and local governments and households that are at record highs."[136] In response to this combination of factors, interest rates surged upward. Yields on six-month federal agency issues shot up from 4⅜ percent in July 1965 to 5.9 percent a year later. Yields on Treasury bills rose to 5 percent, the highest level since their introduction in 1929.

The surge in interest rates created a bonanza for savers but caused what First National City Bank called a "competitive scramble for available funds by all sectors of the money market"[137] The roots of the scramble dated back to 1961, when the commercial banking industry invented the certificate of deposit, or CD. Most CDs were three to six months in duration, were easily renewable, and could be sold or cashed in early at modest penalties. CDs offered depositors a competitive short-term return and offered banks the opportunity to quickly attract additional funds when they needed them. From 1961 to 1965, banks aggressively promoted CDs, and the industry's share of total new savings ballooned from 23 percent to 43 percent.

The banks' deposit gains came at the expense of the savings and loan (S&L) industry. This industry, the largest provider of funds to the mortgage market, watched its profit margins shrivel as interest rates rose. S&Ls offered competitive short-term rates for deposits but invested the funds in long-term mortgages. During periods of rising interest rates, S&Ls could not adjust the interest rates on their mortgage portfolios as quickly as banks could adjust the rates on their loan portfolios. The situation was even more complicated during the summer of 1966, because both the S&Ls and the banks were losing deposits as investors moved their savings into direct purchases of Treasury securities. These financial institutions were offering rates up to 5 ¼ percent for six-month deposits, but were losing one-third of their potential deposits as savers snapped up Treasury bills offering a risk-free 5 percent yield.

By June, the problems in the S&L industry spilled fully into the public view. On 27 June, Joseph Horne, the chairman of the Home Loan Bank Board, the Fed's counterpart that oversaw the S&L industry, harshly criticized the Fed: "The Federal Reserve Board has taken minimal action . . . to deter further escalation in competitive interest rates and to reduce the drain on available mortgage funds."[138] The allowable maximum yield on bank CDs was set by the Federal Reserve System under Regulation Q of the Federal Reserve Act. Horne wanted the Fed to give the S&L industry a comparative rate advantage by limiting allowable interest rates on bank CDs.

Wright Patman stepped into the fray by proposing a bill in the House of Representatives to roll back the ceilings on bank time deposits and smaller CDs so that S&Ls could compete more effectively. Martin visited Capitol Hill to argue that a rollback would cause banks to lose deposits and "penalize the growing and capital short parts of the country — States such as Texas, California and Arizona — and the related loss of access to credit facilities by small businesses."[139] As usual, Martin's logic failed to impress Patman, but the determined Texan was unable to persuade his committee to report his bill out to the full House. Martin knew the Fed could not continue to remain aloof from the problems of the S&L industry without running unacceptable political risks. As delegations from the S&L industry visited congressional offices to plead their case, Wright Patman gained supporters. As Martin later observed, "When Congressmen begin to believe that the Fed is off base — men like Patman will have the strength of ten."[140]

The months of July and August were a time of trial for the Fed leaders as the tightening cycle reached a climax and public concern reached new peaks. The problems of the savings and loan industry did not get any worse, but hundreds of smaller S&Ls simply could not continue to hang on and were merged or liquidated. Comparatively healthy S&Ls relentlessly reduced the size of their mortgage portfolios. The powerful combination of reduced bank construction lending and sharply reduced S&L mortgage financing caused the rate of home building to decline by a staggering 50 percent over the first eight months of 1966. In selected states where home building had been booming, a majority of residential construction companies suspended operations or went bankrupt.

The Fed continued to tighten credit throughout the summer. Faced with ballooning loan demand, banks were forced to liquidate more of their portfolios of Treasuries and municipal bonds to generate the resources to lend. The banks wanted to sell, but few wanted to buy. One Fed historian wrote that in late August 1966: "For a few days, there was virtually no market for municipal bonds; the imminent failure of two leading bond houses, which were caught with large inventories of unsold municipals, was rumored on Wall Street. The news media was filled with talk of financial panic."[141] "At that time," Treasury Undersecretary Fred Deming said, "the [S&L] crunch was so heavy that people whose judgment I respect . . . in the financial community, were scared to death."[142]

This period was literally painful for Martin because he had prostate surgery in late June and began a slow two-month recovery. He usually enjoyed excellent health due to his daily regimen of tennis or squash racquets and his teetotal lifestyle, and this was one of his rare hospitalizations. There were postoperative complications, and it was not an easy time to be flat on his back. During Martin's absence, the failure of the Fed's credit restraint to slow bank lending enlarged the majority on the FOMC in favor of further tightening. Governor George Mitchell kept Martin updated on developments, but Martin "was not comfortable dictating to the FOMC from his home."[143]

In the 26 July FOMC meeting, Governor Andrew Brimmer took a strong stand for "as much firmness as possible . . . and an increase in the discount rate when the time is propitious."[144] Brimmer also wrote to Ackley that "higher rates are inevitable. We need fiscal action to relieve the monetary load."[145] By the 23 August meeting, a strong majority of the FOMC voted for further tightening despite some foot-dragging by the FOMC staff. Martin must have been gratified by the actions of his fellow FOMC members. He could enjoy knowing that the FOMC was pursuing the tightening he supported, but he did not have to be the spokesman and constantly emphasize his differences with the president.

On his return to work in early September, Martin grasped the nettle of how to slow bank lending. An informal program begun in May, in which the Reserve Bank presidents were to talk with individual member banks about reducing the growth of their loan portfolios, had failed. Martin approved sending a letter, which he made public, advising member banks that those who failed to reduce their rate of lending would find it harder to borrow reserves from the Fed. Member banks reacted angrily to this invasive move. One big-city banker told Martin that "a number of large corporations have about run out of money . . . my question is whether it is really prudent to curtail business loans to the extent that seems to be indicated."[146] Despite the bankers' objections and undiminished market turmoil, FOMC policy stayed on its path of restraint.

Bill Martin's willingness to run a substantial risk of overtightening the economy during 1966 reflected his resolve to slow the economy's growth to a more sustainable rate—and equally important, to force the administration to consider a significant tax increase to finance the cost of the Vietnam War. Martin's tax-increase campaign began in mid-1965, when he already knew about the ballooning costs of the Vietnam War. He then learned that the administration's social and health programs were increasing as well. He informed the FOMC that he had told the president that he expected the Treasury to have problems financing any increase in the deficit, and that to assist the Treasury in placing its debt, the Fed would be forced to ease credit against its wishes. He also confided to Governor Dewey Daane in the fall of 1965 that he had "a number of go-rounds with Johnson on this [the impact of war spending]."[147] Martin was normally very reluctant to give any administration advice about fiscal matters, but he was concerned that without fiscal restraint, monetary policy would be asked to do more than it could in order to slow down the economy. Throughout his chairmanship, Martin was extremely conscious of the limitations of monetary policy and felt a personal responsibility for persuading the administration to supplement the Fed's efforts with appropriate fiscal policy.

During the clash over the discount rate increase in December 1965, Martin told members of the Quadriad that lower interest rates were dependent on a tax increase. Both Martin and CEA Chairman Ackley returned to Washington after a late-December visit to the LBJ ranch convinced that Johnson accepted the need for a tax increase.[148] Johnson asked aide Joe Califano to organize a few highly secret meetings at the White House on the subject in January 1966. In one of them, Wilbur Mills, the canny and powerful head of the House Ways and Means Committee, which had jurisdiction over tax legislation, said, "[A] tax increase is out of the question."[149] The president quietly ordered the issue dropped from the administration's agenda.

The tax increase also fell victim to Lyndon Johnson and Robert McNamara's disastrous decision to withhold the true costs of the Vietnam War from the fiscal 1967 budget. Johnson was actively concealing the administration's commitment to the war because he feared that Congress would not fund both his social agenda and sharply increased war spending. In January 1966, McNamara brazenly defended allocating only $10.2 billion for the war by offering the "admittedly arbitrary" assumption that the war would end by 30 June 1967.[150] Both McNamara and Johnson knew full well that the administration's plan was to more than double the 184,000 men then in Vietnam and that the full year's budgetary spending could be twice the budgeted amount. The misleading budget showed a modest deficit. Henry Fowler was so poorly advised by McNamara that Fowler "firmly stated throughout most of calendar year 1966 . . . that the budgetary deficit for 1967 will not exceed $1.8 billion."[151] By August 1966, Ackley and the CEA were working with a 1967 deficit that had increased to $4.5 billion. Although Ackley gave a series of memoranda to Johnson about a tax increase during 1966, they do not convey a consistent sense of urgency about the issue, nor is there any indication that he pursued this issue personally with Johnson. During this same period, Henry Fowler gave little support to a tax increase.[152] Bill Martin could not count on any meaningful support from within the administration in his struggle to carry the tax issue to Lyndon Johnson.

One of the many ironies of the tax struggle was that both Ackley and Fowler knew better than to believe Department of Defense estimates. Fowler had served as assistant general counsel for the War Production Board in World War II and had run the National Production Authority and the Office of Defense Mobilization during the Korean War.[153] Gardner Ackley, who had served as assistant director of the Office of Price Stabilization during the Korean War, is quoted as saying: "In the Korean War, the [cost] estimates were enormously inaccurate . . . I didn't trust them at all."[154] Despite their experience, neither man supported serious contingency planning for the possibility of higher war outlays until the latter part of 1966. The United States would pay a high price for the willingness of these two men to disregard their own experience during this critical period. The economists at the Fed, using public information about manpower planning and military purchases, developed much higher budgetary estimates. The differing views of the war's future costs and resulting budget deficit added to the fissure between the Fed and the administration.

Though he knew he would find little support, Martin kept the tax issue in front of Lyndon Johnson. Martin sent carefully argued memos to the president in March, April, and June of 1966, urging the president to "share the burden of economic restraint among all the tools of economic policy."[155] He carried the argument into Quadriad meetings as well. Late in 1966 he told Johnson: "I feel now, as in every meeting [with you] since January, that you should go forward with a tax increase on the assumption that expenditures in Vietnam are going to rise," but he made no progress.[156]

Martin also sent copies of Fed staff studies on the tax increase to Henry Fowler. Martin and Fowler's relationship was badly strained during the December 1965 struggle over the rate increase, but Martin kept pushing him because he believed "you could express your doubts to him [Fowler]."[157] The Fed's tight money policy also kept pressure on Johnson. As interest rates continued to rise, Johnson angrily asked Ackley why he hadn't predicted that this would happen. Ackley referred to memoranda in which he concluded that higher interest rates were the lesser evil compared to a tax increase. Johnson's reply conveyed his state of mind: "It may be a lesser evil, but it's hard for a Texas boy to ever see high interest rates as a lesser evil."[158]

Ackley's artful position on the tax increase did not reflect the thinking of the majority of the country's economists. Many economists had come out in favor of a tax increase by mid-1966. Walter Heller worried that if the expansion spiraled into a boom-bust cycle because the political will to increase taxes did not exist, the theoretical basis for the "new economics" would be jeopardized. He wrote to Johnson in May and again in June, arguing that the combination of "Lyndon Johnson . . . and the most powerful economy in history" needed to employ "the full use of the weapons of modern economics."[159] Paul Samuelson publicly backed an increase in February. At the end of February, five of the six economists on the Treasury Department's consultative board were in favor of an increase. Hobart Rowen reported in the *Washington Post* in April that his poll of thirty economists resulted in a 70 percent majority in favor of an increase. Ackley's ambivalent approach toward a tax increase reflected his conflicting instincts. He could not ignore the emerging consensus among his peers, but his determination to publicly support his president overrode his professional judgment. And his president did not want to spend any of his political capital on a tax increase.

In June 1966, Johnson undertook a shrewd maneuver to educate Martin about the political realities of the tax issue and (as a long shot) to improve the political prospects for a tax increase. Johnson asked Martin to talk with Representative Wilbur Mills about changing his position on an increase in taxes. Martin had a good relationship with Mills, resulting in part from Martin's earlier visit to speak at an Arkansas college commencement at which Mill's daughter graduated. Mills and Johnson had entered the House of Representatives together in 1938 and both represented districts in the rural Southwest. They had worked together for decades, but their politics and economics had diverged over the years. Mills had become a powerful member of the conservative wing of the Democratic Party and usually described Johnson as a fiscal liberal: "Lyndon Johnson always was a spender. He thought you could always stimulate the economy better through public spending than through private spending. That's the old Roosevelt doctrine."[160] In their conversation, Mills made it clear to Martin that he was upset with Johnson's spending for the war and his social programs, but if "Lyndon will ask for a supplemental [appropriation] on Vietnam, and offer a reduction on spending, and these two goals are accomplished, I think he can then get a tax increase."[161] Martin also reported that Mills wanted the president to "summon" him to the White House to discuss the matter.

As Martin listened to Lyndon Johnson react to Mills's suggestions, he could see that the relationship between the two men had soured badly. Johnson recounted his anger after a previous White House meeting when Mills had gone public with information Johnson had wished to treat privately, concluding: "I can't bring him down here. Wilbur will have it in the *Wall Street Journal* the next day."[162] Martin's credo was to modify even his most dearly held and publicly stated beliefs if the nation's long-term welfare required it. Here was the president of the United States letting personal pique stand in the way of resolving a crucial national issue. Martin offered to work with Henry Fowler and Budget Director Charles Schultze to negotiate further with Mills, but Johnson would have none of it. When Martin was most exasperated with Johnson, he labeled him an uncompromising "egomaniac."[163] This must have been one of those times. It looked to Martin that the cause of a tax increase was dead until economic conditions got much worse.

By August 1966, the pleas coming from the financial community for relief from the tight monetary conditions finally galvanized Treasury Secretary Fowler to action. As the Fed's tightening gathered strength during the summer of 1966, leaders of the investment banking community, with whom Fowler had a long relationship, came to him "expressing great fear that a financial panic is likely" if something weren't done to relieve the Fed's tightening.[164] He concluded that the Fed's monetary policy was threatening the economy and the future of the Johnson administration. In late August, Fowler called Martin, who was still recovering from his surgery, to convey his concern about the economic situation. Martin told Fowler that the Fed could relieve the pressure on the S&L industry but "needed to see some sign of fiscal restraint" first.[165] Martin and Fowler also discussed the pressure Congress was receiving from constituents affected by the credit squeeze. Both of them knew that it was only a matter of time until ill-conceived legislative proposals regarding the Fed and interest rates would begin circulating. Fowler concluded that "we just had to take some action."[166]

Changes of heart can be powerful events in human affairs, and Fowler's was of crucial importance to the ultimate prospects for any tax increase. Fowler was trusted by Lyndon Johnson and was a highly skilled and tenacious policy advocate. In September, he began a forceful lobbying campaign to convert LBJ, telling him that "the hard facts" made it plain that a tax increase was necessary. Faced with the agreement of Fowler, Ackley (who supported Fowler's initiative), and Martin that the economy must be cooled, Lyndon Johnson finally accepted the need for fiscal action. He agreed to suspend the Investment Tax Credit (ITC) along with a $3 billion cut in spending and the suspension of bond issues by government agencies. Fowler aptly described the proposal in late September during hearings before the Ways and Means Committee: "The proposal is designed to relieve the pressures, clearly observable in the money markets and capital goods sector, which are producing . . . the highest interest rates in forty years and a perceptible trend toward a general condition of economic instability."[167] Martin saw the ITC suspension, worth only $1.5 billion a year, as only a first installment on the added tax revenue that that was needed. But the administration was no longer stonewalling the issue of fiscal restraint.

In the middle of December 1966, the need for a more significant tax increase became an undeniable reality. The administration produced its first firm projections for fiscal year 1968 along with a revised estimate for the current fiscal year ending in June 1967. The results were staggering, even to Johnson's economic team. The military buildup in Vietnam was nearing completion — 455,000 Americans were in the country along with masses of aircraft, patrol boats, and armaments. The U.S. Navy operated throughout the South China Sea, and a logistical support system spanned Asia. The budget impact of the war could no longer be covered up, as McNamara had cleaned out all the hidden military spending reserves and the fiction of an early end to hostilities was stripped away. Spending on the war in Vietnam for fiscal 1967 was now forecast to grow by $13 billion instead of the original forecast of $5.8 billion. Total budgetary spending was also expanding at a frightening pace: budgetary outlays for fiscal 1967 were growing from the original estimate of $112 billion to $129 billion and were forecasted to grow to $140 billion in fiscal 1968. Revenues, on the other hand, were growing slowly, and consequently budgetary deficits were exploding. The fiscal 1967 deficit widened from $4.5 billion, estimated as recently as August 1966, to $11.9 billion. The fiscal year 1968 deficit was forecast at a horrific $19 billion, the largest deficit, even on a percentage basis, since World War II.

This was the nightmare Bill Martin had been fighting so hard to avoid. The Fed's tightening was visibly slowing the economy, but government spending of these magnitudes would bring the economy, and inflation, roaring back to life. The tight-money policy could not be pushed further without at best a recession and at worst a financial panic with its frightening possibility of an economic collapse. Worse yet, the fiscal 1968 assumptions on the war could be just as wrong as those of fiscal 1967 were proving to be. A tax increase was now a matter of the highest possible urgency, and Martin knew he had to use all his resources to force the issue. The consequences of further delay were unthinkable.

Martin took on the tax issue at a meeting on the afternoon of 12 December 1966 with the president, Ackley, and Robert McNamara. The meeting began badly when McNamara was evasive on the adequacy of defense-spending estimates, and Ackley observed that due to the slowing economy, projected budget revenues might be slightly optimistic. Martin struggled with his feelings of dread and sweeping anger. He argued that "it would be disastrous to come out with budget deficits of virtually unprecedented size without coming out for an increase in taxes."[168] Once again he tried to persuade Johnson that "[a] candid presentation of the facts, giving full weight to the costs of our efforts in Vietnam . . . would ensure prompt enactment [of a tax increase]. I am far more concerned about the effects at home and abroad of a failure to propose an increase in taxes than I am about the effects of proposing one."[169] Finally he dispelled any justification for the administration to look to the Fed for further tightening: "[M]onetary policy has done about all that it properly can."[170]

These were words that a president rarely, if ever, heard from a Federal Reserve chairman, and certainly not from Bill Martin. He had violated two of his most dearly held rules of his chairmanship: to avoid acting in outright opposition to his president and to avoid giving advice on matters properly the responsibility of the administration. His outburst could destroy his already strained relationship with Johnson. He had told the president how he saw the situation: the chips would fall where they might.

Ackley, who had advised Johnson only a few days before that "the tax increase should be put on the shelf" due to the predicted softness in the economy, offered half-hearted resistance to Martin's assault.[171] The very size of the deficits defied justification. The president kept his own counsel, and the meeting broke up with Johnson promising again to do some "deep praying and heavy thinking."[172] The next day, Ackley told the president that "Martin's performance was disgraceful, his worst in a long time."[173]

The size of the projected deficits discussed in the 12 December meeting, no doubt aided by Martin's outrage, finally broke through the last of Lyndon Johnson's resistance on the tax issue. The next day, the president asked Ackley and the CEA to review the economy and the impact of a tax increase. He also asked aide Joe Califano to organize an administration review of the question. The final recommendations were carefully hedged, both politically and economically. The plan included a 5 percent increase in corporate and personal taxes along with an easing of monetary conditions by the Fed. It provided Johnson with options for damage control if the economic results were different from those anticipated. The tax increase was proposed to start on 30 June 1967, when the CEA expected the current economic softening to be over. The tax would be considered temporary, lasting only as long as the war continued. Johnson's political advisors had mixed reactions to the plan but accepted the value of a lower fiscal 1968 deficit as long as the plan would keep the economy on course through the 1968 elections. It was a practical, flexible plan, and it must have infuriated Martin that it hadn't been proposed at least a year earlier. The only questions were whether Johnson would really sell it — and if he did, whether Congress would buy it.

On 9 January 1967, Martin received a late-night call from Lyndon Johnson: "I've decided to bite the bullet on taxes and after long agonizing, I have decided to follow your advice."[174] Johnson had a knack for making each advisor feel that he was the instrumental factor in a presidential decision. In reality, Johnson policy decisions had numerous authors, usually forged into a consensus by Joe Califano. Johnson went on: "I don't want you to run out on me . . . labor will be very mad and a lot of business people will be very mad . . . saying I should have let monetary policy do this thing and not at this late date invoke fiscal policy."[175] Exasperated at Johnson's constant need for reassurance, Martin replied, "I never run out; I gave you the best advice I had and I will be glad to stand or fall on it. I might prefer a different timing, but you can rest assured that I will support your position fully."[176] It was a promising call, but with Lyndon Johnson, nothing was certain until it actually happened.

True to his word, in his 1967 State of the Union speech the next day, the president did propose a 6 percent surtax on individual and corporate incomes "to last for two years or so long as the unusual expenditures associated with our efforts in Vietnam continue."[177] It was a deeply gratifying moment for Bill Martin — the culmination of nearly two years of effort in which he had repeatedly risked his relationship with the president. Lyndon Johnson finally accepted that he could not get the "guns and butter" he wanted without asking the American people to pay for more of it. Martin had told Johnson of his confidence that "[c]ongressional and public understanding of the need to demonstrate the fiscal responsibility of the U.S. and the willingness of its citizens to share in the burdens of the war in Vietnam will assure prompt enactment."[178] Now Martin would find out how correct he was. In any event, the Fed and the administration would again be able to work together to bring the economy under control. Martin's renewed hope for the future was colored by the apprehension that even if Congress supported the legislation, it might be too little and too late. But that was a worry for another day.

IO

Reaping the Whirlwind: The Late Johnson Years

The half-life of the Johnson administration's surtax proposal of January 1967 was less than a month. Johnson aide Joe Califano described the congressional response to the president's initiative: "No one welcomed Johnson's announcement. Republican opposition had been anticipated, but it hurt when Wilbur Mills and Senate Finance Committee Chairman Russell Long . . . doubted out loud that Congress would pass one."[1] Privately, Mills told CEA Chairman Ackley that he would not hold hearings on a tax proposal tied to the CEA's forecast of an economic recovery in the second half of 1967: "You can't legislate on the basis of economic forecasts. You have to legislate on the basis of reality."[2] It did not require much political opposition to end Johnson's already ambivalent support for the tax increase. By early February, the increase had disappeared from the presidential agenda even though the administration's economic team and Bill Martin continued to speak out in favor of it.

The Joint Economic Committee hearings on the president's economic report carried unusual significance in 1967. For committee members it was a chance to probe the policy decisions behind the Fed's dramatic monetary tightening of 1966, and for Bill Martin it was a chance to urge congressional support for a tax increase. The hearings were led by the new committee chairman, Senator William Proxmire. Proxmire, a Democrat from Wisconsin, was known as a no-nonsense leader who was less likely than his predecessor Paul Douglas to use the chairmanship as a bully pulpit and more likely to forge a committee consensus. Martin knew his defense of the tax increase would have to offset the mixed message coming from the administration and the opposition of most of the academic economists who were also scheduled to testify.

Martin appeared before the committee on 9 February and began his presentation by reviewing economic developments in 1966: "We could have been wiser if we had followed a more restrictive monetary policy from mid-1965 on. Also, if we had reduced [budgetary] expenditures and increased taxes, we would have had a better and smoother flow of funds through the economy."[3] Going on the offensive, he indicted Congress for failing to remove the 4¼ percent interest rate ceiling on long-term borrowing that forced the Treasury to borrow exclusively in the Treasury bill market in 1966: "If we had removed the ceiling on longer term Treasury maturities . . . we would not have had a [record high] 5.58 percent Treasury bill rate this [past] summer."[4] He announced his overall satisfaction with the results of the tightening program: "The monetary and fiscal actions undertaken to convert an overly exuberant economy to one expanding at a slower but healthier rate were successful. The six-month Treasury bill rate is now just over 4½ percent."[5]

He went on to deal with the tax increase. He knew that selling the increase in the midst of the current slowdown would not be easy. A few weeks earlier, Paul Samuelson had publicly cautioned the administration: "It has become too late in the expansion to raise taxes. It might bite just when our economic expansion is running out of steam."[6] However, most economists in and outside the Fed agreed that the slowdown would be temporary, reflecting an adjustment by manufacturers to bring inventories in line with sales. Strong economic growth was expected to resume in the second half of the year. To accommodate this forecast, Gardner Ackley had convinced Johnson to propose that the tax increase take effect on 1 July 1967. Martin told the committee that the Fed expected inflationary pressures to return in the second half, and unless the tax increase were enacted, another Fed tightening was in store: "We are still dealing with the problems of inflation. The tax increase is designed to be a defense against what might occur in late 1967. . . . A tax increase will be desirable as a means of preventing a recurrence of what happened last year when almost the entire brunt of this was borne by monetary policy."[7] Martin was well aware that leading his FOMC associates through another painful tightening would be difficult, if not impossible, but it did not stop him from threatening Congress members with one.

To justify his concern about inflation, Martin took on the disciples of economist John Maynard Keynes on whether a limited amount of inflation was acceptable in the pursuit of full employment. Martin mentioned his conversations with the great man himself, the last of which was shortly before Keynes's death: "Before the end of the war, Keynes was convinced that the main problem of the postwar period was going to be unemployment, but he explained to me that his views had completely changed, and he was now convinced that the problem of the postwar world was going to be dealing with inflation. He was going to do a book or similar work on it. I think he has been misquoted a great deal with respect to his attitude toward inflation and deflation."[8] Martin then attacked the unwillingness of many Keynesian economists to emphasize the discipline of budgetary surpluses during strong economic conditions: "We have failed to compensate. We have been relying too much on deficit finance without ever having a surplus. You have got to have a balance. If deficit financing becomes permanent, then it is just a matter of time before you undermine your currency."[9] The link between a country's financial discipline and the esteem in which its currency is held was one of Bill Martin's most transcendent ideals, first expressed in his public speeches in the 1930s and repeated regularly in one of his stock speeches titled "Good Money Is Coined Freedom."[10]

Bill Martin was correct that most of the economists who followed him into the JEC hearing room assigned little urgency to the tax increase. Walter Heller, now back in academia, indicated that his support for the tax increase had declined since mid-1966, and if the economy continued to be soft well into 1967, "I would forego [*sic*] the tax increase if we can get monetary easing and adequate support for essential programs." Former CEA member James Tobin was more pessimistic about the strength of the economy: "In spite of the anticipated growth in public expenditures, the restraints of current taxes and monetary policies, taken together, are likely to be too severe. Therefore, I do not now see a case for the proposed six percent surcharge."[11] Even Arthur Burns did not recommend a tax increase in the current environment and accepted the inevitability of increasing government deficits. On inflation, he observed: "Once an inflationary spiral gets underway, I am afraid there isn't a great deal that can be done constructively. A severe recession would bring it to a halt, but no one of us wants that. If we move back toward a policy of severe credit restriction, chances are that we will bring on a recession."[12]

Martin was disappointed that Burns, the economist most likely to reinforce Martin's arguments, made few supportive comments and reached some very unhelpful conclusions. Martin's search for allies in the battle over taxes and inflation would have to continue.

If Martin had hoped for thoughtful media coverage of his JEC presentation, he was doomed to disappointment. What followed his presentation was a flurry of speculation about whether Lyndon Johnson would reappoint Martin

230 Reaping the Whirlwind

as Fed chairman when Martin's term ended six weeks later. The issue arose in early January 1967, when a reporter from the *Washington Post* news service wrote: "William McChesney Martin, Jr. has told the White House he would like to resign from the Federal Reserve Board. Sources close to Martin said they feel he will stay on in the job if President Johnson asks him to."[13] A stream of articles in business sections across the country followed that raised questions about Martin's health, his unhappiness with his more liberal FOMC associates, his problems with the president, and his general desire to escape the "burdens and harassments" of his job.[14] Lyndon Johnson's penchant for delaying important appointment decisions until the last minute and his absolute passion for secrecy added fuel to the speculative fires.

The original reporter was on the right track; Martin had tried to resign on three separate occasions, but Johnson simply ignored his offers. When the speculation over Martin's situation erupted, Johnson ordered a staff study on the extent of support for Martin. John Macy, the shrewd head of the Civil Service Commission who advised Johnson on personnel matters, recommended Martin's reappointment: "His world prestige is unequaled. More on the hill are pro-Martin than against him."[15] CEA member James Duesenberry reported that "95 percent of the Business Council members want Martin reappointed."[16] Gardner Ackley wrote: "Andy [Brimmer] and the other governors have no idea if Martin will accept reappointment if offered, but Andy, Mitchell, Daane, Robertson, and probably Maisel favor reappointment."[17] One of the most unexpected testimonials came from Fed Governor George Mitchell, who often disagreed with Martin but pointedly told Gardner Ackley: "Martin is increasingly becoming a follower of the new economics. Bill is very much inclined to go along with the majority of his Board and his staff. Now that the new economics is firmly in the saddle in both places, Bill can be counted on to cooperate."[18] There was little likelihood that Martin would have agreed with Mitchell's observation, but Mitchell's support did not hurt Martin's reappointment prospects.

In the absence of any indication from the White House about its intentions, the public debate became more active. Senator Russell Long of Louisiana, the chairman of the Senate Finance Committee and a longtime Martin opponent, demanded that "Johnson take the simple course of not renaming Mr. Martin as Chairman."[19] Unable to resist this golden opportunity to call for Martin's replacement, Representative Wright Patman claimed: "$200 billion of excess interest charges can be traced to Mr. Martin's policies . . . it is a gross betrayal of the public trust."[20] Arthur Burns publicized the story about Martin's popularity among international bankers by observing: "I have heard men, including a high administration official, say that Bill Martin is worth a billion dollars in gold [to the U.S. balance of payments]."[21] As 31 March approached, Lyndon Johnson received more free advice from the media.

At the end of a long Tuesday, 14 March 1967, Bill Martin sat down with Lyndon Johnson to discuss his reappointment. In a diary memorandum, Martin wrote that he told Johnson: "If I am reappointed I will be beginning my fifth four-year term as Chairman, and I think this is too long. You and I have had some sharp disagreements. I do not want to complicate the problems you are facing, and I will merely say to the press that I turn the job over to my successor with all good wishes."[22] "Then," Martin wrote: "in his characteristic way, the president seized the initiative." Staring intently at Martin, Johnson said, "Bill, you and I have had our differences, but I respect you and like you. I am convinced that you're the best man available for the job. The country has confidence in you, and I desperately need you to continue. I am going to have a very difficult time in the next two years and I am pleading with you to continue. The Vietnam War is going to get hotter. I have a bear by the tail and I don't know how to let go. In my judgment, your word is your bond, and if the U.S. goes back on its word, we are betraying everything this country has stood for. If it were not for Vietnam, I would be willing to let you retire."[23] If this were not sufficiently stunning, Martin was totally unprepared for what came next.

Johnson began again: "Now I am going to tell you something that I want you to keep in complete confidence. I have decided not to run again in 1968 and, in spite of what the press writes, I expect to turn the Government over to someone else at the start of 1969. I am asking you to stay with me, if your conscience permits, until the inauguration of a new president in 1969."[24]

Although his mind and emotions were reeling, Martin tried to assess the situation. Johnson's ability to manipulate people was legendary, and his resignation plans could be changed numerous times in the next eighteen months. On the other hand, Martin had never heard Johnson be so candid about the war in Vietnam or about his view of Martin. If the war continued to grow in intensity, the country's economic turmoil would increase, and it would take a great deal of independence and determination by a Fed chairman to pressure Lyndon Johnson to make sound economic decisions. He might not be able to persuade Johnson to do the right thing, but if he acceded to Johnson's plea, Martin would have a much better chance of succeeding than anyone who might replace him. Although he intensely wanted to retire, a lifetime commitment to public service made it impossible for Martin to refuse a president who asked for his help.

If he were going to continue, Martin at least wanted to exact some presidential help in making his life easier at the Fed: "I will have to have some assurance that whoever is appointed to replace [retiring Governor Charles] Shepardson will be acceptable to me."[25] Johnson was immensely relieved to know that the discussion had moved on to bargaining and was immediately back on the offensive, complaining about the pressures coming from Senators Long and Gore, who, along with Wright Patman, were "demanding that you not be reappointed."[26] Martin "waited for him to run down" and would not change the subject until the president "assured me he would not appoint anyone until I gave my approval."[27] Finally, Martin addressed the most sensitive issue between them: "I am inclined to accept if you are asking me to run the Federal Reserve Board and do not want to run it yourself by indirection. If you want me to run it and are completely sincere in this, I am disposed to continue, much as I would like to retire."[28] When Johnson, who was rarely at a loss for words, offered no opposition, Martin was satisfied.

As the two men sat considering their bargain, Johnson tried to lighten the moment: "I have liked you since the first time we met, and I hope you like me."[29] It was a typical reminder of Lyndon Johnson's incessant search for affection and generated characteristic candor from Martin: "Mr. President, I have said some unkind things about you behind your back, and don't want to be two-faced and pretend I haven't . . . but I honestly like you when you are reasonable about things, but sometimes you are not reasonable."[30] Johnson laughed heartily and said, "That is exactly what Lady Bird says to me." On that note Martin left the White House and walked into the dark night toward his parked car. The possibility of a changed relationship with Lyndon Johnson was intriguing, but the pragmatic side of Martin did not give it much likelihood.

On the morning of 31 March, the White House made an uncharacteristically brief statement: "[T]he president has decided to re-appoint William McChesney Martin, Jr. as Chairman of the Federal Reserve Board."[31] The usual White House press office management of the announcement was noticeably muted. With the exception of Wright Patman's comment that "Martin will cause this administration much sorrow in future years," most public commentary on the reappointment was positive.[32] The *New York Times* editorialized that Martin "has become so celebrated a symbol of monetary respectability that the president could not let Mr. Martin go without casting doubts, here and abroad, on his own desire for effective fiscal and monetary policies."[33] Lyndon Johnson could not have been pleased that his poor bargaining position with Martin was so widely recognized.

Now that the fates had conspired to keep him in office, Martin returned to the issue of a tax increase. His campaign took a surprising turn in May 1967. Martin's continuing conversations with Senator Richard Russell and Deputy Defense Secretary David Packard confirmed that actual spending on the war for the 1967 fiscal year ending in a few months would indeed be twice the estimated amount and that future commitments were still escalating. Martin remained convinced that Congress and the public would support a tax increase, but they needed the facts about war spending to appreciate the urgency of the situation. In his determination to change the situation, he took a remarkably uncharacteristic step.

He invited Hobart Rowen, the chief *Washington Post* financial reporter and a longtime confidant, to lunch to discuss the war costs. Martin agonized over this step because he knew the revelation would create an uproar. By early 1967, the Vietnam War had become a highly contested subject, and disclosing the future cost increases would fan the flames of dissent. Martin believed deeply in resolving policy conflicts out of the glare of the public spotlight and that manipulating the press to influence policy decisions was extremely destructive to the democratic process. Nevertheless, he believed that Lyndon Johnson's deceit was distorting the country's economic policies. The tax issue had been crippled by half-truths and dissembling for too long. It was time for the facts to come out in the open so the national debate could be based on reality. Though the action totally contradicted his personal values, Martin met with Rowen.

Rowen's subsequent disclosure and reference to a "high government economic official" was met with anger and astonishment.[34] It confirmed a future manpower increase that had only been rumored before and that "escalation of U.S. troop commitments in Vietnam might require a substantial 1968 tax increase."[35] Senator William Proxmire, chairman of the Joint Economic Committee, who had unsuccessfully tried for over a year to pin the administration down on the war, wondered publicly how the United States could continue to underestimate the costs of the war. The more informed debate Martin sought was under way, but Martin knew that Lyndon Johnson would inevitably learn of his disclosure. He could only pray that subsequent events would soon confirm the validity of his accusation. Four months later, presidential aide McGeorge Bundy publicly confirmed Martin as the source of the leak. Rowen, quick to defend his source, wrote in the *Washington Post* that Senator Proxmire and the JEC had recently authorized a study of Vietnam spending: "According to the Joint Economic Committee, the facts are bearing out Martin's concerns almost exactly."[36] It was hardly a moment of satisfaction for Bill Martin. The Vietnam War was poisoning everything, Martin's operating methods included.

Lyndon Johnson's promise that the replacement for retiring Fed Governor Charles Shepardson would be acceptable to Martin was scheduled to come due in April 1967. On 21 March, the White House informed Martin that the proposed candidate was William Sherrill, currently a member of the board of the Federal Deposit Insurance Corporation (FDIC). Sherrill had been a banker and investment manager in Houston prior to joining the FDIC board and fit Martin's profile of an experienced businessman who was knowledgeable in national financial issues. It would not have surprised Martin if he had known that Sherrill had also been selected because of his loyalty to the president. Johnson aide Jack Valenti recommended Sherrill to Johnson with the comment, "He is your man—LBJ all the way—active in your campaign. Totally loyal without a doubt. His is the new Johnson look — young, brilliant, articulate, but loyal."[37] Personnel decisions in the Johnson administration carried a heavy political ingredient, and Fed governor candidates would not be treated differently. Martin at least got the noneconomist governor that he was seeking.

During the spring and early summer of 1967, the Fed attempted to counteract the economic slowdown by adopting a more expansionary policy. For the first five months of the year, the money supply (M1) increased at an annual rate of 10 percent and bank credit at 12 percent, the highest rates in sixteen years. The flood of liquidity caused rates on three-month Treasury bills to tumble from 5 ½ percent in October 1966 to 3 ½ percent in early June 1967. In the third week of April, the Fed governors reduced the discount rate from 6 percent to 5 ½ percent, the first cut since 1960. As the Fed had anticipated, banks and corporations rushed to rebuild the liquidity that had been drained away during the credit squeeze of 1966. Even the badly hit housing industry began to recover as funds flowed into the mortgage market. By June, the contraction of the monetary aggregates experienced in 1966 was fully offset: for the twelve months ending May 1967, the money supply had expanded at an overall rate of 2 ½ percent and bank credit by 6 percent.

The CEA was also concerned about the economic slowdown, and this concern cooled its enthusiasm for the tax increase proposal. In February 1967, Gardner Ackley announced that the administration was delaying its request for a tax increase in view of the uncertainties about the economy. By 10 May, with the prospects for the second-half recovery firming up, Ackley flip-flopped. He wrote to Johnson with his strongest defense of the tax increase but still gave the president the opportunity to defer requesting one until the economic recovery was certain. On 5 June, the Quadriad held its first meeting since late November 1966, and Martin grasped the opportunity to take the tax issue directly to Johnson.

Gardner Ackley initiated the meeting by focusing on the "sluggishness of the economy," but Martin moved directly to the issue of the tax increase. He "stressed as hard as I could the feeling of the bond market that the administration was not pursuing a tax increase actively enough and that defense expenditures would increase.[38] Martin, who was struggling to maintain a temper that always troubled him, often resorted to old-fashioned phrases to express himself when he was emotional: "There should be no shilly-shallying around about this, and it is essential to make clear that it is the size of the deficit . . . that makes this action necessary."[39] Johnson's only response was, as it was so often, to ask if Martin was publicly supporting the tax increase proposal. Their argument was becoming ritualized, but Martin sometimes felt that he was the only government official willing and able to directly confront Lyndon Johnson about the tax issue.

Lyndon Johnson was stung by Martin's outburst, but he was alarmed a few weeks later when the Troika concluded that even after the impact of a 6 percent tax increase beginning on 1 October 1967, the deficit for the fiscal year 1968 was projected at $15 billion, or 12 percent of the budget. Henry Fowler told the president that without a tax increase "the fiscal year 1968 deficit could soar to $23 to $28 billion."[40] Once again Johnson turned to Joe Califano to marshal an administrationwide review of support for the tax increase. This time, Lyndon Johnson sent him off with the admonition: "Get agreement, for God's sake."[41] Califano forged a consensus around the arguments of Treasury Secretary Fowler, who had resumed his role of administration proponent for the tax increase. During the discussions, Fowler advised Johnson that "the overwhelming preponderance of economic opinion is that there is no longer any real danger that the imposition of this temporary [tax] increase will cause an economic downturn."[42]

To keep the pressure on Johnson during the administration's review, Martin announced in a speech on 26 June: "I would support income tax increases amounting to 10 percent to bring federal income and expenditures closer to balance."[43] In the 21 July Quadriad meeting, the president went around the table asking the members to state their recommendation for the amount by which taxes should be increased. When Budget Director Charles Schultze raised his suggested rate from 6 to 8 percent, bringing him closer to the other Quadriad members, Fowler advised him that "you have a great future in pricing at Sears."[44] At the end of a series of bids resembling a poker session, the president announced the conclusion: "the 10 percent surtax increase recommended by Chairman Martin."[45] The process was hardly the result of disciplined economic reasoning, but Martin had to take some comfort with the outcome. In late July, the White House announced that the tax increase legislation would go to Congress in early August. Despite Wilbur Mills's warning to Califano that "I am distancing myself from the legislation until the president delivers spending cuts," the proposal contained no spending reductions.[46] The troubled prospects for the tax increase continued.

Treasury Undersecretary Joseph Barr had the unenviable task of negotiating the surtax legislation with Wilbur Mills. Recognizing that Mills would demand his pound of flesh, Barr initiated a tentative and highly confidential discussion of a $2 billion expenditure cut. The *Washington Star* printed an unconfirmed report that the Johnson administration was lining up specific spending cuts. Predictably, the president flew into a rage and told Barr that "you are not authorized to move one inch from my tax message" that offered no expenditure cuts.

Despite the fact that his hands were now tied, Barr pleaded with Mills and the president to keep the hearings and the dialogue going, but his urging came to naught. Johnson did not see Mills between the 3 August tax message and early October. Cut off from the president and offered no compromise on spending cuts, Mills suspended the tax legislation hearings. Lyndon Johnson's anger boiled over into public view. In a 17 November press conference he said, "Mr. Ford [House Republican leader] and Mr. Mills have taken the position that they cannot have any tax bill now. They will live to rue the day when they made that decision because it is a dangerous decision . . . an unwise decision."[47] The response from Chairman Mills's office was: "The president will rue the day he made that statement."[48] The conflict was becoming bitter and personal.

As the two branches of government moved toward a standoff, Bill Martin used his public pulpit to urge the administration to accept the need for both a tax increase and expenditure cuts. In September he told Wilbur Mills and the House Ways and Means committee: "It would be grossly imprudent not to take quick action specifically by passing the tax increase."[49] He also said, "I heartily endorse reductions in government spending."[50] In a speech in Dallas on 9 November, he said: "The United States cannot go on trying to have guns and butter . . . we are trying to do too much too fast."[51] Recognizing Lyndon Johnson's concern about the possible gutting of his domestic programs in any spending cuts, Martin said, "You don't have to be against any of these programs, but you do have to space them out some. We ought to increase taxes . . . and reduce expenditures. We need both."[52] Martin was giving a public voice to what was becoming apparent to economists in and outside the administration. The tax increase, projected to raise $7.5 billion per year, would not make a sufficient dent in a $28 billion deficit. Significant spending reductions were an economic as well as a political necessity.

As the financial markets began to appreciate the burgeoning budgetary deficit, interest rates began to rise in anticipation of a flood of Treasury issues to finance it. During the four months prior to mid-September, three-month Treasury bill rates increased from 3.71 percent to 4.32 percent, and five-year Treasury bond rates rose from 4.58 percent to 5.39 percent. As First National

City Bank reported: "Net government borrowing could be in the neighborhood of $20 billion in the second half of 1967 [compared to $5 billion in
calendar 1966]. Investors obviously will not suddenly increase their holdings
of Government securities by such a large amount without some yield incentive."[53] At the 24 October FOMC meeting, Martin made a similar observation: "[L]arge deficits in the budget are rapidly generating inexorable forces
that might prove more important than any decisions [on credit conditions] the
committee might take."[54] The Fed's "even-keel" policy of maintaining stable
market conditions in support of Treasury bond issues often required substantial open-market purchases of Treasury securities and virtually precluded any
serious attempt to tighten the economy. The failure to achieve a tax increase
was severely compromising the Fed's ability to pursue an independent monetary policy.

Of all the problems that the high interest levels caused for the Fed, the
prospect of a repeat of the credit squeeze of 1966 was the worst. The September 1967 interest rate on a three-month Treasury bill of 4.32 percent was only
1.26 percent below the 1966 high, and five-year Treasury rates were only 0.37
percent lower than their peak. With only a modest increase in rates, banks
would again encounter Regulation Q ceilings on the amount of interest they
could pay on CDs, and there would be a replay of the competitive struggle for
savings deposits with savings and loans. Home building would again suffer as
mortgage money dried up. Martin, well aware of the sharp criticism that had
rained down on the Fed during 1966, had admitted earlier in 1967: "I am not
sure the things we were driven to were the wisest."[55] As late as November
1967, Martin was still affirming: "We have no desire to produce a disastrous
crunch in the money market."[56]

The credit squeeze of 1966 exposed both the effectiveness of the Fed's monetary powers and the unhappiness of the public and politicians with the impact
of the Fed's policy. If the Fed were forced into a repeat performance in 1967 or
early 1968, the reaction by politicians might not be as restrained as it was in
1966. This time around, the Fed's independence could be permanently compromised. If tightening credit was politically dangerous, fiscal action became
even more essential.

During the second half of 1967, Bill Martin adopted a remarkably risky
tactic to force consideration of a tax increase. He concluded that the FOMC
should not tighten credit because it would encourage Congress to avoid action
on the tax increase by letting the Fed do the job of slowing the economy.
Martin was aware of Wilbur Mills's negative attitude toward the tax increase,
typified by his comment to CEA member Arthur Okun: "I don't see this boom
again. You're solving the problem of the first half of 1966 and here we are in

August 1967."[57] On the other hand, the administration, led by Henry Fowler, was finally pushing for the tax increase. The Fed could support the administration by keeping monetary policy easy and letting Wilbur Mills witness his boom. There was a risk that the administration and Congress would not reach an accommodation soon enough to prevent inflation from taking off, but Martin concluded that the risks to the Fed associated with a 1966-style tightening were greater. Neither alternative was desirable, and Martin sought the lesser evil.

Martin expected to have a difficult time maintaining an FOMC consensus around his approach, and by the 12 September meeting of the FOMC, resistance was building up. New York Bank President Hayes repeated an argument he had been making for the two prior meetings by urging the FOMC to consider "the desirability of some modest move toward less monetary ease."[58] Martin expressed sympathy for those who favored restraint: "[T]he simple logic of the economic situation implies the desirability of changing monetary policy, as it did two months ago."[59] But he concluded: "The overriding need at this point is to get some restraint from fiscal policy through a tax increase, and my judgment is that it will be less likely if Congress believes that adequate restraint is being exercised by monetary policy."[60] Martin was taking the most difficult step a Fed chairman could take. By refusing to lead the Fed toward restraint when the economic conditions clearly justified it, he gambled that he could push the political process into an unnatural act, raising taxes. Balancing the economic necessities with the political realities is at the heart of what Arthur Burns later eloquently labeled "The Agony of Central Banking."

Though Martin was able to hold off the FOMC hawks, his success gave him little comfort about the risk he was running. The September statistics were terrible. Retail sales were up strongly in July and August, and unemployment was back down to 3.7 percent. Wage settlements averaged a horrific 6 percent increase and guaranteed further cost-push pressures on prices. The CPI was increasing at a 3 ½ percent annual rate, and worse yet, wholesale prices were now rising at a 3 percent annual rate. These conditions would normally have caused Martin to forge a consensus around tightening credit, but he was committed to letting inflation run. The critical question was whether these statistics were bad enough to convince Wilbur Mills to change his mind.

At the end of November, Martin came face-to-face with the difficulties of moving Congress toward a tax increase. Following an administration plea, Wilbur Mills agreed to resume hearings on the tax increase. On 29 November, Martin and Fowler made another effort to persuade Mills to support the tax increase. Fowler had heroically breached Johnson's resistance to spending cuts and offered an "Administration Economy Program" that would cut $2.6 billion from fiscal 1968 spending. When Mills expressed disappointment in the size of the cuts, Martin tried to bridge the gap between the administration and Mills by observing: "The proposed reductions are meaningful, but I had hoped they would be larger."[61] Despite Martin's plea for prompt action on the proposed tax increase, Mills noted: "Although as Chairman Martin suggests, a demand-pull situation could develop early next year, I have not yet seen any evidence of an inflationary situation which requires immediate action."[62] With that comment, Mills adjourned the hearings indefinitely.

When the FOMC met on 12 December, Martin recognized the failure of his gamble with Congress: "I have done everything I could to help the administration persuade Congress of the need for enactment of a tax increase, but those efforts have been futile."[63] He agreed with the FOMC's consensus for tightening and spoke of the importance of sending a clear message: "The most important need is for an indication by the Committee that it is willing to resist inflationary pressures. Many observers apparently have become convinced that the Committee will not, under almost any conditions, move toward restraint. The existence of that attitude . . . is unfortunate."[64] The battle against inflation was reengaged, but it could bring the worst of both worlds: a tightening that came too late to control the buildup of inflationary momentum and yet played into the hands of the opponents of a tax increase.

Martin's preoccupation with the tax increase was interrupted during mid-November by yet another crisis involving the British pound. Even though it had achieved a strong recovery from the massive sterling bailout of 1964, the Labour government of Prime Minister Harold Wilson had not fashioned a long-lasting solution to Britain's balance of payments problems. The high level of interest rates prevailing in the United States and Germany during 1966 and into 1967 put sterling under a continuing selling pressure that was building toward a climax in the fall of 1967. On 17 November, Sir Leslie O'Brien, governor of the Bank of England, informed Martin and Fowler that sterling would be devalued by 14.3 percent. Martin and Fowler met with Lyndon Johnson to tell him the bad news and to produce a now predictable statement by the president that "I reaffirm unequivocally the commitment of the United States to buy and sell gold at the existing price of $35 per ounce."[65] They also urged the president to use the crisis as an opportunity to push for his tax increase, and later that afternoon, the three met with the congressional leadership. Mills reluctantly agreed to reopen the tax hearings in the next two weeks but observed: "What the outcome might be, I cannot predict at this time."[66]

Fowler and Martin knew that the devaluation would put strong pressure on the dollar and that trading on the London gold market would be chaotic. Trading on 21 November opened with the news that France had withdrawn from the London gold pool and rumors that Italy and Belgium were about to do the same. Treasury Undersecretary Deming and Fed Governor Daane conducted an unsuccessful telephone campaign to secure a joint public statement by gold pool members that they would continue to support the pool. After pleas from Fowler and Martin, Karl Blessing, the respected head of the German Bundesbank, agreed to convene a meeting of pool members in Frankfurt on Saturday, 25 November, to see if a joint commitment could be reached. The Frankfurt meeting was rancorous and ended with a fig leaf of commitment to "continue all-out pool operation for one more week before reaching a final decision."[67]

Officials at the Fed and the Treasury agreed that the only solution was for the Fed to restore confidence in the dollar by forceful intervention in the foreign-exchange markets. During the week of 27–31 November, the Fed's foreign-currency desk in New York executed "heavy" purchases of dollars in the futures market. These purchases had the desired effect, and gold sales by the gold pool slowed from a peak of $260 million a day to an encouraging two-week total of $100 million. The scheduled review by the gold pool participants was delayed a week, then two, and finally evolved into watching and waiting as sterling's recovery took place.

As he looked back on the experience, Martin had many reasons for concern. The deficit in the U.S. balance of payments undermined confidence in the international monetary system and was a major contributor to sterling's problems. Under normal conditions, the Fed would respond to the payments deficit by raising interest rates to attract foreign investment funds and reduce domestic demand for imports. This time, domestic economic considerations made it impossible to raise rates, and the Fed was forced into a massive support program for the dollar. In Martin's view, the inability of the U.S. political system to address the fiscal problem was forcing the Fed further and further away from market-oriented monetary policies that produced long-term economic stability.

The strain of the sterling crisis also exposed the outright anger that the traditional European allies now felt toward the United States. Al Hayes had reported that Bundesbank's Karl Blessing, one of the "most loyal" allies of the United States, expressed "concern about U.S. fiscal policy. The lack of congressional action is raising questions in the minds of European monetary authorities as to the willingness of the U.S. to come to grips with its problems."[68] Even more devastating, Hayes quoted Blessing as saying: "[I]f the deficit in the U.S. balance of payments remains large, the group's discussions [on strengthening the gold pool] might as well be brought to an end, because they would be futile."[69] As if to confirm Blessing's criticism, Robert Solomon, the Fed's director of international research, observed in the 12 December FOMC meeting: "The outlook for the balance of payments next year is not promising."[70] To Martin's mind, it was hard to argue with the Europeans. They had endured a U.S. balance of payments problem that began almost a decade earlier. Despite various initiatives by presidents Eisenhower, Kennedy, and Johnson, no real improvement had been realized, and European central banks were constantly being asked to hold more dollars as reserves. The weakness of sterling and the dollar were tearing the international monetary system apart.

As Martin shifted his attention back to domestic issues, he returned to the on-again, off-again battle over the surtax. On 22 January 1968, Mills reopened his hearings on the tax increase and reviewed a proposed budget for fiscal 1969 that Schultze characterized as "containing painful cuts." He castigated Martin, Fowler, and Schultze for "no change in attitude toward [lower] government spending."[71] The prospects for the tax increase appeared as remote as ever, and the extended struggle was taking a toll on the administration. CEA member Arthur Okun described Henry Fowler's attitude: "In early 1968, Fowler would have paid any price, taken any cut in domestic spending, to get the tax increase."[72] At one point, the hearing degenerated into a shouting match between Schultze and Representative John Byrnes over the extent of spending cuts. The next day, Mills told Schultze to take another look for additional spending reductions, and once again suspended the hearings for an indefinite period.

A few days later, Martin tried to minimize his disappointment in the hearings when he advised the FOMC that "it is important to press for a tax increase however questionable the prospects are."[73] At the same time he dismissed the concern of the FOMC's economic advisors that the tax increase, together with the Fed's tightening, could cause an economic slowdown in the second half of 1968: "Whatever the future risks of . . . too much economic restraint, the risks of inaction are greater."[74]

Though Martin felt that the surtax issue deserved his undivided attention, the recurrent pressures on the international monetary system demanded that he put aside his domestic agenda. Following the British devaluation in November 1967, European foreign-exchange markets continued to be unsettled and in early March, a new tidal wave of gold sales rattled the London gold market. On 7 March, $180 million of gold changed hands, and that evening Martin canceled his appointments and flew to Basel, Switzerland, where he made an unexpected appearance at a routine gathering of European central leaders. Encountering an atmosphere of "heavy gloom" among his counterparts, Martin "raised the specter of a collapse of the international monetary system" and won a further commitment by the participants in the London gold pool to continue supporting the $35 official price.[75] When he was asked about the commitment, Sir Leslie O'Brien, head of the Bank of England, was quoted as saying: "I am very pleased with the result and I hope the world will be, too."[76] Later he told Charles Coombs, the Fed's special manager for international finance, "[A] major duty of every central banker is to learn how to exude confidence without positively lying."[77]

In the following week, the gold market shrugged off the hopeful words of the central bankers, and gold demand surged again. On 14 March, Martin and Fowler had to "forcefully reject" the opposition of White House and CEA staff members to an expansion of existing Fed swap credits by $2 billion.[78] Martin also encountered strong resistance to the swap proposal when he convened a telephone meeting of the FOMC. In the middle of the meeting, Sir Leslie O'Brien called to tell Martin some ominous news: the British wanted to close the London financial markets. As the FOMC discussion continued, the members were evenly split over the swap increase. Only after strong arguments by New York Reserve Bank President Al Hayes and Governor Dewey Daane, who led the negotiations with other central bankers, did the FOMC eventually go along.

Martin and Fowler then requested an emergency White House meeting, and they described the stark picture to the president.[79] The United States and its allies were running their gold reserves down to a dangerous level through their unlimited support of the London gold pool. The gold pool arrangements must be changed or the pool closed. If the pool were closed, confidence in the dollar would plummet, and a worldwide financial crisis of unpredictable proportions would inevitably be triggered. American embassies were already reporting that American exporters and travelers were having serious problems exchanging their dollars in Europe. Wilbur Mills later described Johnson's reaction: "He was scared almost out of his body when he heard that people in Europe were having trouble exchanging dollars for foreign currency."[80] Martin proposed a temporary closing of the London market and offered to convene an emergency meeting of the heads of the leading central banks to agree on a solution to the gold crisis.

Johnson was concerned that a meeting would produce only stopgap measures. Martin admitted that if a U.S. tax increase were not passed, there was no guarantee that another "gold rush" would not develop in the future. Ever the financial historian, Martin discussed the importance of a cooling-off period when financial markets became panicked and reviewed the bank holiday that FDR initiated in 1933. Fowler pushed for an immediate decision; "the damage from a day's delay could be incalculable."[81] After a hiatus during which Johnson conferred with congressional leaders, the president said he was prepared to go along. Martin called O'Brien with Johnson's agreement to the closing. Two hours later the Queen of England, roused from her bed by a delegation of Labour Party ministers, formally agreed to the closing.

During 15 March, the day before the start of the weekend meeting of central bankers, the U.S. position was "hammered out." It preserved the $35 per ounce fixed price for gold, which represented a pillar of Bill Martin's monetary philosophy. A month before the gold crisis, Martin eloquently defended his position in a speech to the National Industrial Conference Board. He argued that the dollar's role as the world's leading reserve currency made the United States the world's banker, but it was defaulting on that role by allowing its short-term liabilities in the form of dollars held by foreigners to far exceed its short-term assets in the form of readily available gold. The United States had to address the short-term imbalance by "strengthening its underlying [balance of] payments position . . . and by pursuing effective stabilization policies that promote price stability and a competitive cost structure."[82]

Martin acknowledged the problems of the Bretton Woods system but urged his listeners to support the international cooperative efforts to strengthen it: "Those who recommend an increase in the price of gold seem to me to have decided that monetary management is impossible on an international scale. Given the magnificent record of international monetary and economic cooperation we have witnessed in the past twenty years, I refuse to accept the cynical and desperate view that man must turn back to greater dependence on gold."[83] Martin observed that even if confidence in the dollar were restored, the world must support the plan for a new form of international monetary reserves. The new reserve, to be called Special Drawing Rights (SDRs), was the product of the collaborative effort Martin supported so wholeheartedly. SDRs represented the so-called paper gold proposed to be issued by the IMF, and Martin observed: "The deliberate creation of international reserves as a supplement to existing reserves . . . means that the world will be assured of a growing supply of reserves at the present price of gold."[84] Since his days at the NYSE, Bill Martin steadfastly maintained that financial systems must evolve in response to fundamental changes in the underlying economy.

On the morning of 16 March, a blustery spring day, the leaders of the seven central banks of the gold pool assembled in the Fed's boardroom. Fed staff member Robert Solomon remarked: "Central bankers are always described as somber, but somber and tense was particularly apt for this occasion."[85] Martin outlined the issues facing the participants and, as expected, reaffirmed the U.S. government's position to hold the $35 per ounce gold price. He then asked Guido Carli, the head of the Bank of Italy, to offer a proposal. As William Scammell, a representative from the Bank for International Settlements, wrote: "It was apparent from Martin's calling on Carli to lead off with his scheme, that the U.S. had come around to this way out of the crisis."[86] Carli had been promoting a plan to create two parallel markets in London, one for official settlements to be conducted at the $35 price and another for nonofficial trading at prices determined by market forces. The United States had in fact thrown its support to Carli even though Martin and Fowler knew that his proposal was controversial.

After Carli's presentation, Sir Leslie O'Brien of the Bank of England quickly proposed an increase in the official price of gold as an alternative, and the head of the Dutch central bank and the general manager of the Bank for International Settlements were quick to support him. A noisy debate followed, with each side raising objections to the other's proposal, and as Fed representative Charles Coombs observed, "Martin imperturbably followed his usual practice in FOMC meetings of letting everyone talk himself out."[87] But then, as Solomon observed, "he closed the bazaar." Martin told the delegates: "The price of gold cannot be raised this weekend. It is necessary to come to a practical solution before the market opens on Monday."[88] Martin's tone was unmistakable; the gold increase was a dead letter. The United States was calling in its chips as the protector of Western Europe and the unflagging supporter of the Bretton Woods system. The delegates understood they should be prepared to discuss the Carli proposal the next day.

On Sunday after a short debate, the delegates were presented with a draft communiqué outlining the commitment to the Carli plan. The most crucial sentence was "As the existing stock of monetary gold is sufficient, in view of the prospective establishment of the facility for Special Drawing Rights, the governors no longer feel it necessary to buy gold from the market."[89] The statement effectively forced all the pool members to rely primarily on SDRs for new reserves and, as Charles Coombs wrote, "carried hints of secret policy understandings to phase out gold in official settlements."[90] There was hard bargaining over the implications of this statement, and Treasury Undersecretary Deming had to promise that the United States would make a major borrowing from the IMF with the proceeds used to purchase some of the dollars accumulated by gold pool participants during the crisis. As Scammell unhappily observed: "The U.S. finally got its way."[91]

The weary bankers traveled home that evening with "grave forebodings of an explosion of speculation when the exchange markets opened the next day."[92] But the markets were unexpectedly calm. Searching for an answer, Coombs observed: "Curiously enough, with all the technical expertise assembled around the table in Washington, we had lost sight of the simple fact that the gold speculators were now saturated with inventory."[93] The billions of dollars worth of gold purchased by private investors in anticipation of a higher price now created a huge overhang of supply. These speculators found themselves with an asset that was unlikely to appreciate significantly and paid no interest or dividends. They had to find a way of selling off their positions without destroying the new private market for gold.

Like many others, Bill Martin was under no illusions about the staying power of the new arrangements, dubbed the "Two-Tier System." In a speech given the day after the conference ended, he observed: "The two-tier system . . . will not solve our fundamental [balance of payments] deficit problem."[94] He revealed his view of what was happening to the monetary system and his sense of isolation in dealing with it: "The U.S. dollar may be on the road to being devalued in terms of gold . . . but I, for one, am going to stick in here as long as I can, fighting to keep it from being devalued."[95] Then he emphasized what he saw as the solution by adding: "Others in the world seeing the [balance of payments] deficits are doubtful we have the capacity to handle our affairs, and this is what is causing a loss of confidence in the dollar. Once the world sees that we have a sound economy and a sound base, they'll no longer worry about the dollar and our gold."[96] Henry Fowler also reflected on the gold crisis and the failure to increase taxes: "Events were proving the case that we had made out on a forecast basis."[97]

It is difficult to appreciate the unbearable pressures on Lyndon Johnson and his economic team that culminated in the events of the first quarter of 1968. The projected budget deficit for 1968 was the largest since the Korean War, and the administration's inability to forecast the actual deficit had exacerbated relationships between the White House and congressional leaders for over two years. The gold crisis of 1967–68 was the most serious threat to the international monetary system since 1945, and was in great part the result of the continuing U.S. payments deficit. Lyndon Johnson and Wilbur Mills were locked in a test of wills that paralyzed progress on the surtax. The Fed was embarked on a program of tightening credit that most observers acknowledged was the right course but carried heavy risks of an overtightening. The impact of these events on Lyndon Johnson and his administration are apparent in their comments at this time.

Henry Fowler had carried much of the administration's message to Congress through continual presentations to a variety of congressional hearings. He and Martin had just been through an emotionally exhausting campaign to resolve the gold crisis. Surveying his efforts on the tax increase during this period, Fowler said: "[M]y job was a backbreaking bone-breaking job which demanded and received every conceivable energy and tactic that I could think of . . . to get the job done."[98] In early April, CEA Chairman Arthur Okun, who had replaced Gardner Ackley, summarized his advice to Johnson in a memorandum titled "Explanation of Possible World Financial Crisis" in which he tried to help Johnson understand what could happen if the tax increase legislation could not be passed. Okun foresaw another 1966-style credit tightening, the world losing faith in the U.S. dollar, another gold crisis, and the fracturing of the international monetary system.

Bill Martin made a well-publicized speech in mid-April in which he "apologized several times for appearing to be emotional."[99] He concluded: "We have, to a certain extent, been living in a fool's paradise. We face a financial crisis that is not understood by the public."[100] He said that he had tried to make himself heard, but "there is no disposition on either side of the aisle in Congress to face up to the problems."[101] These three overworked men [Fowler, Okun, and Martin] could no longer hide the strain of trying to control events that were moving inexorably against them.

For Lyndon Johnson, occupying the desk that Harry Truman had decorated with his "the buck stops here" sign, the strain was even greater. As one historian later wrote about the first half of 1968: "[T]his was one of the most dreadful periods any American President ever faced."[102] Johnson was pursuing a war that he and his advisors believed was in the country's national interest. Despite his protestations that he could see "light at the end of the tunnel," the North Vietnamese Tet offensive in mid-January indicated that peace was a long way off. In January, the U.S. spy ship *Pueblo* was captured by the North Koreans. On 12 March, Senator Eugene McCarthy, campaigning as a peace candidate, received 43 percent of the vote in New Hampshire, and four days later Johnson's nemesis, Robert Kennedy, announced his candidacy for the presidency. Johnson's economic issues were equally urgent. He was convinced that a tax increase was of paramount importance, but he could not bring himself to sacrifice one of his greatest legislative achievements, the war on poverty, to accomplish it. His economic advisors were united in their concern that an economic collapse would occur if current economic policy did not change. The most excruciating knowledge was that his handling of the presidency was the source of these many dilemmas. In addition, he was beginning a presidential election season that would galvanize the contending forces and heighten the conflict over the war.

On 31 March, at the very end of a speech on his Vietnam War peace initiatives, Johnson cut the Gordian knot of his embattled presidency by declaring that he "would not seek nor would he accept" the Democratic nomination for the presidency in 1968. He coupled that announcement with a plea: "We must have a responsible fiscal policy in this country. The passage of a tax bill now, together with expenditure control that Congress may desire and dictate, is absolutely necessary."[103] Johnson's decision took every one of the administration's economic team, with the exception of Bill Martin, by surprise, and they accepted his forcefully expressed determination on the tax increase at face value.[104] True to his word, the president mapped out his plan with the Quadriad two days later. The following day, he invited the congressional leaders to the White House to begin his first sustained presidential leadership role in the campaign to secure approval for his tax legislation.

On 2 April, the surtax was rescued from the impasse between Johnson and Mills by an unlikely source, the U.S. Senate. Members of the Senate, impressed by the gold problems and Lyndon Johnson's dramatic announcement a few days earlier, voted 57–31 to approve legislation containing an amendment offered by Senators Williams of Delaware and Smathers of Florida that simply attached the administration's 10 percent tax increase and a $6-billion expenditure-reduction program. The Senate's more flexible legislative procedures enabled the amendment to be part of a routine extension of existing excise taxes. The Senate had legislation ready for a conference committee and Mills, now outflanked, had to begin serious negotiation for the tax increase legislation in the House.

While the politicians girded for a final showdown, the economic news provided a forbidding backdrop. First-quarter 1968 nominal economic growth was at a breathtaking 10 percent annualized rate, a rate matched only a few times in history. The CPI was escalating at an annual rate of 4.1 percent, the highest rate in seventeen years. Workers in the aluminum and telecommunications industries received three-year contracts with 6¾ percent and 6.2 percent annual increases respectively, sending the wage-price guideposts into greater oblivion. The balance of merchandise trade for the first quarter recorded the first deficit in five years, which CEA Chairman Arthur Okun called "disastrous and shocking."[105] Given the discouraging statistics, it was easy for the Fed's board of governors to unanimously approve increasing the discount from 5 percent to 5½ percent on 18 April. Okun advised Johnson: "Without the tax increase, the rate change makes a lot of sense."[106] If the unemotional and realistic Okun had replaced Walter Heller instead of Gardner Ackley, Lyndon Johnson's false sense of well-being in 1966 and 1967 might not have occurred.

The uncertain prospects for the tax increase and the certain prospects for an economic boom goaded Martin into speeches that reflected his anger and frustration with the lack of progress in dealing with the country's economic problems. Martin's speech on 18 April to the Society of Newspaper Editors was extemporaneous and, for Martin, highly personal. He described his problems in dealing with foreign central bankers unhappy with U.S. fiscal policies, senators who were indifferent to the country's problems, an administration that for years would not address the budget deficit, and a public that did not understand the financial crisis confronting it. He concluded: "We are in the midst of the worst financial crisis that we have had since 1931. . . . I think it will take a long time to recover from it."[107]

On 10 June, in a speech at Yale University described as a "long, rambling and at times emotional address," Martin described the economy as "living on the edge of an abyss" if taxes and spending were not addressed.[108] He then observed that if nothing were done, "the first trouble would be . . . some basic questions regarding the convertibility of the dollar."[109] Completing the bleak picture, Martin went on: "[T]he government will be forced to consider imposing direct controls over wages, prices, and credit."[110] Martin knew that his speeches pushed the limits of what a Fed chairman was expected to say in public, but it did not stop him.

Martin agonized over these speeches, worrying that his comments could be interpreted as overly harsh and pessimistic. He had painful memories of the public's reaction to his Columbia University speech in 1965. Finally, as he told the executive secretary of the American Society of Newspaper Editors, he had decided to provide "unvarnished accounts of matters of importance to us all."[111] He could not have been surprised that a number of editorials criticized him for being an "alarmist." Hobart Rowen in the *Washington Post* compared his 18 April speech to George M. Humphrey's infamous statement on a possible economic slowdown — "I predict you will have a depression that will curl your hair" — which virtually sunk his career as Treasury secretary in 1957. Ed Dale, the *New York Times* chief economic reporter, referred to the speech and repeated an old canard that "an optimistic central banker is one who believes the situation is deteriorating somewhat less rapidly."[112] The *Times* editorialized that "even though Mr. Martin's zeal to break the impasse on fiscal policy is understandable, his warning created fear and uncertainly throughout the financial markets."[113] It would have given Martin little satisfaction to know that most of his predictions would come to pass within a few years. The business press response was generally muted, perhaps because administration spokesman Henry Fowler was making forecasts that were almost as pessimistic.

There was little time for Martin to muse on the question of media support because the international monetary system was again coming under pressure. The debate within the Fed over how to respond revealed the ongoing shift in the balance of power between the regional Reserve Banks and the board in Washington. The issue was the continuing failure of the British government to resolve its exchange problems. In April 1968, after three months of continual negotiations about the Fed's support for various British payments programs,

Charles Coombs, a vice president of the New York Fed, expressed his pessimism about the economic prospects for Britain. "[T]he devaluation of last November has to be considered a failure."[114] The original projection of a trade surplus following the devaluation had recently been revised to a deficit. Britain was reaching the limit on many of its existing credit lines, and "there is risk of a British decision to go onto a floating exchange rate."[115] In addition, Britain was making poor progress in negotiating a drawdown on a proposed $1.4-billion loan from the IMF. In Coombs's opinion, "the British situation has come very close to being hopeless."[116] Coombs's pessimism reflected the hard-nosed realism of the New York financial markets.

Coombs, who administered the Fed's swap network, was most troubled by the prospect that at the end of June, a large portion of the Fed's outstanding swaps with Britain would have been outstanding for a year. Coombs reminded the FOMC that the swap program was specifically for short-term accommodation. All other Fed swaps had been repaid within six months, and "such a development with the Bank of England clearly would lead to abuse of the swap network."[117] When Governors Brimmer and Mitchell as well as several Reserve Bank presidents indicated varying degrees of agreement with Coombs, Martin moved to counter their pessimism by extending the debate and marshalling his supporters.

In a late May FOMC meeting, Martin called on Robert Solomon, an FOMC advisor who led the Fed's negotiating efforts at the ministerial level, to be spokesman for the British commitment. In terms that were harsh for FOMC discussions, Solomon argued: "If the British were forced onto a floating exchange rate while a substantial portion of the [Fed] swap remained unused, the FOMC would have to bear the responsibility for the chaos into which the international monetary system would be thrown. A run on the dollar by foreign central banks would undoubtedly follow."[118] Solomon added: "The risk of international monetary chaos with a round of competitive devaluations must be balanced against the risks to the quantity of System assets."[119] Solomon broadened the debate beyond the issue of an individual nation's credit-worthiness to the impact of a U.K. collapse on the whole international monetary system. Now that the risks to the Fed in either situation were clearly drawn, Martin had to design a consensus that both sides could live with.

Martin agreed with Coombs that existing and any further drawings under the Bank of England's swap line "could become frozen" and extend beyond the twelve-month limit.[120] Recognizing the risks facing the British, Martin observed carefully that "it is quite possible that sterling will weather the current storm. There is at least divided opinion as to whether the $2.40 parity can survive."[121] He then echoed Solomon: "Despite the hazards, I am clearly in favor of going the last mile with the British."[122] He advised his colleagues that the prospects for the surtax legislation were improving and that "fiscal action in this country will certainly buttress the position of the pound."[123] Governors Daane, Robertson, and Maisel agreed with Martin, and the momentum of the debate had changed. The swap position would be extended.

Martin had indeed "walked the extra mile" with the British. Since the beginning of his international experience at the Export-Import Bank in 1945, Martin had grappled with the never-ending problems of the British economy and sterling. During the early years, Martin had charged British economic policy makers with failing to attack the country's fundamental problems. More recently, his own inability to decisively influence the solution of similar problems in the United States had taught him humility. He knew the cause of the failures all too well; as he told the FOMC: "The line between political and economic decisions has been almost obliterated."[124] Politicians who once left economic issues to technicians were no longer willing to do so, and "that was causing a great deal of trouble on a world-wide basis."[125]

As May drew to a close, the natural beauty of Washington's blossoms offered a sharp contrast to the hothouse atmosphere on Capitol Hill. Despite parliamentary roadblocks erected by House Speaker John McCormack, Wilbur Mills regained control of the tax increase issue. By working with Senate Republicans, Mills had led the House-Senate conference committee to a package consisting of the tax increase and $6 billion of spending cuts in the 1969 budget. Lyndon Johnson had very reluctantly committed to a $4-billion spending cut and was furious at what he considered a "betrayal" by Mills. Goaded by aide Joe Califano to "come out fighting," he pleaded with Congress to pass legislation with lower spending cuts: "[B]ite the bullet . . . and do what ought to be done for the country. Don't hold the tax bill up until you can blackmail someone."[126] Rumors of a presidential veto cast a pall on the negotiators as they tried to reach an accommodation.

The stalemate may well have continued, but Johnson's beleaguered economic team could resist compromise no longer. In mid-May, Henry Fowler wrote to Johnson: "It does not seem reasonable to turn down a proposal that reduces the deficit by $20 billion for $2 billion of difference."[127] The next week, he publicly endorsed the conference package. A week later, James Duesenberry, a CEA member, stated that "the conference report would impose somewhat more economic restraint than was needed, but . . . it would still do a great deal of good."[128] Johnson's economic team had thrown in the towel.

As he did so often with decisions he did not want to make, Johnson agonized endlessly over the spending cut. One of the many ironies of the surtax debate was that Johnson had quickly cut $5 billion out of John Kennedy's fiscal 1965 budget to gain congressional approval for a tax cut. Only four years later, he could not bring himself to cut $2 billion out of a budget that was 80 percent larger than that of 1965. After the resounding defeat of an effort by Speaker John McCormack to propose a $4-billion spending cut from the floor of the House, Lyndon Johnson put up the white flag. On 20 June, representatives from all persuasions climbed on the oft-delayed bandwagon. The final tally was 268–150 in favor of the legislation. The Senate approved the conference report the next day in a vote of 64–16. A week later, Lyndon Johnson signed the tax and spending bill in the Rose Garden in front of his exhausted economic team. Almost three years after Martin had begun to press Lyndon Johnson for a tax increase, it was finally a reality. It had taken a series of domestic and international economic crises to push America's political leadership to achieve the tax increase. The question was whether the plan would be sufficient to deal with the forces the crises had unleashed.

As the White House basked in the afterglow of its accomplishment, Johnson's economic team wrestled with the question of managing the economy, now that the tax increase was a reality. In a Quadriad meeting on 24 June, Arthur Okun urged the Fed to ease monetary policy to offset the restraining effect of the tax package: "If the money supply is not increased, there could be a recession in 1969, and possibly a slowdown as early as Election Day, 1968."[129] CEA economists expected economic growth to decline from an annual rate of 10 percent in the first half of 1968 to 4.5 percent for calendar 1969. Unemployment would rise above 4 percent. Interest rates were still historically high, and in the eyes of CEA economists, it would not take much tightening to bring on a recession.

The concerns about a slowdown reflected the thinking of Keynesian economists in the administration and in academia. For Keynesians, the primary objective of economic policy makers is to achieve maximum long-term economic growth by influencing aggregate demand for goods and services through fiscal and monetary policies. The stimulative impact of the $25-billion budget deficit would completely disappear in fiscal 1969, and $25 billion was a significant amount of demand to withdraw from an $830-billion economy. Such a withdrawal would slow economic growth, and monetary policy should accommodate the transition by an appropriate degree of ease. The Keynesians believed that once the transition to slower growth was achieved, inflationary cost and price pressures would decline.

The Fed economics staff was also populated primarily by Keynesian economists, and their recommendations paralleled those of Keynesians outside the Fed. The summary recommendation of the FOMC economics staff at the 16

July FOMC meeting was typical: "The risk of a resumption of overheating appears small. The greater risk, given the lag in policy effects on real demands, is too sharp a deceleration of economic growth and too high a rise in unemployment."[130] At the 13 August FOMC meeting, the summary recommendation of the FOMC economics staff highlighted a modest rise in interest rates, concluding: "It would be unfortunate if such a reversal [of interest rates] occurs at a time when the economy is in transition to a significantly slower pace of real growth and diminishing pressure on resources."[131] According to economist Allan Meltzer, there were a few noted economists who argued that the surtax would have only a moderate impact on economic growth, but their conclusions were ignored within the administration and the Fed.[132]

Bill Martin also believed that the Fed should be moving toward ease, but for different reasons than the Keynesians. Martin's highest concerns were those that traditionally motivated him: maintaining orderly financial markets during economic transitions and eliminating inflationary pressures. To Martin, the most significant development in the financial markets was that the Treasury would not have to borrow to finance a large budget deficit. Less Treasury competition for savings, along with a slowing economy, meant that "a trend toward easier monetary conditions is inevitable."[133] Martin believed that the Fed had to work with these major forces rather than stand in their way by trying to pursue monetary restraint.

Martin also urged persistence in dealing with inflation. The years of delay in passing the tax increase created inflationary pressures that were strong and growing stronger. Martin described the situation to the FOMC as early as December 1967. "The horse of inflation is out of the barn and already well down the road. We cannot return the horse to the barn . . . but we can [through monetary policy] prevent it from trotting too fast."[134] With the exception of a few quarters after the squeeze of 1966, the CPI had been increasing at an annual rate of 3.5–4 percent since the beginning of 1966. Two and one-half years of inflation had embedded inflationary expectations into the behavior of American citizens. Martin believed that it could take an extended period for the Fed to squeeze out those expectations. Moving too quickly to monetary restraint in the current high-interest environment could cause a repeat of the 1966 crunch without achieving an immediate impact on inflation. The transition to slower growth and a reduction of the pressures on interest rates had to be negotiated before a serious anti-inflation campaign could begin. Martin's challenge was to achieve a controlled level of ease during the transition.

By September 1968, the first solid signs of the economy's response to the tax increase were visible. Those economists who had forecast that Americans would respond to the increase in their tax witholdings by cutting down on spending and maintaining their savings rates were proved wrong. Consumers maintained their lifestyle and cut into their savings to pay for it. In the FOMC meeting on 10 September Dan Brill, the Fed's director of research and the FOMC economic advisor, lamented his forecasting failure: "Perhaps I should intensify my search for alternative occupations. If consumer spending continues strong . . . it could influence economic psychology and impact the prospects for moderation of price pressures."[135]

New York Reserve Bank President Al Hayes was alarmed by the growth of bank credit and the persistence of inflationary pressures. He pressed the FOMC to begin restricting bank credit and emphasized that others agreed with him: "Some of the Reserve bank presidents, who are in a position to observe developments in their respective Districts and the strength of inflationary pressures there, are concerned about the danger of excessive credit expansion."[136] Martin noted that interest rates were trending downward and again cautioned against a premature tightening: "The existing momentum of inflationary pressures is because both fiscal and monetary restraint have come much too late. It is asking too much of the available tools of monetary policy to expect them to deal with the inflationary psychology that resulted from the delay."[137] Martin achieved a unanimous vote to maintain current credit conditions, but the strong economy was fraying his consensus.

To better understand the perplexing economic trends, the Fed economics staff completely recomputed its forecast for the economy through the middle of 1969. It is important to note that by October 1968, economic forecasts had become an integral component in the FOMC policy-making process. Despite Bill Martin's skepticism about their reliability, he had supported Governor Sherman Maisel's 1966 initiative to integrate formal forecasts into FOMC deliberations. Eventually, two primary groups of forecasted information were developed. The first focused on macroeconomic elements such as GNP, prices, and employment, while the second focused on money and credit elements such as interest rates, reserves, the money supply, and bank credit, as well as how these elements might behave under alternative monetary policies.

After two years of experience, the Fed economics staff had gained confidence in the reliability of their forecasts, and economic analysis based on the forecasts began to play a significant role in FOMC discussions. Meeting-briefing materials were heavily oriented toward analyzing current economic statistics in light of the forecasts, and meetings always began with detailed commentaries by FOMC staff advisors. During the meetings, those FOMC members with strong economics backgrounds were often the most articulate and influential contributors to deliberations. These developments gave particular significance to the staff reforecast of October 1968.

FOMC advisor Dan Brill summarized the reforecast as "reflecting a significantly different assessment," but the conclusions hardly changed.[138] The economics staff admitted that in the first four months after the tax increase, "the fiscal bite is much less severe" due to stronger consumption and higher levels of production to meet the demand.[139] Inexplicably, the staff chose to ignore the possibility that their original assumptions might be incorrect and concluded: "It is imperative to distinguish temporary aberrations from developments of longer lasting significance."[140] The decline in the annual growth rate was reduced fractionally from the initial estimate, but the staff observed: "It would be premature to conclude that hopes for slowing the pace of aggregate demand have been lost."[141] The revised forecast called for economic growth to decline from a nominal annual rate of 10.5 percent in the first half of 1968 to 5 ½ percent in the first half of 1969.

The revised forecast for inflation was similarly unchanged. Brill ascribed the unexpected strength in consumption to inflationary expectations: "Inflationary pressures have been with us so long already that expectations of further cost and price rises are beginning to be fundamental factors in the spending decisions of businesses and consumers."[142] Despite this conclusion, the staff maintained its forecast that the price deflator would decrease from 4 percent in calendar 1968 to 3.5 percent in 1969.[143] In view of this analysis, the staff's recommendation that monetary policy remain unchanged was no surprise: "We believe that maintaining interest rates at around current levels would serve to hold down credit expansion and GNP."[144]

The staff recommendation failed to persuade FOMC members to become more supportive of Martin's tenuous FOMC consensus for moderate ease. In late November, Al Hayes ignored the implications of the staff recommendations and went back on the attack against inflation. He was incensed that bank credit continued to expand at an annual rate in excess of 10 percent in the face of inflation that was still increasing at 4 percent annually and estimates that the economic growth would pick up again in the second half of 1969. He pressed for greater restraint on bank credit growth because "it is consistently exceeding projected rates by a wide margin."[145] Martin accepted Hayes's criticism, but again emphasized the difficulties of dealing with inflationary expectations: "To affect the prevailing inflationary psychology, the System would have to take more drastic firming action . . . that might result in massive disintermediation for banks."[146] Martin was still looking for further interest rate moderation and hoped that by raising the specter of the 1966 squeeze, he could maintain a majority against a move toward restraint.

This time Al Hayes did not accept Martin's caution, and he led three other bank presidents to dissent from Martin's majority. Martin's carefully crafted consensus was fractured and would, with the release of the Fed's year-end summary of FOMC decisions, soon be a matter of public knowledge. The differences of opinion were becoming entrenched, and the FOMC's next consensus would be formed by events rather than by a reconciliation of opposing views.

Al Hayes's unusual split with Martin revealed his frustration with Martin's reluctance to move toward restraint when inflation was at a historically high level. Based on past experience, it is not hard to understand Hayes's confusion about Martin's priorities in October 1968. Hayes and Martin began to work together in 1956, and they had voted together during the Fed's forceful campaigns to deal with inflation in the late 1950s. It was true that in the past, Martin would have moved decisively to deal with inflation rates as high as 4 percent and would have publicly warned the nation of the prospects of a boom followed by a bust. He would have supported a rise in interest rates sufficient to allow an "adjustment process" in which higher interest costs forced consumers and businesses to slow their spending and borrowing plans. There are no clear indications in Martin's public statements or private documents about his motivation during the second half of 1968. We are left to speculate as to why he did not move more decisively against inflation when its effects were so plainly visible.

The most obvious consideration that could have influenced Martin in the fall of 1968 was the possibility of re-creating the 1966 credit squeeze by moving too quickly to tighten credit. Martin often expressed this concern to the FOMC to justify his determination to delay a return to tightening. By mid-1968, short-term interest rates were back at their 1966 peak, and the Fed's discount rate was a full percent higher than in 1966. The threat of disintermediation, a key element of the 1966 credit crunch, was clearly an issue for Martin. This concern about high interest rates might have been lessened if either Martin or the FOMC's economic advisors had given serious consideration to whether interest rates included an inflation premium. However, few economists were focusing on this issue at the time, and so it is not surprising that there was no effort to quantify this possibility. Martin's FOMC comments confirm that he was sensitive to creating another credit crunch and that it influenced his thinking, but they do not indicate that this was a decisive consideration for him.

Another potential factor that might have persuaded Martin to move cautiously was his often-repeated commitment to the administration that if fiscal restraint was enacted, monetary restraint could be eased. Martin had made statements to this effect for over three years, first to persuade Lyndon Johnson to propose a tax increase and later to persuade Congress to approve the legislation. In August he admitted to the FOMC that he was guilty of tying future interest rate levels to passage of the tax increase. If the Fed returned too quickly to restraint after passage of the surtax, the political pressures coming from angry Congress members and administration officials would be fierce. But Martin had endured worse criticism when he believed he was doing the right thing, and it is difficult to see this consideration as decisive.

Another equally important consideration was Martin's possible concern about the reaction of the financial markets if the Fed disappointed investors and financial officers who were operating on the assumption of a Fed easing. During the 1960s, both financial and nonfinancial institutions regularly engaged in hedging or short-term investment activities that could destabilize the financial markets if they were reversed en masse. The Fed periodically had to modify its policy moves to reduce the potential negative effect of these hedging operations. In the 1950s, Martin rarely had to deal with the implications of large-scale investment behavior by sophisticated financial investors, but in the 1960s, Martin could not ignore it.

The prevalence of Keynesian economists serving as economic advisors to the FOMC and on the FOMC itself was another element that inhibited Martin's ability to attack inflation. In the 21 November FOMC meeting, the economic staff reached the same conclusion as its CEA counterparts: monetary policy should tend toward ease because restraint, in addition to the tax increase, would run an unacceptable risk of causing a recession and jeopardize the benefits of full employment. A solid minority of FOMC members shared this view, and Martin would have been hard-pressed to persuade any of them otherwise. Martin had watched as Al Hayes passionately and repeatedly argued the case for tightening. However, Hayes made no converts among the Keynesians, and not all of the Reserve Bank presidents supported restraint. If Martin actively supported Hayes, they might make progress in swaying additional FOMC members, but a consensus was a long way off — and Martin led through consensus.

Economist Thomas Mayer analyzed FOMC decision making and how it contributed to the inflationary era of the 1970s and early 1980s. He assigned primary responsibility for the reluctance to attack inflation to "[t]he intellectual atmosphere, or more specifically the preponderant opinions of macroeconomists. By and large they did not consider inflation to be a disaster and were much more concerned about unemployment."[147] This consideration would certainly have influenced Martin but does not go to the core of his beliefs about his responsibility for leading the Federal Reserve System.

One factor that could have been decisive was Martin's frequently expressed goal of a monetary policy that both fostered stable economic growth and was compatible with the administration's economic plans. In late 1968, the American economy was in a transition to slower economic growth, and the most difficult time to make monetary policy was during a transition period. In addition, the Fed's relationship with the Johnson administration had entered a period of limbo. With the passage of the tax increase, the Johnson administration sat back and waited for the economy to slow down in response. Distracted by the presidential election, the administration left managing the economy up to the Fed, with the admonition to keep credit conditions easy.[148] The situation changed dramatically on 8 November 1968, when Richard Nixon won the presidential election.

The new administration's position on inflation was potentially more constructive than that of the Democrats, since Nixon had pledged to bring inflation under control. Whether this pledge would be honored would depend on the economic conditions when the new administration took office and the views and capabilities of Nixon's economic advisors. Until the new administration's economic priorities became clear, Martin had no idea whether they would be compatible with the Fed's monetary policy. Fed economist Robert Hetzel observed: "It would be typical of Martin to want to establish a rapport with the Nixon administration before he seriously moved on inflation."[149]

Waiting for the new administration to settle in made sense for another reason. On 31 January 1970, slightly more than a year away, Bill Martin's nonrenewable fourteen-year term as a Fed governor would expire. While Martin no doubt thought of retirement with a profound sense of relief, he could not ignore the importance of leaving the Fed in the strongest possible position. The very last thing he wanted to do was to leave the Fed when its monetary policy was under fire or its independence threatened in any way.[150] This consideration was at the heart of Bill Martin's legacy to the Federal Reserve System and to his country. In only a few months the new administration would be in place, and he could begin to build support for the Fed's policies. The campaign against inflation could be long and painful, and a supportive administration would be an absolute necessity. Until then, there was every reason to plot a moderate course.

As 1968 drew to a close, it was clear that the economic uncertainties mirrored the social turmoil of the time. The year saw the assassinations of Martin Luther King and Robert Kennedy, riots in the streets of Detroit and Paris, continuing protests over the Vietnam War, and Russian tanks invading Prague. Perhaps it is not surprising that Congress could not agree on the tax increase or that agreement on long-term solutions to the problems of the international monetary system proved unattainable. The economic tragedy lay in the missed opportunities to address the economic imbalances that were becoming more deeply entrenched and infinitely more costly to ultimately resolve.

Bill Martin and Lyndon Johnson shared a quiet moment in the White House in the early evening of 12 December, in which they shared memories of their time together. There is no record of their conversation, but it is not difficult to speculate on it.[151] As was his style, Martin would have taken the opportunity to repeat comments made to Johnson in earlier conversations: that he had enjoyed working with him, that he appreciated how Johnson would always listen when Martin raised difficult issues, even if he did not agree. Johnson could have repeated that he enjoyed kidding Martin because he liked him and always knew where Martin stood, even if Johnson didn't always like the stand he chose. They could have reminisced about the December 1965 confrontation, and Martin could have reminded Johnson of how the president had called him "every name in the book." Johnson could have responded by reminding Martin that he had "pulled the rug out from under me" by raising interest rates. Martin would respond by observing that he regretted that he hadn't done it earlier so that Johnson "would not have had to fly half so high."

The tide of events would soon intrude on this bittersweet moment for two men who had struggled against each other for the better part of four eventful years. Each had seen the other as the symbol of forces that put his own deepest-held beliefs at risk. In Bill Martin, Johnson saw the bankers who protected the established order and, through high interest rates and denying access to credit, took away the hopes and opportunities of the disenfranchised. In Lyndon Johnson, Martin saw a man of supreme ego, a politician whose unchecked political appetite and unwillingness to compromise ended in the pursuit of policies that ignored financial realities and mortgaged the future of his constituents. Intertwined by their respective institutional responsibilities and joined in a common cause of trying to do their best for their nation, they had forged an uneasy alliance.

The complex relationship between the president of the United States and the chairman of the Federal Reserve Board had withstood stresses that could have easily led to a breakdown in the relationship between the two institutions or the impairment of Federal Reserve independence. Their differing personal philosophies and goals for their respective institutions put Martin and Johnson in conflict throughout most of Johnson's five years in the presidency. It is unlikely that Lyndon Johnson ever had to work continually with anyone with whom he disagreed more frequently, and the same can be said for Bill Martin. Yet it is a tribute to both men that their conflict never became personal and to the end, each said they genuinely liked the other. The relationship was also buttressed by their pragmatic appreciation that neither could survive without a functional relationship with the other. At the end of their time together, the relationship between the president and the Fed chairman was as open and resilient as it was when they had first met.

From Martin's perspective, the last years of the Johnson presidency produced more than their share of problems. The most disappointing and potentially dangerous outcome was the administration's failure to achieve the tax increase soon enough. Through a consistent policy of restraint throughout much of 1966, the Fed had reduced the rate of inflation by half, to 1.7 percent, between the first half of 1966 and the first half of 1967. Had the administration passed a tax increase beginning by mid-1967, it might have been possible to deal decisively with inflationary expectations, but the opportunity had been squandered. To increase the pressure on Congress to pass the surtax, Martin made a hazardous decision to ease restraint in the fall of 1967. The Fed's action failed to impress Congress, and by the time the tax increase was finally passed, it was clear that the Fed's pause had enabled inflationary forces to regain a dangerous momentum. Moreover, in the months that followed the surtax passage, the continued strength of the economy and the resilience of inflation confirmed that neither the tax increase nor the comparatively high level of interest rates was capable of slowing the economy down. The Fed again faced the prospect of having to tighten credit, with all the economic and political risks such a step entailed.

The situation was little better on the international front. The loss of confidence in the U.S. dollar due to the continuing balance of payments deficit required a series of stopgap solutions to strengthen the international monetary system. Despite the Fed's leadership and the innovative quality of some of the modifications, these solutions could not resolve the fundamental cause of the system's instability: the U.S. payments deficit. As long as that deficit continued, the fixed-rate international monetary system remained extremely vulnerable. It remained to be seen whether the new administration would have the fortitude to decisively address the payments problem.

Bill Martin could now look forward to his fifth president, Richard Nixon. Nixon was known to bear grudges. He believed that he had lost the presidency in 1960 in great part because the Federal Reserve had kept monetary policy tight during the year, giving credence to John Kennedy's pledge to end the "stop-and-go" policies of the Republican administration. It would be an awkward start, but Bill Martin had been in that situation before. He had taken a considerable risk to delay any resumption of credit restraint until he could gauge the likely support of the Nixon administration. Its campaign rhetoric had been encouraging, but it remained to be seen if the administration would honor it.

Passing the Torch: The Nixon Administration

Richard Nixon did not trust Bill Martin. Aide John Ehrlichman wrote that in Nixon's mind, "Martin was a stereotypical tennis-playing Eastern, Ivy League banker who considered himself wholly independent of the administration."[1] Moreover, it was widely known that Nixon felt the Fed's tight-money policy during the 1960 presidential campaign was a crucial contributor to his narrow defeat. In his book *Six Crises*, Nixon described Arthur Burns's advice in March 1960 that monetary policy must be eased to avoid an "economic dip just before the elections," but Nixon failed to sway Eisenhower and Martin to change course.[2] In one of the more telling conclusions in the book, he wrote: "Unfortunately, Arthur Burns turned out to be a good prophet. The bottom of the 1960 dip did come in October and the economy did move up in November — after it was too late to affect the election returns. All the speeches, television broadcasts, and precinct work in the world could not counter that one hard fact."[3] Despite another embarrassing political defeat in the California governor's race and eight years in the political wilderness, Richard Nixon had persevered and triumphed. One of his early questions as president-elect was how to deal with Bill Martin.

On 9 December, Martin met Richard Nixon in his temporary office at the Pierre Hotel in New York City. Nixon surprised Martin by asking him to join his cabinet as the secretary of the Treasury, telling him, "I have great confidence in your ability to serve as the chief fiscal officer of the United States."[4] Nixon also told Martin that he intended to appoint Arthur Burns as Fed chairman. Martin questioned the choice of Burns, advising Nixon: "It is a mistake to appoint another professional economist to the board, especially one in his 60s."[5] Martin thanked Nixon for his show of confidence in him, telling the president-elect: "I intend to serve out the balance of my term."[6] Nixon replied that he was "disappointed that I will not be able to name Burns chairman of the Federal Reserve at the outset of my administration. Instead I will bring Burns into the White House as counselor and then appoint him when your term ends."[7] It was an awkward beginning, but if Nixon were true to his word, Martin would at least be succeeded by a pragmatic business economist with substantial experience in economic policy making. That was some consolation.

During the meeting at the Pierre, Martin also told Nixon that "inflation is the primary economic problem facing the nation. Close relations and policy coordination [between the administration and the Fed] are important since monetary policy will need the help of fiscal policy to cope with inflation."[8] For Martin, the most important economic issue facing the nation was the extension of the Johnson surtax that was scheduled to expire in June 1969. The surtax had been the major factor in eliminating the large budget deficit of fiscal 1968 and if it lapsed, deficits would return and fiscal policy would again become excessively stimulative. Nixon had come out against the surtax during the campaign, and Martin was determined to change his mind. Martin went on: "Your administration has to deal with inflation effectively from the beginning if it is not to get out of control."[9] In a theme he would repeat, Martin advised Nixon that his administration should move during its "honeymoon" period to deal firmly with inflation. Nixon's bland response informed Martin that he had his work cut out for him.

In part, Nixon's response to Martin reflected the low priority the president-elect assigned to economic issues. As Nixon economic historian Allen Matusow writes: "Economic policy was at the outset hardly one of Nixon's main concerns. If the good times of the sixties had kept on rolling . . . Nixon would have gladly delegated supervision of the economy to a subordinate strong enough to manage it and wise enough not to pester him with issues he found both boring and baffling."[10] His choice for CEA chairman, Paul McCracken, is quoted as saying, "Mr. Nixon may even have had an almost psychological block about economics. He approached the subject somewhat like a little boy doing required lessons."[11] Though he was able to ignore economic issues at the beginning of his presidency, Nixon would not enjoy this luxury for long.

Nixon's preoccupation with other issues led him to pay little attention to picking his economic team, and the results showed. In the tradition of Republican administrations, he chose a corporate executive, midwestern banker David Kennedy, for his secretary of the Treasury. Kennedy had spent sixteen years at the Fed in Washington, ending his career there as special assistant to fellow Mormon and Fed chairman, Marriner Eccles. Lured away by Continental Illinois Bank in Chicago, within ten years he became its president. Kennedy drove the bank's expansion and by 1964, it was the eighth largest U.S. bank. Kennedy kept his Washington ties, including a year spent as special assistant secretary for Treasury Secretary George Humphrey. Kennedy soon proved to be an orthodox economic thinker, given to making doctrinaire statements that unnerved his more experienced Treasury staffers. His limited political instincts resulted in a series of gaffes that revealed that he was poorly equipped for his new job. He refused to make the ritual statement that the United States would defend the dollar, and when a run on the dollar resulted, he had to be bailed out with a clarifying statement by Nixon. It was clear that Kennedy would not be the spokesperson for the Nixon economic team.

Nixon's choice for chairman of the Council of Economic Advisers was Paul McCracken, a Harvard economics Ph.D. with an ideal background for the position. He also began his career in the Federal Reserve System and eventually served as director of research at the Minneapolis Reserve Bank. After five years at the Fed, McCracken became a professor at the University of Michigan and eventually a spokesman for mainstream Republican economics. In 1956, he was selected as a member of the Eisenhower-era CEA under Chairman Raymond Saulnier. At the CEA, he was a leader of an unsuccessful move to implement a tax cut in 1958, for which he received a degree of fame by anticipating the Kennedy/Johnson tax cut of 1964. McCracken kept his hand in Washington economic affairs by serving on government task forces and appearing before congressional committees. McCracken was well versed in providing cogent economic advice in a presidential format, but his low-key presentation and measured speaking style were ineffective in dealing with Richard Nixon's short attention span. The president was unwilling to invest his attention in what McCracken had to say and, before very long, began listening to other advisors.

The administration's economic policy began to emerge in mid-February during McCracken's presentation to the Joint Economic Committee. Unable to resist the understandable temptation to blame the Democrats, McCracken began by saying: "We have inherited a difficult situation," but then preceded to put on the rose-colored glasses that the Johnson administration CEA used to forecast the economy in 1969.[12] The Nixon CEA accepted the Johnson estimate of a first-half economic slowdown followed by a resumption of growth in the second half of the year. The Nixon men highlighted a similar pattern of a six-month slowdown followed by a recovery in 1967, and concluded: "[W]e find it worrisome that by the end of 1967 the rate of inflation was again accelerating."[13] Then, ignoring its own caveat, the Nixon team forecast that during 1969 the GNP deflator would decline from 4 percent in the last quarter of 1968 to 3½ percent by the end of the year. Based on its forecast, the administration signaled its intention to follow a fairly standard Republican economic policy. It would seek a balanced budget and offered its general support for monetary restraint.

Martin was gratified by the administration's public support for the Fed's policy of restraint, however tentative it might be in reality. However, the administration's own commitment to fighting inflation was unclear. The CEA's forecasted decline in inflation not only flew in the face of the economy's performance in 1967, but also was questionable in view of the uncertainty of the surtax extension. The fight against inflation was left up to the Fed, and Martin was prepared to move forcefully and in a highly visible campaign.

When his turn before the Joint Economic Committee on the Economic Report of the President came, Martin began by confessing to past errors in judgment: "It appears that the Federal Reserve was overly optimistic in anticipating immediate benefits from fiscal restraint . . . but now we mean business in stopping inflation."[14] Martin conceded: "A credibility gap exists in the business and financial community as to whether the Federal Reserve will push restraint hard enough to check inflation. The board means to do so and is unanimous on that point."[15] He cited his concern that the administration would back away from fiscal restraint too quickly because "[t]he government has raised the ghost of [anti-inflationary] overkill at the first sign of a cloud on the horizon."[16] Then, as the *New York Times* reported, "Martin strongly implied that this will not happen again and that restraint will persist even when there are clear signs the economy is slowing and in the face of some increase in unemployment."[17]

Under question from JEC members, Martin agreed that there were risks that the policy of restraint could be pushed too far and bring on a recession, but he replied that in order to stop inflation, "[y]ou must take risks. In the last few years we have not taken real risks."[18] Martin explained why the Fed expected a second-half recovery, ending with the admonition: "Whether such a surge in demand will occur cannot be predicted with any assurance, but it is foolhardy to increase the risk by adding the fuel of easy credit."[19]

On April Fools' Day, 1969, the FOMC spent a dreary meeting grappling with the meaning of the first quarter's economic statistics. Once again, the economic forecasters were proved wrong: the economy was shrugging off the effect of tighter fiscal and monetary policies. First-quarter real economic growth was at an annual rate of 2.8 percent compared to the forecast of 2 percent, and private consumption was unexpectedly strong. The price deflator increased to 4.5 percent from 3.9 percent in the last quarter of 1968, instead of falling to 3 percent. The estimated yearly increase in business-spending estimates was revised upward from 9 percent to 14 percent. The economy's performance occurred despite the Fed's success in clamping down on credit. The money supply M1, which had grown at a 6 percent rate during 1968, grew only 2.3 percent in the first quarter of 1969. Similarly, the bank credit proxy registered the sharpest decline since World War II, dropping from an annual increase of 11.4 percent in 1968 to a 1.2 percent increase in the first quarter of 1969. The Fed's program of restraint was only a few months old, and it usually took a minimum of six months for the impact of tight credit to become visible. The precipitous decline in the monetary aggregates indicated that the Fed's policy of restraint was working its way through the economy, but the statistics indicated that the economy was still growing faster than expected.

In view of the disheartening statistics, the FOMC concluded that the Fed had to adopt a more visible posture of restraint. Governor Daane spoke for the majority when he observed: "The time has come for concerted System action, involving all of the policy instruments."[20] A week later, the board of governors raised the discount rate by ½ percent, to 6 percent, the highest rate since 1929. In a small but symbolic move, the governors also increased reserve requirements for smaller member banks by $0.6 billion. Most bankers grumbled about the added tightening; a Cleveland banker's comment was typical: "It now appears the Fed is going in the direction of a recession."[21] Martin had to have been pleased by the rejoinder of James L. Robertson, the board vice chairman, rejecting both the banker's criticism and the administration's "gradualism" policy: "We have to brake inflation as fast as we can brake it."[22] Since becoming vice chairman in 1967, Robertson had adopted a broader view of his role at the Fed and became much more supportive of Martin's efforts to generate a FOMC consensus.

The Fed's tightening actions got Richard Nixon's attention. At a meeting of the Cabinet Committee on Economic Policy on 10 April, Nixon asked about the Fed move and was told that it was designed to cool off the economy.[23] Referring to the 1958 midterm elections, which were a disaster for the Republican Party, Nixon said: "I remember 1958. We cooled off the economy and cooled off 15 Senators and 60 congressmen at the same time. I want to give a special charge to the Council [CEA] and this group — watch this thing."[24]

Paul McCracken did not have to be told twice. At the next Quadriad, he told Martin that if current monetary restraint were continued, "[w]e could face the maximum danger of a soft economic situation in middle or late 1970" and pressed Martin to ease restraint by the third quarter of 1969.[25] Martin could see that he would have to work harder to stiffen the administration's spine about continuing the battle against inflation. One encouraging development was that in April Nixon finally agreed to ask Congress to extend the surtax for another year, even though Republican congressional leaders forced him to cut it from 10 percent to 5 percent for the second six months.

In late May, Ed Dale, the chief economics writer for the *New York Times,* wrote an article detailing the evolution of Nixon administration economic policy. Dale highlighted four fundamental Keynesian tenets that were now "officially" abandoned by the Nixon administration: (1) the U.S. economy was inherently unstable; (2) the federal government should compensate for economic fluctuations by modifying its taxing or spending policies; (3) influencing the cost and supply of credit by the Fed is "relatively unimportant" compared to fiscal policy; and (4) pricing power by unions and large corporations create an inflationary bias to the price level, and government efforts at "guideposts" are ineffective. In its place, the Nixon administration put new principles: (1) the U.S. economy has a bias toward relatively steady growth; (2) the money supply matters a great deal and should be allowed to grow in line with the "normal" growth of the economy; (3) Federal Reserve monetary policy should be less interventionist and change much less frequently than in the past; and (4) the federal government should produce a budget surplus under "normal economic conditions," although the budget need not be balanced at all times or at all costs. The administration defined the "normal" growth rate for the economy as 4 to 4½ percent a year, reflecting the average growth of the labor force and average increases in productivity.

McCracken and his CEA associates were hardly breaking new theoretical ground, but they were acknowledging that the Keynesian gospel was being rewritten in view of the failures of the Kennedy/Johnson administrations to maintain the Keynesian discipline of budgetary surpluses during a strong economy. The new economic gospel was a return to more traditional Republican economics with a nod toward monetarism. Monetarism was a new approach to achieving stable economic growth articulated most effectively by Professor Milton Friedman of the University of Chicago. Monetarists believed that the private economy would self-correct cyclical downturns and would tend toward full employment if not impeded by governmental action. There was no need for countercyclical fiscal policy, and achieving stable economic growth depended on the central bank to provide stable growth in the money supply.

Paul McCracken had formulated a flexible version of monetarism that provided fiscal support in the form of a balanced budget and allowed the Fed a modest amount of discretion setting monetary policy. The new administration philosophy was a long way from Bill Martin's concept of actively leaning against the winds of inflation and deflation. Martin would have to bend with the wind of economic theory to gain the administration's support for the Fed's fight against inflation.

Martin's approach to accommodating the administration's new philosophy was complicated by the difference between the Fed and the administration over dealing with inflationary expectations. The administration's approach was to gradually slow the economy. When demand was sufficiently reduced and enough excess capacity created, inflation would ease. Martin believed that inflationary pressures might be reduced by slowing demand, but they would not be fully controlled until inflationary expectations were extinguished. Dealing with the psychological element of inflation had long been an essential element of Martin's monetary policy philosophy. During the Fed's much criticized anti-inflation campaign of 1960, he focused on the importance of eliminating the vestiges of the "inflationary psychology" by encouraging the "adjustment process" through which individuals and businesspeople adapted their behavior to accommodate a noninflationary environment.[26] Martin often referred to the success of that campaign and its contribution to the low-inflation environment during the early 1960s. Throughout the decade of the 1960s, Martin did not change his basic attitude toward the role of "psychology" or "expectations" in sustaining inflationary pressures.

Building support for a policy to deal with inflationary expectations was not a simple matter. Keynesian economists generally downplayed inflation and did not support the Fed's attack on inflationary expectations if it meant rising unemployment or keeping the economy from operating at full capacity. Governor Maisel spoke for Keynesians in April 1969 when he justified a dissent from the policy of restraint by observing: "I believe that attempts to influence psychology and spending directly by Federal Reserve action is an incorrect policy objective."[27] At the same time, during the 1960s, the impact of inflationary expectations could not be easily isolated in economic statistics, and it was very difficult to determine whether progress was being made in dealing with them. In a period of rising prices, expectations of future inflation contributed to a wide range of economic behavior: strong consumer demand, rising corporate spending for real assets, increased borrowing by individuals and corporations, the inclusion of an "inflation premium" in long-term interest rates, and significant increases in wages and prices.

Experience taught Martin that it took an agonizingly long time to squeeze inflationary expectations out of the economy. Slowing the economy could be achieved much more quickly than controlling inflationary expectations. Once the economy began to slow down, public and political resistance to continued restraint built up quickly. Staying the course required a supportive president, and Dwight Eisenhower was the last president with the requisite type of economic philosophy and political courage to pursue that goal.

Experience also taught Martin that Americans needed to be convinced that the Fed and the administration were fully committed to controlling inflation and would not back away when their policies began to bite. Using the Fed chairman's bully pulpit, Martin voiced his concerns in a speech in May 1969: "I am disturbed by the defeatist attitude that inflation cannot be brought under control or the cynical conviction that the Government will not see the anti-inflation measures through."[28] Admitting that "[p]rogress is slow because of inflationary momentum," Martin maintained that "patience, perseverance — and considerable fortitude as well — will be necessary."[29] It was the kind of speech Martin had given numerous times before. What Martin hoped for was an equally forceful and public anti-inflation commitment from the Nixon administration.

Martin almost got his statement. "Suppose we pushed housing down now?" Nixon asked at the 16 May meeting of his Cabinet Committee on Economic Policy in the middle of a discussion about the impact of fiscal and monetary policy on housing. "If we can hit this price thing now, we would all be better off. It is better to take the bad medicine now. We cannot cool it next year — politically, it's impossible."[30] Turning to Labor Secretary George Shultz, he asked: "George, couldn't we do it now? Let's take the bad news, but if it would have some effect on prices, perhaps we should take the risk."[31] It was a moment filled with possibility.

Nixon's turn toward George Shultz at this moment was no accident. Shultz was a fast-rising star of the Nixon administration. He had joined the administration at the recommendation of Arthur Burns, for whom Shultz had served as a senior staff economist during Burns's CEA chairmanship in the 1950s. Shultz was nationally known as an expert in labor-management issues and was serving as the dean of the University of Chicago School of Business when he was selected to be Nixon's secretary of Labor. While at Chicago, Shultz came under the influence of Milton Friedman and became an articulate spokesman for Friedman's version of monetarism. Once in the administration, Shultz acquired the reputation of a man who could get things done. It is not surprising that Nixon, who never had high hopes for his economic team but appreciated a realist who could produce results, would gravitate to Shultz for advice on economic issues.

Shultz, the monetarist, believed that the first quarter's decline in the growth of the money supply was already too severe and certainly did not justify further tightening moves. He counseled patience, advising Nixon: "The rate of increase in the real GNP has been declining. I think that what we have done already will begin to show up."[32] Arthur Burns, Nixon's other behind-the-scenes advisor, agreed: "If you cut down now, it may hurt you next year. I do not believe we should permit housing starts to fall below [the current level of] 1.5 million units."[33] The conversation continued on, but the moment had passed. Nixon closed the discussion with, "I see my hunch was wrong."[34] The possibility of raising the visibility of the administration's anti-inflation policy and convincing the public that both the Fed and the administration were committed to ending inflation was lost. The tragedy of this missed opportunity was that this offhand discussion by Nixon's informal economic advisors short-circuited the careful analysis and study of alternatives prepared at the working-party level in the Treasury and CEA. But neither Kennedy nor McCracken could persuade Richard Nixon to consider them.

At the end of the second quarter, the FOMC wrestled with a confusing set of statistics on bank lending. The Fed normally would have expected member-bank reserves to decline in the face of the Fed's credit restraint and the impact of disintermediation as investors moved their savings into three-month Treasury bills that offered a 1 percent yield advantage over the maximum rates banks could pay on CDs. This deposit erosion could be expected to force banks to cut back on their lending activity, but by mid-1969, bankers had discovered alternative ways to fund their new loans. Banks with overseas offices were borrowing massive amounts of Eurodollars in European money markets and by July, Eurodollar borrowing was at an annual rate of $12 billion.[35] This amount of Eurodollar borrowing was significant when compared to the total business lending of the banking industry of $78 billion. Similarly, those money-center banks with a new organizational entity, the one-bank holding company, were using this entity to issue billions of dollars of commercial paper in the New York credit market. The importance of commercial paper was described by Walter Wriston, chief executive of the newly christened First National City Corporation: "The CD funded the world for ten years, more or less, and then commercial paper came in for bank holding companies for another ten years."[36]

These new funding sources were a headache for the Fed. They were not counted in any of the statistics that defined the credit proxy and consequently undermined the policy-making value of this crucial indicator. When staff member Lyle Gramley discussed a staff study of these new sources, he observed, "Recent innovations by banks affect bank credit as an indicator of policy. . . . They [commercial paper and Eurodollar borrowings] are not reflected in bank balance sheets and have made bank credit growth more difficult to interpret."[37] The Fed experimented with new definitions of the money supply to reflect these new sources, and the first calculation of the modified money supply numbers revealed how out of date the traditional calculations had become. According to the revised numbers, the money supply had grown by 4.3 percent during the first half of 1969, compared to zero growth calculated by traditional means. These new data were a staggering surprise to the Fed staff, but provided a crucial understanding of why the financial markets and financial institutions had weathered the Fed's tightening so well.

The new information also gave a fresh insight to battered economic forecasters who were desperately reengineering their econometric models to compensate for the forecasting failures in 1967 and 1968. Bill Martin was not surprised by the revised bank credit numbers because he had always been skeptical of relying too heavily on statistical indicators of credit availability. He had a similar view of the problems involved in predicting changes in the money supply and referred to the overreliance on numerical indicators as "statisticalitis."

Eurodollar funding was particularly problematic in the eyes of the Fed because Eurodollars conveyed two important competitive advantages to those banks able to secure them. They were available only to those banks with access to European capital markets, and they did not require a 12 percent reserve deposit. The FOMC staff recommended bringing Eurodollar deposits under the Fed regulation: "The objective is to close loopholes that have given certain banks special advantages in resisting general monetary restraint."[38] Before the year was out, the Fed both redefined the credit proxy to make it more reliable and brought Eurodollars under its reserve requirements. These changes were part of the constant evolution of the Fed's regulatory practices in order to adapt to changing conditions in the U.S. banking industry.

During a hearing on bank regulatory issues in late February, Martin's personal credit philosophy came in for discussion. In an aside, Martin volunteered that he occasionally had to borrow money from friends "to get out of a restaurant." Amid the laughter over the image of the nation's money manager with empty pockets, Martin admitted, "I don't have any credit cards and . . . I wish I could establish credit."[39] Some committee members immediately began fulminating about this indignity and proposing to investigate credit bureaus. Martin tried to calm the storm by saying, "But it's because I haven't tried."[40] The congressional indignation then veered off to excoriate the inequity of cash-paying customers carrying the costs associated with credit card–paying customers before it finally ran out of steam. The next day an American Express card in Martin's name was hand delivered to Martin, courtesy of Howard Clark, the chairman of the corporation. To Martin there was no inconsistency when the man who gave speeches extolling the development of consumer credit for its contribution to the well-being of individual Americans decided not to use any of it himself.

Another part of Martin's personal situation became a topic of conversation about this time: the impending completion of his fourteen-year term as a Fed governor. Initially, Martin had filled the remainder of his predecessor Chairman Thomas McCabe's term and in 1956 was appointed to a full fourteen-year term of his own. That term would end on 31 January 1970. In June, a reporter from the *New York Times* observed that Martin's determined efforts against inflation indicated that "he is prepared to seek vindication of Federal Reserve policies down to his final day in office."[41] He also concluded that Martin's replacement should be "a man of command, capable of winning respect from his staff and fellows and their adherence to common policies. He should have considerable achievement, but not necessarily be an economist. He should not be wedded to any particular pattern of financial organization, but capable of adapting . . . to a rapidly changing financial community. He should speak softly and carry a big stick."[42] Ironically, the author wrote a perfect description of a young Bill Martin. Complimentary as it was, the article highlighted Martin's vulnerability in dealing with Congress and the administration. Would they listen to him or just wait for his successor?

As summer ripened into fall, evidence of the Fed's tightening grew more widespread, but inflationary pressures were as strong as ever. In July, staff economist Steven Axilrod concluded that banks and S&Ls were reaching the limits of their liquid resources and that is was "prudent at this juncture to take a little of the edge off monetary restraint."[43] In mid-August, the staff concluded that since bank lending had fallen by 30 percent over the last eight months, "[t]he time has come for the Committee to consider backing off slightly from its current posture of severe restraint."[44] By September, Charles Partee, the FOMC's principal economics advisor, was less subtle: "I feel that the time for backing off from the present degree of monetary restraint cannot be postponed much longer if we are to avoid a recession beginning early next year."[45] Even Al Hayes, Martin's staunch ally in the fight against inflation, acknowledged that there was a risk that the Fed's posture "could lead, after sufficient time, to a major slowing of the economy."[46] The unhappiness of expansion-minded Governors Maisel and Mitchell paralleled the staff's urgency, and by August they were formally dissenting from the policy of restraint, even though formal dissents were still relatively rare in the Martin-era FOMC.

Martin fought to hold the largest majority he could. He knew that the FOMC staff's concern about a possible recession was based on its economic forecasts, and he was angry that they continued to place so much faith in the projections despite their past failures. In the July FOMC meeting, he reminded the committee that "the System was overly hasty in moving toward ease in the summer of 1968, in part because of faulty projections. No one can make projections with assurance at this moment."[47] Then he gave vent to his deep frustration: "If the decision were mine alone, I would dispense with the kind of analysis presented in the blue book [the briefing book containing staff economic forecasts]."[48] It was a remarkable outburst for Martin and revealed his profound ambivalence toward the FOMC's growing dependence on economic statistics and projections to make monetary policy. Though he could still command the floor and set the terms of the policy debate, he was finding less support for his calls to apply judgment to the growing flood of analytical information that accompanied so much of the policy deliberation. During his more pessimistic periods, Martin foresaw the end of the tenuous balance between the statistically oriented FOMC members and those who favored a more judgmental decision-making process.

The next month Martin returned to the attack. The 1968 easing resulted from "too much emphasis on the prospective turnaround in the fiscal position of the Federal Government and not enough on the underlying inflationary expectations which had been building up over an extended period. The mistake was compounded for several months by the rationalization that some moderation of the inflationary pressures was imminent."[49] Recounting a conversation with a corporate executive who was skeptical about the Fed's commitment to fighting inflation, Martin observed that "the main danger is a new outburst of inflationary sentiment that could be generated if it becomes apparent that the administration and the Federal Reserve are implementing easing policies."[50] To Martin, any move toward ease, no matter how modest, would be taken as a sign that the Fed was backing away, and all it might hope to achieve in its 1969 tightening would be lost.

Martin had used similar arguments many different times, but rarely did he advance them with such passion. He was asking his fellow FOMC members to maintain a rigorous anti-inflation stance in the full knowledge that they were increasing the risk of recession. They would have to trade the comfort of basing their decision on projections of a slowing economy that were widely accepted by economists in exchange for the uncomfortable position of being the only actor in the battle against inflation. Whether it was through faith or loyalty, Martin was able to limit the FOMC dissenters to his persistent expansionists, Maisel and Mitchell.

Martin's pessimism about the intentions of the administration to deal with inflation colored his farewell speech to a group of international bankers in Copenhagen on 20 June. He started with a proposition that he deeply believed but rarely stated: "It is more important to settle the problem of inflation than to settle the war in Vietnam."[51] Saying that he was not predicting a financial crash, he observed: "[T]here will be a good deal of pain and suffering before the U.S. eliminates inflation."[52] With his eye on a difficult future and the limits of monetary policy, he concluded: "I might favor even sterner restraints such as voluntary credit controls, forced savings, and a higher tax increase, if these should be needed to bring the severe United States inflation under control."[53] It was not Martin's last address, but it was his last admonition to America's political leaders that the fight against inflation would have to continue long after he had left the Federal Reserve chairmanship.

Though Martin held his support within the FOMC and continued his public campaign against inflation, he could not persuade the administration to support the Fed's anti-inflation campaign. On 7 October, George Shultz wrote to the president that the Fed's restraint was slowing the economy down, but its move to an even tighter policy in May could bring on a recession in 1970. He advised Nixon that the Fed should be told to "return to the gradualist policy immediately."[54] Nixon responded by inviting Martin to the 15 October meeting of the Cabinet Committee on Economic Policy. He opened the meeting by asking Martin point-blank if he planned to keep money tight. Martin replied: "Mr. President, I have been fooled too many times by statistics. The momentum of inflation was stopped in mid-summer, but the psychology of inflation has accelerated again. When the four percent inflation figure came out, a lot of people said we would soon be throwing in the towel."[55] As he had before, Martin tried to persuade the president to hold the line on inflation by emphasizing the political benefits: "Do you want to face the 1970 elections with a surge of inflation or do you want to face the possibility of overkill. We shouldn't relax the pressure prematurely. The risk of underkill [a return to inflation] is worse than overkill [a recession]. I personally discount the threat of recession."[56]

As the discussion went around the table, Nixon's advisors offered conflicting views. David Kennedy agreed with Martin: "Any [easing] signal from the Fed will turn on the inflation psychology again." Paul McCracken adopted a Hamlet-like indecision: "The basic question is when should our policy be eased? When basic economic activity softens or when there is renewed confidence in the price level?" Arthur Burns advised Nixon against further tightening because "[y]ou have four percent unemployment and an election coming up."[57] George Shultz restated his advice to Nixon: "I think the right policy is moderate restraint, the kind we had in the beginning of the year." Martin tried again to gain more time for restraint: "It is my judgment that we have more to lose by easing the pressure than anything else," but Shultz cut him off with another appeal for immediate ease.[58] Frustrated by Shultz's constant needling, Martin faced him directly and said, "There is a disease called statisticalitis that could wreck us. This is not a statistical question, it's a judgment question and I have been at this at least as long as you."[59] Shultz finally backed off by observing, "[Y]ou have been at this a lot longer." The inconclusive meeting finally ground to an end, and Nixon asked Martin to accompany him into the Oval Office.

Once they were seated in the office in which Martin had had so many momentous presidential meetings, Nixon informed Martin that in a few days he would nominate Arthur Burns to succeed him. The news came as no surprise. A month earlier, Nixon aide Robert Haldeman had talked with Martin about the possibility of his retiring early, and Martin had ignored the request. In early October, rumors of Burns's impending appointment began to circulate in Congress, and the White House could wait no longer. Now that Nixon was confirming his intention, Martin was angry that the announcement would make him an official lame duck earlier than he felt necessary. There was little he could do about it.

Nixon's decision was not unexpected, but combined with the Cabinet Committee meeting, it was a body blow. Nixon's obvious lack of involvement in the debate over the future of economic policy was terribly discouraging. His only active participation in the Cabinet Committee meeting concerned the public-relations effect of presidential jawboning, when he commented: "It will make people feel better if only to know that someone is concerned about inflation."[60] Nixon's advisors were divided about the economy, and the president appeared to be content to let them disagree rather than forcing them to face reality and come to a consensus about what to do about it. Worse yet, Nixon appeared to be relying on his behind-the-scenes advisors, Burns and Shultz, neither of whom wanted continued restraint. It was easy to see that once Nixon had Arthur Burns in the Fed chairmanship, he would expect Burns to get the economy growing and keep unemployment from becoming a political problem. Burns would take over in about three months, and Martin was running out of time to keep restraint in place.

Though he told the FOMC in October that "I am more discouraged than I have been for some time," Martin had no intention of giving up his fight against inflation.[61] After the October Cabinet Committee meeting, Nixon ordered Paul McCracken to press Martin to begin easing. There is no record of the conversation but, as historian Allan Matusow wrote about this period, "Martin converted McCracken."[62] Indeed, shortly after his discussion with

Martin, the CEA chairman began to describe the administration's situation in terms that were distinctly Martinesque. On 3 November, McCracken advised Nixon: "Evidence that the economy is cooling is only tentative. Belief that the budget will slip from surplus back to deficit is growing. If on top of that there is premature monetary relaxation, this would congeal fears that Washington has given up, and that we are off to the inflationary races once more."[63]

McCracken knew that the public concern about the prospect of a budget deficit was well justified. The modest surplus of fiscal 1969 and that projected for fiscal 1970 were achieved only because of the surtax, and it was scheduled to end on 30 June 1970. Nixon had announced spending plans for revenue sharing and a guaranteed income for low-income Americans that could increase fiscal 1972 spending by $9 billion and fiscal 1973 by $11 billion. If the Senate had its way, the tax-reform plan working its way through Congress could cost the administration up to $6 billion in fiscal 1972 and a staggering $10 billion in fiscal 1973. The most recent budget estimate for fiscal year 1971, based on congressional and administration spending requests, forecast a deficit of $5 billion. Unless spending were controlled, McCracken told the president, "We are in trouble . . . for FY 1972 and FY 1973."[64] McCracken could foresee problems getting Martin and the Fed to move toward ease once the budget problems became known, and he advised Nixon "[W]e need, paradoxical as it may sound, a stringent fiscal policy and an easier monetary policy . . . and the needed easier monetary policy will be delayed by evidence of softening on the budget."[65]

McCracken suggested that Nixon establish "[a] Special Cabinet Committee to review existing programs . . . and report a strategy for timed reduction over the next five years."[66] He also recommended that "[t]he Treasury should present a program for revenue increases . . . including possible new additions to the system, such as the value-added tax."[67] The Republican Party would soon be heading into midterm elections, and Paul McCracken wanted spending cuts and tax increases — the last things politicians running for office wanted to consider. The chance that McCracken's proposal would be unpalatable was very high, but at least someone in the Nixon administration was concerned about the dangerous drift of the administration's policy of gradualism and was willing to propose a concrete plan to deal with it.

On 18 December, Arthur Burns appeared before the Senate Finance Committee for his confirmation. As Martin expected, Burns predicted that the Fed would ease monetary conditions. But then, reflecting Paul McCracken's budget concerns, Burns added a condition on his support for easing: "only when the right foundation has been laid in the form of balanced budgets for both the present and the next fiscal year."[68] Asked what he would recommend if the budgets could not be balanced, Burns replied, "We must raise taxes, as unpopular as that may be. . . . We must rely on a sound fiscal policy and not leave it to the monetary authorities to do it all by themselves."[69] In response to a question about the Fed's independence, Burns observed, "I fully believe that the Federal Reserve should not become the handmaiden of the Treasury. We may have to go to war with the Treasury, but I hope it will not happen."[70]

Burns's brave statements would have to be lived out in the months and years to come as the Fed continued its struggle with inflation. Arthur Burns was drawing a line in the sand, signifying that he was no longer Richard Nixon's economic counselor. He was on his way to becoming a central banker.

Martin spent his 1969 Christmas week as he had many others, on a small island in the Bahamas called Harbour Island. There he walked the beach in the gray early mornings clad in his pajamas and a raincoat, "picking up all the seashells before most visitors were up," played his usual noontime game of tennis, and spent well-earned time with his beloved "chief," Cynthia. Back in Washington, the Nixon administration was wrangling over whether the president should sign the swollen tax-reform legislation that "would add $3.7 billion to revenues during FY 70, but by FY 1972 would cost Nixon $7 billion [annually]."[71] Nixon, alternately threatening to veto a bill he considered "screwed up" and listening to McCracken's advice — "Sign the tax bill. Clear the air. Build the case for easier money" — could not make up his mind.[72] Nixon twice called Martin at his island retreat with his dilemma, and Martin advised him to veto the bill because "I am convinced it is inflationary."[73] Martin thought he had Nixon persuaded, but when Nixon finally decided to sign it, he was not surprised. Martin told syndicated columnist Marquis Childs, "That veto was more than could be expected of any president."[74]

As 15 January 1970 and his last FOMC meeting approached, Martin could take scant comfort in the economic situation. During 1969, the nation's GNP increased by 8 percent, only slightly less than the 9 percent in 1968. Despite monetary restraint that reduced real growth to zero in the fourth quarter, the CPI increased by 6 percent, well over the 4.7 percent of 1968. Many wage settlements called for a total of 30–35 percent increases over a three-year contract period. Under strong pressure from Arthur Burns, Richard Nixon was in the process of cutting his spending plans for fiscal 1971, but the skeptical view of the financial markets was reflected in First National City Bank's conclusion that "fiscal policy is getting out of control despite the administration's attempt to keep the reins tight."[75] The termination of the surtax in June would leave the Fed alone in the battle against inflation, and its policy of restraint was already exerting maximum pressure on the banking system. The FOMC generally agreed with the staff that "there is not much more that monetary policy can do."[76]

Had he been slated to remain in the chairmanship, Martin would undoubtedly have tried to maintain a consensus for continued restraint. But he knew that Arthur Burns was publicly committed to easing monetary conditions sooner rather than later. The FOMC staff had been urging a turn toward ease for months, and Martin's majority for restraint was eroding. There were three dissents now, and the number would grow as the economic slowdown became more apparent. Moreover, Governor Maisel had taken the highly unusual step of holding a press conference to explain his differences with the majority. A few months earlier, Martin had tried to buy time for restraint by telling Nixon: "Our next move will be in the direction of easing monetary policy, but not now."[77] The pragmatist in Martin traditionally avoided fighting against the inevitable, and a move toward ease was inevitable. Since it was just a question of time, why not begin a modest easing now? Perhaps it was only human nature for Martin to want to soften the contrast between his policy and that of his successor. In the meeting Martin acknowledged that with three-month Treasuries yielding a historic high of 8 percent, money-market conditions justified relief. Using a favored metaphor — "On the theory that steel which bends is better than iron which breaks" — he led the FOMC toward ease.[78]

On Saturday, 17 January, the Nixon White House held an official farewell for Bill and Cynthia Martin in the State dining room. It was a typical black-tie presidential affair with crystal, tuxedoed waiters, champagne, filet mignon, baked Alaska, and lively conversation among the 110 guests. In his toast to Martin, Nixon graciously repeated an accolade he had offered at the time he announced Arthur Burns as Martin's replacement: "It is difficult to think of any economic policy maker, since the time of Alexander Hamilton, whose influence has been as considerable as Chairman Martin's over such an extended period of time."[79] Nixon also used the theme of "service" to link Martin's tennis career with his role as a public servant.[80] One of the more memorable toasts came from Representative Wilbur Mills, whom Martin considered a "real" friend but who had caused him more anguish than anyone else in the room. Mills observed: "Bill has almost, but not quite, made me a sound money man."[81]

When it came Martin's turn to speak, he quieted the convivial gathering with his heartfelt words: "I wish I could turn the bank over to Arthur Burns as I would have liked. But we are in very deep trouble. We are in the wildest inflation since the Civil War."[82] After apologizing for his role in creating the current situation, Martin sat down amid "uneasy applause."[83] It was the last time he would, in the words of a famous Martin quote: "take away the punch bowl just as the party got going." What followed was a fine irony so often typical of the nation's capital. In the midst of this somber moment, that evening's entertainment burst into the room. It was a group of enthusiastic young singers and dancers from a touring theater company, singing songs from a review called "The Decline and Fall of the Entire World as Seen through the Eyes of Cole Porter."[84] It was poetic justice for a man who tried to keep from taking himself too seriously and yet regularly offered the most pessimistic of forecasts.

Martin expressed his personal disappointment again at his last lunch with his fellow governors. As FOMC Secretary Bob Holland wrote: "He [Martin] said simply 'I've failed.' He felt that the inflation that had crept into the American economy was too much. It had happened on his watch, and he saw it as his failure."[85] Holland went on: "His colleagues argued that he had *not* failed. Given all the circumstances he had to deal with, they insisted, he had done a splendid job."[86] The next day, he began a schedule to meet individually with each of the Fed's nine hundred employees, most of whom had never been in the chairman's office, to thank them personally for their contribution to the Fed over his years in office. At 5:00 p.m. on 31 January 1970, Martin climbed into his white 1951 Cadillac convertible and drove out of the Fed basement garage to the gracious Georgian house at 2861 Woodland Avenue, where he and Cynthia would begin the next phase of their life together.

The public accolades rolled in. His critics turned nostalgic, and Martin's supporters had their final say. James Reston of the *New York Times* wrote: "Farewell to the happy puritan. He makes such gloomy predictions in such a pleasant way that even Wright Patman may regret not having him in office to kick around."[87] Paul Samuelson, a frequent critic, wrote glibly but with some appreciation: "Martin enters the Valhalla of American central bankers. Let Benjamin Strong, Marriner Eccles, and Allan Sproul give him a hero's welcome."[88] Then he criticized Martin for paying too little attention to monetary aggregates, but in an unacknowledged tribute, gave a Martin-like definition of a central bank's role: "Nature created the central bank so that it might lean successfully against the winds of cyclical disturbance."[89] *Time* magazine attempted to put him in historical perspective: "Martin's adroit leadership helped to change the Reserve Board from a cloistered temple of orthodoxy to an institution responsive to national and social goals. For all the political tantrums he provoked, Bill Martin has been the pivotal economic figure of two tumultuous decades."[90] Martin rarely paid attention to public commentary on his performance. Reflecting on public criticism of one of his recommendations, Martin once replied: "Well, that's a matter of judgment. I don't worry about those things."[91] It is unlikely that he paid much attention to it now.

Martin's thirteen-month association with the Nixon administration is too brief to draw many far-reaching conclusions, but he did accomplish a few of his goals. Martin built a consensus within the FOMC to reestablish monetary restraint during a period when a majority of economists in and out of the Fed did not feel it was necessary. He carried the fight against inflation to the administration and forced it to recognize that the public was not convinced that the administration would deal decisively with it. He maintained a majority of the FOMC in favor of restraint for a sufficient period for its results to become visible, and he gave way gracefully to the inevitable by initiating a move toward ease.

At the end of his chairmanship, Martin was able to bequeath to Arthur Burns a Federal Reserve System with its reputation for considered independence and nonpartisanship intact. Its relations with the administration were somewhat distant but generally cooperative. Relations with Congress, while always sensitive, were stable, and the Fed had very strong supporters in the most important congressional oversight committees. The banking industry was fundamentally sound, and while it occasionally chafed at the Fed's regulatory policies, the industry could be relied on to support the Fed if it faced unreasonable political pressures. Internally, the Fed's highly competent leadership was bolstered by the belief that a career in the Federal Reserve System was a high calling requiring dedication, integrity, and ability. The Fed's economic research capability, on which so much depended, was regarded as the best in the nation, if not the world. Working-level relations with the Fed's sister agencies were close and highly cooperative. Martin had done all he could to leave behind a tradition of institutional excellence.

12

The Public Private Citizen: Retirement

Bill Martin had been retired for only a few months when he was contacted by Randolph Burgess, one of his oldest friends and the man who had created the position of undersecretary of the Treasury for Monetary Affairs during the Eisenhower administration. Burgess was serving as chairman of a foundation established in honor of Per Jacobsson, the illustrious former managing director of the International Monetary Fund. The foundation sponsored an annual address on international monetary issues, given in connection with the annual meetings of the World Bank and International Monetary Fund. Burgess asked Martin to give the fall 1970 speech, and Martin readily agreed. He had been seeking just such an opportunity for a valedictory speech on an issue he had been thinking about for some time: the creation of a world central bank. As the recently retired leader of the most important central bank in the world, Martin believed he was in a unique position to propose the compromises that powerful nations would have to make in order to make such a world institution possible. He would use his experience, along with whatever reputation and influence he might have, to urge consideration of this worthy prospect.

Pulling together his thoughts on the subject must have been deeply satisfying to Martin. His experience in international cooperative efforts had begun in 1945 with his position as an observer in the Bretton Woods conference that had established the IMF. As a member of the National Advisory Council on

International Monetary and Financial Problems, he had participated in the policy decisions to implement the IMF and to establish the system of fixed exchange rates. During his Treasury years, he had worked with European finance ministers to nurse the Bretton Woods exchange system through its early postwar trials. During his years at the Fed, he had joined with other central bankers through the Bank for International Settlements (BIS) to negotiate short-term interbank loans in support of currency stabilization. In view of Martin's twenty-five years of experience in international monetary cooperation, it is hardly surprising that he could envision the evolution of these cooperative efforts into the creation of a world central bank. He asked Bob Solomon, who served as advisor to the board of governors, to help him. Solomon remembered: "Bill and I worked long and hard on that lecture. It was one of Bill's most important speeches."[1]

Martin delivered his speech on 14 September 1970 in the ornate Aula lecture hall at the University of Basel. Basel was famous for conservative banking, and it was here that Martin had first encountered the slogan he used throughout his Fed career: "A sound currency is coined freedom."[2] Standing next to a life-sized portrait of Jacobsson, Martin reflected on his own life experiences and voiced his hopes for the future. He reviewed the success of postwar cooperative efforts to create and maintain the international monetary system. He highlighted the activities of existing institutions such as the IMF, the Organization for Economic Development (OECD), and the BIS that already represented those powers usually associated with a central bank, including advice to individual countries with balance of payments problems and serving as the lender of last resort to help those countries address their currency problems.[3] He emphasized that he did not propose a new institution but rather the extension of the powers of existing institutions.

Martin observed that one of the most significant milestones in the development of a world central banking capacity occurred in 1968 when the IMF was authorized to create new international monetary reserves through Special Drawing Rights (SDRs). SDRs took their place alongside the existing reserve sources; newly mined gold, IMF loans, and dollars accumulated as the result of the U.S. balance of payments deficit. The non-SDR sources were completely unmanaged, and Martin argued that the uncontrolled creation of international reserve assets demanded the creation of a world central bank just as the uncontrolled creation of credit by a national banking system demanded a national central bank: "It was only with the development of central banking in all our countries that the rate of expansion of bank credit and money came to be deliberately regulated in the public interest."[4]

Then he grasped one of the nettlesome issues in international monetary economics: the current dependence of central banks on the U.S. balance of payments deficit to generate dollars to add to their reserve assets: "I don't want to see the world on a dollar standard. . . . If the U.S. puts its balance of payments in order . . . the SDR and the two-tier gold system give us the means of keeping the gold exchange standard functioning without chaos."[5] This was an important statement for an American central banker. Many of Martin's fellow central bankers believed that the United States did indeed want a world dollar standard, and it was a major source of tension, undercutting cooperative efforts at strengthening the monetary system.[6]

Martin went on to describe the capabilities of a world central bank that were not yet being carried out. The most important was to promote worldwide economic stabilization through global open-market operations that "bring about somewhat greater variation in the rate of growth of world reserves . . . as a means of offsetting cyclical tendencies in the world economy."[7] Another was to regulate behavior in the international financial markets by international regulatory supervision of the burgeoning Eurodollar and Eurobond markets and by monitoring the activities of multinational corporations in these markets. Finally, a world central bank could promote "harmonization of the policies of the member states and maintenance of payments equilibrium among them."[8] Martin made no effort to propose how these added responsibilities might be apportioned among the existing international organizations. He knew his general thesis would meet considerable resistance, and he did not want to get enmeshed in additional arguments over the mechanics of implementation.

Martin concluded by addressing the hurdles facing his proposal. The most difficult was convincing the major trading nations to give up some of their individual economic sovereignty to a series of multilateral financial institutions. Martin reminded his audience that the economic and political progress of the postwar years had resulted primarily from individual nations ceding some of their sovereignty to multilateral organizations: "It could be said that what were once the principal objectives of sovereign powers, the maintenance of economic prosperity and effective defense, can now only be achieved by the acceptance of cooperative international arrangements which impose limitations on the sovereignty of all the nations concerned."[9] Then he tried to change the terms of the debate by observing that a national commitment to a world central bank "[i]nvolves no loss of sovereignty, but rather a pooling of sovereignty." He hoped that national leaders would not view cooperation as a zero-sum game and that each nation, by limiting some of its freedom for independent action, could reap the benefits that a world central bank could bring to the world economy.

Then he addressed the Achilles' heel of his position: the U.S. balance payments deficit. The U.S. deficit poisoned the atmosphere for international cooperation because the Americans refused to abide by the rules of the Bretton Woods system, and their trading partners were forced to live with the knowledge that their growing dollar reserves could one day be devalued. Knowing that the best he could do was to add his plea to the chorus already urging the U.S. government to do something, he concluded: "The United States must make every effort to keep its payments position more or less in balance."[10] As usual, he balanced this advice with its corollary: "Such a goal is achievable only if other countries also adopt reasonable balance of payments goals and take actions to attain them."[11] Martin had tried for almost fifteen years to convince three U.S. presidents of the need to take the unpopular steps that would bring a fundamental improvement in the U.S. balance of payments and had failed. His advice was even less likely to be taken now that he was a private citizen, but he would not abandon his efforts to persuade the U.S. government to be a more constructive force in the community of nations.

He ended with a plea to his fellow central bankers, those with whom he had worked through the years, to bring the decades of cooperative efforts to full realization: "I think we have come a long way in international cooperation in financial affairs in the past generation. [There is] a general acceptance of the thought of a world central bank and it seems to me that we are not being overly optimistic to believe that we can go forward."[12] His final words were an apt summation of Martin's goals for international monetary cooperation and regulation: the achievement of sustainable worldwide economic prosperity. A prosperous world would become a peaceful world: "Further evolution along the lines we have been examining today will enhance world political stability and with it, the probability of peace."[13]

It was no surprise to Martin that the world was still not ready for the reality of a world central bank. In a comment following Martin's speech, Karl Blessing, the admired leader of the German Bundesbank with whom Martin had worked closely for over a decade, spoke for central bankers frustrated with the U.S. indifference to its balance of payments problems: "Let us put our own houses in order. . . . It would be wise not to strive for utopian goals but to try to make less dramatic progress within the existing machinery."[14] In another typical critique, Martin was attacked from the monetarist perspective by Professor Harry G. Johnson, an academic economist held in high regard at the Fed.[15] He argued that Martin's belief that a world central bank could moderate world economic cycles by managing the creation of new reserves "is a highly tempting idea for any central banker . . . but the evidence shows that they are poor indeed at the job. I have little confidence that a world central bank could sit there skillfully 'fine tuning' the world economy. My view is that we should try first to get a stable growth of the ultimate reserves of the system."[16]

There were positive comments on Martin's speech but they were drowned out by the dissents. After an all-too-brief flurry of discussion, Martin's speech joined the accumulated inventory of forgotten proposals for a world central bank.[17] Bill Martin was rarely deterred by the likelihood of failure and was usually content to make the best case he could for promoting the public interest. His approach to his "Toward a World Central Bank" speech was no different. Eight years later, Martin replaced Randolph Burgess as the chairman of the board of the Per Jacobsson Foundation. The annual address that year, given by Gabriel Hauge, included a reference to a world central bank. At the conclusion of the address, Martin remarked from the podium: "I cannot help but comment on Gabe Hauge's remark about the central bank—that we all recognize in him the Man of La Mancha who dreams the impossible dream."[18] In fact, Martin was referring to himself and his own lonely quest for the world central bank.

During his preparation for his Jacobsson address, Martin was approached by Bernard "Bunny" Lasker, the chairman of the board of governors of the New York Stock Exchange, to discuss the current problems at the Exchange. The Exchange was once again experiencing a tumultuous period and was besieged on many fronts. The board of governors concluded that an independent review of its situation was required, and after considering almost two hundred names, agreed that Bill Martin was the best-qualified individual to lead such a review. Martin initially turned Lasker down, agreeing to the request only when Lasker promised him a complete carte blanche and that the report would be made public. Later Martin told the press: "I really didn't want the job. I guess what led me to say yes was my puritan concern that it was a job that needed doing and it would be a good thing for me to do it."[19]

The problems at the Exchange were almost as serious as those Martin had struggled with during 1938–41. After a boom in the mid-1960s ended with the puncture of a speculative bubble, the NYSE index had declined by almost one-third between December 1968 and the spring of 1970. The decline consumed a significant slice of the net worth of investors and brokerage firms alike. Trading volume plummeted, and NYSE member firms began to lose money. By early 1971, a frightening 129 of the 759 member firms had merged or gone out of business, a greater number than had disappeared during the years immediately following the Great Depression. In addition, institutional investors such as mutual funds and insurance companies were aggressively lobbying the SEC to end the NYSE system of fixed commissions on stock transactions. When the NYSE rejected their request, these institutions began using "third-market" brokers who specialized in handling large blocks of shares, at significantly lower commissions, through their membership on regional stock exchanges. By early 1970, third-market volume was equal to 20 percent of total NYSE trading, and there was no telling how high the share might go.

If these problems were not enough, a surge in volume in 1968 caused a massive paperwork backlog as the Exchange's unautomated documentation system became overloaded. To ease the crunch, trading hours were shortened, and then the NYSE went to four trading days a week. By the end of 1969, the added staff costs and belated investments in automation raised the break-even volume for the Exchange as a whole from five million shares a day to twelve million, just as volume began to decline. Responding to the pressure from institutions, the SEC weighed in with a demand that NYSE trades worth more than $500,000 must be negotiated. Hearings to examine Wall Street's problems were scheduled in both the House of Representatives and the Senate, and it was widely believed that new securities legislation would result. The Exchange was at another crossroads in its stormy existence.

Lasker appointed a seven-person "advisory" committee for the study, which included the heads of the most powerful Wall Street firms, and offered Martin as much staff support as he would need. Martin surprised Lasker by telling him that he would need only a lawyer, a computer expert, and an administrative assistant. The report would be completed in six months, and Martin would take no salary. Lasker was probably even more surprised when Martin announced to the press in January 1971: "We will deal with everything and anything. I certainly will not duck in making judgments. I want clear judgments to come out of this—nothing fuzzy."[20] Bunny Lasker might or might not like the report that he would be getting, but one thing was certain—the conclusions would be unambiguous.

Then Martin went to work. He spent weeknights in the apartment on 5th Avenue that he and Cynthia had used during the Lyndon Johnson years when they wished to be incommunicado. Each morning he would go to the Edwardian Room of the Plaza Hotel for breakfast, where he would meet with a representative of an organization involved with the stock market. This routine was repeated at lunch and usually dinner as well. Martin's companion might be a CEO of a very large brokerage firm with capital problems, the president of a mutual fund company seeking Exchange membership, a technical director of a brokerage firm that had successfully automated its data-processing requirements, or the head of a small brokerage firm worried about getting forced out of business by negotiated commission rates. For a man who enjoyed talking with people from all walks of life, these months were rejuvenating and stimulating. Wearing his off-the-rack pinstriped suits, round wire-rimmed glasses, and irrepressible smile, Martin would ask questions that could be broad or remarkably technical. During the course of the six months, Martin once recalled, he had close to 150 of these meetings.

Martin soon learned that he had to move quickly to keep up with events. On 10 March, the SEC released its long-awaited *Institutional Investor Study Report,* which criticized the NYSE for exercising monopoly power to restrict trading in NYSE-listed stocks in other markets: "Our objective is to see a central market system in which all investors have access . . . and which is controlled not only by appropriate regulation but also by the forces of competition."[21] Regarding fixed commission rates, the study concluded: "Fixed minimum brokerage commissions, by providing a built-in incentive for many investors to trade off the major exchanges, are incompatible with the development of a truly national, central market system."[22] Martin's fundamental premise was the creation of a national stock market using a strengthened NYSE as the umbrella organization. If the study's conclusions represented the opinion of the SEC commissioners, Martin would probably not be able to win SEC support for his recommendations.

The central tenet of Martin's vision for the future of the stock market was that it had to become truly national: "It must provide a continuous, fair, and orderly market with centralized disclosure of all executions of buy and sell orders and other material facts."[23] Martin believed that the keystone of a national market was the NYSE, which he described as "having, to some extent, all of the characteristics for the proposed national exchange system."[24] The NYSE dominated the business of trading stocks and bonds. The total market value of its listed securities represented almost 50 percent of all the stock market value in the world. The Exchange's self-regulatory apparatus needed strengthening, but it was the most comprehensive of any of the financial markets. The auction process offered the fairest pricing mechanism, and the stock specialist system provided the most effective market-making capacity of any stock market in the United States. It alone could serve as the umbrella organization for integrating the activities of the other U.S. stock exchanges.

However, Martin concluded that for all its strengths, the NYSE could not serve as an effective keystone in a national market system until it was truly dedicated to the public interest. His 1938 reorganization of the Exchange had only partially converted the Exchange into such an institution, and the few efforts at further reform had been snuffed out by change-resistant members. The fates had conspired to give Martin another opportunity to reform the Exchange, and he drew up his recommendations with that goal in mind.

The first step in completing the reform of the Exchange was to reduce the ability of floor-trading members to control the board and policy decisions. Martin focused on a proposal being promoted by a broker-dealer firm for transferring voting power in the NYSE from those who held "seats" on the Exchange to those who actually contributed the daily trading volume. This step would take voting control of the Exchange from individual floor traders, who were often trading for their own accounts, and place it in the hands of the larger broker-dealer organizations, who were largely dependent on the investment activity of the investing public. Martin also proposed that the board be reduced from thirty-three to twenty-one members, ten of whom would be public representatives drawn from "all segments of the investing public." The chairperson of the board would be the full-time chief executive and would appoint the president to serve as the chief operating officer. This step would finally put policy making in the hands of a board dedicated to investor interests and put policy implementation in the hands of professional managers.

One of the most controversial issues was the third market and its ability to take business volume from the NYSE. Martin met with Donald Weeden, the brash, outspoken thirty-eight-year-old president of Weeden & Co., the most aggressive third-market brokerage house. Weeden had dozens of traders working computers and telephones to comb through the holdings of institutions to find potential buyers or sellers for large blocks of stock held by other Weeden institutional clients. Weeden argued forcefully that NYSE specialists and member firms were unable to place institution-sized blocks of stock as quickly or as cheaply as Weeden. During his visits to the trading rooms of major institutions, Martin learned that Weeden was not exaggerating. His firm was indeed offering a service and a cost that his customers wanted, and NYSE members were not. Martin also learned about the problems of the third market from an executive of a regional brokerage executive who told him that "the third market suffers from at present, limited regulatory control, as compared to the [NYSE] specialist, and in the event of further erosion [i.e., the imposition of negotiated rates] of the commission structure, diminishing profitability."[25]

The third-market issue presented Martin with his greatest dilemma. His analysis convinced him that although the third market provided a real service at a competitive cost, its main appeal was that it was poorly regulated. He was also concerned that unlike the specialists on the NYSE, the third-market brokers had no commitment to maintaining a market during times of market stress. In a decision that he knew would generate heavy criticism, he recommended that NYSE member firms expand their block placement capacity, that the NYSE tighten its regulation over these trades, and that the third market be closed down.

Institutional membership in the Exchange was another knotty issue. Martin came away from his discussions with institutional executives convinced that they wanted to join the Exchange only to lower commission costs. He felt that "institutions probably should not be joining any Exchange in order to recapture commissions."[26] Martin believed very deeply that the securities business had unique characteristics and that "perhaps the paramount consideration [on institutional membership] is the necessity of recognizing and preserving the difference between the securities business and other businesses."[27] By their very nature, financial markets needed contrarian investors and market makers, those willing to move against the market in search of gain. In so doing, they counteracted the actions of the majority of investors and provided a vital buffer against market overreactions. Most other financial businesses, such as insurance or commercial banking, did not present this profile. If they were allowed heavy ownership of Exchange members, they might decide to reduce their financial exposure in a crisis, just at the time their capital was most needed. In 1931, Martin had written anonymously about the importance of short sellers, and his attitude toward their role had not changed over the years. Despite the likely complaints from Exchange members who wanted investment in their firms by well-heeled institutional buyers, Martin decided against institutional ownership.

Martin had determined at the outset of his study that the potential for computerization would be a fundamental element in the reorganization of the financial markets. As the months wore on, he became more convinced of this conclusion. Many NYSE member firms were finally spending heavily to automate their "back office" operations for processing trades, but they were still only scratching the surface of automation's potential. Visits to large bond-trading houses such as Salomon Brothers & Hutzler confirmed the potential for electronically processing and communicating high volumes of trading activity. Engineers at IBM described a system that could lead to the complete elimination of the stock certificate, and representatives of Digital Equipment Corporation described the potential for electronically linking the nation's stock exchanges. The electronic ticker tape that kept brokers and traders across the country informed of the latest trades could carry transactions from every stock exchange, and the market that offered the best pricing would be available for all to see. The existing capabilities of computers and electronic communications networks meant that Martin's vision of a centralized trade reporting system was less than two years of intense development away from becoming reality.

When Bill Martin presented his report on 5 August 1971, a month before the promised delivery date, the NYSE Board of Governors vehemently objected to creating an independent chief executive and to the prohibition on institutional ownership. Martin concluded: "They wanted me to put it [the organizational structure] into the same straightjacket as it was before. I fought that."[28] Martin forcefully reminded the leaders of their initial promises, and the report was published unchanged.

The report was brief, only nineteen single-spaced pages, and Martin made no effort to provide a detailed analysis of the stock market: "The issues have been extensively documented elsewhere. My recommendations are intended to identify goals to be pursued in the public interest."[29] Martin highlighted the Exchange's self-regulatory process operated under the supervision of the SEC. To strengthen that process, Martin recommended a twenty-person board, half representing the public and half representing the industry, but particularly the large broker-dealers. A paid chief executive officer would serve as board chairperson. He proposed strengthening the market-making mechanism by requiring stronger capital structures for specialist firms and higher performance standards for continued market-making eligibility. He also argued for more time for member firms to prepare for the financial impact of fully negotiated commission rates. He castigated the NYSE for failing to embrace technology in the past, and in view of the complexity of the changes that lay ahead, advocated giving the industry time to move toward the unified ticker tape and to do away with the stock certificate. He urged the SEC to seek uniform rules for all the major stock exchanges. Finally, using the Federal Reserve System as a model, Martin urged the SEC to become more understanding of the problems faced by the industry it regulated.

As he expected, the report generated a firestorm of controversy. Most of the criticism concerned Martin's allegiance to the NYSE as the linchpin of his national market system and his recommendation that the innovative third market be eliminated. The *New York Times* editorialized: "The securities business must have freer competition if a new and more closely integrated national market is to come into being. Neither the New York Stock Exchange nor the nation's investors will be benefited by an effort to construct a securities monopoly, complete with price fixing."[30] A more influential group of critics were nineteen economists, including Milton Friedman, Paul Samuelson, and a half dozen of the most well-regarded financial market theorists, who urged congressional leaders to oppose Martin's recommendations. They argued that self-regulation had failed to prevent the current conflicts of interest at the NYSE; "Self regulation by the exchange . . . is a little like having the rabbits guard the lettuce."[31] The group also accused Martin of contradicting the goals of the SEC: "The SEC has generally favored strengthening competition while the Martin report favored eliminating some kinds of competition [such as the third market]."[32]

Other economists criticized Martin for not forcing the NYSE to do more to support institutional trading: "Martin is preoccupied with the small investor. . . . The point we are making is that the NYSE's basic problem has resulted from a decline in the relative importance of the small investor and an increase in the volume of institutional block trading."[33] The criticism did not surprise Martin, but he hoped the critics would be more understanding of his goals.

Martin's report received mixed reviews from those who would have to implement his recommendations. Despite the complaints of SEC staff members about the report, *Newsweek* reported that SEC Chairman William J. Casey was "pleased with its contents though he would have preferred to come out in favor of competitive rates."[34] Ralph Saul, the well-regarded former chief executive of the American Stock Exchange, defended the concept of uniform rules for all exchanges: "Much of the growing competition among the different markets today stems from the different rules and regulations of those markets. The imposition of common standards would put this inter-market competition on a healthy footing."[35] Martin anticipated that Exchange members would not like his proposals for reorganizing the Exchange and prohibiting institutional membership. But he was disappointed that Lasker and his deputy, Ralph DeNunzio, could not persuade their associates to appreciate the changes needed to justify the central role the Exchange would play in Martin's proposed national market of the future. Martin concluded: "I don't think it got the reception that I hoped it would get in the street."[36]

While he could not have foreseen it in 1971, most of Martin's recommendations have stood the test of time. In 1972, the NYSE reorganized itself by reducing the board of governors to twenty-one members and appointing both a full-time chairman and chief executive. Although subsequent NYSE chairmen fought to reduce the influence of floor members and specialists, these members resolutely opposed any further diminution in their power. The Exchange also dragged its feet on the issue of a national market until 1975, when the Securities Acts were amended to mandate a national market. By 1978, the Intermarket Trading System linked nine exchanges, and trading desks at brokers were automatically presented the lowest available price on any linked exchange. By 1973, the creation of the Depository Trust Company provided electronic registration of shares, and certificates were on their way out. Computerization at the Exchange facilitated a steady increase in trading volume. Daily capacity, which was 10 million shares in the mid-1960s, grew to 100 million shares in 1982, and trading volumes in 2004 approached 2 billion shares. By 2004, the NYSE still transacted 85 percent of the total trading volume in NYSE-listed stocks.

In hindsight, Martin was disappointed that the institution he made the centerpiece of his study had to be forced by the SEC into the national market era. The critics were right; the Exchange had always been change-resistant, except during times of crisis, and probably would always be so. Martin had two unique opportunities to push the Exchange toward reform, and he made as much progress toward that elusive goal as any other single individual in the Exchange's history.

In the following years, Martin finally entered his well-deserved retirement. He served as a director of a dozen large corporations, including Royal Dutch Shell, Caterpillar Tractor, and IBM. He also served as a trustee of twelve nonprofit organizations, including the National Geographic Society, the Carnegie Foundation, and the Mayo Clinic. Ironically, Lyndon Johnson was also a Mayo trustee at the time, and Martin chuckled at the hard-driving president's new role as a long-haired Texas patriarch, consumed with building the biggest and best presidential library. In 1977, he retired from the board of trustees of Berry College, a small college in northwest Georgia emphasizing work-study programs in agriculture and other applied arts. Martin served as chairman of the board of trustees for eighteen years and once, during a year of financial difficulty and leadership transition, he had served as acting president of the college.

There were regular opportunities to offer comments on current economic issues, but he scrupulously avoided criticizing his successors at the Fed. In a February 1972 speech to the Conference Board, he "reluctantly" accepted Richard Nixon's decision to devalue the dollar and bring down the curtain on the Bretton Woods monetary system, but observed: "That it became necessary and even desirable cannot obscure the fact that it represents a failure of United States economic policy — a failure to restrain inflation and failure to improve our balance of payments."[37] As the international monetary system was buffeted by the German decision to let the deutsche mark float and a second U.S. devaluation, Martin appealed to the U.S. government in June 1973 to take the lead in restructuring the international monetary system. "This marks the end of an era on international economic and monetary cooperation envisaged in the Bretton Woods Agreements Act. . . . I am sure it will take time, as we are presently learning, to reconstitute our international monetary system, but it is essential that the IMF should be converted as rapidly as possible into some form of World Central bank."[38] Despite some encouraging words from Paul Volcker, the current undersecretary of the Treasury for Monetary Affairs, Martin's words went unheeded.[39]

Martin returned briefly to the spotlight in early 1976 as a member of a three-person panel to review the financial condition of the New York State government. Martin, along with Eugene R. Black, the former president of the World Bank, and William H. Morton, a retired president of American Express

Company, were asked by State Comptroller Arthur Levitt to examine the state's financial condition to determine if it was strong enough to justify fresh borrowing in the municipal bond market. After three weeks, the panel publicly announced its conclusion that the state and its associated agencies would have sufficient cash flow to service new borrowing. After the hubbub died down, Martin returned eagerly to retirement.

During the decade of the 1970s, the economic conditions Martin warned about and fought against became a reality. Government budget deficits widened and inflation grew worse. International monetary cooperation reached a low point as the U.S. balance of payments deficit grew and exchange rates gyrated more frequently. In his public statements, Martin tried to repeat the principles he had espoused over his career without engaging in "I told you so" comments. Occasionally his dark side would color his comments. On the fiftieth anniversary of the stock market crash of September 1929, he observed: "The country is floating on a sea of credit. The average consumer's debt repayment burden, in terms of income, is at the highest level in history. I believe there's a good chance that we'll have another depression within the next three to five years."[40] Martin could not foresee that his successor, Fed Chairman Paul Volcker, would take advantage of the independence that Bill Martin had created for the Federal Reserve System; by applying his political skills, understanding of the economy, and personal courage, Volcker brought an end to almost seventeen years of inflation. In an interview in 1985, Martin gave Volcker credit: "He is very good on monetary policy."[41]

There were accolades, a few of which were memorable. On 2 February 1972, Martin was inducted as a commandeur of the French Legion d'Honneur by the French ambassador. For a central banker who had led the opposition to President Charles de Gaulle's policy of relying exclusively on gold for France's monetary reserves, the award had a fine irony. Earlier, on 4 April 1971, Bill Martin dug a silver-handled shovel into the earth of an empty lot behind the Federal Reserve Building. It was the symbolic start of the construction of the William McChesney Martin Jr. building, a new marble and smoked glass edifice designed to house the Fed's expanding operations. It was the first building in Washington, D.C. constructed for an agency of the federal government to be named for a living public servant. When Representative Wright Patman learned of this honor for his old nemesis, he was enraged. He protested on the floor of the House: "There is no excuse for the Congress to allow the Federal Reserve to build a monument to high interest rates down on Constitution Avenue — a monument to mistaken monetary policies and classic disregard for the wishes and needs of the American People."[42] Typically, Patman's impassioned plea fell on deaf ears, and the building now graces official Washington.

One of the pleasures of Martin's retirement was the opportunity to devote

292 Public Private Citizen

more time to his enduring love of tennis. He played in his age category in tournaments around the country. When he was seventy-five, he was quoted as saying: "They even have a new category for over 80. I'd like to last long enough to play in one of those."[43] The official birthplace of championship tennis in the United States is the Newport Casino, a lawn tennis club that hosted the first U.S. National Championship in 1881. Through his wife Cynthia's father, Dwight F. Davis, who had donated the Davis Cup in 1900, Martin had a long connection with official tennis organizations. In 1977, he became involved in a plan to merge two struggling tennis historical associations and launch a major fund-raising campaign to rebuild the neglected facilities at the Newport Casino and create an International Tennis Hall of Fame to honor past champions. Working with his old friend Joseph F. Cullman III, an energetic and public-spirited tennis partner, the money was raised and the museum completed in 1979. Martin served as president of the combined organization from 1979 to 1988. In a memorial tribute to the Hall of Fame, he summed his feelings for tennis: "From my schooldays on, I have made more good friends through tennis than any other sporting or social activity. The Tennis Hall of Fame has preserved those long-standing friendships."[44]

To the very end of his life, Martin believed that change was inevitable in the financial markets, and that in the long run, the changes would be for the best. In 1984, in one of his last interviews, he was asked to reflect on the current state of the financial markets: "They have many imperfections, but I think they'll be corrected in time and I just wish them well."[45] Martin's philosophy about that struggle was summarized in his favorite poem, "Say Not, the Struggle Nought Availeth," by Arthur Hugh Clough:

> Say not, the struggle nought availeth,
> The labor and wounds are vain,
> The enemy faints not, nor faileth,
> and as things have been, they remain.
>
> For while the tired waves, vainly breaking,
> Seem here no painful inch to gain,
> Far back, through creeks and inlets making,
> Comes silent, flooding in, the main.
>
> And now by eastern windows only,
> When daylight comes, comes in the light;
> In front, the sun climbs slow, how slowly,
> But westward, look, the land is bright.

The last years of Martin's life were etched in physical pain. He did not make it into the eighty-plus tennis tournament circuit; a painful fall in 1981 and a partial recovery forced him to walk with a cane. A few years later, the athletic body that had served him so well began to break down, and arthritis and back problems reduced him to his bed and a wheelchair. By the time he was ninety, the continual pain required him to be on powerful pain medicines that dulled his consciousness, and he became bed-bound. On 27 July 1998, at the age of ninety-one, Bill Martin died in his sleep. As was his nature, he slipped quietly away. There was no solemn memorial service at Washington's National Cathedral with eulogies by friends and retired dignitaries. He was buried in a family plot in St. Louis, and a simple stone marks his resting place. His true memorial lies elsewhere, in America's financial markets, where the Federal Reserve System and the New York Stock Exchange fulfill the promise he created for them.

Epilogue: Bill Martin's Legacy

The evolution of the Federal Reserve System has been driven forward by the great men who conceived, shaped, and led it through periods of challenge and transition. The honor roll includes Senator Carter Glass, H. Parker Willis, Benjamin Strong, Marriner Eccles, Allan Sproul, Paul Volcker, and Alan Greenspan, as well as many who are not so well known. Each of these men has contributed to the development of the institution that has been described as "America's greatest contribution to the science of government."[1] But the leader whose handiwork is most visible in the Federal Reserve System that we know today is William McChesney Martin Jr.

Bill Martin's reputation as the "Creator of the Modern Fed" rests on how he shaped the Federal Reserve System as an institution. The Fed Martin inherited had a tarnished reputation for monetary management, policy-making tools that had been suspended, poor relations with the administration, and an organizational structure at odds with its institutional purpose. When Bill Martin retired from the Fed, he bequeathed an institution with its federal structure revitalized, the effectiveness of its reconstituted monetary policy tools no longer subject to doubt, and a well-recognized reputation for nonpartisan competence and dedication to the public interest. These qualities form the core of Martin's contribution to the Fed and are as much a part of the Fed today as when he left in 1970.

One of Martin's greatest contributions was to reinvigorate the federal structure envisioned in the original Federal Reserve legislation. Martin remade the full nineteen-member (with twelve voting members) FOMC into the Fed's primary monetary policy-making body. Equally important, he introduced a consensus-driven leadership style that incorporated the contributions of the twelve Reserve Bank presidents into policy decisions. Martin estimated that he spent one-third of his time on "system issues" directed primarily at strengthening the leadership and other capabilities of the Reserve Banks. He also traveled to the Reserve Banks to meet with officials, maintain contacts with leading regional bankers, and carry the Fed's message to local business leaders. He believed that these relationships could cement a strong base of national support if the Fed needed to counteract pressure coming from Washington.

Another of Martin's singular contributions was to change the goals and techniques for implementing monetary policy. Martin was a pragmatist who described his macroeconomic policy for promoting long-term economic growth with the homely aphorism of "leaning against the winds of inflation and deflation — whichever way they are blowing." Under the philosophy of a flexible monetary policy, Martin encouraged early, but measured, Fed action to combat inflationary pressures or to moderate recessionary tendencies in the economy. Because he believed that a stable price level was an essential condition for long-term economic growth, Martin publicly committed the Fed to preserving the purchasing power of the dollar. Martin implemented the "Bills Only" policy to minimize the disruptive impact of open-market transactions on the Treasury bond market and encourage a bond market with "depth, breadth, and resiliency." Finally, in order to assure a better balance between national economic policy considerations and the reality of the financial markets, he transferred the responsibility for supervising the Fed's open-market operations from the New York Reserve Bank to the FOMC in Washington, D.C.

Bill Martin realigned the Fed's relationship with other parts of the U.S. government by establishing a delicate balance between cooperation and independence. He believed that the Fed was most effective when it was working with the administration, and he sought opportunities to coordinate monetary and fiscal policies. He fashioned the Fed-Treasury Accord as a "partnership of equals" between the two agencies and brought this vision to reality. While Martin emphasized cooperation, he and Allan Sproul redefined the position of the Fed as "independent within the government, not independent of the government." For Martin, staking out an independent position was justified only after attempts at cooperation had failed, and the nation's interest and the Fed's mandate justified it. Independent action was always carefully considered, clearly communicated, and followed by efforts to reconcile the disagreement without compromising the integrity of the Fed's posture.

Bill Martin encouraged the Fed to take a leading role in international monetary issues. Despite few precedents, a somewhat shaky legal justification, and a strong minority of dissenters, Martin initiated a network of currency swaps to help deal with recurrent currency crises. He worked with a series of secretaries of the Treasury to deal with the U.S. balance of payments problems, and he supported and occasionally led joint efforts by central bankers to strengthen the structure of the international monetary system. Subsequent Fed chairmen have followed Martin's example of personal involvement in international issues to varying degrees, but at the working level, the Fed's cooperation with the Treasury and leading foreign central banks has been continuous.

Martin was the first chairman to actively build an understanding of the Fed's goals and support for its policies within the various constituencies impacted by the Fed's decisions. Martin sought to obtain support, or at least to minimize opposition, from the administration by emphasizing communication and consultation. He developed personal relationships with selected congressional leaders. He believed that effective regulation of the banking industry required that the Fed be sympathetic to the issues confronting the industry and, to the extent possible, to secure its understanding for the Fed's regulatory decisions. He was highly concerned that the financial markets and the general public understand the Fed's policies and its motivations. He wanted the Fed to be viewed as a private-public partnership operating in the public interest, not just another Washington-based government agency. These educational activities are carried on today.

Lastly, one of Martin's important contributions to the Fed was to set a new standard for the qualities and capabilities we have come to expect in our Fed leaders. Before the Martin era, the Fed had experienced several episodes of weak leadership, the most disastrous occurring during the Great Depression. Martin's background in the financial markets and in the leadership of public institutions enabled him to endow the Fed and the chairmanship with a reputation for competence and nonpartisanship. His personal integrity gave him the moral authority to speak out on behalf of the nation's economic well-being. His widely acknowledged belief in traditional economic disciplines and his commitment to international monetary cooperation gained him the respect of the world's central bankers. The skill with which he maintained the Fed's independence enabled him to differ forcefully with a president without it becoming personal or causing an intragovernmental crisis. These are the expectations by which subsequent candidates for the Fed chair have been evaluated.

To be sure, the Fed has evolved in ways that Martin did not anticipate or influence. To the end of his term, Martin gave only grudging acceptance to economic forecasting and using a variety of indicators, including not only money market conditions but also indicators such as the monetary aggregates, to evaluate the impact of Fed policies. Since the Martin era, the consideration of a variety of indicators has become standard procedure for determining monetary policy goals. Martin himself eventually abandoned his inflexible commitment to "Bills Only" for open-market operations, although most of these transactions remain in the short-term end of the Treasury market. Martin's concern about overreliance on economists for the Fed's leadership positions seems misguided today. Managing the complexity of the twenty-first-century economy demands a solid grounding in economics; since the 1960s, nearly all Fed leaders have been economists. The ongoing U.S. balance of payments deficit that concerned Martin and successive Treasury secretaries has become a permanent feature of the international monetary system. Martin would be astounded to see the continued willingness of foreign investors and governments to finance the U.S. deficit. Finally, the fixed-rate exchange system that Martin and others worked so hard to preserve could no longer overcome its inherent instability and gave way to floating rates. Despite these unforeseen developments, when it came to anticipating the future of the Fed, Bill Martin got it right more often than not.

A review of Bill Martin's Fed career would not be complete without a discussion of the great question of his chairmanship: how could a chairman so committed to fighting inflation allow it to get out of control? There is no disagreement that Martin and the Fed extinguished the inflationary pressures of the mid-1950s, although it took two recessions (1957–58 and 1960) and five years of 2.5 percent average real economic growth to achieve it. Inflationary pressures returned in 1965 as a result of the Johnson administration's spending programs and the tax cut of 1964. It took Martin the better part of 1965 to build an FOMC consensus for tightening credit, but during 1966 the Fed proved that a sustained program of monetary restraint could slow down the economy. The impact of the 1966 restraint fell unevenly, and faced with the growing anger of politicians over the collapse of the housing industry and the prospect of irreparable damage to the financial system, the Fed backed off its restraint.

During the years 1966–69, Martin led the Fed into alternate periods of ease and restraint as it leaned against recessionary winds in early 1967 and late 1968 and against inflationary headwinds during late 1967 and again in 1969. At his last FOMC meeting in January 1970, Martin noted that the CPI had increased by 5.8 percent during 1969 and concluded that he had failed to control inflation, his primary responsibility as Fed chairman.

There is no question that the Fed made mistakes in dealing with the resumption of inflation. By 1967, the FOMC concluded that its traditional indicators of the impact of monetary policy, the net reserves of the banking system and short-term interest rates, were inadequate. However, it made little concerted effort to use a broader range of available indicators such as the monetary aggregates, bank reserves, or longer-term projections for the appropriate growth of the money supply. Because of its singular focus on nominal short-term interest rates, the FOMC was reluctant to force rates higher than the peaks during the 1966 tightening for fear of igniting another runoff of bank and savings and loan deposits as they encountered Regulation Q ceilings. Finally, the Keynesians on the Fed staff and on the FOMC accepted a resumption of inflation as the unavoidable cost of achieving full employment, and they opposed any credit restraint that would increase unemployment.

Martin compounded these mistakes by his efforts to influence fiscal policy. His ill-advised attempt to pressure Congress to pass the surtax in late 1967 by "letting Congress experience its boom" allowed inflationary pressures to build. Similarly, he supported the FOMC's desire to loosen credit after the surtax was finally passed in June 1968. There are several justifications why Martin advocated these easing moves, but the most important was to generate political support for the surtax, and once it was in place, to put monetary policy in a supporting role. Nevertheless, the fact remains that these decisions contributed very significantly to the rebuilding of inflationary momentum. For a man who argued persuasively about the difficulty of extinguishing inflationary expectations, Martin underestimated them when it counted most. By 1969 and the time he rededicated the Fed to fighting inflation, he had too little time left in his term to assure a successful campaign, and the "great inflation" was well under way.

In Martin's defense, much of the criticism of late-1960s monetary policy during recent decades has come from those who believe there should have been more restraint on the growth of the money supply, bank credit, and total reserves. This criticism discounts the economic problems generated by the 1966 credit restraint, Martin's inability to bring the Keynesians on the FOMC and in the Fed economics staff into a consensus for fighting inflation, and the unwillingness of either the Johnson or Nixon administration to accept a recession in order to control inflation. It would have required a heroic change of heart for Martin, who led by consensus and did not believe that the Fed could operate in opposition to the president for any extended period, to have pushed a forceful program of restraint throughout 1966–68 and to ignore the consequences of much higher interest rates that would have resulted. But in a larger sense, Martin's reputation does not depend on whether he should have done more to control the great inflation that began in 1965.

Bill Martin's legacy is the reputation the Fed enjoys in the White House, among its sister agencies, and the Congress, as well as in foreign central banks and countless banks in U.S. and foreign financial centers. Those in the Fed are seen as capable public servants who skillfully manage monetary policy, produce outstanding economic analysis and research, and oversee the financial markets. Bill Martin might not recognize the particulars of today's monetary issues, but he would be pleased that the Fed's operating principles continue to include transparency, respect for free markets, and independence from political interference, all goals that he worked so hard to promote.

When Bill Martin left the Fed, he was followed by two chairmen, Arthur Burns and G. William Miller, who took monetary policy on a different tack. They downplayed the importance of dealing with the inflationary psychology at work in the financial markets and they failed to embrace the Fed's responsibility for restoring price stability in the economy. The result was almost a decade of inflation. When Fed Chairman Paul Volcker took on the great inflation in 1979, he was able to capitalize on the Fed's reputation for acting in the nation's interest, possessing the tools needed to do the job, and pursuing the task "until inflation was licked." Today's Federal Reserve System, which is as capable and trusted as it has ever been, is Bill Martin's lasting gift to us.

Appendix

Selected Economic Statistics of the Martin Era at the Fed

The graphs in this appendix are based on data published by various U.S. government sources, including the Commerce Department and the Bureau of Labor Statistics as well as the Federal Reserve System.

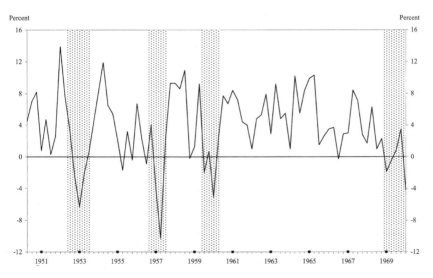

Figure 1. Real GDP growth, 1951–70 (%). *Note:* Quarterly observations of annualized percentage changes in real GDP. Shaded areas indicate recessions denoted by the National Bureau of Economic Research (NBER). Heavy tick marks indicate fourth quarter.

Percent   Percent

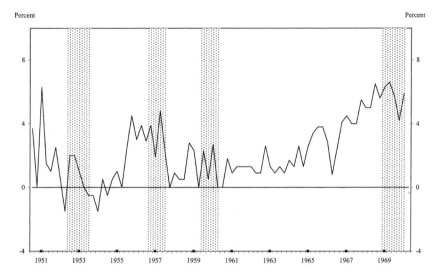

Figure 2. Inflation, 1951–70 (%). *Note:* Quarterly observations of annualized percentage change in the Consumer Price Index (CPI). 1951 Q1 inflation was 17.2%. Shaded areas indicate recession denoted by the NBER. Heavy tick marks indicate fourth quarter.

Percent   Percent

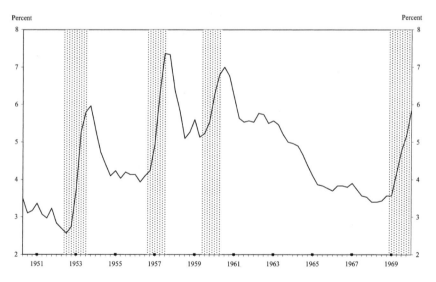

Figure 3. Unemployment, 1951–70 (%). *Note:* Civilian unemployment rate. Shaded areas indicate recessions denoted by the NBER. Heavy tick marks indicate fourth quarter.

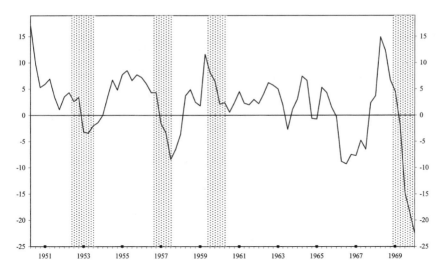

Figure 4. Federal government surplus or deficit, 1951–70 ($billions). *Note:* Shaded areas indicate recessions denoted by the NBER. Heavy tick marks indicate fourth quarter. Seasonally adjusted annual rate.

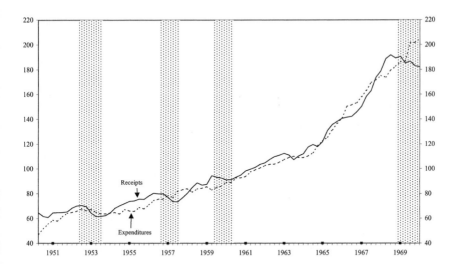

Figure 5. Federal government receipts and expenditures, 1951–70 ($billions). *Note:* Shaded areas indicate recessions denoted by the NBER. Heavy tick marks indicate fourth quarter. Seasonally adjusted annual rate.

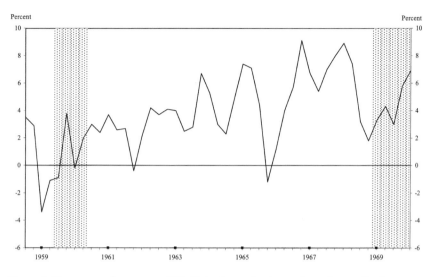

Figure 6. Money growth, 1951–70 (%). *Note:* Quarterly observations of annualized percentage changes in M1. Shaded areas indicate recessions denoted by the NBER. Heavy tick marks indicate fourth quarter.

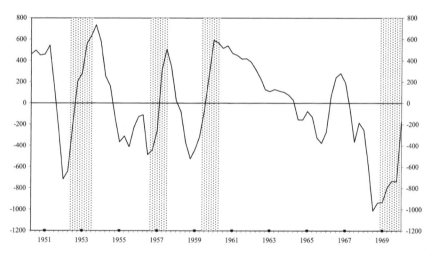

Figure 7. Free reserves, 1951–70 ($millions). *Note:* Excess reserves minus borrowed reserves of commercial banks. 1951–59 data obtained from Federal Reserve Board of Governors, *Banking and Monetary Statistics, 1941–1970* (Washington, D.C., 1976); 1959–70 data from Federal Reserve Board of Governors. Shaded areas indicate recessions denoted by the NBER. Heavy tick marks indicate fourth quarter. Not seasonally adjusted.

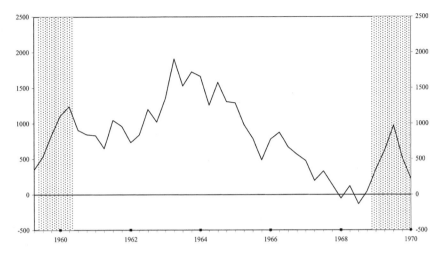

Figure 8. Current account, 1951–70 ($millions). *Note:* U.S. international transactions: balance on goods and services, income, and net unilateral transfers. Seasonally adjusted.

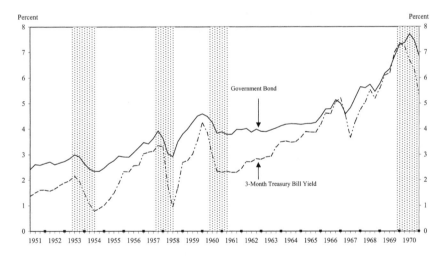

Figure 9. Government bond and 3-month Treasury bill yields, 1951–70 (%). *Note:* Quarterly observations of U.S. (long-term) government bonds from 1951–53 from Federal Reserve Board of Governors, *Banking and Monetary Statistics*. Data from 1953 Q1 on are U.S. Treasury 10-year constant maturity bond yields from Federal Reserve Board of Governors, "Selected Interest Rates," Statistical Release G.13. Shaded areas indicate recessions denoted by the NBER. Heavy tick marks indicate fourth quarter.

Abbreviations

BGFRS	Board of Governors, Federal Reserve System, Washington, D.C.
CCEP	Cabinet Committee on Economic Policy of the Nixon Administration
DDEPL	Dwight D. Eisenhower Presidential Library, Abilene, Kansas
FOMCM	Memorandum of discussion of meetings of the Federal Open Market Committee, Board of Governors, Federal Reserve System, Washington, D.C.
HSTPL	Harry S. Truman Presidential Library, Independence, Missouri
JFKPL	John F. Kennedy Presidential Library, Boston, Massachusetts
LBJPL	Lyndon B. Johnson Presidential Library, Austin, Texas
MPMHS	William McChesney Martin Jr. Papers, Missouri Historical Society, St. Louis
NA	National Archives II, College Park, Maryland
NPM	Nixon Presidential Materials, National Archives II, College Park, Maryland
NYSE	New York Stock Exchange
SECA	Securities and Exchange Commission Archives, Washington, D.C.
WHCF	White House Central Files

Notes

Introduction

1. Johnson to Fowler, telephone call, 3 December 1965, tape library, LBJPL.
2. William McChesney Martin Jr., oral history, 11, LBJPL.
3. Ibid., 9.
4. Martin, testimony to U.S. Senate, Committee on Banking and Currency, *Nomination of William McChesney Martin, Jr.*, 84th Cong., 2nd sess., 1956, 5.
5. Retired Fed governors and bank presidents, tribute to Martin, commemorative booklet, Fall 1999, BGFRS.

Chapter 1. A Family of Substance

1. Recession statistic from Allan Meltzer, *A History of the Federal Reserve* (Chicago: University of Chicago Press, 2002), 1:8.
2. William McChesney Martin Sr., "The Proposed Plan for a National Reserve Association," speech to the Missouri Bankers Association, 1911, 4, Martin File, Federal Reserve Bank of St. Louis library.
3. Malcolm W. Martin, brother of William McChesney Martin Jr., interview by author, 31 January 1995.
4. Martin Sr., "The Proposed Plan for a National Reserve Association," 4.
5. Ibid., 16.
6. Ibid., 10.
7. The initial board consisted of five men selected by the president and two ex officio members, the secretary of the Treasury and the comptroller of the currency.

8. Martin Sr., "The First Two Years of the Federal Reserve Bank," speech to the Memphis Institute of Bankers, 14 November 1916, 11, Martin File, Federal Reserve Bank of St. Louis library.

9. Malcolm W. Martin, interview by author, 8 October 1997.

10. Martin Sr., speech at his retirement celebration (as reported in the *St. Louis Post Dispatch*, 9 April 1941), box 9, MPMHS.

11. Clifford went to Washington D.C. during World War II and began his public service as an aide to an advisor of President Harry Truman. He subsequently became a counselor to a succession of presidents and served as secretary of Defense in the Johnson administration.

12. Benjamin Edwards III, interview by author, 22 February 1998.

13. *New Haven Register,* 12 June 1928, 44.

Chapter 2. Into the Maelstrom

1. William McChesney Martin Jr., oral history (1984), 2, NYSE.

2. Donald Kettl, *Leadership at the Fed* (New Haven: Yale University Press, 1986). Kettl wrote: "The reserve banks' confusion only further encouraged stock speculation while the board watched quietly from the sidelines," 34.

3. Kettl, *Leadership at the Fed.* The Treasury secretary and comptroller of the currency sat on the Fed board from 1913 to 1935.

4. J. P. Klingaman, *1929, the Year of the Great Crash* (Boston: Houghton Mifflin, 1960), 10.

5. *New York Times,* 30 October 1929, 2.

6. *A. G. Edwards & Co.: Historical Summary* (St. Louis: A. G. Edwards & Co., n.d.), 12.

7. Jan Broderick, corporate historian for A. G. Edwards & Co., interview by author, 9 October 1997.

8. In a retrospective on 7 March 1933, the *St. Louis Globe Democrat* quoted Finley McElroy, an A. G. Edwards & Sons analyst: "They didn't like it at the time, but in retrospect, he [Martin] saved their necks."

9. *A. G. Edwards & Sons,* 12.

10. Martin, oral history, 3, NYSE.

11. James Neal Primm, *A Foregone Conclusion* (Boulder: Pruett, 1981), 10.

12. Martin Towey, "St. Louis Had the Largest Hooverville," *Gateway Heritage* (Missouri Historical Society) 1 (Spring 1982): D22.

13. Joseph Seligman, *The Transformation of Wall Street,* rev. ed. (Boston: Northeastern University Press, 1995), 6.

14. Robert Sobel, *A History of the New York Stock Exchange* (New York: Weybridge & Talley, 1974), 18.

15. Seligman, *Transformation of Wall Street,* 20.

16. Raymond Moley, *After Seven Years* (New York: Harper & Brothers, 1939), 183.

17. Seligman, *Transformation of Wall Street,* 71.

18. Martin, oral history, 11, NYSE.

19. Martin to Presley Edwards, 4 November 1935, box 2, MPMHS.

20. Martin and Mead published the *Economic Forum* until March 1934, when they sold it to Frank Vanderlip, the former president of National City Bank of New York.

21. "Introduction," *Economic Forum Quarterly* (Winter 1932): 13.

22. Ibid., 21.

23. Martin, oral history, 21, NYSE.

24. Martin to Presley Edwards, 25 July 1935, box 2, MPMHS.

25. Martin, oral history, 22, NYSE.

26. Martin to his father, 24 September 1935, 3, box 2, MPMHS.

27. Ibid.

28. Ibid.

29. Martin to Presley Edwards, 25 May 1935, box 2, MPMHS.

30. Martin to Presley Edwards, 10 November 1935, box 2, MPMHS.

31. Martin to Presley Edwards, 21 October 1935, box 2, MPMHS.

32. Martin, notes for an undated speech, box 8, MPMHS.

33. William O. Douglas, *Go East, Young Man: The Autobiography of William O. Douglas* (New York: Dell, 1974), 155.

34. Douglas Gilbert, "New Brooms on Wall Street," *New York World Telegram*, 22 February 1938, vol. 3, MPMHS.

35. *New York Times*, 15 October 1937, 1, 12.

36. Ibid.

37. Ibid.

38. Ibid.

39. Ibid.

40. Ibid.

41. Sobel, *History of the New York Stock Exchange*, 34.

42. Ganson Purcell, memo, "Problems of Organization and Administration of the New York Stock Exchange," n.d., Douglas SEC Commissioner Files, box 13, SECA.

43. Conway Committee Commemorative Volume, NYSE.

44. Paul Shields, interview, Conway Committee Commemorative Volume, NYSE.

45. Ibid.

46. Ibid.

47. Martin, oral history, 40–47, NYSE. See also Sobel, *History of the New York Stock Exchange*, 38.

48. Summary of Conway report, reprinted in the *New York Herald Tribune*, 28 January 1938.

49. Sobel, *History of the New York Stock Exchange*, 43; minutes of New York Stock Exchange Governing Board meetings, 1937 volume, NYSE.

50. Sobel, *History of the New York Stock Exchange*, 44.

51. Dean Acheson, "Report upon the Circumstances Surrounding the Failure of Richard Whitney & Co.," NYSE.

52. In his NYSE oral history, Martin states that he discovered that Whitney had misappropriated assets belonging to Whitney's cousin and firm client, Mary Stevens Baird. The Baird misappropriation was ultimately one of the actions used by the NYSE to expel Whitney.

53. Douglas, *Go East, Young Man*, 289.

54. John W. Hanes, SEC commissioner, memo, "The Events of March 7 and 8, 1938," Douglas SEC Commissioner Files, box 13, SECA.

55. *New York Times,* 24 March 1938, Leslie Gould Papers, box 30, Hofstra University.

56. Carle Conway to Lawrence Oakley, 11 March 1938, box 1, MPMHS.

57. Malcolm W. Martin, interview by author, 31 January 1995.

Chapter 3. Cleaning the Augean Stables of Capitalism

1. "Symbol of the Wall Street Revolt," *New York Times,* magazine section, 15 May 1938, vol. 3, MPMHS.

2. Joseph Seligman, *The Transformation of Wall Street,* rev. ed. (Boston: Northeastern University Press, 1995), 176.

3. *New York Times,* 16 May 1938, vol. 2, MPMHS.

4. Ibid.

5. Ganson Purcell, memo, "May 18 Conference," Douglas SEC Commissioner Files, folder 19, SECA.

6. *New York Times,* 5 February 1938, Leslie Gould Papers, box 33, Hofstra University.

7. *New York Times,* 25 April 1938, vol. 3, MPMHS.

8. Seligman, *The Transformation of Wall Street,* 176.

9. The reformers Martin promoted to positions of Exchange Committee leadership were all experienced and influential members of the Exchange, but they faced majorities of Old Guard members on their committees.

10. William McChesney Martin Jr., oral history, 74, NYSE.

11. Ibid., 75.

12. Ibid., 76.

13. Ibid., 78.

14. Ibid., 79.

15. NYSE press release, 31 October 1938, box 7, MPMHS.

16. *New York Times,* 1 November 1938, 1, Leslie Gould Papers, box 33, Hofstra University.

17. Ibid., 21.

18. William O. Douglas to Martin, 1 November 1938, accompanying SEC report "In the Matter of Richard Whitney," box 7, MPMHS.

19. William O. Douglas, *Democracy and Finance* (New Haven: Yale University Press, 1940), 8.

20. Douglas to Roosevelt, 12 April 1939, Douglas SEC Commissioner Files, box 14, SECA.

21. Douglas to General Robert Wood, 5 January 1939, Douglas SEC Commissioner Files, box 25, SECA.

22. Martin, notes for an undated speech, box 8, MPMHS.

23. Seligman, *The Transformation of Wall Street,* 211.

24. Douglas press release, as quoted in Douglas, *Democracy and Finance,* 123.

25. For a description of Douglas's poker playing experiences with Roosevelt, see Douglas, *Go East, Young Man: The Autobiography of William O. Douglas* (New York: Dell, 1974), 330–39.

26. Ibid., 441.

27. Robert Sobel, *A History of the New York Stock Exchange* (New York: Weybridge & Talley, 1974), 66.

28. Earle Bailie to William O. Douglas, 22 June 1939, accusing Douglas of leaking the story, box 8, MPMHS.

29. *New York Times,* 1 September 1939, carried the Public Examining Board's report and recommendations in full.

30. Ganson Purcell, "Conference with William McChesney Martin, September 15, 1939," Frank SEC Commissioner Files, box 30, SECA.

31. For more information on the Exchange during these years, see Sobel, *History of the New York Stock Exchange,* chapters 4 and 6; "Letter from a Blighted Area: Wall Street," *Fortune,* November 1941, 38–41.

32. Martin, "Meeting with the Securities and Exchange Commission, March 6, 1940," box 8, MPMHS.

33. Ibid., 3

34. Ibid.

35. Ibid.

36. Martin, speech to NYSE members, 5 March 1941, quoted in Sobel, *History of the New York Stock Exchange,* 98.

37. Sobel estimates in *History of the New York Stock Exchange,* 94, that the OTC represented 30–40 percent of total volume in the "more actively traded NYSE issues."

38. Representative John McCormack to SEC Chairman Jerome Frank, 15 April 1940, Frank SEC Commissioner Files, box 20.

39. Frank to McCormack, 17 April 1940, Frank SEC Commissioner Files, box 20. SECA.

40. U.S. Securities and Exchange Commission Report, "On the Problem of Multiple Exchange Trading," 1–3, 22 October 1940, SEC Archives.

41. The RFC was in the process of increasing its borrowing capacity by $1.5 billion and already had been involved in financing the expansion or creation of over eight hundred defense plants with a total value of $2 billion. The resources of the private financial markets, and particularly the Exchange, were a small fraction of the RFC's capacity. On an average day, U.S. Steel, one of the most active stocks on the Exchange, would trade shares worth no more than $450,000, and trades of blocks of shares were typically done on the OTC market

42. NYSE press release, 27 February 1941, Press Release File, NYSE.

43. Martin, "Address to a General Meeting of the Membership of the Exchange," speech to NYSE membership, 5 March 1941, President Martin Speeches, NYSE.

44. Ibid., 22.

45. Ibid., 11.

46. Ibid., 13.

47. Ibid.

48. Ibid., 20.

49. Sylvia F. Porter, "Democracy Goes to Town," *New York Herald Tribune,* 6 March 1941, Leslie Gould Papers, box 35, Hofstra University.

50. Philip Russell, managing partner of Fenner & Beane, to Martin, 6 April 1941, box 8, MPMHS.

51. Lawrence Oakley, former governor of the NYSE, 22 April 1941, box 8, MPMHS.

52. Editorial, *Newsweek*, 17 March 1941.

Chapter 4. From President to Private and Back Again

1. Hershey, quoted in a *Time* magazine profile of Martin, 14 September 1956.

2. Sources are an article in the September 1998 issue of the *Federal Reserve Bank of Minneapolis Monthly* by former Fed Governor Andrew Brimmer, and Malcolm W. Martin, interview by author, 8 October 1997.

3. Obituary of Martin, *Washington Post,* 29 July 1998, B10.

4. William McChesney Martin Jr., oral history, 98, NYSE.

5. H. H. Arnold to General O. W. Griswold, box 1, MPMHS.

6. Peter J. Michel, "Mission to Moscow: William McChesney Martin Jr.'s World War II Trip to the Soviet Union," *Gateway Heritage* (Missouri Historical Society) (Summer 1993): 55.

7. William H. Standley, quoted in Robert H. Jones, *The Roads to Russia: U.S. Lend-Lease to the Soviet Union* (Norman: University of Oklahoma Press, 1969), 81.

8. Martin, quoted in Michel, "Mission to Moscow," 50.

9. Ibid., 51.

10. Ibid.

11. Jones, *The Roads to Russia,* 101.

12. Ibid., 122.

13. Ibid.

14. Martin, "Aid to Russia," unpublished and undated speech, box 9, MPMHS.

15. Ibid.

16. Martin, speech to the American Institute Dedicated to American-Soviet Postwar Relations, 19 October 1944, box 9, MPMHS.

17. Ibid.

18. Ibid.

19. Ibid.

20. Jones, *The Roads to Russia.* Jones wrote: "Mounting evidence indicated that the Russians had abused American generosity, giving or selling lend-lease supplies to Iran, Poland, Rumania, and Bulgaria, and ignoring repeated American protests" (104).

21. Ibid., 286.

22. Martin to Colonel Hilton Railey, 27 September 1945, box 9, MPMHS.

23. Ibid.

24. Martin to Matthew Connelly, secretary to Truman, 26 November 1945, President's Official File, box 27B, HSTPL.

25. Vinson to Truman, 29 August 1945, President's Official File, box 27B, HSTPL.

26. Report of the National Advisory Council on International Monetary and Financial Problems, 8 March 1946, box 12, MPMHS.

27. Martin's position was explained in a letter to Truman, 6 February 1946, President's Official File, box 27B, HSTPL.

28. Earl Mazo, "The Export-Import Bank of the U.S., 1934–1974" (U.S. Export-Import Bank, Washington, D.C., 1976), 115.

29. "U.S.-French Financial Negotiations, Top Committee Meeting Minutes," 25 March 1946, NAC File, NA.

30. NAC, minutes of meeting, 25 April 1946, 3, NAC Files, NA.

31. Ibid., 4.

32. NAC, minutes of meeting, 20 March 1946, 3, NAC Files, NA.

33. Ibid.

34. In his NYSE oral history, 98, Martin remarked: "One of the few people in power that I ever got to know well was general Marshall. I'd been running the Marshall Foundation . . . I became very fond of him."

35. Malcolm W. Martin, interview by author, 31 January 1995.

36. These respective positions are described in Martin's letter to Truman dated 20 December 1946, the day of the meeting. President's Official File, box 27B, HSTPL.

37. "Big Risk in Political Loans," *Washington Daily News,* 26 March 1947, 18.

38. Martin expressed his gratitude for Truman's words of support in a letter to Truman, 20 December 1946, box 18, MPMHS.

39. Ibid.

40. Mazo, "The Export-Import Bank of the U.S.," 118.

41. *Business Week,* 2 June 1951, 60.

42. Martin to Truman, 20 December 1946.

43. U.S Export-Import Bank, *5th Semiannual Report to Congress* (Washington, D.C.: Government Printing Office, 1947), 3.

44. NAC, minutes of meeting, 25 March 1948, 4, NAC Files, NA.

45. Ibid., 5.

46. Ibid.

47. Martin, "Trip to Bogota," 28 March 1948, box 15, MPMHS.

48. Ibid., 6.

49. George C. Marshall, speech to International Conference of American States, 1 April 1948, box 15:5, MPMHS.

50. Ibid.

51. Martin, "Trip to Bogota," 6.

52. Cynthia Martin, interview by author, 10 February 1997.

53. Malcolm W. Martin, interview by author, 31 January 1995: "It hit Bill pretty hard and was one of his biggest disappointments at that time."

54. Martin to Truman. cable, 9 November 1948, President's Personal File, box 27B, HSTPL.

55. Mazo, "The Export-Import Bank of the U.S.," 118.

56. Ibid., 119.

57. NAC, minutes of meeting, 4 February 1949, 2, NAC Files, NA.

58. Martin to Truman, 19 January 1949, President's Official File, box 27B, HSTPL.

Chapter 5. From Crisis to Crisis

1. William McChesney Martin Jr., statement to U.S. Senate Committee on Banking and Currency, *Nomination of William McChesney Martin Jr.,* hearings, 82nd Cong., 1st sess., 1951, 7.

2. Leon Keyserling, oral history, 10 May 1971, 156, HSTPL.

3. *U.S. News and World Report,* 17 October 1947, 48.

4. Martin, quoted in Richard Austin Smith, "Bill Martin: A Talent for Timing," *Fortune,* October 1955, 154.

5. Cripps, quoted in E. H. Collin, "U.K. Government Firm on Devaluation Issue," *New York Times,* 23 May 1949, 9.

6. NAC, minutes of meeting, 28 June 1949, 4, NAC Files, NA.

7. Ibid.

8. Ibid.

9. Alec Cairncross and Barry Eichengreen, *Sterling in Decline* (Oxford: Basil Blackwell, 1983), 118.

10. Ibid.

11. Ibid.

12. A task force consisting of three junior ministers — Hugh Gaitskell, Harold Wilson, and Douglas Jay — also was a pivotal influence in persuading the Attlee cabinet to approve devaluation. B. W. E. Alford, *Britain and the World Economy since 1880* (New York: Longman, 1996), 197.

13. Martin to McCloy, 18 September 1949, box 14, MPMHS.

14. *Business Week,* 2 June 1951, 60.

15. Ibid.

16. Marriner Eccles, testimony to U.S. Congress, Joint Committee on the Economic Report of the President, hearings, 82nd Cong., 1st sess., 1951, 158.

17. Truman repeatedly referred to losses he had sustained on government Liberty savings bonds when he sold them upon his return home from World War I. Snyder tried to point out that savings bonds from World War II could not lose their principal value as long as the bonds were held to maturity, which Truman had not done. Truman made no effort to understand the difference.

18. In a 1954 oral history, Truman referred to his decision on Eccles: "I didn't like the way Eccles first spoke in the Senate. He talked one way to them and another way to the President. I didn't want a chairman like that." HSTPL.

19. Allan Sproul, "The Accord: A Landmark in the First Fifty Years of the Federal Reserve System," *Monthly Review* (Federal Reserve Bank of New York), November, 1964, 230.

20. Harry S. Truman, *Public Papers of the Presidents: Harry S. Truman: 1950* (Washington, D.C.: Government Printing Office, 1957), 113–14.

21. Allan Sproul, confidential files, note dated 28 September 1950, quoted in an unpublished article, "Allan Sproul and the Treasury-Federal Reserve Accord," Federal Reserve Bank of New York library.

22. FOMCM, 31 January 1951, 24.

23. Truman to McCabe, 1 February 1951, Snyder Papers, Federal Reserve 1951, box 13, HSTPL.

24. FOMCM, 31 January 1951, 25.

25. Editorial, *New York Times,* quoted in *Newsweek,* 12 February 1951.

26. *New York Times,* 2 March 1951, 21.

27. McCabe to Truman, Federal Reserve Board, box 20, MPMHS.

28. Smith, "Bill Martin," 236.

29. Martin's version of these negotiations was made public during an extended interview with Smith in connection with his *Fortune* article, "Bill Martin." Other commentary is from Herbert Stein, *The Fiscal Revolution in America,* rev. ed. (Washington, D.C.: AEI Press, 1990); Sproul, "The Accord"; and brief personal schedules and notes from the Martin Papers at the Missouri Historical Society.

30. E. A. Bartelt, "A proposal" draft Accord agreement, presented to the FOMC on 1 March 1951, box 19, MPMHS.

31. In fact, the interagency report was not completed until 31 May 1951, even though the results of the Accord were available and incorporated into it.

32. FOMC correspondence, attachment to notes dated 26 February 1951, Sproul Papers, Federal Reserve Bank of New York library.

33. FOMCM, 1–2 March 1951, 13.

34. Smith, "Bill Martin," 238.

35. FOMCM, 1–2 March 1951, 18.

36. Ibid., 19.

37. Ibid., 20.

38. Ibid., 20–21.

39. FOMCM, 3 March 1951, 12.

40. *Federal Reserve Bulletin,* March 1951, 267.

41. Smith, "Bill Martin," 238.

42. Sproul, "The Accord," 236.

43. In his comments, Snyder remarked, "Allan Sproul . . . was constantly needled by the New York bankers. The financial center of the country used to be in New York, but now it's moved to Washington . . . they decided that it was time to recapture control of government financing and bring it to New York where the decisions would be made." John Snyder interview, 10 August 1954, 31, Post-Presidential Files, HSTPL.

44. Snyder, oral history, HSTPL; Truman interjection during joint interview on 8 October, 1954, 33.

45. Ibid.

46. Although both Martin and McDonald were residents of Washington, D.C., their home districts were considered to be the location in which they had spent the majority of their nongovernmental career.

47. See note 17.

48. James Reston, "Farewell to the Happy Puritan," *New York Times,* 26 January 1971, 25.

49. Martin, Transcript from a talk, "Reminiscences and Reflections," reprinted in *Hot Springs (Virginia) News,* 26 January 1971, vol. 7, MPMHS.

50. Ibid.

51. Martin, testimony, *Nomination of William McChesney Martin Jr.,* 25.

52. Ibid., 26.

53. Ibid.

54. Ibid., 12.

55. Ibid.

56. *The Federal Reserve Act*, Public Law 43, 63rd Cong., 2nd sess., 1913, sections 12, 13, 14.

57. Treasury Secretary McAdoo, quoted in Donald Kettl, *Leadership at the Fed* (New Haven: Yale University Press, 1986), 23.

58. Carter Glass, speech recorded in the *Congressional Record*, quoted in Benjamin Klebaner, *American Commercial Banking: A History* (Boston: Twayne, 1990), 115.

59. The Committee of Governors (the original title for Reserve Bank presidents was governor) on Centralized Execution of Purchases and Sales of Government Securities by Federal Reserve Banks was formed in 1922.

60. Quote from oral history of Eccles associate, Merritt Sherman, included in Kettl, *Leadership at the Fed,* 52.

61. Kettl, *Leadership at the Fed,* 53.

62. Robert Hetzel, interview by author, 23 March 2001.

63. FOMCM, 13 March 1951, 13.

64. Ibid.

65. FOMCM, 17 May 1951, 9.

66. Ibid.

67. First National City Bank of New York, *Monthly Letter,* April 1951, 40.

68. FOMCM, 4 October 1951, 9.

69. First National City Bank of New York, *Monthly Letter,* January 1952, 5.

70. U.S. Congress, Joint Committee on the Economic Report, Subcommittee on General Credit Control, *Monetary Policy and Management of Public Debt,* 82nd Cong., 2nd sess., 1952, 78.

71. Robert Holland, former FOMC secretary and later Fed governor, interview by author, 27 January 2000.

72. Joint Economic Committee, *Monetary Policy and Management of Public Debt,* 76.

73. Ibid., 86.

74. Kettl, *Leadership at the Fed,* 76. The widely quoted concept was often credited to Sproul, but was actually originated by Robert Roosa, a vice president at the New York Fed at the time.

75. Joint Economic Committee, *Monetary Policy and Management of Public Debt,* 508.

76. Ibid., 96.

77. Ibid., 94.

78. Ibid., 56.

79. Ibid.

80. A quote from Frank Morris, president of the Federal Reserve Bank of Boston, as told to him by Martin. Recorded in a memorial tribute to Martin at the Federal Reserve Board in 1999.

81. Herbert Stein, *The Fiscal Revolution in America,* rev. ed. (Washington, D.C.: AEI Press, 1990). Stein points out that a public opinion poll on 26 February 1951 showed that only 26 percent of those surveyed approved of the way Truman was handling the presidency, 288–89.

Chapter 6. By Fits and Starts

1. Dwight D. Eisenhower, *Public Papers of the President of the United States: Dwight D. Eisenhower, 1953* (Washington, D.C.: Government Printing Office, 1960), 19.

2. Quoted in John W. Sloan, *Eisenhower and the Management of Prosperity* (Lawrence: University Press of Kansas, 1991), 70.

3. Quotation from Eisenhower's State of the Union address in Raymond Saulnier, *The Constructive Years: The U.S. Economy under Eisenhower* (Lanham, Md.: University Press of America, 1991), 9.

4. William McChesney Martin Jr., remarks to Reserve Bank Chairman's Conference, 8 December 1953, Martin Speeches, 10, Federal Reserve Library.

5. FOMCM, 6 January 1953, 8.

6. Emmett John Hughes, *The Ordeal of Power* (New York: Atheneum, 1963), 3.

7. Elmo Richardson, *The Presidency of Dwight Eisenhower* (Lawrence: Regents Press of Kansas, 1979), 6.

8. Dwight Eisenhower to Milton Eisenhower, 6 January 1954, Milton Eisenhower Papers, DDEPL.

9. Hughes, *Ordeal of Power,* 73.

10. U.S. Congress, Joint Committee on the Economic Report, *Conflicting Views on Monetary Policy;* 84th Cong., 2nd sess., 1956, 74.

11. Ibid., 101.

12. Martin, "The Transition to Free Markets," speech reprinted in the *Federal Reserve Bulletin,* May 1953, 333.

13. Ibid., 331.

14. The phrase "depth, breadth and resiliency" originated with Winfield Riefler, who was so enamored of it that it was rumored he named his son Donald B. Riefler so that he would have the same initials.

15. Martin, "The Transition to Free Markets," 332.

16. Ibid., 333.

17. Allan Sproul to Henry Alexander of J. P. Morgan & Co., 12 March 1954, Sproul Papers, FOMC correspondence, 1954, folder 1, Federal Reserve Bank of New York library.

18. FOMCM, 24 September 1953, 17.

19. FOMCM, 11 June 1953, 19.

20. Sproul, personal notes for speech to presidents of Federal Reserve Banks, 12 March 1954, Sproul Papers, FOMC correspondence, 1954, folder 1, Federal Reserve Bank of New York library.

21. Martin, presentation to Joint Economic Committee on the Economic Report, 11 March 1952, Martin Speeches, 2, Federal Reserve Library.

22. Martin, speech to the Chairman's Conference for Federal Reserve Bank directors, 8 December 1953, Martin Speeches, 7, Federal Reserve Library.

23. Martin, speech to the American Cotton Manufacturers Institute, 27 March 1953, Martin Speeches, 3, Federal Reserve Library.

24. Robert Holland, interview by author, 27 January 2000.

25. FOMCM, 24 September 1953, 29.

26. Robert Holland, interview by author, 27 January 2000.

27. Malcolm W. Martin, interview by author, 8 October 1997.

28. Robert Holland, interview by author, 19 June 2000.

29. Ibid.

30. *New York Herald Tribune,* 15 April 1953, 75.

31. FOMCM, 6 May 1953, 2.

32. Martin, speech to Pacific Northwest Conference on Banking, 9 April 1954, Martin Speeches, 14, Federal Reserve Library.

33. Ibid., 15.

34. Ibid.

35. Ibid., 13.

36. FOMCM, 23 June 1953, 8.

37. Ibid., 12.

38. Applying the commonly accepted deposit-expansion multiplier, a $1.1 billion reduction in reserve requirements would enable the banking system to expand loans or investments by $6.6 billion without increasing reserves. Such a loan increase would amount to 7 percent of existing loans, a substantial increase in the short term.

39. First National City Bank of New York, *Monthly Letter,* July 1953, 75.

40. The impact of capital losses on Treasury portfolios can be very significant. If the banks had been forced to sell 25 percent of their $65 billion in Treasury securities, in theory they would have to absorb $800 million in capital losses between October 1952 and June 1953. This amount represented about 40 percent of their before-tax earnings in 1953.

41. James Knipe, *The Federal Reserve and the American Dollar* (Chapel Hill: University of North Carolina Press, 1965), 89.

42. Allan Sproul argued that Fed purchases in the long-term market would have produced a much quicker result. There are many studies critical of the "Bills Only" policy; see Daniel Ahearn, *Federal Reserve Policy Reappraised: 1951–1959* (New York: Columbia University Press, 1963) for an extended discussion. The "Bills Only" policy is Martin's most controversial decision.

43. FOMCM, 11 June 1953, 13.

44. "A Five Year Balancing Act," *Newsweek,* 11 February 1956, 148.

45. FOMCM, 7 July 1953, 10.

46. FOMCM, 6 October 1953, 5.

47. FOMCM, 23 November 1953, 11.

48. Martin, quotation from Martin's 1956 renomination hearing, in Bernard S. Katz, *Biographical Dictionary of the Board of Governors of the Federal Reserve* (New York: Greenwood, 1994), 197.

49. FOMCM, 5 January 1954, 10.

50. Martin, testimony to U.S. Congress, Joint Economic Committee on the Economic Report of the President, *Hearings on the Economic Report of 1954,* 83rd Cong., 2nd sess., 1954, 168.

51. Minnich cabinet notes, 2 April 1952, 52, DDEPL.

52. FOMCM, 3 March 1954, 33.

53. FOMCM, 8 September 1954, 6.

54. William McChesney Martin III, interview by author, 2 July 2001.

55. Arthur Burns, speech to the Detroit Economic Club, 18 October 1954, *U.S. News & World Report*, 29 October 1954, 44.

56. Ibid., 46.

57. *New York Times* editorial attached to letter of congratulations from D. Eisenhower to Arthur Burns, dated 23 October 1954, Burns Papers, 1956–57, DDEPL.

58. FOMCM, 9 November 1954, 10.

59. Ibid., 13.

60. FOMCM, 7 December 1954, 6.

61. Ibid., 7.

62. FOMCM, 2 March 1955, 64.

63. Ibid.

64. Ibid.

65. George Humphrey, Minnich cabinet notes, 4 March 1955, 39, DDEPL.

66. Sproul, notes from presentation to American Bankers Association Monetary Conference at Arden House, 18 March 1955, Sproul Papers, FOMC correspondence, 1955, New York Federal Reserve Bank library.

67. FOMCM, 2 March 1955, 8.

68. Ibid.

69. FOMCM, 12 April 1955, 14.

70. FOMCM, 2 August 1955, 14.

71. FOMCM, 23 August 1955, 8–9.

72. First National City Bank of New York, *Monthly Letter*, December 1955, 135.

73. FOMCM, 6 June 1955, 12.

74. Martin, quoted in "A Five Year Balancing Act," *Business Week*, 12 February 1956, 147.

75. Ibid., 150.

76. Ibid.

77. Martin, testimony to U.S. Congress, Joint Committee on the Economic Report of the President, *Hearings on the Economic Report of 1956*, 84th Cong., 2nd sess., 1956, 302.

78. FOMCM, 30 November 1955, 4.

79. Martin, testimony, *Hearings on the Economic Report of 1956*, 302.

80. Ibid., 304.

81. Arthur Burns, presentation to the cabinet, 23 January 1956, Staff Secretary Records, 1952–61, box 4, file C31, DDEPL.

82. Burns, telephone call to President Eisenhower relating Martin's intention, 24 January 1956, Ann Whitman Files, DDE Diary Series, box 12, DDEPL.

83. FOMCM, 24 January 1956, 16–17.

84. Ibid., 17.

85. Cabinet meeting, 20 April 1956, W. H. Office of the Staff Secretary, Cabinet Series, file C31 (3), 66, DDEPL.

86. Saulnier, *The Constructive Years*, 86.

87. Humphrey, Minnich cabinet notes, 20 April 1956, 62, DDEPL.

88. Ibid., 63.

89. FOMCM, 9 May 1956, 22.

90. Saulnier, *The Constructive Years,* 87.

91. Sproul, quoted by Malcolm W. Martin, interview by author, 8 October 1997.

92. FOMCM, 27 November 1956, 9.

Chapter 7. Trying to Manage Prosperity

1. Dwight Eisenhower, Minnich cabinet notes, 9 January 1957, DDEPL.

2. Transcript from Humphrey's press conference, quoted in Raymond Saulnier, *The Constructive Years: The U.S. Economy under Eisenhower* (Lanham, Md.: University Press of America, 1991), 103.

3. Fed document, 18 February 1957, "Conversations with Federal Reserve Board Chairman, 1957–60," Saulnier Papers, 1938–86, DDEPL.

4. FOMCM, 5 March 1957, 8.

5. Saulnier, minutes of meeting, 12 April 1957, "Conversations with Federal Reserve Board Chairman."

6. William McChesney Martin Jr., "A Financial Education," speech, 26 March 1936, 3, MPMHS.

7. Ibid., 5.

8. Martin, presentation to the Senate Finance Committee, 13 August 1957, *Wall Street Journal,* 19 August 1957.

9. Ibid.

10. Ibid.

11. Ibid.

12. Ibid.

13. Henry C. Wallich, "Postwar United States Monetary Policy Appraised," in *United States Monetary Policy,* ed. Neil H. Jacoby (New York: Columbia University Press, 1958), 101.

14. Martin, testimony to the Joint Economic Committee, 5 February 1957, Martin Speeches, 7, Federal Reserve Library,

15. Ibid.

16. Ibid., 6.

17. Martin, speech to the Association of American Soap Producers, 24 January 1957, *Commercial and Financial Chronicle,* 31 January 1957.

18. Ibid.

19. Ibid.

20. FOMCM, 16 April 1957, 37.

21. Dwight Eisenhower, *Mandate for Change* (Garden City, N.Y.: Doubleday, 1963), 235.

22. *Time,* 29 November 1959, 22.

23. FOMCM, 28 May 1957, 34.

24. FOMCM, 9 July 1957, 13.

25. Ibid., 35.

26. Reported by Robert Holland, interview by author, 27 January 2000. Holland relates that Martin's comment—which became legendary within the Fed—was applied to meetings in which it seemed almost impossible to paper over the differences.

27. FOMCM, 20 August 1957, 38.

28. Holland, interview.

29. FOMCM, 30 July 1957, 38.

30. Sumner Slichter, "Five Trends Shape the Business Future," *Nation's Business,* February 1957, 96.

31. Edwin L. Dale Jr., "Martin Criticizes 2% Inflation," *New York Times,* 16 March 1957.

32. Martin, testimony to Senate Finance Committee, *Wall Street Journal,* 19 August 1957.

33. Ibid.

34. Saulnier, minutes of meeting, 8 August 1957, "Conversations with Federal Reserve Board Chairman."

35. Ibid.

36. Saulnier, oral history, "The Oral History Project," 1967, 37, Columbia University.

37. According to Donald Kettl in *Leadership at the Fed* (New Haven: Yale University Press, 1986), the Roosevelt administration established the Monetary and Fiscal Advisory Board to meet with the president. The group included the secretary of the Treasury, the Fed chairman, the director of the budget, and the chairman of the Advisory Commission on Natural Resources. The group fell into disuse, but served as the model for Hauge.

38. Saulnier, minutes of meeting, 24 September 1957, "Conferences with Federal Reserve Board Chairman."

39. Kettl, *Leadership at the Fed,* 95.

40. FOMCM, 12 November 1957, 48.

41. Ibid.

42. Edwin L. Dale Jr., *New York Times,* 24 October 1957.

43. Sauliner, minutes of meeting, 31 December 1957, "Conferences with Federal Reserve Board Chairman."

44. Robert Anderson, Minnich cabinet notes, 18 October 1957, DDEPL.

45. First National City Bank of New York, *Monthly Letter,* January 1958, 4.

46. FOMCM, 11 February 1958, 33.

47. Robert Hetzel, interview by author, 17 December 2000.

48. FOMCM, 25 March 1958, 10.

49. Martin, testimony to Senate Finance Committee hearings, 22 April 1958, Martin Speeches, 8, Federal Reserve Library.

50. Ibid., 8.

51. Martin, Hauge minutes of ad hoc committee meeting, 15 May 1958, staff notes, DDE Diary Series, DDEPL.

52. Ibid.

53. Dwight D. Eisenhower, *The Public Papers of Dwight David Eisenhower: 1958* (Washington, D.C.: Government Printing Office, 1960), 452.

54. James Mitchell, quoted in Herbert Stein, *The Fiscal Revolution in America* (Washington, D.C.: AEI Press, 1990), 344.

55. FOMCM, 27 May 1958, 40.

56. First National City Bank of New York, *Monthly Letter,* August 1958, 89.

57. FOMCM, 8 July 1958, 42.

58. First National City Bank of New York, *Monthly Letter,* August, 1958, 90.

59. FOMCM, 29 July 1958, 18.

60. Ibid., 52.

61. FOMCM, 9 September 1958, 11.

62. Ibid.

63. Ibid., 53.

64. FOMCM, 16 December 1958, 37.

65. Walter Heller, testimony to U.S. Congress, Joint Committee on the Economic Report of the President, *Hearings on the Economic Report of 1959,* 86th Cong., 1st sess., 1959, 204.

66. Samuelson, testimony, ibid., 208.

67. Stein, testimony, ibid., 244.

68. Martin, testimony, ibid., 467.

69. Ibid.

70. Ibid., 468.

71. Robert Hetzel, interview by author, 18 December 2000.

72. Saulnier, oral history, part 2.

73. Ibid.

74. FOMCM, 13 October 1959, 33.

75. FOMCM, 15 December 1959, 42.

76. Ibid., 44.

77. Net reserves were used in and outside of the Fed as an indicator of the Fed's pressure on the banking system. A condition of net free reserves existed when total member bank excess reserves (reserves in excess of required reserve levels) exceeded member bank reserve borrowings from the Fed. A condition of net borrowed reserves existed when the opposite was true. Net free reserves indicated easy credit conditions and vice versa.

78. FOMCM, 1 March 1960, 32.

79. These targets are described primarily in terms of "net reserve" amounts, but the account manager was usually given latitude to "feel his way" toward these targets and to exercise judgment in meeting the targets or achieving another amount deemed appropriate in view of credit conditions.

80. FOMCM, 9 February 1960, 39.

81. Ibid., 40.

82. FOMCM, 15 December 1959, 44.

83. FOMCM, 9 February 1960, 40.

84. Arthur Schlesinger Jr., quoted in Max Ways, "A New Mask for Big Government," *Fortune,* April 1960, 115.

85. Henry Wallich, undated article submitted to the *Yale Review.* The article was circulated within the Eisenhower administration by Gabriel Hauge. Central files OF 114, 1956, box 558, DDEPL.

86. Stein, *The Fiscal Revolution in America,* 354.

87. Saulnier, *The Constructive Years,* 125.

88. Stein, *The Fiscal Revolution in America,* 357.

89. Martin, testimony to the U.S. Congress, Joint Economic Committee on the Economic Report of the President, *Hearings on the Economic Report of 1960,* 86th Cong., 2nd sess., 1960, 167.

90. Ibid., 169.

91. Saulnier, Minnich cabinet notes, 26 February 1960, DDEPL.

92. FOMCM, 12 April 1960, 6.

93. Ibid., 39.

94. FOMCM, 26 July 1960, 46.

95. John F. Kennedy, quoted in "Kennedy Firm on Dollar," *New York Times,* 22 October 1960, 48.

96. Robert Anderson, quoted in "Anderson Reassures Central Bankers," *New York Times,* 21 October 1960, 54.

97. FOMCM, 13 September 1960, 43.

98. John Maynard Keynes, box 28, MPMHS.

99. FOMCM, 22 November 1960, 41.

100. Ibid.

101. John Sloane, *Eisenhower and the Management of Prosperity* (Lawrence: University Press of Kansas, 1960), 154.

102. Ibid.

Chapter 8. Gunfight on the New Frontier

1. FOMCM, 13 December 1960, 36.

2. FOMCM, 22 November 1960, 42.

3. W. H. Lawrence, "Kennedy Denies Deal with Dillon on Treasury Job," *New York Times,* 24 December 1960, 1.

4. Ibid.

5. Martin reviewed his thought process at this time a few months later in a discussion with Heller and the other CEA members. See James Tobin, memo, 30 May 1961, Heller Papers, box 19, JFKPL.

6. Ibid.

7. Samuelson Report, quoted in *U.S. News and World Report,* 16 January 1961, 86.

8. "Mr. Kennedy and the Recession," *New York Times,* 22 January 1961.

9. Douglas Dillon, quoted in Richard Mooney, "Dillon Foresees a Budget Deficit," *New York Times,* 12 January 1961.

10. Walter Heller, oral history, in *The President and the Council of Economic Advisers,* ed. Erwin Hargrove and Samuel Morley (Boulder: Westview, 1984), 189.

11. Ibid.

12. Walter Heller, CEA oral history, 186, JFKPL.

13. "The Economics of the Candidates," *Fortune,* October 1960, 138.

14. British economist John Maynard Keynes posited that government spending, not monetary policy, was the primary mechanism for pushing an economy toward full utilization of its resources. He also argued that the government should be willing to incur budgetary deficits to counteract economic declines.

15. *Time,* 7 November 1960, 29.

16. Malcolm W. Martin, interview by author, 8 October 1997.

17. FOMCM, 25 October 1960, 17.

18. FOMCM, 13 December 1960, 42.

19. FOMCM, 7 February 1961, 45.

20. Ibid.

21. Ibid., 46.

22. Young to Martin, confidential memo, 20 February 1961, FOMC Memoranda Files, Federal Reserve Library.

23. FOMCM, 7 February 1961, 48.

24. Paul Samuelson, quoted in James Knipe, *The Federal Reserve and the American Dollar* (Chapel Hill: University of North Carolina Press, 1965), 277.

25. Daniel B. Ahearn, *Federal Reserve Policy Reappraised* (New York: Columbia University Press, 1965), 108.

26. Quoted in ibid.

27. Irving Bernstein, *Promises Kept: John F. Kennedy's New Frontier* (New York: Oxford University Press, 1991), 123.

28. Ibid.

29. Theodore Sorensen, *Kennedy* (New York: Harper & Row, 1965), 394.

30. Heller, oral history, in Hargrove and Morley, *The President and the Council of Economic Advisers,* 176.

31. Kennedy to Martin, 25 March 1961 (drafted by Heller for Kennedy's signature), President's Official Files, box 78, JFKPL.

32. Douglas Dillon, quoted in "A Dillon, a Dollar," *Fortune,* February 1961, 220.

33. Ibid.

34. Ibid., 95.

35. Ibid., 220.

36. Walter Heller, testimony to the Joint Economic Committee, 9 March 1961, reported in *U.S. News and World Report,* 20 March 1961, 99.

37. CEA, memo to Kennedy, "A Second Look at Economic Policy in 1961," 17 March 1961, Heller Papers, box 6a, JFKPL.

38. William McChesney Martin Jr., testimony to the Joint Economic Committee, 7 March 1961, Martin Speeches, Federal Reserve Library.

39. Ibid.

40. Heller, CEA oral history, 322, JFKPL.

41. John F. Kennedy, transcript of Kennedy press conference, *New York Times,* 16 March 1961.

42. Heller to Ken O'Donnell, in Donald Kettl, *Leadership at the Fed* (New Haven: Yale University Press, 1986), 93.

43. Heller to Kennedy, 31 May 1961, Heller Papers, box 19, JFKPL.

44. There is some indication that the open-market desk at the New York Fed knew how much activity in medium- and long-term Treasuries would be enough to satisfy the CEA analysts, leaving the Fed free to pursue its major open-market campaigns in the short-term end of the market.

45. Heller, oral history, 2:10, LBJPL.

46. Martin, oral history, 17, LBJPL.

47. Heller, CEA oral history, 2:9, LBJPL.

48. Heller, CEA oral history, 351, JFKPL.

49. Ibid., 349.

50. Heller recounted his recommendation to Kennedy in a telephone call to Dillon, 21 June 1961, "Notes of Telephone Conversations," Dillon Papers, JFKPL.

51. Heller, oral history, 349, JFKPL.

52. Heller, ever the wordsmith, initially called the campaign to tilt the yield curve "Operation Nudge." When he became frustrated with the Fed's lack of enthusiasm, he called for more decisive action and elevated the campaign title to "Operation Twist." Kettl, *Leadership at the Fed*, 99.

53. Editorial, *Journal of Commerce,* 3 November 1961, JFKPL.

54. Sorensen, *Kennedy,* 452.

55. Bernstein, *Promises Kept,* 142.

56. Sorensen, *Kennedy,* 459.

57. Ibid., 457.

58. Bernstein, *Promises Kept,* 145.

59. Heller to Kennedy, 3 May 1962, President's Official Files, box 89, JFKPL.

60. Sorensen, *Kennedy,* 423.

61. This description of the meeting is based on Sorensen's interpretation in *Kennedy* and Malcolm W. Martin in an interview by the author on 31 January 1995.

62. Richard Reeves, *President Kennedy: Profile of Power* (New York: Simon & Schuster, 1993), 319.

63. Charles A. Coombs, *The Arena of International Finance* (New York: John Wiley & Sons, 1976), 71.

64. FOMCM, 12 September 1961, 57.

65. FOMCM, 5 December 1961, 49.

66. Ibid.

67. Ibid.

68. Ibid., 51.

69. Ibid., 59.

70. Ibid., 69.

71. Ibid., 63.

72. Ibid., 69.

73. Ibid., 71.

74. Coombs, *The Arena of International Finance,* 16.

75. Robert Roosa, oral history, "The Oral History Project," 1966, 57, Columbia University. This statement is all the more remarkable in that Martin's decision to support Al Hayes for the presidency of the New York Fed ended Roosa's long-shot candidacy (he was only thirty-nine) for that job.

76. Robert Roosa, letter to the FOMC, included in the minutes of the FOMC meeting, 19 December 1961, 85.

77. Ibid., 86.

78. The general counsel of the Treasury concurred with this conclusion. See FOMC minutes of meeting on 9 January 1962, 61.

79. FOMCM, 13 February 1962, 78.

80. Ibid.

81. Ibid.

82. Coombs, *The Arena of International Finance,* 62.

83. FOMCM, 12 September 1961, 43.

84. Dillon to Kennedy, 22 December 1961, President's Official Files, box 89, JFKPL.

85. FOMCM, 19 December 1961, 99.

86. Ibid.

87. Coombs, *The Arena of International Finance,* 73.

88. James Tobin, CEA oral history, 336, JFKPL.

89. Heller, CEA oral history, 329, JFKPL.

90. *New York Times,* 8 February 1963, 10.

91. Walter Heller and James Tobin, discussion of the Martin reappointment, CEA oral history, 195, JFKPL. Heller commented that Kennedy emphasized Heller's effective working relationship with Martin and said, "Frankly I need Martin and Dillon."

92. Dillon to Kennedy, 16 January 1963, Dillon Papers, box 34, JFKPL.

93. Ibid.

94. Ibid.

95. Tobin, confidential addendum to the CEA oral history, JFKPL.

96. Ibid.

97. Ibid.

98. Editorial, *New York Times,* 10 February 1963.

99. Ibid.

100. Paul Samuelson and Robert Solow to Kennedy, 13 July 1962, President's Official Files, box 89, JFKPL.

101. Kennedy, press conference, 7 June 1962, in Bernstein, *Promises Kept,* 148.

102. Ibid.

103. Paul Samuelson and Robert Solow to Kennedy, 15 November 1962, President's Official Files, box 90, JFKPL.

104. Sorensen, *Kennedy,* 430.

105. FOMCM, 18 December 1962, 61.

106. Ibid., 29.

107. U.S. Congress, Joint Committee on the Economic Report of the President, 88th Cong., 1st sess., *January 1963 Economic Report of the President,* 1963, 355.

108. Ibid., 322.

109. Ibid., 375.

110. Ibid., 394.

111. Walter Heller, speech to President's Advisory Committee on Labor-Management Policy, 14 November 1962, President's Official Files, box 63A, 11, JFKPL.

112. First National City Bank of New York, *Monthly Letter,* March 1963, 27.

113. Dillon's attitude toward Martin's position is indicated in his oral history at the Kennedy Presidential Library.

114. FOMCM, 5 March 1963, 42.

115. Ibid., 82.

116. FOMCM, 7 May 1963, 60.

117. FOMCM, 5 March 1963, 84.

118. Ibid.

119. Dillon to Kennedy, 17 April 1963, President's Official Files, box 90, 3, JFKPL.

120. FOMCM, 5 March 1963, 83.

121. Ibid.

122. Quadriad meeting minutes, 15 July 1963, President's Official Files, box 76, JFKPL.

123. Ibid.

124. Ibid.

125. *New York Times*, 21 July 1963, 1.

126. By early September, Heller's irritation was visible in an unusually critical memorandum to Kennedy, dated 9 September 1963, describing the Fed's weakening commitment to open-market operations in longer-term Treasuries and the Treasury Department's cooperation with the Fed. He titled it "The Twist [the administration's term for "Operation Nudge"] or the Screw." Heller Papers, box 20, JFKPL.

127. Heller, CEA oral history, 358, JFKPL: "Bob Roosa was certainly against Seymour Harris."

128. Seymour Harris to Kennedy, 27 September 1962, President's Official Files, box 90, JFKPL: "A ten year incumbency is enough for anyone."

129. Seymour Harris, *Economics of the Kennedy Years* (New York: Harper & Row, 1964). Harris wrote: "I have grave doubts about the whole theory of [Fed] independence,"113.

130. Dillon to Kennedy, 16 September 1963, Dillon Papers, box 35, JFKPL.

131. Ibid.

132. Heller to Kennedy, 2 October 1963 and 10 October 1963, Heller Papers, box 20, JFKPL.

133. Paul Samuelson, CEA oral history, 81, JFKPL.

134. Ibid.: "The president, before he was assassinated, still assumed he was going to appoint him [Harris] to the board." Heller: "That's absolutely unquestionable." 361.

135. Dillon to Kennedy, 23 September 1963, Dillon Papers, box 35, JFKPL.

136. FOMCM, 12 November 1963, 59.

137. Ibid.

138. Ibid.

139. Ibid., 60.

140. *Wall Street Journal*, 25 November 1963.

141. Ibid.

142. Coombs, *The Arena of International Finance*, 105.

143. Ibid., 106.

144. Tobin, addendum to CEA oral history, 193, JFKPL.

145. Martin Mayer, *The Fate of the Dollar* (New York: Times Books, 1980), 82.

146. FOMCM, 17 December 1963, 55.

Chapter 9. Sowing the Wind

1. Lyndon Johnson, speech to a joint session of Congress, *New York Times*, 28 November 1963.

2. Anthony Lewis, "Johnson Style," *New York Times,* 24 November 1963, 1.

3. Walter Heller, notes on meeting, 23 November 1963, Heller Papers, box 13, JFKPL.

4. Heller, oral history, LBJPL.

5. Johnson, speech to a joint session of Congress, *New York Times,* 28 November 1963.

6. Heller to Johnson, 31 December 1963, Heller Papers, box 20, JFKPL.

7. Heller to Johnson, 5 January 1964, box 21, MPMHS.

8. Ibid.

9. William McChesney Martin Jr., draft memo to Johnson, 9 January 1964, Martin Papers, box 21, MPMHS.

10. Taken from a calendar of Martin's meetings with Johnson, "The White House, Meetings with the President," Martin Papers, LBJPL.

11. Lyndon Johnson, *The Vantage Point* (New York: Holt Rinehart & Winston, 1971), 36.

12. "The President's Economic Report for 1964," *New York Times,* 26 January 1964, 1.

13. Paul Duke, "Banking Battler," *Wall Street Journal,* 30 April 1963, 1.

14. *Time,* 14 February 1964, 85.

15. Martin, quoted in "The Fed Remodels Itself," *Business Week,* 16 May 1964, 67.

16. Martin, oral history, 6, LBJPL.

17. Ibid.

18. "The Fed Remodels Itself," 70.

19. Erwin Hargrove and Samuel Morley, eds., *The President and the Council of Economic Advisers* (Boulder: Westview, 1984), 206.

20. FOMCM, 5 May 1964, 6.

21. FOMCM, 17 June 1964, 18.

22. Heller to Johnson, 15 September 1964, WHCF, 1963–65, LBJPL.

23. Martin, quoted in Hobart Rowen, "Fed Chief Concerned about Inflation," *Newsweek,* 5 October 1964, 36.

24. The Troika forecast for 1965 was complete in late September 1964. On 6 October, Heller presented his plans for additional expenditures and a tax cut to Johnson.

25. FOMCM, 10 November 1964.

26. Rowen, "Fed Chief Concerned about Inflation," 36.

27. Ibid.

28. *Time,* 4 December 1964, 99.

29. Lee Cohn, "Johnson Agreed on Discount Rate Reluctantly," *Washington Star,* 26 November 1964.

30. Ibid.

31. FOMCM, 24 November 1964, 5.

32. Martin and Johnson, telephone call, 24 November 1965, tape library, LBJPL.

33. Robert Roosa, "The $3 Billion Bail Bond," *Time,* 4 December 1964, 33.

34. Martin to files, 8 December 1964, Martin Papers, LBJPL.

35. Ibid.

36. Ibid.

37. Martin, testimony to the Joint Economic Committee, First National City Bank of New York, *Monthly Letter,* April 1965, 44.

38. Joseph Slevin, "Managing the Dollar," *Washington Post,* 27 February 1965.

39. *New York Times,* 27 February 1965, 41. Johnson's balance of payments program of 10 February 1965 added further restrictions on overseas investments and loans by U.S. banks and corporations.

40. "The Economy under New Management," *Fortune,* May 1965, 224.

41. Ibid., 228.

42. Ibid.

43. Ackley, oral history, 2:9, LBJPL.

44. Ibid., 2:6.

45. Ibid., 2:11.

46. Ibid., 2:7–8.

47. Martin to files, 11 March 1965, Martin Papers, LBJPL.

48. Ibid.

49. Ibid.

50. William Greider, *Secrets of the Temple: How the Federal Reserve Runs the Country* (New York: Simon & Schuster, 1989), 73. Quotation from the Federal Reserve Act of 1913.

51. FOMCM, 13 April 1965, 33.

52. Ackley to Johnson, "Quadriad Briefing Notes," 8 February 1965, WHCF, LBJPL.

53. Ibid.

54. "Good Economic News Is Given to President," *Washington Post,* 11 May 1965.

55. "A Prosperity Dialogue," *Washington Post,* 19 May 1965.

56. *New York Post,* 17 May 1965, Martin Speeches, Federal Reserve System Library.

57. "A Prosperity Dialogue."

58. Martin, speech delivered at Columbia University commencement, 1 June 1965, Martin Speeches, Federal Reserve Library.

59. Ibid.

60. Ibid.

61. *Washington Post,* 4 June 1965.

62. "Federal Reserve Aide Disputes Martin View," *Washington Post,* 10 June 1965.

63. Editorial, *New York Times,* 5 June 1965.

64. S. Menshikov, translation of an article in the 27 June 1965 issue of *Isvestya* (Moscow), Martin Papers, LBJPL.

65. *Newsweek,* 14 June 1965, 79.

66. "President Seeks to End Anxieties on the Economy," *New York Times,* 11 June 1965.

67. Transcript of presidential press conference, 10 June 1965, WHCF, file FG110, LBJPL.

68. Ibid.

69. Ibid.

70. Katzenbach to Johnson, 6 July 1965, WHCF, Confidential, file FG 212, LBJPL.

71. FOMCM, 10 August 1965, 45.

72. Robert Holland, interview by author, 30 January 2002.

73. Dewey Daane, in Hargrove and Morley, *The President and the Council of Economic Advisers,* 249.

74. Ackley, oral history, LBJPL. Ackley observed: "There may have been a real effort in the middle of the summer . . . by LBJ to conceal what he thought his commitment was to the Defense Department." Hargrove and Morley, *The President and the Council of Economic Advisers,* 249. In January 1966, Fowler said, "I would have to defer any questions about the magnitude of the defense expenditures to Secretary McNamara. I am not familiar with them in any detail." Fowler to files, "Public Statements of Secretary in 1966 concerning Vietnam," 10 January 1967, Fowler Papers, LBJPL.

75. FOMCM, 28 September 1965, 93.

76. FOMCM, 12 October 1965, 69.

77. Martin to Johnson, 6 October 1965, Martin Papers, LBJPL.

78. Ibid.

79. Ackley to Johnson, 5 October 1965, WHCF, Confidential, file FG 212, LBJPL.

80. Ibid.

81. Paul Volcker, tribute to Martin, commemorative booklet, Fall 1999, BGFRS. Volcker was serving in the Treasury Department at the time.

82. Ackley to Johnson, 6 November 1965, CEA Administrative History, volume 2, LBJPL.

83. Arthur, Okun, oral history, 24, LBJPL.

84. Ackley to Johnson, 6 November 1965.

85. Okun, oral history, 25. LBJPL.

86. Holland, interview, 30 January 2002.

87. Ibid.

88. "Weak Link between Federal Board and Government," *Financial Times* (London), 15 December 1965, Martin family scrapbook.

89. Fowler to Johnson, 3 November 1965, WHCF, file FG233/A, LBJPL.

90. Malcolm W. Martin, interview by author, 31 January 1995.

91. "Weak Link between Federal Board and Government."

92. Board of governors, minutes of meeting, 3 December 1965, Federal Reserve System Archives, Washington, D.C., 7.

93. Ibid., 19.

94. Ibid., 3–4.

95. Ibid., 28.

96. FOMCM, 12 October 1965, 69.

97. Board of governors, minutes, 3 December 1965, 28.

98. FOMCM, 23 November 1965, 84.

99. Board of governors, minutes, 3 December 1965, 28.

100. Ibid.

101. Ibid., 29.

102. FOMCM, 23 November 1965, 82.

103. Joseph Califano, *The Triumph and Tragedy of Lyndon Johnson: The White House Years* (New York: Simon & Schuster, 1991).

104. Fowler and Johnson, telephone call, 3 December 1965, tape library, LBJPL.

105. Ibid.

106. Martin, oral history, 8–9, LBJPL.

107. Ibid., 13.

108. Ibid., 11.

109. Ibid., 13.

110. Ibid., 11. Martin was referring to his agreement to delay any rate increase until after Johnson's gall bladder operation in October 1965.

111. Ibid.

112. Ibid., 9.

113. *Time*, 17 December 1965, 18.

114. Ibid.

115. Richard Debs, retired Fed official, Martin memorial service, Fall 1999.

116. Califano, *The Triumph and Tragedy of Lyndon Johnson.*

117. Eisenhower to Martin, 4 January 1966, Martin Papers, box 75, LBJPL.

118. Martin to Johnson, 2 February 1966, Martin Papers, box 75, LBJPL.

119. Ibid.

120. Martin, "Memorandum of Conversation with the President," 26 February 1966, Martin Papers, box 75, LBJPL.

121. Ibid.

122. Martin to Johnson, April 1966, WHCF, Confidential, Finance, 1966–68, LBJPL.

123. Fowler repeated Martin's comment to John Macy, the head of the Civil Service and an advisor to Johnson. Macy to Johnson, 1 February 1966, WHCF, Macy File, LBJPL.

124. Martin to Johnson, 2 February 1966, Martin Papers, box 75, LBJPL.

125. Martin, "Memorandum of Conversation with the President."

126. First National City Bank of New York, *Monthly Letter,* February 1966, 15.

127. Martin to Johnson, 15 March 1966, Martin Papers, box 75, LBJPL.

128. FOMCM, 8 February 1966, 85.

129. Sherman Maisel, *Managing the Dollar* (New York: W. W. Norton, 1991), 85.

130. Ibid.

131. FOMCM, 12 April 1966, 25.

132. Ibid., 77.

133. Ibid., 21.

134. Thomas Mayer, *Monetary Policy and the Great Inflation in the United States* (Cheltenham: Edward Elgar, 1999), 18.

135. FOMCM, 7 June 1966, 104.

136. First National City Bank of New York, *Monthly Letter,* August 1966, 89.

137. Ibid.

138. Joseph Horne, quoted in "Rate War Joined by US Agencies," *New York Times,* 28 June 1966.

139. Martin, testimony to the House Committee on Banking and Currency, 8 June 1966, Martin Speeches, Federal Reserve Library.

140. *Fortune,* December 1968, 176.

141. George L. Bach, *Making Monetary and Fiscal Policy* (Washington, D.C.: Brookings Institution Press, 1991), 128.

142. Frederick Deming, oral history, LBJPL.

143. Holland, interview, 30 January 2002.

144. FOMCM, 26 July 1966, 77.

145. Ackley to Johnson, 30 July 1966, CEA Administrative History, vol. 2, LBJPL.

146. U.S. Federal Reserve System, minutes of Federal Advisory Council meeting, 20 September 1966, 11, Federal Reserve System Archives, Washington, D.C., 15.

147. Daane, comment in Ackley, oral history, in Hargrove and Morley, *The President and the Council of Economic Advisers,* 249.

148. Ibid., 250.

149. Ibid., 251.

150. Deborah Shapley, *Power and Promise: The Life and Times of Robert McNamara* (New York: Little Brown, 1993), 373.

151. King to Fowler, 10 January 1967, Fowler Papers, box 258, LBJPL.

152. Okun, oral history, in Hargrove and Morley, *The President and the Council of Economic Advisors,* 301. Okun said of Fowler, "In that period Fowler was not signing Troika memos, not signing memos jointly with Ackley urging tax increases. It wasn't clear whether Fowler really recognized that Johnson just wasn't ready to accept a tax increase recommendation and consequently didn't want to launch a crusade."

153. Deming, oral history, 32, LBJPL. Treasury Undersecretary Deming quoted Fowler as saying that "the only safe assumption about any war you're in is that it's going to continue, and it's going to expand."

154. Ackley, oral history, tape 2:14, LBJPL.

155. Martin to Johnson, 8 April 1966, Surcharge Chronology, vol. 2, Fowler Papers, LBJPL.

156. Martin to files, "Meeting with the President," 17 November 1966, Martin Papers, box 75, LBJPL.

157. Martin, oral history, 4, LBJPL.

158. Okun, oral history, in Hargrove and Morley, *The President and the Council of Economic Advisers,* 274.

159. Heller to Johnson, 13 May 1966, Heller Name File, LBJPL.

160. Wilbur Mills, oral history, 21, LBJPL.

161. Martin and Johnson, telephone call to discuss Mills's reaction, 30 June 1966, Martin Papers, box 75, LBJPL. Notes taken by Martin.

162. Ibid.

163. Martin, oral history, 23, LBJPL.

164. Fowler, oral history, 29, LBJPL.

165. Martin's reaction described by Ackley to Johnson, 28 August 1966, WHCF, Confidential, file FG233, LBJPL.

166. Fowler, oral history, 29, LBJPL.

167. Henry Fowler, testimony to House Ways and Means Committee, quoted in First National City Bank of New York, *Monthly Letter,* October 1966, 113.

168. Martin summarized his arguments in a memorandum to Johnson the next day. Fowler Papers, box 257, LBJPL.

169. Ibid.

170. Ibid.

171. Ackley to Johnson, 1 December 1966, CEA Administrative History, vol. 2, LBJPL.

172. Martin to files, 12 December 1966, Martin Papers, box 75, LBJPL.

173. Ackley to Johnson, 13 December 1966, WHCF, Confidential, box 32, LBJPL.

174. Martin to files, 10 January 1967, Martin Papers, box 75, LBJPL.

175. Ibid.

176. Ibid.

177. Johnson, State of the Union address, 10 January 1967, *Public Papers of the President of the United States: Lyndon B. Johnson, 1967* (Washington, D.C.: Government Printing Office, 1969), 20.

178. Martin to Johnson, 13 December 1966, Fowler Papers, box 257, LBJPL.

Chapter 10. Reaping the Whirlwind

1. Joseph Califano, *The Triumph and Tragedy of Lyndon Johnson: The White House Years* (New York: Simon & Schuster, 1991), 242.

2. Ackley, oral history, in *The President and the Council of Economic Advisers,* ed. Erwin Hargrove and Samuel Morley (Boulder: Westview, 1984), 257.

3. Martin, testimony to U.S. Congress, Joint Economic Committee on the Economic Report of the President, *Hearings on the Economic Report of 1967,* 90th Cong., 1st sess., 1967, 394.

4. Ibid., 392–93.

5. Ibid.

6. *Newsweek,* 2 January 1967, 59.

7. Joint Economic Committee, *Hearings on the 1967 Economic Report of the President,* 406.

8. Ibid., 409.

9. Ibid.

10. William McChesney Martin Jr., speech to the Economic Club of Detroit, 18 March 1968, Martin Speeches, Federal Reserve Library.

11. Joint Economic Committee, *Hearings on the 1967 Economic Report of the President,* 581.

12. Ibid., 551.

13. Frank C. Porter, "Martin Reported Set to Quit FRB," *Los Angeles Times–Washington Post* news service, 6 January 1967, Martin family scrapbook.

14. "Chief Martin Wants to Resign," *Los Angeles Times,* 9 January 1967.

15. Macy to Johnson, 20 February 1967, Macy Name File, LBJPL.

16. Duesenberry to Ackley, 10 January 1967, WHCF, file FG232A, LBJPL.

17. Ackley to Johnson, 20 February 1967, WHCF, Confidential, file FG212, LBJPL. Ackley did not mention Charles Shepardson, Martin's strongest supporter, because he was scheduled to retire on 31 March.

18. Ibid.

19. "Martin's Future Is Johnson's Problem," *New York Times,* 26 March 1967.

20. "Patman Urges President Not to Reappoint Martin," *Washington Post,* 7 March 1967.

21. Joint Economic Committee, *Hearings on the 1967 Economic Report of the President,* 557.

22. Martin, "Memorandum of a Conversation with President Lyndon B. Johnson," 14 March 1967, box 60, MPMHS.

23. Ibid., 2.

24. Ibid., 2–3.

25. Ibid., 5.

26. Ibid.

27. Ibid.

28. Ibid., 6.

29. Ibid.

30. Ibid.

31. *New York Times,* 30 March 1967, 1.

32. *Time,* 3 April 1967.

33. Editorial, *New York Times,* 30 March 1967.

34. Hobart Rowen, "Major Tax Hike Seen if Troop Need Grows," *Washington Post,* 5 May 1967, D7.

35. Ibid.

36. Hobart Rowen, "Panel Supports Martin on War Cost Prediction," *Washington Post,* 9 September 1967.

37. John T. Woolley, *Monetary Politics: The Federal Reserve and the Politics of Monetary Policy* (London: Cambridge University Press, 1984), 51.

38. Martin to files, 5 June 1967, Meetings with the President, folder 3, Martin Papers, LBJPL.

39. Ibid.

40. Califano, *The Triumph and Tragedy of Lyndon Johnson,* 242.

41. Ibid.

42. Fowler to Johnson, 11 July 1967, Surcharge Chronology, Fowler Papers, LBJPL.

43. Martin, speech reported in the *Toledo Times,* 27 June 1967, Martin family scrapbook.

44. Martin to files, 22 July 1967, Martin Papers, box 74, LBJPL.

45. Ibid.

46. Califano, *The Triumph and Tragedy of Lyndon Johnson,* 244.

47. Ibid., 245.

48. *New York Times,* 18 November 1967.

49. "Martin Sees Slump without Tax Rise," *Washington Post,* 15 September 1967.

50. Ibid.

51. "Fed Chief Says Butter Must Give Way to Guns," *Dallas Morning News,* 9 November 1967.

52. Ibid.

53. First National City Bank of New York, *Monthly Letter,* September 1967, 99.

54. FOMCM, 24 October 1967, 66.

55. *Business Week,* 22 April 1967, 81.

56. "Fed Chief Says Butter Must Give Way to Guns."

57. Okun, oral history, in Hargrove and Morley, *The President and the Council of Economic Advisers,* 305. Okun observed: "I believe there was a conscious feeling at the Fed and on our part that you had to let the economy take on somewhat of a booming mood before Congress would take you seriously."

58. FOMCM, 12 September 1967, 31.

59. Ibid., 73.

60. Ibid.

61. *New York Times*, 30 November 1967, 1.

62. U.S. Congress, House Committee on Ways and Means, *President's 1967 Surtax Proposal*, 90th Cong., 1st sess., 1967, 200.

63. FOMCM, 12 December 1967, 97.

64. Ibid.

65. FOMCM, 27 November 1967, 4.

66. Ibid., 36.

67. Charles A. Coombs, *The Arena of International Finance* (New York: John Wiley & Sons, 1976), 162. The London gold pool was established in 1962 by the United States and seven other countries in order to provide a mechanism for stabilizing the free-market price of gold at $35 an ounce.

68. FOMCM, 12 December 1967, 17.

69. Ibid.

70. Ibid., 45.

71. "Four Officials Fear Blow to Economy without Tax Rise," *New York Times*, 23 January 1968.

72. Okun, oral history, in Hargrove and Morley, *The President and the Council of Economic Advisers*, 303.

73. FOMCM, 6 February 1968, 109.

74. Ibid., 110.

75. Robert Solomon, *The International Monetary System, 1946–76* (New York: Harper & Row, 1976), 118.

76. *New York Times*, 11 March 1968, 1.

77. Coombs, *The Arena of International Finance*, 166.

78. Ibid., 167. The Fed intended to exercise the swaps to buy dollars accumulated by European central banks. The central banks had purchased the excess dollar inventories of commercial banks in their jurisdiction that had participated in the dollar support program.

79. Martin to files, "White House Meetings with the President," 21 March 1968, Martin Papers, box 74, LBJPL. The memo describes the presentation Fowler and Martin made to Johnson.

80. Wilbur Mills, oral history, 35, LBJPL.

81. Henry Fowler, oral history, 23, LBJPL.

82. Martin, speech to the National Industrial Conference Board, 14 February 1968, Martin Speeches, 6, Federal Reserve Library.

83. Ibid., 14.

84. Ibid., 12.

85. Solomon, *The International Monetary System, 1946–76*, 118.

86. William M. Scammell, *International Monetary Policy: Bretton Woods and After* (New York: Wiley, 1975), 145.

87. Coombs, *The Arena of International Finance*, 168.

88. Scammell, *International Monetary Policy*, 147.

89. Solomon, *The International Monetary System, 1946–76*, 122.

90. Coombs, *The Arena of International Finance,* 171.

91. Scammell, *International Monetary Policy,* 147.

92. Coombs, *The Arena of International Finance,* 173.

93. Ibid.

94. Martin, answers to questions after his speech to the Economic Club of Detroit, 18 March 1968, Martin Speeches, 21, Federal Reserve Library.

95. *New York Times,* 19 March 1968, 61.

96. Ibid.

97. Fowler, oral history, 18, LBJPL.

98. Irving Bernstein, *Guns or Butter: The Presidency of Lyndon Johnson* (New York: Oxford University Press, 1996), 373.

99. "Martin Sees Crisis in U.S. Inflation," *New York Times,* 18 April 1968.

100. Martin, speech to American Society of Newspaper Editors, 18 April 1968, Martin Speeches, Federal Reserve Library.

101. Ibid.

102. Bernstein, *Guns or Butter,* 372.

103. *New York Times,* 1 April 1968, 1.

104. Johnson had advised Martin of his intention not to run in a conversation on 14 March 1967.

105. Okun to Johnson, 24 April 1968, CEA Administrative History, vol. 3, LBJPL.

106. Okun to Johnson, 18 April 1968, CEA Administrative History, vol. 3, LBJPL.

107. Martin, speech to American Society of Newspaper Editors.

108. *New York Times,* 11 June 1968, 61.

109. Ibid.

110. Ibid., 64.

111. Martin to Gene Giancarlo, 8 May 1968, Martin Papers, box 74, LBJPL.

112. *New York Times,* 28 April 1968, 3.

113. *New York Times,* 21 April 1968, 12.

114. FOMCM, 28 April 1968, 10.

115. Ibid., 12.

116. Ibid., 15.

117. FOMCM, 30 April 1968, 12.

118. FOMCM, 28 May 1968, 19.

119. Ibid.

120. Ibid., 23.

121. Ibid.

122. Ibid.

123. Ibid.

124. FOMCM, 2 April 1968, 24.

125. Ibid.

126. Bernstein, *Guns or Butter,* 374.

127. Fowler to Johnson, 9 May 1968, WHCF, files FI11–4, LBJPL.

128. Lawrence C. Pierce, *The Politics of Fiscal Policy Formation* (Pacific Palisades, Calif.: Goodyear, 1971), 168.

129. "How the Battle Is Going Over Tight Money," *U.S. News and World Report,* 12 August 1968, 79.

130. FOMCM, 16 July 1968, 34.

131. FOMCM, 13 August 1968, 24.

132. Allan Meltzer, interview by author, 1 July 2003: "Franco Modigliani, Milton Friedman, and Ed Phelps were all predicting that a temporary tax increase would have a short-term impact at best and that consumers would ignore the surtax by borrowing over it."

133. FOMCM, 16 July 1968, 96.

134. FOMCM, 12 December 1967, 98.

135. FOMCM, 10 September 1968, 25.

136. Ibid., 69.

137. Ibid., 68.

138. FOMCM, 29 October 1968, 20.

139. Ibid., 33.

140. Ibid., 20.

141. Ibid., 21.

142. Ibid., 33.

143. The price deflator reflected price changes throughout the economy and tended to be less volatile than the CPI, which tracked consumer price changes only.

144. FOMCM, 29 October 1968, 34.

145. FOMCM, 26 November 1968, 57.

146. Ibid., 93.

147. Thomas Mayer, *Monetary Policy and the Great Inflation in the United States* (Northampton, Mass.: Edward Elgar, 1980), 119.

148. Okun to Johnson, 25 December 1968, CEA Administrative History, vol. 2, LBJPL. Okun wrote a final update of the administration's forecast for fiscal year 1969. Optimistic to the end, the CEA forecast that inflation would be at 2½ percent and that the Fed needed to achieve more monetary ease.

149. Robert Hetzel, interview by author, 7 March 2002.

150. Ibid., Hetzel observed: "All Fed chairmen want to preserve the System's institutional integrity. Martin would not want to expose the Fed to the political repercussions of a 1966-style tightening."

151. All of the following comments are actual statements by Martin in his oral history for the Johnson Presidential Library (see section 1, p. 11) or comments made by Johnson in his meeting with Martin on 14 March 1967, recorded in Martin's memo to files, box 60, MPMHS.

Chapter 11. Passing the Torch

1. John Ehrlichman, *Witness to Power* (New York: Simon & Schuster, 1982), 247.

2. Richard Nixon, *Six Crises* (New York: Doubleday, 1962), 309.

3. Ibid., 310.

4. Andrew Brimmer, *Federal Reserve Bank of Minneapolis Monthly,* September 1998.

5. Ibid.

6. Ibid.

7. Ibid.

8. FOMCM, 14 January 1969, 72.

9. Ibid.

10. Allen Matusow, *Nixon's Economy* (Lawrence: University Press of Kansas, 1998), 4.

11. Ibid., 16.

12. *New York Times,* 18 February 1969, 1.

13. Ibid., 20.

14. *New York Times,* 27 February 1969, 1.

15. Ibid.

16. Ibid

17. Ibid., 23.

18. Ibid.

19. Ibid.

20. Ibid., 70.

21. Noel McBride, economist for the Cleveland Trust Co., quoted in "Bankers Unhappy with Fed," *Business Week,* 12 April 1969, 31.

22. Ibid.

23. Nixon created the Cabinet Committee on Economic Policy (CCEP) as the domestic economic equivalent to the National Security Council. Nixon's directive was that the committee "should look at economic policies long range." It was designed to give Arthur Burns, George Shultz, and several cabinet members the opportunity to influence the policy proposals of Nixon's economic team.

24. CCEP, minutes of meeting, 4 April 1969, President's Office Files, Memos, box 77, NPM, NA.

25. McCracken to Nixon, 15 April 1969, WHCF, Staff, McCracken, box B40, NPM, NA.

26. See chapter 7, p. 123.

27. FOMCM, 1 April 1969, 106.

28. *New York Times,* 23 May 1969, 65.

29. Ibid.

30. CCEP, minutes of meeting, 16 May 1969, President's Office Files, Memos, box 78, NPM, NA.

31. Ibid., 3.

32. Ibid., 6.

33. Ibid.

34. Ibid.

35. Eurodollars are dollar balances in the hands of foreign private and public holders.

36. Phillip Zweig, *Wriston: Walter Wriston, Citibank, and the Rise and Fall of American Financial Supremacy* (New York: Crown, 1995), 268.

37. FOMCM, 14 June 1969, 39.

38. FOMCM, 12 August 1969, 24.

39. *Wall Street Journal,* 27 February 1969, Hearings FRB, February–April 1969, Martin Papers, LBJPL.

40. Ibid.

41. "The Fed's Next Chairman," *New York Times,* 25 June 1969.

42. Ibid.

43. FOMCM, 15 July 1969, 37.

44. FOMCM, 12 August 1969, 23.

45. FOMCM, 9 September 1969, 24.

46. Ibid., 33.

47. FOMCM, 15 July 1969, 82.

48. Ibid.

49. FOMCM, 12 August 1969, 78.

50. Ibid.

51. *New York Times,* 21 June 1969, 1.

52. Ibid.

53. Ibid.

54. Shultz to Nixon, 7 October 1969, WHCF, Subject Files FG131, NPM, NA.

55. CCEP, minutes of meeting, 15 October 1969, WHCF, Subject Files, BE, box 46, NPM, NA.

56. Ibid, 2.

57. Ibid., 6.

58. Ibid., 7.

59. Ibid., 8.

60. Ibid., 5.

61. FOMCM, 7 October 1969, 90.

62. Matusow, *Nixon's Economy,* 31.

63. McCracken to Nixon, 3 November 1969, WHCF, Staff, McCracken, box 40, NPM, NA.

64. McCracken to Nixon, 17 November 1969, WHCF, Staff, McCracken, box 46, NPM, NA.

65. McCracken to Nixon, 15 November 1969, WHCF, Subject Files, BE, box 46, NPM, NA.

66. Ibid.

67. Ibid.

68. *New York Times,* 19 December 1969, 1.

69. Ibid., 107.

70. Ibid.

71. Matusow, *Nixon's Economy,* 50.

72. Ibid., 51.

73. Marquis Childs, "Nation Will Miss Fed's Uncompromising Martin," *Washington Post,* 21 January 1970, A19.

74. Ibid.

75. First National City Bank of New York, *Monthly Letter,* December 1969, 136.

76. FOMCM, 15 January 1970, 34.

77. CCEP, minutes of meeting, 15 October 1969, WHCF, Subject Files, BE, box 46, NPM, NA.

78. FOMCM, 15 January 1970, 101.

79. *New York Times,* 18 October 1969, 19.

80. Malcolm W. Martin, interview by author, 31 January 1995. Martin attended the dinner.

81. Comment referred to in Martin to Mills, 21 January 1970, Martin Papers, box 138, LBJPL.

82. Victor Riesel, *New Haven Register,* via the *Washington Post* news service, 23 January 1970, Martin Papers, box 138, LBJPL.

83. Ibid.

84. Ibid.

85. Retired Fed governors and bank presidents, tribute to Martin, commemorative booklet, Fall 1999, BGFRS.

86. Ibid.

87. James Reston, "Farewell to the Happy Puritan," *New York Times,* 25 January 1970.

88. Paul Samuelson, "Bill Martin's Legacy," *Newsweek* Magazine, 2 February 1970, 73.

89. Ibid.

90. *Time,* 2 February 1970, 66.

91. Martin, oral history, NYSE, 91.

Chapter 12. The Public Private Citizen

1. Robert Solomon, tribute to Martin, commemorative booklet, Fall 1999, BGFRS (videotape copy).

2. This motto was contained in a pamphlet produced by the Swiss Bankers Association, file "Pearls of Wisdom," Martin Papers, LBJPL.

3. The OECD began life in 1948 as the Organization for European Economic Cooperation (OEEC) to coordinate Europe's response to the U.S. Marshall Plan. Douglas Dillon reorganized the OEEC into the OECD in 1950–51 to coordinate foreign aid and monetary policy planning between the United States and Western Europe.

4. William McChesney Martin Jr., "Toward a World Central Bank," Summary of Proceedings, Per Jacobsson memorial address (Washington, D.C.: Atlantic Council of the U.S., 1970).

5. Ibid., 9.

6. Solomon, tribute to Martin. Solomon wrote: "Charles DeGaulle wanted to reduce the " 'exorbitant privilege' of the United States that resulted from the special status of its currency." According to Solomon, other European countries held similar opinions.

7. Martin, "Toward a World Central Bank," 7.

8. Ibid., 8.

9. Ibid., 5.

10. Ibid., 6.

11. Ibid.

12. Ibid., 11.

13. Ibid., 9.

14. Commentaries on "Toward a World Central Bank," 35.

15. In 1968, Johnson's critique of recent monetary policy was circulated to the FOMC, one of the few academic analyses to receive this treatment.

16. Commentaries on "Toward a World Central Bank," 47.

17. One of the more recent efforts was made by Jeffrey Garten, a former member of the Clinton administration, in 1998. Garten said later, "It was seen as too visionary and did not help my reputation within the administration." Discussion with the author, June 1999.

18. Atlantic Council of the U.S., official transcription of the 1978 lecture and commentary, 1978, p. 46. The reference is to a then-popular Broadway musical about Don Quixote.

19. *Business Week,* 30 January 1971.

20. *New York Times,* 25 January 1971, 46.

21. Donald Farrar, the director of the SEC study, *Financial Analysts Journal,* September–October 1971, 2.

22. Ibid., 5.

23. Ibid.

24. Martin, "The Securities Markets," report to the board of governors of the New York Stock Exchange, 5 August 1971, Martin Papers, box 12, LBJPL.

25. Richard Wescott, draft presentation to Senate Finance Committee, 1971, Martin Papers, LBJPL. Wescott, an executive of a regional brokerage firm in Nebraska, was a supporter of Martin's recommendations and was a primary defender of the Martin Report before Congress.

26. Martin, transcript of press conference following release of the report, *Magazine of Wall Street,* 30 August 1971, 38.

27. Martin, "The Securities Markets," 13.

28. Martin, oral history, NYSE, 91.

29. Martin, "The Securities Markets," 1.

30. Editorial, *New York Times,* 7 August 1971.

31. "Martin Study Hit by 19 Economists," *New York Times,* 28 December 1971.

32. Ibid.

33. Richard R. West and Seha M. Tinic, "Crisis in the Stock Market: The Martin Report and the Public Interest," *Public Policy Quarterly,* Winter 1971.

34. *Newsweek,* 16 August 1971, 62.

35. Guthrie Backer, "Blueprint for Constructive Reform," *Financial Analysts Journal,* November–December 1971.

36. Martin, oral history, NYSE, 90.

37. Martin, speech to the Conference Board, 24 February 1972, Martin Papers, box 243, LBJPL.

38. Martin, presentation to the Subcommittee on International Finance of the Senate Finance Committee, 1 June 1973, Martin Papers, box 243, LBJPL.

39. Paul Volcker to Martin, 2 July 1973, Martin Papers, box 237, LBJPL. Volcker wrote: "I am not at all ready to say this is the end of the era of cooperation, but we (and almost everybody else) are inevitably going to have to face up to this more clearly if there is to be any monetary reform at all."

40. *Wall Street Journal,* 17 September 1979, 1.

41. Robert Hershey, "In Remembrance of Real Money," *New York Times,* 10 December 1985.

42. *Congressional Record*—House of Representatives, 29 April 1971, Martin Papers, box 243, LBJPL.

43. *Newsweek*, 12 January 1981, 13.
44. Commemorative booklet, the International Tennis Hall of Fame, Newport, Rhode Island, 1979.
45. Martin, oral history, NYSE, 100.

Epilogue

1. Martin, quoted in tribute to Martin, commemorative booklet, Fall 1999, 6, BGFRS.

Acknowledgments

Every biography depends on a determined author, sources of financial support, an editor willing to fight for the book, candid and quotable contemporaries of the subject, a few expert advisors willing to help the author strive for balance, and one or more critics who will review the manuscript honestly and constructively.

There are four members of this cast without whom this book would not exist. One is Malcolm Woods Martin, Bill Martin's younger brother. Malcolm was always close to his brother, shared his family's commitment to a life of purpose and public service, and is gifted with a remarkable memory. Robert Hetzel, vice president and economist of the Federal Reserve Bank of Richmond, shared his understanding of the economic realities that Martin dealt with, offered crucial insight into the institutional environment of the Fed and the pressures on the chairman, and reminded me regularly that Martin's biographer had to be accurate and fair. Joseph F. Cullman 3rd, an indefatigable friend of Martin's, added funding for the research of this book to the long list of causes he so ably supports. Finally, Professor Edwin Perkins, an economic historian and author, read every tangled line of prose and challenged every unsupported conclusion. The finished product bears his inspection stamp.

This book has numerous other midwives. Tim Wells and Mark Pachter educated me on the skills and dedication required to bring a biography into being. My first editor, Charles Grench, introduced this project to the Yale

University Press and badgered his colleagues into taking a risk on a first-time author. Other members of the Martin family have been generous with their memories and scrapbooks, particularly Bill Martin 3rd and Cynthia Martin, Bill Martin's beloved "chief," who has graced my life with her friendship. All authors depend mightily on the help of archivists and reference librarians. They are a generous community, but a few stand out. I spent hours at the Federal Reserve Library in Washington, where Cathy Tunis and Krista Box were indispensable. Martin's papers are at the Missouri Historical Society in St. Louis, where Dennis Northcott was always available and helpful. The presidential libraries are invaluable resources, and Barbara Constable at the Eisenhower Library, Bob Tissing at the Johnson Library, and particularly Dennis Bilger at the Truman Library were delights to work with.

Among the many who made signal contributions to the insights presented in this book are some of Martin's contemporaries, including former Treasury Undersecretary Charls Walker, former CEA Chairman Ray Saulnier, former Fed Board Advisor Bob Solomon, and particularly former Fed Governor and FOMC Secretary Bob Holland, who personified the qualities of character and wisdom so typical of long-serving Fed officials.

This book was not created in a vacuum. One of its inspirations was Donald Kettl's innovative look at a series of Fed chairmen in his book *Leadership at the Fed*. Another was Allan Meltzer's authoritative *A History of the Federal Reserve,* vol. 1. Dr. Meltzer also shared his research and insights about the Martin era, some of which will be included in his second volume. This book also benefited from a wealth of minutes of meetings held in the White House and of the meetings of the FOMC. I am exceedingly grateful to those who labored to capture the significant details of discussions, many of which were of considerable significance to the economic policies that evolved. My goal has been to portray Martin and other policy makers as they struggled to exercise their responsibilities and to help the reader appreciate how and why they made their decisions. The individuals and documents mentioned were crucially important to my task.

Writing is a lonely and hard business, but there are always those who make it less so. I am extremely grateful to those who did the yeomen's share of the research: Coralee Paul, Sydney Soderberg, Anna Watkins, and the irrepressible, persistent Chris Findlay. Added thanks go to my steady and supportive editors at the Yale University Press, John Kulka and Mike O'Malley. The remaining gratitude goes to my wife, Lucy, and my three children, who would gamely ask, "How is the book coming?" knowing full well that a litany of small gains, frustrating delays, and laments on the world's indifference to biographers would follow.

Index

Balderston, Canby, 141, 205
Bank for International Settlements (BIS), 280
Bank holiday, 242–243
Banking Act of *1935*, 3, 84, 100, 160
Barr, Joseph W., 161, 235–236
Bartlett, Edward E., 33
Bean, Atherton, 212
Berle, Adolph, 29
Bevin, Ernest, 71
"Bills Only" policy: acceptance of, 99–103; criticism of, 154–155; and current practice, 103; decision to abandon, 297; implementation of, 94, 295; initial goals for, 94, 102; suspension of, 135, 153–154
Black, Eugene R., 290–291
"Black Thursday," 18
Blessing, Karl, 240, 282
Blough, Roger, 163–164
Bond debacle of *1953*, 103–106
Boylan, Robert P., 47
Bretton Woods Agreements Act, 59
Bretton Woods System: abandonment of, 290; creation of, 59, 167–168; efforts to strengthen, 243, 244, 280; inherent weaknesses, 166, 243; review of, 169
Brill, Daniel, 192–193, 206, 253
Brimmer, Andrew, 212–213, 214, 219
British pound: devaluation of *1949*, 69–72; devaluation of *1964*, 194–196, 239–240; devaluation of *1967*, 239, 248–250
"Brokers' banks," 43–44, 46
Bryan, Malcolm, 126, 141, 169
Budget deficits. *See* Deficits, budget
Bundy, McGeorge, 233
Burgess, W. Randolph, 97–98, 279
Burns, Arthur: on adjustment of economy, 106; appointment of as Fed chairman, 261, 273, 274–276, 299; on economic prospects of *1956* presidential year, 115–116; on end of recession, 110; on housing, 268; on Martin's

reappointment, 230–231; on monetary policy, 260; and tax cuts, 176; on tax cuts and recession of *1957–1958*, 133; on tax increase, 229
Burns, James, 53, 55
Byrd, Robert, 188
Byrnes, James, 62
Byrnes, John, 241

Cairncross, Alec, 71
Califano, Joe, 209, 225, 226, 227, 235, 250
Canada: collapse of dollar, 173; devaluation of dollar, 165
Carli, Guido, 243–244
Casey, William J., 289
Certificates of deposit (CDs), 217–218
Chiang Kai-shek, 61
China and Ex-Im Bank loans, 61
Civil rights and Johnson administration, 212–213
Clay, Lucius, 96
Clayton, William, 60, 62
Clifford, Clark, 14
Closing of London financial markets, 242–243
Cohen, Benjamin V., 22
Columbia University, 24
Combs, Charles, 170, 173, 244, 249
Computerization and NYSE, 287
Congressional hearings. *See* Hearings
Conway, Carle, 29, 44
Cook, Donald, 197
Cotton-loan fund, 13
Credit crunch of *1966*, 215–219, 237
Credit ease: consensus for moderate ease in *1969*, 254; during negotiations of surtax debate in *1967*, 237–239; in *1968*, 6; prior to recession of *1953–1954*, 105–106; during recession of *1957–1958*, 130–131, 134, 138
Cripps, Stafford, 70
Crowley, Leo, 57, 58, 59

Daane, J. Dewey, 181–182, 207, 240, 264

Dale, Ed, 265

Davis, Cynthia (wife), 52, 53–54, 190, 275, 276, 277

Davis, Dwight F. (father-in-law), 53–54

Davis, Howland, 32

Deficits, budget: Eisenhower Administration, 93–94; Johnson administration, 214, 217, 219–221, 224–225, 226–237, 247–248; Martin's predictions on, 291; Nixon administration, 274; Truman administration, 93–94

DeNunzio, Ralph, 289

Depository Trust Company, 289

Depression. *See* Great Depression

Dewey, Thomas E., 32

Dillon, Douglas: appointment as Treasury Secretary, 151, 156–158; and balance of payments, 196; and Bank of England's rate increase, 194–195; on expiration of Martin's term, 174; and governor selections, 181; on interest rate hikes, 183; and Johnson administration, 188; and "Kennedy Bear Market," 164–165; and proposal for increase in resources of IMF, 166–167; resignation of, 197; on swaps, 172; on tax cuts, 178

Dodge, Joseph, 94

Dollar: continuing weakness, 165–166; and gold crisis, 242; postwar shortages, 168; supporting, 167, 240

Douglas, Paul: criticism of Fed by, 115; on independence of Fed, 90; and Martin confirmation, 82; on role of Fed in Accord, 89; on support of Federal Reserve, 75, 85; and tax cuts, 132–133, 177

Douglas, William O.: appointment to Supreme Court, 42; biography of, 27; and collapse of Old Guard, 32; on J. P. Morgan partners, 40–41; and Martin's NYSE presidency, 38; on Martin's

reform agenda, 40–42; reform agenda of, 36–38; SEC appointment of, 27–30; and Whitney case, 40–42; working relationship with, 3, 35–36, 37–38, 49

Duesenberry, James, 230, 250

Eccles, Marriner, 3, 5, 73, 75, 84–85, 87

Economic forecasts, 252–254, 296–297

Economic Forum Quarterly, 23–24, 168

Economic growth, 142–144

Edwards, Albert N., 17, 19

Edwards, Presley, 14, 27

Edwards & Co. *See* A. G. Edwards & Sons

Ehrlichman, John, 260

Eichengreen, Barry, 71

Eisenhower, Dwight: on authority of Federal Reserve, 117; on budget surplus, 137; on economic goals, 93; election of, 92; financial education of, 95; on importance of financial issues, 95; and letter following 1965 interest rate increase, 211; on need for Fed action, 131; years of administration, 93–148

Employment Act of 1946, 132, 143

Eurodollar market, 268–269, 281

Exchange Act of 1934, 22, 25

Export-Import (Ex-Im) Bank: chairmanship of, 58–67; Chinese relations, 61; conflict with the World Bank, 63–64; and ECA loans, 66; and French loans, 60; funding of, 62–63; history and role of, 4, 59; as independent institution, 5, 61–62; and international financial experience, 168; and Israeli loans, 66–67; Latin American initiative, 63–66; Martin's goals for, 61–62; and NAC, 59; and politically motivated loans, 60–62

Federal Open Market Committee (FOMC): and Accord implementation, 86–87; Executive Committee of, 112; Martin reorganization of, 100, 102,